WRITING BACKWARDS

LITERATURE NOW

Literature Now offers a distinct vision of late-twentieth- and
early-twenty-first-century literary culture. Addressing contemporary literature
and the ways we understand its meaning, the series includes books that are
comparative and transnational in scope as well as those that focus
on national and regional literary cultures.

Matthew Hart, David James, and Rebecca L. Walkowitz, Series Editors

■ ■ ■

For a complete list of titles, see page 339

WRITING BACKWARDS

*Historical Fiction and the
Reshaping of the American Canon*

ALEXANDER MANSHEL

Columbia University Press
New York

Columbia University Press
Publishers Since 1893
New York   Chichester, West Sussex
cup.columbia.edu
Copyright © 2024 Columbia University Press
All rights reserved

Library of Congress Cataloging-in-Publication Data
Names: Manshel, Alexander, author.
Title: Writing backwards : historical fiction and the reshaping of the American canon / Alexander Manshel.
Description: New York : Columbia University Press, [2023] | Includes bibliographical references and index.
Identifiers: LCCN 2023019017 (print) | LCCN 2023019018 (ebook) | ISBN 9780231211260 (hardback) | ISBN 9780231211277 (trade paperback) | ISBN 9780231558822 (ebook)
Subjects: LCSH: Historical fiction, American—History and criticism. | American fiction—20th century—History and criticism. | American fiction—21st century—History and criticism. | Canon (Literature) | LCGFT: Literary criticism.
Classification: LCC PS374.H5 M36 2023 (print) | LCC PS374.H5 (ebook) | DDC 813/.08109054—dc23/eng/20230712
LC record available at https://lccn.loc.gov/2023019017
LC ebook record available at https://lccn.loc.gov/2023019018

To my parents,
David Manshel and Sandra Manshel

CONTENTS

Acknowledgments ix

Introduction 1

1 Contemporary Fiction in Reverse 41

2 The Making of the Greatest Generation 81

3 Colson Whitehead's History of the United States 121

4 Reading the Family Tree 165

5 The Rise of the Recent Historical Novel 205

   Coda: Excavating the Present 241

Notes 249
Works Cited 299
Index 325

ACKNOWLEDGMENTS

THIS BOOK would not exist without the support of a great many individuals and institutions. These brief words are not enough to honor the time, energy, expertise, and care of each of the following people, but I hope that they might serve as a small gesture of my profound gratitude.

I am thankful to the teachers and professors who first sparked my interest in literature's capacity to represent the historical past: Joel Thomas-Adams, Michael Newbury, Brett Millier, Amy Hungerford, and Stuart Sherman.

I owe much to my mentors and friends in the English Department at Stanford University. For years, Mark McGurl has been this project's best reader, its toughest critic, and its staunchest supporter. Mark Algee-Hewitt and Paula Moya pushed me to think differently about what the study of American literature can and should be. Important conversations with Michaela Bronstein, Amir Eshel, Mark Greif, Sianne Ngai, Vaughn Rasberry, and Ramón Saldívar encouraged and shaped this project at key moments.

ACKNOWLEDGMENTS

My colleagues in the Department of English at McGill University have made Montreal a vibrant place to think, teach, and write. I am grateful to Sandeep Banerjee, Peter Gibian, Erin Hurley, Maggie Kilgour, Eli MacLaren, Trevor Ponech, Monica Popescu, Fiona Ritchie, Ned Schantz, Richard So, Michael Van Dussen, Paul Yachnin, and Katie Zien for their warm welcome and ongoing fellowship. Tabitha Sparks lent her considerable insight to this manuscript and helped me to sharpen my arguments. Allan Hepburn's keen editorial eye has made these pages both more incisive and more readable, and I am grateful for his counsel. Derek Nystrom shows me daily what it means to live one's values. Ara Osterweil's courage and her commitment to artistry are an inspiration, and her friendship is a gift.

My students at McGill have been nothing short of luminous, and I am thankful for their intellectual seriousness as well as their sense of play. Conversations with Nicole Huang, Richard Joseph, Matthew Molinaro, Andy Perluzzo, and Jaede Shillingford energized my thinking, as did those with Emily Barber, Alexandra Colby, Nived Dharmaraj, Adam Hill, and Mathias Orhero, whose editorial labor significantly improved this book.

I am enormously grateful to the members of my writing group—Sam Huber, Laura McGrath, Samantha Pergadia, Anna Shechtman, Arthur Wang, and Kathryn Winner—whose intelligence and generosity mark many of the chapters that follow. Morgan Frank, Ben Libman, J. D. Porter, and Dan Sinykin offered helpful feedback at crucial junctures, and I only wish I could have taken more of their advice. Thank you to the scholars and organizers who make up the Association for the Study of the Arts of the Present for the many opportunities to share this work and to learn from my brilliant colleagues in the field. Thanks especially to Gloria Fisk for her advice on the publishing process, and for modeling what it means to do this job with grace.

My thanks to Matthew Hart, David James, and Rebecca Walkowitz, the editors of the Literature Now series at Columbia University

ACKNOWLEDGMENTS

Press, for their support of this project. I am particularly thankful to Matt for believing in the best version of this book, and for helping me to bring it into being. Philip Leventhal has been a thoughtful, generous, and patient editor, and I appreciate the care with which he has handled this work. Three anonymous readers provided invaluable encouragement and critique, and I owe them a debt of gratitude for how they have shaped this book and my thinking. Thanks also to Ben Denzer, Meredith Howard, Zachary Friedman, Caitlin Hurst, Leslie Kriesel, Monique Laban, Milenda Lee, Gregory McNamee, and Sarah Osment for lending their talents to this project.

Sue Luftschein, Louise Smith, and Masoud Farajpour made it possible for me to consult the Ronyoung Kim archives at the University of Southern California and to reproduce some of that material here. My thanks also to the Joseph Cornell Estate, VAGA at Artist Rights Society (ARS), and the Museo Nacional Centro de Arte Reina Sofía in Madrid, for allowing me to include Cornell's *Untitled (To Marguerite Blachas)* in chapter 2. The "Family Tree" in chapter 4 is from *Homegoing* (copyright © 2016 by YNG Books, Inc.), and used by permission of Alfred A. Knopf, an imprint of the Knopf Doubleday Publishing Group, a division of Penguin Random House LLC (all rights reserved). Every effort has been made to identify copyright holders and obtain their permission for the use of copyright material.

An earlier version of chapter 5 was published in *Post45* in 2017, and I am grateful to Merve Emre, Amy Hungerford, Sean McCann, Sarah Chihaya, Theodore Martin, Palmer Rampell, Anna Shechtman, and Arthur Wang for shepherding my research into the world for the very first time. An earlier version of chapter 3 was published in *MELUS* in 2020, and I am thankful to Gary Totten, Jolie Sheffer, Cathy Schlund-Vials, Michael Bérubé, and an additional anonymous reviewer for their advice and support. The research, writing, and production of this book have also been supported by generous grants from the Social Sciences and Humanities Research Council (SSHRC) and the Fonds de Recherche du Québec Société et Culture (FRQSC).

ACKNOWLEDGMENTS

I owe so much to the friends, near and far, new and old, whose kindness and good humor have sustained me over the last several years: Ellen Adams, Daniel Barrett, David Baumflek, Oona Baumflek, Dale Bernier, Lee Bilsky, Rachel Heise Bolten, Jude Dry, Ramin Eshraghi-Yazdi, Allen Frost, Molly Johnsen, Katy Laird, Omri Moses, Julia Sehmer, Stefan Spec, Woodrow Travers, and Claire Yeo. Special thanks to Nina Cherney, Rob Doyle, Andrew Doyle, Amelia Walker, Madeline Doyle, and Phil Vegrytsky for helping me to find family in Montreal.

Laura McGrath and Kathryn Winner belong in nearly every section of these acknowledgments. There is not a single draft or question or cry for help to which they have not lent their expertise, intellect, wisdom, wit, and compassion. I wasn't sure whether to list them among my colleagues, mentors, friends, or family, so I will put them here, with deepest gratitude for being, at various times, all of the above.

When I began writing this book, I did not yet know Sophie Doyle, a situation that eventually became untenable. She is pure light, and I am grateful for every day I spend with her. While I am not sure I could have finished this without her, I am certain that there is no one I would rather celebrate it with. For everything past, and the future we are building together, I thank you.

Finally, I am grateful to my family. My brother, Jeffrey Manshel, will not get to read these pages, but I hope that I have honored his memory and the history that we share. My parents, David Manshel and Sandra Manshel, taught me to read and write and remember where I came from; they worked without end, while telling me that my only job was to learn; they said, *Don't be afraid of hard work* and *Never put books on the floor*, *Keep asking why*, and *Remember words matter*. This book is dedicated to them.

INTRODUCTION

AMERICAN FICTION PAR EXCELLENCE

BY VIRTUALLY any measure, Toni Morrison's *Beloved* (1987) is the single most canonical work of contemporary American fiction.[1] Pulitzer Prize winner, finalist for the National Book Award and the National Book Critics Circle Award, *Beloved* is one of the most taught novels in university English classrooms, and *the* contemporary novel most cited by scholars.[2] In many ways, Morrison's haunting novel of American slavery stands out from the contemporary canon even as it typifies that canon's thematic and aesthetic preoccupations.[3] The novel takes place during a crucial moment in the historical past, documenting the horrors of history with a startling closeness and tracing their resonances across several generations. In the decades since its publication, *Beloved* has proved a model for a diverse group of writers interested in narrating the past, as well as a touchstone for teachers and scholars invested in recovering that past.

Among a great many other things, the novel is about the relationship between Sethe, a formerly enslaved woman struggling to reconcile her traumatic past with her life in the present, and her two daughters: Beloved and Denver. Throughout the novel, Morrison mines the complexity of this triangular relationship, often setting the two young women, who represent two possible paths for the family's future, against one another. Beloved is frighteningly childlike, while Denver struggles to mature. Beloved is frail, while Denver is hearty. Beloved is born into slavery (and dies because of it), while Denver comes into the world crossing a river into freedom. Importantly, Sethe's two daughters also serve opposing, yet complementary, structural functions in the novel. Denver is a kind of proxy for the reader, a semi-naïf confronted with a horrifying history that she must make sense of in order to understand her family, her community, and her nation.[4] By contrast, Beloved is the very figure of that history, the complex phenomenon that Denver and the reader alike must decipher: a traumatized and traumatizing specter, returned from the grave (or a white man's cell, or the belly of a slave ship) to make the present speak her name. Beloved represents the horror of the past, Denver the possibility of a future.

If one of the inciting incidents of the novel is the reunion of these two sisters, then its conclusion narrates their scattering once again. On the verge of giving birth herself, Beloved is cast out by the praying, singing, shouting women of the larger community. At the same time, Denver returns to that very community, to work and to school. In the final pages of the novel, Morrison lays out two paths for the inheritance of this family's troubled history and, by extension, history itself: one daughter banished but pregnant (literally) with the promise of future hauntings, the other reabsorbed into the social collective by way of education, learning "book stuff" on her way to Oberlin College (314). And while the dichotomy of Sethe's two daughters may invite a kind of either/or thinking on the part of the reader, the end of Morrison's *Beloved* suggests that both are in fact correct. History is inescapable and irreconcilable, and yet also knowable and recuperable. *Beloved* is a story that, as its final lines attest,

INTRODUCTION

cannot be *passed on*, and yet must not be passed over. Like the contemporary literary field that it both emerged from and shaped indelibly, Morrison's novel is fixated on a traumatic past that, in the final account, becomes exorcized and institutionalized all at once.

For Sethe, and those who have come before her, there is "nothing in the world more dangerous than a white schoolteacher" (314). The archvillain of the novel, who bears that name, not only prevents Sethe from educating herself but victimizes her repeatedly within the schoolroom itself. Schoolteacher dehumanizes Sethe by overseeing her rape at the hands of his pupils, but also by inviting them to catalogue her human and animal qualities in a side-by-side comparison.[5] What is more, he forces Sethe to make the ink that teacher and student alike use to write her out of humanity. As she laments at the close of the novel, "I made the ink. . . . He couldn't have done it if I hadn't made the ink" (320). A generation later, her daughter is on her way to a liberal arts education. For mother, the school is a site of terror; for daughter, possibility. One generation makes the ink, the next wields the pen.

When *Beloved* became a finalist for the National Book Award in the late 1980s, Morrison was one of only a handful of Black novelists to be shortlisted for the prize in the decades since Ralph Ellison's *Invisible Man* (1952) won it in the early 1950s.[6] Whereas *Invisible Man* opens with the protagonist being expelled from college, following him as he is employed to paint the world "Optic White," *Beloved* closes with Morrison's own young protagonist at the precipice of college admission, so that she might write a different story with the ink her mother made. While the tale the invisible man tells is his own, its setting the contemporary world in which he lives, Denver's narrative is one of *rememory*, of grappling with the world that came before her. The same is true of Ellison and Morrison respectively: the former celebrated for narrating the nation as it is, the latter canonized for chronicling it as it was. And though neither Morrison nor *Beloved* inaugurated this shift in literary value singlehandedly, novel and

INTRODUCTION

novelist alike came to exemplify it for the generation of readers, teachers, scholars, and writers that followed.

One way of understanding this book is as the story of how American literature moved from Ellison to Morrison to where we are now—of how, in other words, the past came to supplant the present in contemporary American fiction. Yet another way to think of the chapters that follow is as a narrative of the afterlives of Sethe's two daughters, of what happened when Denver went off to college, and of what, exactly, Beloved gave birth to.

■ ■ ■

In the decades since the 1980s, the American literary field has undergone two major and interrelated transformations. The cultural organizations that fund, publish, prize, teach, and canonize literary fiction have become increasingly diverse, recognizing racially and ethnically minoritized writers that they had previously overlooked.[7] At the same time, these literary institutions have fundamentally reorganized themselves around the aesthetic, pedagogical, and political value of the historical past, privileging historical fiction above all other literary genres. Nearly every metric of contemporary canonization bears this out. Historical fiction makes up 70 percent of the post-1945 novels that are most taught in American universities.[8] Likewise, while historical fiction accounted for just over half of all novels shortlisted for a major American prize between 1950 and 1979, in the 1980s works of historical fiction were shortlisted eighty times, a full two-thirds of the decade's shortlisted novels. This trend only intensified at the turn of the twenty-first century, with novels set in the past comprising nearly three-quarters of all shortlisted novels between 2000 and 2019, and reaching a whopping 80 percent in the first decade of the twenty-first century alone.[9] Scholarly attention—as evidenced by the number of articles and book chapters on a given work listed in the Modern Language Association's International

INTRODUCTION

Bibliography—also heavily favors historical fiction.[10] Given all this, it is safe to say that historical fiction now stands at the very center of the American literary canon.

This overwhelming turn toward the historical past has both motivated, and been motivated by, the increasing recognition of Black, Asian American, Latinx, and Indigenous writers within the literary canon. Over the past five decades, minoritized novelists have been canonized almost exclusively for the writing of historical fiction.[11] Of the top ten most-taught novels by writers of color published after 1945, eight are works of historical fiction. Of the fifty-four novels by writers of color to be shortlisted for a major American prize between 1980 and 2010, all but four are works of historical fiction. Richard Jean So has argued that racial disparities in twentieth-century publishing constituted a kind of "cultural redlining," wherein writers of color were largely unrepresented.[12] While the literary canon of the early twenty-first century is markedly more inclusive, a different sort of redlining still exists: not the outright refusal of literary institutions to enfranchise minoritized writers, but a selective elevation that enfranchises those writers only in a single sector of the literary field.[13] Though the pantheon of American literature may be more racially and ethnically diverse than it has ever been, the criteria that consecrate minoritized writers have never been more homogeneous.

Previous scholarship has attributed American fiction's fascination with history to a post–Cold War "absence of an overarching narrative," "symbolic compensation" for a postmodern "crisis" in historical consciousness, and shifting theories of historiography.[14] By contrast, I argue that American literature's historical turn is the product of a series of phenomena far more local to the literary field itself. In the early 1980s, for example, the National Endowment for the Arts (NEA) adopted an anonymous selection process for their literature fellowships—the main channel of federal funding for American writers—that led to the use of a work's historical setting as a way of identifying its author's identity. In the years that followed these

INTRODUCTION

reforms, the NEA not only sponsored scores of minoritized authors, but minoritized authors of historical fiction in particular.[15] Throughout the 1980s, and in the decades since, several key institutions of literary canon formation—from literary prize organizations to university English departments—transformed in ways that either expressly or implicitly promoted historical fiction as contemporary literature's most prestigious and politically potent genre. These transformations impacted the careers of twentieth-century writers such as Leslie Marmon Silko, Julia Alvarez, and David Bradley, and they shaped those of twenty-first-century writers such as Colson Whitehead, Julie Otsuka, Jesmyn Ward, and Tommy Orange.

This book investigates the work of these and other contemporary novelists, examining it both at the level of the sentence and within a complex system of social relations. Here again, Morrison's example is instructive. Though *Beloved* is now firmly ensconced in the American literary canon, its status in the late 1980s was far less assured. The novel was one of only a handful of finalists for the 1987 National Book Award and National Book Critics Circle Award, but it failed to win either prestigious prize. And although *Beloved* was still in the running for the Pulitzer Prize for Fiction, that award had gone to an African American writer only twice before in its nearly seventy-year history. In advance of the Pulitzer committee's decision, a group of nearly fifty Black authors, critics, and scholars published a statement in the *New York Times Book Review* praising Morrison's novel and stressing its importance in and to contemporary literature. Amid the 1980s culture wars, both the statement—seen by some as an effort to influence the prize committee's aesthetic impartiality—and the novel that it lauded were met with significant conservative opposition.[16] By 1987, debates over the status of history in fiction, and which novelists in particular would be rewarded for writing it, were already well underway.

By 1987, major literary awards like the National Book Award and the Pulitzer Prize had already gone to Alice Walker for her

INTRODUCTION

historical novel *The Color Purple* (1982), and shortlisted David Bradley's and Louise Erdrich's historical fiction as finalists. In fact, in the ten years before *Beloved*, these two prizes and the National Book Critics Circle award shortlisted more works of fiction by writers of color than they had in the three decades before that. At the same time, Black and ethnic studies curricula were becoming the object of a concerted backlash, both institutionally and on the national political stage. At the height of the so-called canon wars, when revising literary history was construed by some as an effort to erase it altogether, historical fiction by minoritized writers emerged as the ideal literary form to placate "traditionalists" and "multiculturalists" alike. It also offered an ideal object of study for the growing cadre of New Historicists, literary scholars eager to embed and investigate fiction within its historical contexts. Modernizing the syllabus while endowing it with historicity, diversifying the canon while engaging canonical history, historical fiction not only stood at the intersection of literary disputes over methodology and multiculturalism in the late twentieth century but also operated as those debates' central yet invisible category. In the late 1980s, Stephen Greenblatt's and Toni Morrison's "desire to speak with the dead" may have been different, but they were not discontinuous.[17]

In retrospect, it becomes clear that Morrison's career was both a catalyst for and an index of the myriad structural changes that were taking place in the central institutions of the literary field in the late twentieth century. While her body of work stands as a monumental literary achievement in its own right, Morrison's curriculum vitae reads as a veritable catalogue of the organizations that assess and announce such an achievement. These include Howard University (as an undergraduate English major); Cornell University (as a graduate student in English and American literature); the National Endowment for the Arts (as an advisor to its literature program); Random House (as an editor); the *New York Times* and *New York Review of Books* (as a critic); Oprah's Book Club (as a four-time featured author);

INTRODUCTION

the Pulitzer and Nobel prizes (among others, as an honoree); Yale University, Bard College, Rutgers, SUNY Purchase, and Princeton (among others, as a member of the faculty); Harvard University Press (as a scholar of literary history); and various other arts organizations, including the Princeton Atelier writers workshop (as its founder). As Morrison herself put it in one interview, "I know it seems like a lot.... But I really only do one thing. I read books. I teach books. I write books. I think about books. It's one job."[18]

Although the work of contemporary authorship, as Morrison's résumé makes clear, is in fact not one but many different kinds of jobs, it is in the best interest of novelists and many others in the literary field to maintain the illusion of literary production by overlooking the decidedly unenchanting, nonmiraculous work of these institutions. But Morrison's career is a testament to the power of behind-the-scenes and often bureaucratic literary labor. At Random House she edited the work of Toni Cade Bambara, Angela Davis, and Gayl Jones. She shepherded iconic anthologies such as *Contemporary African Literature* and *The Black Book* into the world.[19] And she understood the importance of the university—its classrooms and curricula—as a central venue for the making of literary careers.[20]

Even in her scholarship, Morrison was deeply attuned to the structures that make artistic production possible as well as shape its thinking. In 1990, she delivered the Massey Lectures in the History of American Civilization at Harvard University, which were later published as *Playing in the Dark: Whiteness and the Literary Imagination* (1992). Given the occasion and the author's status as the nation's preeminent historical novelist, it is perhaps unsurprising that Morrison turned in her lectures toward the past. More specifically, she turned to the history of the American literary canon and the conspicuous absence of African American voices in "the silence of four hundred years."[21] Narrating the process of discovery that had motivated her lectures, Morrison explained: "It is as if I had been looking at a fishbowl—the glide and flick of the golden scales... the castles at the bottom, surrounded by pebbles and tiny, intricate fonds of green; the barely disturbed water . . . the tranquil bubbles traveling to the surface—and suddenly I saw the bowl, the structure that transparently (and invisibly) permits the ordered life it contains to exist in the larger world."[22]

This book follows Morrison in that pursuit by recognizing, examining, and critiquing the structures that have authorized American fiction for the last five decades. As Pierre Bourdieu has argued, world-historical phenomena like "economic crises, technical transformations, [and] political revolutions . . . of which traditional social history seeks the direct manifestation in [artistic] works, can only be exercised by the intermediary of the transformations of the structure of the field which these factors may determine."[23] In other words, the *Brown v. Board of Education* decision, the election of Ronald Reagan, the fall of the Berlin Wall, the rise of the internet, the 9/11 attacks, the 2008 financial crisis, and the Covid-19 pandemic all come to bear on literary history, but they can do so only by way of the mediating actors, organizations, and logics of the literary field. James F. English has called this "the middle-zone of cultural space," the area between individual writers and history writ large.[24] A wealth of recent scholarship has taken seriously the connections between literary form and the literary institutions that occupy this middle zone: the tremendous influence of creative writing programs such as the Iowa Writers' Workshop; the complex and increasingly important work of literary agents; the politics of contemporary publishing, from the conglomerated Big Five to independent presses like Holloway House and McSweeney's; the internationalization of those publishers and its influence on the language(s) of fiction; the formation and organization of contemporary reading practices; the continuously contested power of literary prizes; and the relation between university English departments, evolving scholarly paradigms, and an ever-changing canon.[25]

While many of these studies have focused, broadly speaking, on either the production or reception of contemporary fiction, this book

INTRODUCTION

traces the continuous feedback loop that exists between the two: the way that discourses of canon formation in university English departments or on literary prize juries mediate booksellers' promotion protocols, and the acquisition priorities of publishers and agents, which inflect the training of the coming generation of novelists and literary scholars. Though it is tempting to try to locate the originary forces of the contemporary literary field, the greatest explanatory power lies in the investigation of this dynamic circulatory system of aesthetic value. If a central insight of Mark McGurl's work on the creative writing program is that literary historians have overlooked the importance of their colleagues across the hall in creative writing, then this book argues that it is equally essential to consider how those writers were influenced by the evolving priorities of their own departmental neighbors. American fiction's turn toward the historical past has as much to do with individual authors and world-historical phenomena as it does the clash, or rather the convergence, of critical and institutional paradigms like the New Historicism and literary multiculturalism. To understand how historical fiction, and historical fiction by minoritized writers in particular, came to define the contemporary American literary canon, it will first be necessary to define and describe those constituent terms.

HISTORICAL FICTION AND THE NEW HISTORICAL SINCERITY

Imagine a novel published earlier this year that takes place in the historical present and narrates a woman taking a trip to visit her friend for a weekend. The two go out to dinner, and afterward dancing, and they spend much of their time examining the significance of their relationship in one another's lives. (Perhaps you have read a novel like this, perhaps even earlier this year.) Now imagine that that same novel, with its same characters and plot, is set in the late 2010s, and

INTRODUCTION

we know this simply because of the style of pants the woman is wearing, the functionality of her friend's phone, and the music that is playing as they dance. Now imagine a novel that makes use of those same types of details to set itself ten years earlier, two decades prior to its publication, in the early 2000s.

Now perhaps it takes place in 2001 specifically, and the woman's friend lives in New York City. Perhaps the novel takes place on the weekend before Tuesday, September 11, 2001, and the woman's friend works on the 107th floor of the South Tower of the World Trade Center. Or perhaps it is set in 1995 and the woman is Hillary Rodham Clinton, visiting South Asia as First Lady of the United States. Or imagine it takes place on a weekend in 1965, and the woman is Hillary Diane Rodham, the President of Wellesley College's Young Republicans, talking with her friend about the Vietnam War. Or it is 1865, and the woman is Mary Todd Lincoln, accompanying her husband to a performance of *Our American Cousin* at Ford's Theatre.

Now imagine a novel that closely follows Abraham Lincoln through that very evening, as well as the four years of his presidency that preceded it, documenting in nearly biographical detail the central crises of that crucible in American history. Or one that transforms Lincoln into a buffoonish caricature, riddling his speech with anachronisms and narrating as escaped slaves watch his assassination live on satellite television from Canada. Or one that registers the news of Lincoln's death only obliquely, as it follows several generations in a family of enslaved persons from 1750s Gambia to the 1970s United States. Or a novel in which the name Lincoln never appears, which follows three women living in a gray and white house outside of Cincinnati, Ohio, in 1873.

While, to some readers, only a select few of these would be considered examples of *the historical novel*, I consider all of them except the first to be works of historical fiction. Though the terms *historical fiction* and *the historical novel* are often used interchangeably, they name two related yet distinct literary objects. *Historical fiction* describes a broad continuum of fictionalizations of the historical past.²⁶ *The historical novel* describes a specific sector of that continuum occupied by narratives that are primarily concerned with world-historical figures and events, and that take place anywhere between one generation and several centuries before their publication. Yet between a novel concerned with the amorphous historical present ("a woman takes a trip to visit her friend") and a meticulously researched novel that conventionally portrays major persons or events ("Abraham Lincoln is assassinated at Ford's Theatre") lies a wide spectrum of narratives that represent the historical past. These novels fictionalize history variously, and to various extents, by way of the events, figures, and periods that they narrate; the relative historical significance of those events or figures, and the proximity of their central characters to them; the vaguely remembered or highly researched period details that they describe; the fact-laden realism or unruly fabulation of their narrative styles; the breadth and depth of their meditations on history and historiography; and the historical distance between when they are published and when they take place. Each of these factors lends more or less historicity to a work of fiction, and taken together they demonstrate that the fictional representation of the historical past is not a binary matter (i.e., a book either *is* or *is not* a historical novel), but rather an issue of degree.

In this way, the archive of this book is also part of its argument: namely, that both the definition of historical fiction and the critical understanding of its narrative strategies must expand in order to accurately describe the great wealth of historical fiction that has been produced over the last five decades. Diverse in form and focus as twentieth- and twenty-first-century historical fiction has become, it seems less accurate to describe it as a single, monolithic genre than as a kind of contemporary literary mode, a more capacious term that unites multiple and increasingly porous genres of historical narratives while acknowledging their shared aesthetic, political, and pedagogical projects. Just as a novel that takes place on a distant planet would

INTRODUCTION

be considered a work of science fiction, regardless of whether its narrative was primarily an epic or a romance or a mystery, so too can a novel set in the historical past, regardless of the exact distance or significance or facticity of that past, be considered a work of historical fiction.

In the 1980s and 1990s, Fredric Jameson argued that one of the many failings of contemporary historical fiction was its "omnivorous, and well-nigh libidinal historicism," its "random cannibalization of all the styles of the past."[27] More than twenty years later, Jameson doubled down on that claim in an essay titled "The Historical Novel Today, or, Is It Still Possible?" There he lamented that "the historical novel seems doomed to make arbitrary selections from the great menu of the past, so many differing and colorful segments or periods catering to the historicist taste, and all now ... more or less equal in value."[28] Surveying the most notable works (and authors) of historical fiction over the past forty years, however, quickly reveals that this assessment is both too narrow and too broad. On the one hand, measuring such a varied collection of texts against a preordained and restrictive definition of what *the* historical novel can and should do overlooks what a great many contemporary historical novelists have actually produced. On the other, the charge that beyond aesthetic orthodoxy lies only arbitrariness (i.e., random selections from "the great menu of the past") fails to register just how selective—one might even say discerning—writers and readers have been when it comes to their appetites for history.[29]

Though the historical settings of contemporary American fiction are as diverse as the authors who create them, a significant portion of this work falls within a highly specific constellation of historical subgenres: contemporary narratives of slavery, Holocaust fiction and the World War II novel, the multigenerational family saga, narratives of immigration, and the novel of recent history. Testifying to the prominence of these individual subgenres, many of the works discussed in this book fall under the rubric of not one but two or more of them. Ruth Ozeki's *A Tale for the Time Being* (2013) chronicles the history of Japanese airmen during World War II, as well as the recent history of the 2011 Tōhoku earthquake and Fukushima nuclear disaster. Yaa Gyasi's *Homegoing* (2016) is a multigenerational historical novel that narrates two halves of a family tree divided by enslavement but regrafted two centuries later by way of immigration from Ghana to the United States. Margaret Wilkerson Sexton's *A Kind of Freedom* (2017) is a World War II novel, a multigenerational family saga, and a novel of recent history that follows three generations of a Black family living in New Orleans from the 1940s through the 1980s to the period just after Hurricane Katrina. The chapters of Sexton's novel cycle repeatedly through these three periods, and these three historical genres, emphasizing key features of the contemporary American historical imagination. While it may seem odd to assemble works as various as Colson Whitehead's *The Underground Railroad* (2016), Min Jin Lee's *Pachinko* (2017), and Ben Lerner's *10:04* (2014) under the single heading of historical fiction, this more inclusive approach allows us not only to see the forest for the trees—that is, the important subgenres that connect works like *The Underground Railroad* to *Homegoing* or *Beloved*—but also to recognize the larger literary ecosystem that allows those diverse forms to flourish. While each of the historical genres listed here has become central to the contemporary American canon, taken together they represent a sea change in conceptions of literary prestige and a shift in value from narratives of the way we live now to chronicles in which "nothing ever dies."[30]

To understand this transformation fully, it is necessary to move beyond traditional definitions of historical fiction and its proper attention, whether in terms of period, geography, theme, or aesthetics. More than two centuries ago, Walter Scott argued that a historical novel should tell the tales "of the last generation" at a safe distance of "sixty years since."[31] The appeal of such a numeric litmus test for genre, one that draws a bright line between present and past, is clear.

INTRODUCTION

But what to make of novels—by Ozeki, Lerner, and others—that are set only a handful of years before they are published and work to create, or at least emphasize, a historical boundary between those two periods? As I discuss in chapter 5, these "recent historical novels" not only testify to the historical significance of their central events but also assert a meaningful historical distance from them. Defining the historical novel according to Scott's method of counting years would therefore underestimate the proliferation of historical fiction by overlooking new formulations of the genre in contemporary American literature.[32]

We must also enlarge our conception of the geographical scale of historical fiction, which has long been associated with the project of national mythmaking.[33] While the novels and novelists discussed in this book are all, to some extent, American, they are neither monolithic nor uncritical in their Americanness.[34] For some of the authors studied here the United States is their birthplace, or perhaps the place they call home; for others it is a place of self-imposed exile, a nation in which to seek refuge or to seek refuge from. The novels, too, are as ambivalently American as they are insistently transnational in their histories: they move with dexterity from Los Angeles to Ho Chi Minh City, from Accra to Baltimore and San Francisco, from New York to Birkenau, Lisbon, Madrid, Tokyo, Santo Domingo, and back again.[35] Yet they also demonstrate how contemporary historical fiction has worked over the last five decades to push at the borderlines of American history, challenging nationalist narratives of the United States by expanding their scope and diversifying their attention.

All that said, it is important to acknowledge the limits of this book's central thesis. Expanding the ambit of historical fiction does not mean enlarging it to the point where every novel falls within its scope. There are novels narrated in the past tense that are nonetheless not set in the historical past. There are novels that take up the passage of time as a central theme, or meditate on history and historiography (as Ellison does in *Invisible Man*), but nevertheless take

INTRODUCTION

place in the historical present or the speculative future.[36] There are those that with the distance of some years can be read as emerging from their immediate historical context, but that do not distinguish between the time of their writing and the time of what is written. These are works that can *be historicized*, but that do not historicize themselves. Of course, these novels have much to teach us about fictional setting, narrative temporality, and larger questions about the relation between literature and the philosophy of history, but they are not works of historical fiction, nor the subject of this book. My concern here is the wide range of contemporary American fiction set in the historical past and invested in recovering the stories of events, persons, or peoples that have been lost or overlooked.

Likewise, it is not difficult to think of racialized authors who have been canonized for writing about the present, or those who have written historical fiction while resisting the institutions, genres, and aesthetics described here. Regrettably, though necessarily, this book will overlook several important exceptions in favor of the "rules" they prove. Avid readers are skilled at identifying exceptions to any broad claim about literary history, but they are likewise adept at distinguishing between the exceptional and the exemplary. The hope is that what the chapters that follow sacrifice in universal applicability they more than make up for in broad descriptive power. Historical fiction has come to pervade the contemporary American literary canon, and the literary institutions that comprise it, as a result of simultaneous campaigns to both diversify and historicize American literature.

These changes arrived at the tail end of a century in which the status of historical fiction underwent a remarkable renovation. According to Perry Anderson's history of the genre, historical fiction was regarded as both popular and "déclassé" for much of the twentieth century, a literary tradition that consisted of "a few antique jewels on a huge mound of trash."[37] With the exception of high modernist historical novels by the likes of William Faulkner, Willa Cather, and John Dos Passos, the genre that Henry James famously "condemned" for

INTRODUCTION

its "fatal *cheapness*" was for decades associated more with bodice-ripping historical romances than with historiographical revision or recovery.[38] This is partly why so many previous theorizations of historical fiction have worked to mark out what does, and does not, count as *the* historical novel—as if tightfisted classification might protect the genre from its cut-rate reputation.

In the 1960s and 1970s, however, writers like Joseph Heller, E. L. Doctorow, Thomas Pynchon, Ishmael Reed, and Kurt Vonnegut recuperated the genre as a province for serious thinking, even if often couched in comedy. These writers of postmodern historical fiction—what Linda Hutcheon has labeled "historiographic metafiction" and Amy Elias has dubbed "metahistorical romance"—"meld[ed] fantasy, anachronism, metafictionality, and other fabulatory techniques with the facts of history" in order to "project skepticism and irony about the possibilities for true historical knowledge and suspicion of any social or historical narrative."[39] This wave of postmodern historical writing not only reflected developments in the field of historiography (as Hutcheon and Elias make clear, focusing on the work of historians like Hayden White), but it also resuscitated the genre's claims to literary prestige as much as mass-market popularity.

As late as the 1970s, historical novels such as Gore Vidal's *Burr* (1973) and E. L. Doctorow's *Ragtime* (1975) appeared on both the bestseller list and the shortlist for the National Book Award. Beginning in the 1980s, however, these two sectors of the literary field diverged considerably. While as much as 80 percent of bestsellers were "in [a] crudely literal sense, 'about' the contemporary moment," the novels consecrated by cultural institutions like the NEA, literary prizes, and the university became increasingly historical.[40] At least in the United States, literary fiction has never been more historical—nor historical fiction more literary—than it has been over the last forty years. But it is also important to note that the historical turn in American literature is specific to the corner of the literary world invested in cultural prestige, or "symbolic capital," over and above mass readership and its financial returns.⁴¹ As literary fiction is pushed further and further from the center of American culture—displaced by blockbuster bestsellers, and a host of other new and not-so-new media—the institutions involved in its consecration become ever more important, as do their institutional discourses about what defines "literariness" itself. After all, the contemporary canon is not only a list of texts but also a discourse about aesthetic value. One way of understanding literary fiction's turn toward the historical past and the self-evident cultural significance that that past connotes is to say that, amid the ongoing assault on literary fiction's relevance to culture, falling back into history is to some extent a retreat to higher ground.

The privileging of not just historical fiction, but historical fiction by and about minoritized figures, is also a phenomenon specific to the more rarefied sectors of the American literary field. As Richard Jean So has demonstrated, in the second half of the twentieth century, 98 percent of all bestsellers and 97 percent of all novels brought to market by publishing giant Random House were written by white authors.⁴² By contrast, a close examination of university syllabi and the history of literary prizes reveals that more than half of the most-taught novels published after 1945 are by writers of color, and that 35 percent of all novels shortlisted for a major literary award from 2000 to 2019 are by writers of color.⁴³ Though the American literary field as a whole is shockingly homogeneous, the institutions that comprise the contemporary canon are not just *one* venue for investigating the work of marginalized writers, but rather the chief site of their enfranchisement in the American literary field. Moreover, the fact that approximately 80 percent of these most-taught and shortlisted novels by minoritized writers are works of historical fiction suggests that the genre is itself the primary locus of racial diversity in contemporary American literature.⁴⁴

Many of the aesthetic tropes of the postmodern period have lived on in contemporary historical fiction, though repurposed for

INTRODUCTION

altogether different ends. Historical novels by Whitehead, Lerner, and Ozeki (among several others discussed here) employ what might be described as postmodern styles and devices. These works confirm that anachronism, metafiction, and fabulation remain prevalent in historical fiction well into the first decades of the twenty-first century. These novels are historiographic and metafictional, to be sure, but their ambivalent relationship to the historical record is concerned more with revising it than undermining it altogether. Over the last five decades, "the drive to write and know history" has transformed from a potentially "futile endeavor" into the prime directive of American literary fiction. While, according to Elias, "what is left to postmodernists" is only "the ability to theorize and ironically desire history rather than access it through discovery and reconstruction," what sets apart the period of literary history described here is a newly sincere belief in fiction's ability to access, reconstruct, and even recuperate the historical past.[45] The historical novelists examined in the chapters that follow can be characterized by a *new historical sincerity*: a set of literary aesthetics that blends New Historicism's commitment to historical recovery with what Lee Konstantinou and Adam Kelly have respectively described as contemporary fiction's "post-irony" and "new sincerity."[46] For this diverse group of authors, postmodern techniques like genre pastiche, intertextual citation, and metafiction are repurposed not as a means of interrogating the very possibility of historical knowledge, but rather as a method for producing that knowledge in the first place.

THE CANON'S INSIDE MAN

Viet Thanh Nguyen's *The Sympathizer* (2015) provides an especially good example of *new historical sincerity* and its postmodern aesthetics shorn of postmodern irony. In an early chapter of the novel, Nguyen's narrator describes hearing stories of other Vietnamese American

INTRODUCTION

refugees, concatenating them into a single sentence that stretches across two pages. The result combines a Pynchonesque maximalism with a Morrisonian attention to "disremembered" personal histories:

> We learned of the clan turned into slave labor by a farmer in Modesto, and the naive girl who flew to Spokane to marry her GI sweetheart and was sold to a brothel, and the widower with nine children who went out into a Minnesotan winter and lay down in the snow on his back with mouth open until he was buried and frozen, and the ex-Ranger who bought a gun and dispatched his wife and two children before killing himself in Cleveland, and the regretful refugees on Guam who petitioned to go back to our homeland, never to be heard from again . . .[47]

This stunning series of miniaturized elegies emphasizes Nguyen's commitment to the narration of historical experiences, and traumas in particular, that have been previously overlooked. At the same time, this list of literary microhistories also emphasizes the seeming inexhaustibility of this aesthetic and political project. Each of these stories, *all* of these stories, the passage seems to suggest, should be recognized and honored. By dramatizing not only the single narrative of its protagonist but also the practically limitless archive from which it is drawn, Nguyen's novel reflects the new "archival economy" that emerged from historicism's and literary multiculturalism's shared project of recovery, as well as the archival imperative that marks contemporary American fiction.[48] The story of how these movements collided, and intertwined, is the subject of this section.

If the comparison to *Invisible Man* is implicit in *Beloved*, in *The Sympathizer*, it is the novel's opening gambit. The book begins: "I am a spy, a sleeper, a spook, a man of two faces. Perhaps not surprisingly, I am also a man of two minds" (1). Here the similarities to Ellison's iconic opening lines are far from invisible.[49] Both narrators define themselves playfully in relation to mass cultural genres, and both

INTRODUCTION

declare, at the very start, their complex relations to the canon of American literature. Whereas Ellison's invisible man begins by dispensing with canonical figures, asserting that he is decidedly "not a spook like those who haunted Edgar Allan Poe," Nguyen's similarly unnamed protagonist opens by evoking them.[50] The first paragraphs of *The Sympathizer* look to the past in two ways, then: the historical past of the mid-1970s, in the months after the fall of Saigon when the novel is set, and the literary-historical past that the novel cites repeatedly throughout. The first paragraph alludes to the fiction of the 1950s in the figure of Ellison. The second paragraph conjures T. S. Eliot and the high modernist tradition of the early twentieth century ("The month in question was April, the cruelest month"), as well as Charles Dickens and the historical novels of the nineteenth century ("It was a month in which a war . . . would lose its limbs. . . . It was a month that meant everything to all the people in our small part of the world") (1). As the novel continues, Nguyen's allusions to the literary canon are nearly as comprehensive as an exam for the English PhD: Shakespeare, Milton, Emerson, Whitman, Stowe, Twain, Kipling, Kafka, and Faulkner all make appearances, as do Raymond Chandler, Graham Greene, Carlos Bulosan, Noël Coward, Philip Roth, Maxine Hong Kingston, Joan Didion, and Frank Chin.[51]

Given its many references to the pantheon of literary greats, including African American and Asian American writers whose names have been added only in the last several decades, *The Sympathizer* is not just metafictional but specifically *metacanonical*. From its very first lines to its Norton-like anthology of allusions, the novel stakes a claim to canonicity—the writerly equivalent of the baseball player pointing to the stadium fences—while at the same time registering the contingent quality of literary consecration. Nguyen is not the only contemporary novelist whom we might call metacanonical: Colson Whitehead cites Aphra Behn and Toni Morrison in the same breath by naming one of the central characters in *The Underground Railroad* Caesar Garner; Tommy Orange pays homage to Louise Erdrich in

INTRODUCTION

There There (2018), Yaa Gyasi to Nella Larsen in *Homegoing*; and Valeria Luiselli's *Lost Children Archive* (2019) is itself a diverse archive of literary history. For these writers, as for Nguyen himself, insistent allusion to the literary canon, and the newly inclusive literary canon in particular, is not simply an act of literary bravado but a gesture that records the influence of the minoritized writers who came before them and whose work made their own canonization possible.

On one level, this metacanonical style anticipates the attention of literary scholars and their students, and it acknowledges the power of literary institutions like the university to make or break a writer's career in the long term. On another, it emphasizes how the canon itself has long been viewed as an emblem of nationalism and cultural hegemony and has only recently—in these writers' lifetimes—begun to transform. If, as I have argued, Toni Morrison is the novelist who best exemplifies the contentious institutionalization of minoritized writers in the late twentieth century, Nguyen typifies the next generation of American novelists, twenty-first-century writers who came of age during the canon wars that marked Morrison's career and came to prominence in their wake.

In an interview just after *The Sympathizer* was published, Nguyen asserted that while writing the novel, he was "very conscious of what Toni Morrison has said about how she writes" and how she wrote *Beloved* in particular.[52] Not only did Nguyen borrow one of *Beloved*'s most iconic lines for the title of his book on the historical memory of the Vietnam War, *Nothing Ever Dies* (2016), but he also alludes to Morrison's novel directly in an early chapter of *The Sympathizer*.[53] Nguyen's protagonist is instructed by the chair of "the Department of Oriental Studies" at Occidental College to complete a particularly Schoolteacher-esque "homework assignment": "I was to take a sheet of paper and fold it in half vertically. On the top, I was to write *Orient* on the left and *Occident* on the right. Then I was to write down my Oriental and Occidental qualities. Imagine this exercise as an indexing of yourself, the Chair had said" (63). After some trepidation, the protagonist agrees to produce such a chart, which Nguyen copies out on the very next page.

This scene acknowledges the continuity between the experience of Nguyen's protagonist and Sethe's own victimization by figures of educational authority. Yet the differences between these two scenes of forced categorization are significant for what they reveal about each protagonist's—and, indeed, each author's—relation to institutions of higher learning. While Sethe is the unwilling object of scholarly classification, Nguyen's protagonist is coerced into "indexing" himself. While Sethe is barred (by law) from the academy, Nguyen's protagonist is offered both an academic scholarship and a job as "the dour face of the Department of Oriental Studies" (60). Although both characters are subject to the racism inherent in institutions of knowledge production, *The Sympathizer*'s narrator endures this within, and under the auspices of, the university, as a producer of knowledge himself. If Ellison's novel is in large part about the experience of being expelled from cultural institutions, and Morrison's ends with gaining tentative admission to them, then Nguyen's both narrates and thematizes the experience of working within them as a kind of double agent. Not an invisible man, in other words, but an inside man.

Of course, Nguyen's protagonist is literally a double agent, working for communist forces in Vietnam while "undercover" as a political refugee in the United States.[54] As an undergraduate in the late 1960s, the narrator is "part scholarship student, part spy-in-training," pursuing "the mission assigned to [him]": namely, to "read American history and literature . . . becoming expert in all manner of American studies" (12). As his canonical education makes clear, the protagonist is not just a double agent, but an agent of double consciousness à la W. E. B. Du Bois. Nguyen has argued that this particularly literary form of "double consciousness is second nature" to anyone who has been "the only nonwhite person in an academic or literary setting, which happens often." Recalling his own time as an

INTRODUCTION

undergraduate and graduate student of literature at the University of California, Berkeley, in the 1990s, Nguyen cites a member of his PhD cohort, "a scholar of Chicano literature," who declared, "with a note of anger in his voice: 'We have to read their literature, but they don't have to read ours.'"[55] In this light, Nguyen's highly allusive, metacanonical style can be read not only as an homage to his literary forebears but also as a critique of the canon he seeks to amend.[56] While *The Sympathizer* narrates transformations in the American university in the 1970s, it also bears the traces of Nguyen's own literary education in the 1990s, indexing the radical energies that agitated for institutional change as well as the institutional energies that worked to contain that radicalism in the revision of the literary canon alone.

When the protagonist of *The Sympathizer* arrives back on campus to take up his position in the Department of Oriental Studies, he finds that things have changed considerably since his undergraduate days. In the twilight of the civil rights movement, during the late 1960s and early 1970s, student activists concerned themselves not only with the national politics of the Vietnam War but also the campus politics of structures like the Department of Oriental Studies itself. In 1969, the first Asian American studies programs were established at San Francisco State College and the University of California at Berkeley, "as a result of the Third World Strike, a boycott of classes by a multiracial and cross-class coalition of students, activists, and labor and community members."[57] In 1968 and 1969 alone, close to seven hundred institutions of higher learning created a range of "ethnic studies courses, programs, or departments" in an array of interdisciplinary fields such as African American studies, Asian American studies, Chicano studies, and American Indian studies.[58] As Roderick Ferguson has argued, taken together, these programs "denote the moments in which minority difference entered historical narration."[59]

By the time Nguyen's narrator would have returned to campus in the spring of 1975, at least thirteen hundred American colleges and universities offered courses in Black or ethnic studies, and a wave of new novels, collections, and anthologies featuring minoritized writers had been published.[60] Despite these tremendous developments, Nguyen's narrator finds that "the students were of a new breed, not interested in politics or the world like the previous generation" (61). Where then, the reader wonders, has the political ferment and campus activism of a few years earlier gone? One answer comes from the narrator's former English professor, Avery Wright Hammer. "If the bloody history of the past few decades has taught me anything," Hammer says, "it's that the defense of freedom demands the muscularity only America can provide. Even what we do at the college has its purpose. We teach you the best of what was thought and said not only to explain America to the world, as I have always encouraged you to do, but to defend it" (101–2). To wit, American imperialism—previously a military affair carried out by soldiers and protested in the streets—is now a primarily cultural mission, executed via syllabi and contested in university classrooms.

This displacement of national politics onto the politics of the English department, the transmutation of "bloody" conflicts into curricular ones, describes both the mid-1970s, when the novel is set, and the 1980s and 1990s, when Nguyen himself was a student. In a 2018 essay titled "Canon Fodder," Nguyen explains that he "came of age during the so-called culture wars . . . when university debates over what constituted American and Western culture transfixed the nation."[61] This was a period when both sides of the culture and canon wars focused their attentions on the historical past, and in particular how literary texts are uniquely equipped to preserve and disseminate historical memory. The "traditionalist" right was touting the triumphant "end of history," while at the same time decrying the erasure of that history in the form of proposed revisions to the literary canon.[62] Meanwhile, the "multiculturalist" left was demanding the academic recognition of previously disregarded histories and literary traditions. Even John Guillory's influential account of the canon debates, which sought to deconstruct these two positions, emphasizes

INTRODUCTION

their shared investment in historical knowledge. In the early 1990s, Guillory argued that "opening" the American literary canon would require a shift in focus from the past to the present, when marginalized writers had greater access to the means of literary production. Moreover, he cautioned that "no program of multiculturalism will succeed in producing more than a kind of favorable media-image of minority cultures if it is not supported at every point by an understanding of the historical relations between cultures."[63]

As Guillory's claims suggest, this was a period when the dominant methodologies of literary scholarship were changing as a growing number of New Historicists worked to "dissolve 'literature' back into the historical complex that academic criticism [had] traditionally held at arm's length."[64] This movement led to what Joseph North has described as the rise of the "historicist/contextualist paradigm" in the discipline, a "new consensus" that marked "a profound . . . change from reading for the purposes of aesthetic education . . . to reading for the purposes of historical and cultural analysis"; that is, from regarding works of literature primarily as works of art, to regarding them primarily as "diagnostic instruments for determining the state of the cultures in which they were written or read."[65] As Amy Hungerford has memorably put it, from this period onward historicism became "less a critical movement than a simple assumption about literary-critical work . . . not a wave but a tide, or even just the water we all swim in."[66]

In this context, historical fiction, and historical fiction by minoritized writers in particular, emerged as the ideal literary form to mediate between these disparate factions and interests. With a diverse array of historical narratives at its center, American literary studies could diversify the curriculum without sacrificing its historical orientation, all while making ample use of its newly preferred methodology. This is the institutional environment in which Viet Thanh Nguyen, along with a generation of writers including Colson Whitehead, Min Jin Lee, and Jesmyn Ward, received their literary education. And these are the institutional forces that transformed both the university and the larger literary field for writers such as Tommy Orange, Yaa Gyasi, Valeria Luiselli, and Margaret Wilkerson Sexton, who followed soon after.

Given that "widespread classroom adoption" is "the brass ring for publishing" literary fiction, these fundamental transformations in what and how people read in American universities have had outsized effects on the literary field beyond the campus walls.[67] As Black, Asian American, Latinx, and Indigenous writers have won increasing space within the literary canon for the recognition of previously ignored histories, the American literary field has increasingly incentivized this recovery work over and above fictionalizations of present political realities. To borrow from Kenneth Warren, over the last five decades the American literary canon has shifted from a primarily "prospective" orientation—one focused firmly on the present in order to imagine a materially different future—to a primarily "retrospective" one, borne back ceaselessly into the past.[68]

Here it is important to note that these institutional changes and their effects on the American literary field were not without precedent or exclusively racialized. Women writers and feminist scholars in this period worked to excavate women's voices from historical and literary-historical narratives that had continually silenced them. These efforts not only celebrated women authors but also assembled them in a feminist literary tradition that "recovered [and] remembered" literature's "lost foremothers."[69] In the decades since, this focus on revising the literary-historical record has influenced the protocols for canonizing women writers, privileging historical fiction as yet another venue for this type of recovery work. Eight of the ten most taught post-1945 novels by women are works of historical fiction.[70] Of the 183 novels by women writers to be shortlisted for a major American literary prize from 1980 to 2019, 133 (73 percent) are works of historical fiction. In the first decade of the twenty-first century alone, nearly 90 percent of shortlisted novels by women writers were works of

INTRODUCTION

historical fiction.[71] Both the fictional and nonfictional histories of women authors have indelibly shaped the contemporary American literary canon, and as such they also shape the archive of this book.

The history of Jewish writers' incorporation into American literary institutions and the American literary canon is similarly essential to this book's argument, not least because these phenomena provide a clarifying counterexample. As Josh Lambert has documented, over the course of the twentieth century, Jewish writers, editors, and critics gained increasing access to and prominence within the American literary field—so much so that by the 1960s and 1970s, "the idea that Jews possessed too much power in literature and publishing . . . had already begun to circulate in earnest."[72] Despite this antisemitic backlash, American Jews became so thoroughly integrated in the central institutions of American literature that by the end of the twentieth century their status as ethnicized others (at least within those institutions) began to fade. According to Jennifer Glaser, this placed Jewish American authors in "a particularly vexed place" in the culture wars of the 1980s and 1990s, torn between "the canon," which now included them, and "challenges to it."[73]

Nowhere is this ambivalence more apparent than in Philip Roth's *The Human Stain* (2000), a campus novel that chronicles the career of Athena College professor Coleman Silk. Though Silk is among only "a handful of Jews on the Athena faculty" when he is hired and later becomes "the first and only Jew" appointed as Dean of Faculty, he is ultimately forced into early retirement for making what are deemed to be racist remarks about two Black students.[74] While Silk starts his working life as an ethnicized outsider, he ends it counted among (in his words) the very "WASP establishment that ran this place when I first got here."[75] In this way, Silk's career indexes the careers of Jewish American writers like Philip Roth, who "in an era of rising multicultural and feminist literary critique, [were] coming to embody the status quo [they] had once sought to undermine."[76] But what to make of Roth's reveal, later in the novel, that Silk himself is

■ 28 ■

INTRODUCTION

Black and merely passing for Jewish? That it is not clear whether Roth is using this to authorize a critique of 1990s literary multiculturalism, which to some extent regarded him as "just another old white man," or to emphasize the comparative privilege of American Jews with regard to other marginalized groups is precisely the point.[77]

The ambiguous position of Jewish American writers in the late twentieth and early twenty-first centuries—between racialized writers struggling for literary enfranchisement and the largely white literary establishment from which they themselves had once been barred—is reflected in the extent to which they have been celebrated for writing about the historical past. From 1980 to 2019, works of historical fiction accounted for 67 percent of novels by Jewish writers to be shortlisted for a major American literary prize (including a number of historical novels about the Holocaust and World War II, which I take up in chapter 2). The same was true for 72 percent of shortlisted novels by Latinx writers, 76 percent of novels by Black writers, 80 percent of novels by Asian American writers, and 92 percent of novels by Indigenous writers. While the de-ethnicizing of Jewish American writers in the late twentieth century offers one explanation for the disparity in these figures, the fact that Jewish writers had already gained a foothold in the American literary canon prior to the curricular and methodological revolutions of the 1980s and 1990s offers yet another. As the recent history of Jewish American literature demonstrates, the protocols that govern the canonization of minoritized writers are both differentially applied and the product of specific institutional transformations.

Lisa Lowe argued almost thirty years ago that the "ethnic canon" may be compromised "if it is forced to subscribe to criteria defined by the majority canon in order to establish the formal unity of a literary tradition."[78] While this has to some extent taken place, that very process of compromise has transformed the entirety of the contemporary canon, not just the minoritized writers at its center. The discourses that govern the canonization of minoritized writers

INTRODUCTION

have also come to mediate the aesthetic criteria that organize white literary production. Martin Amis's backwards historical novel, *Time's Arrow* (1991), progressively essentializes his protagonist as a startling figure of white identity, just as Julia Alvarez does with her Dominican characters in *How the García Girls Lost Their Accents* (1991). Along with Jewish writers Michael Chabon and Jonathan Safran Foer, Anthony Doerr fashions his World War II novel into an ornate cabinet of curiosities, a collection of eccentricities and arcane fascinations that produces a sense of historical specificity, which can be read as a kind of unconscious compensation for the deracination of whiteness. In *Leaving the Atocha Station* (2011) and *10:04*, Ben Lerner applies the historiographic paradigms of "microhistory" and "history from below" to the tragedies of recent history, reimagining historical fiction on the model of minoritized histories. All this is not to say that these white writers are affecting an interest in history as some kind of canny appropriation of the means by which writers of color have entered the canon. Likewise, this book is not arguing that minoritized writers have a particular penchant for historical fiction as a literary form, but rather that minoritized writers have been particularly celebrated for working within that form—so much so that white writers, too, are incentivized to follow suit and rewarded for doing so. But it is important to note that both phenomena are the results of institutionalized aesthetic judgment, rather than individual aesthetic preference or cynical strategizing.

According to Black and ethnic studies scholars, what does require careful strategizing is how to institutionalize minoritized writers and marginalized histories without also standardizing difference and neutralizing critique. In Mark Chiang's words, this is a question of "what it means for [a] field to become an integral part of the very institution that it initially opposed and sought to transform."[79] Or, to put it in terms of *The Sympathizer* and its protagonist, how to be both "the dour face of the Oriental Studies department" and work, at the same time, as a kind of double agent. As Nguyen himself puts it: "[I] recognize who I am.... I am not the avant-garde artist from the margins who's going to try to destroy the center from the outside.... I'm the guy from inside-out—and that's just my personality, my aesthetic."[80] Like his protagonist, Nguyen's work "from inside-out" is not only about how minoritized subjects are shaped by institutions but also about the challenges of trying to transform those institutions from within. This is especially apparent when *The Sympathizer*'s narrator begins work as a cultural "consultant" on *The Hamlet*, a Hollywood blockbuster of the Vietnam War that bears an unmistakable resemblance to Francis Ford Coppola's *Apocalypse Now* (139). Despite his initial optimism, the narrator ultimately arrives at the novel's most searing indictment of cultural institutions and their co-option of minority difference: "They owned the means of production, and therefore the means of representation, and the best that we could ever hope for was to get a word in edgewise before our anonymous deaths" (179). Yet in Nguyen's novel, this is as true *on set* as it is *on campus*. *The Sympathizer* suggests that the straw man of popular culture may be closer to a red herring, a distraction from how the institutions of literary fiction have themselves fixed on historical fiction in such a way that ultimately contains writers like Nguyen.[81]

Scholars have argued for decades that the representational politics of diversifying syllabi and curricula run the risk of "overvaloriz[ing] aesthetic culture by ascribing agencies to aesthetic culture all by itself, apart from social and material forces."[82] While literature and literary study can be politically galvanizing, they can just as easily aestheticize, and thus pacify, progressive energies. To be sure, the abiding focus on historical fiction in the American literary field has succeeded in elevating scores of minoritized writers and in recognizing a wealth of historical narratives that had been lost, understudied, or actively ignored. That said, and as evidenced by the figures cited earlier, this program of inclusion has become so successful that it may now work to circumscribe minoritized writers, even as it consecrates them. The charge that literary studies has contributed to a displacement of "material forces" onto "aesthetic culture" is actually a doubled one: political representation has been transmuted into literary representation, but the politics of the present have likewise been displaced onto narratives of the historical past.[83]

While the historical novels investigated here are quick to trumpet the promise of fiction's capacity to recover and honor the past, they are just as quick to highlight the limits of such a program, especially if it sequesters minoritized voices and antiracist politics in faraway history. In the opening lines of *The Sympathizer* the narrator declares, "I wonder if what I have should even be called talent. After all, a talent is something you use, not something that uses you. The talent you cannot *not* use, the talent that possesses you—that is a hazard, I must confess" (1). As Nguyen does in *The Sympathizer*'s scenes of forced confession, a number of the novels included here feature episodes of historical narration or reenactment that reflect both the value of these functions in contemporary American literature, and their gradual exhaustion. The protagonist of Whitehead's *The Underground Railroad*, for example, escapes enslavement only to find that the sole employment available to her is *playing* an enslaved woman in a white-owned museum. At the end of Gyasi's *Homegoing* and its three-century chronicle of injustice, the novel's millennial protagonists earn elite degrees for studying history, but they are also disengaged from the political issues of their moment. Likewise, Ozeki's *A Tale for the Time Being* elevates the catastrophes of recent history to canonical status but at the same time expresses an ambivalence about fiction's ability to transform the present by narrating the past. These writers interrogate not only the historical record but also the historical imperative of the contemporary American literary canon.

Finally, it is important to further clarify the term "contemporary canon" and how it shapes this book. The literary canon is often defined as the array of authors and works that, by virtue of their continued reading and appreciation, have achieved a certain artistic timelessness. One of the key insights of Guillory's *Cultural Capital*

INTRODUCTION

(1993) is that the canon as such is an "imaginary totality," an entity that exists either entirely in the imagination or in the ever finite, and therefore always incomplete, form of the university course syllabus.[84] Yet the tremendous growth of the study of contemporary literature over the last several decades requires a revised notion of the canon, given that its central objects of study—recently published writers and works—cannot yet be considered timeless and have only just emerged on university syllabi. At the same time, contemporary literature is even more in need of an agreed-upon canon given both its abundance (tens of thousands of new novels are published in English each year) and the fact that it cannot rely on historical longevity to legitimate its study. As a result, cultural institutions that measure and confer literary prestige—the National Endowment for the Arts, literary prizes, campus "common reads" programs, and so forth—have become increasingly important in winnowing the vast field of contemporary fiction into a coherent, if also provisional, canon.

Aggregating these various organizations and the texts they consecrate under the banner of "the contemporary American canon" acknowledges the part that each plays in "the process by which literary texts come to be preserved, reproduced, and taught."[85] To mention that a novel won this or that literary prize, or remark upon the fact that 80 percent of shortlisted novels have such and such in common, is not to hold up the Pulitzer or the National Book Award as the final arbiter of literary quality, but rather to register the significant effect these institutions have on what readers read, what teachers teach, what scholars study, and therefore what has a better than average chance of being remembered.[86] Likewise, to call a novel published in 2016—or 1987, for that matter—"canonical" is not to say that it will continue to be read for generations, but merely to recognize that by virtue of its institutional consecration it is already far more likely to be than the hundreds of thousands of other, already forgotten, contemporary novels. By elevating historical fiction as contemporary American literature's most prestigious category, these

INTRODUCTION

institutions produce an *effect* of timelessness (if not the thing itself), grounded in a work's historical setting rather than the longevity of its reception. While the very words "contemporary" and "canon" are often considered antithetical, their juxtaposition highlights the centrality of the literary institutions this book investigates, as well as those institutions' reliance on historicity as a metric of artistic seriousness and literary value.

WRITING BACKWARDS

The chapters that follow investigate not only the central writers and texts of American fiction's historical turn but also the logics of contemporary canon formation. These include the funding protocols and the not-so-anonymous review process of the National Endowment for the Arts (chapter 1); the concentration of literary prize finalists around a small group of historical settings (chapter 2); the impact of the changing methodologies of literary studies on a new generation of American authors (chapter 3); the ever-widening historical scope of university literature syllabi (chapter 4); and the influence of news organizations on the priorities of contemporary publishing (chapter 5). At the same time, the book draws its structure from the historical subgenres that best illustrate these transformations in the literary field, whether as exemplars or allegories or both: the historical novel in reverse, the World War II novel and Holocaust fiction, contemporary narratives of slavery, the multigenerational family saga, narratives of immigration, and the novel of recent history. In all, these chapters trace the rise of American literature's historical turn in the late twentieth century, the limits of that aesthetic program in the early twenty-first, and the shapes that contemporary fiction might take in the years to come.

The first chapter, "Contemporary Fiction in Reverse," takes up three works of historical fiction that all proceed backwards: that is,

INTRODUCTION

in reverse chronological order. These novels reimagine the form of the historical novel after postmodernism, and function as allegories of the American literary field's historical turn in the 1980s and 1990s. They also emphasize how the institutions that shape and sponsor contemporary authors—from MFA programs to literary agents and the NEA—came to prize historical setting as a mark of literary ambition and artistic seriousness. Taken together, David Bradley's *The Chaneysville Incident* (1981), Martin Amis's *Time's Arrow*, and Julia Alvarez's *How the García Girls Lost Their Accents* represent a shift from postmodernism's ironizing and "problematizing" of the historical record to a more contemporary conception of history as traumatic, individual, and experiential. At the same time, each operates as a kind of *un-bildungsroman* wherein, by virtue of the backwards structure, the protagonist becomes increasingly disassimilated, ethnicized, and essentialized. For Amis and Alvarez, this move into the historical past represented a crucial turning point in their critical reception and larger careers—a testament to the changing aesthetic values of the literary field in the late twentieth century. For Bradley, however, whose novel acknowledged the horrors of the past expressly to critique their continuities with the present, writing in reverse was met with a far cooler reception from critics and scholars alike. Published in the years before Morrison's novel of American slavery and embodying a more direct (and directly oppositional) relationship to contemporary politics, *The Chaneysville Incident* was not beloved precisely because it was not *Beloved*. Yet Bradley's historical aesthetics, abandoned by writers and largely overlooked by scholars, offer a foreclosed yet important alternate vision of fiction's relation to the historical past.

Chapter 2, "The Making of the Greatest Generation," documents how, as historical fiction by minoritized writers became increasingly prestigious, World War II arose as both the historical setting most prized by major American literary awards and one that was dominated almost entirely by white writers. With this in mind, the chapter

INTRODUCTION

traces the evolving aesthetics of World War II historical fiction, reading white writers celebrated by major literary prizes—from Joseph Heller and Kurt Vonnegut to Michael Chabon and Jennifer Egan—alongside minoritized writers who were overlooked by these awards. Leslie Marmon Silko's *Ceremony* (1977) rejected the prevailing irony of war fiction in the 1960s and 1970s, working instead to ground collective memory of the war in the culture, landscape, and traditions of the Laguna Pueblo people. In the 1980s and 1990s, as depictions of the war became increasingly reverent and the mythologizing of the "greatest generation" took hold, Ronyoung Kim's *Clay Walls* (1986) challenged public perception of the "good war" by reframing it in light of wartime discrimination, segregation, and internment. In the first decades of the twenty-first century, Chabon, Egan, Anthony Doerr, and Jonathan Safran Foer approached the war with an aesthetics of collection and eccentricity in an effort to take the well-known war and make it new. By contrast, Julie Otsuka's *When the Emperor Was Divine* (2002) evacuates both its setting and its sentences, narrating the war not in Paris or Odessa but in the Utah deserts where Japanese Americans were incarcerated. By way of conclusion, this chapter examines how literary prizes both measure and mediate notions of literary seriousness, arguing that the war's enduring prestige also testifies to the enduring divisions at the heart of the newly inclusive American literary field.

The third chapter, "Colson Whitehead's History of the United States," considers how the structural changes described in the first half of the book worked to shape the next generation of American novelists, by looking closely at the career of one of the twenty-first century's most celebrated writers. Despite his reputation for experimenting with a wide array of genres and cultural forms, Whitehead is first and foremost a writer of historical fiction. Whitehead's novels provide a kind of single-author survey course in American history and offer insight into the larger structures of the contemporary literary field. Reading *The Intuitionist* (1999) as an academic satire that is both a product and an allegory of the campus canon wars of the 1980s and 1990s, this chapter demonstrates how Whitehead's first novel dramatizes contemporaneous debates over literary canon reformation in the guise of a formally inventive and "Intuitionist"-influenced historical novel. Situating the work in the context of Whitehead's undergraduate years at Harvard University thus provides a new rubric for *The Intuitionist* and a historical account of the literary-sociological forces that reshaped the American literary canon. Moving from the author's first novel to his more recent work, the chapter turns to *The Underground Railroad* as a case study in the hypercanonical genre of the meta–slave narrative. Focusing closely on the novel's allusive and self-consciously performative relationship to that genre, this chapter argues that *The Underground Railroad* embodies both the recent history and the present limits of contemporary narratives of enslavement. The chapter closes by reading *The Nickel Boys* (2019) and *Harlem Shuffle* (2021) as emblems of the field-specific forces that have supported Whitehead's canonization, as well as the inadequacies of relying on historical analogy as the primary mode of political critique.

Chapter 4, "Reading the Family Tree," examines the genre of the multigenerational family saga alongside the academic and para-academic institutions that have contributed to its growing popularity and prestige. Reading both exemplary and exceptional works in the genre—Yaa Gyasi's *Homegoing*, Min Jin Lee's *Pachinko*, and Margaret Wilkerson Sexton's *A Kind of Freedom*—this chapter argues that multigenerational historical fiction has flourished by appealing to the interpretive strategies shared by institutions as seemingly disparate as the university English department and the middlebrow book club. Although the genre stretches at least as far back as the nineteenth century, its recent focus on the family histories of marginalized peoples is particularly well suited to the "empathetic" and pedagogical reading practices that dominate both the seminar room and the living room. Part of what makes a text like *Homegoing* seem both readable and teachable is the way the novel narrativizes a wide array of historical moments, while also humanizing figures in each era who have been previously overlooked. That said, though the novel conceives of itself as personifying the family tree on its inside cover, ultimately the book instrumentalizes its characters as stand-ins for particular periods in African American history, from slavery and the Harlem Renaissance to the civil rights era. By contrast, *A Kind of Freedom* challenges the long arc of progress suggested by Gyasi's novel, moving circularly rather than linearly through its various historical settings, which (unlike *Homegoing*) include the very recent past. The chapter closes by considering empathetic reading practices writ large, questioning whether they have unintentionally become a recipe for learned and compassionate inaction. While the multigenerational family saga represents the apotheosis of American literature's turn toward the historical past, it also emphasizes the growing disconnect between knowledge of that past and political intervention in the present.

The fifth chapter, "The Rise of the Recent Historical Novel," argues that amid American fiction's fascination with history, a new literary subgenre has taken root: the recent historical novel. Though Walter Scott first imagined the historical novel in English as a tale "of the last generation," these historical novels all take place less than a dozen years in the past. Yet what delimits their recency is not some precise quantity of years, but rather the particular form of historicity that this narrow gap belies. These novels are not (and cannot be) "period pieces," as the historical events that structure them have not yet congealed into a coherent and legible period. By contrast, these works occupy a historiographical middle distance between event and period, specific date and stylized decade. This chapter draws on three contemporary novels—Ruth Ozeki's *A Tale for the Time Being*, and Ben Lerner's *Leaving the Atocha Station* and *10:04*—in order to describe the contours of this genre. By fictionalizing the crises of recent history before they become fully historical, these works

INTRODUCTION

represent both an acceleration of the novel's historical imagination and a decelerating double take at the modern news cycle. In this way, the recent historical novel stands as the paradigmatic form of historical fiction in the age of CNN. Yet while the genre affords its readers the pleasure of seeing the events of their lives become history, it also threatens to foreclose possibilities for the future, since that very pleasure is derived from a kind of teleology of the present. The conclusion of the chapter considers the racial politics of the recent historical novel, arguing that in the context of the overwhelming prestige attached to historical fiction by minoritized writers, another way of understanding the novel of recent history is as a form of white historical fiction.

The book's coda, "Excavating the Present," describes a small but countervailing force emerging as of late in the literary field, and figured in recent novels by Jesmyn Ward, Valeria Luiselli, and Tommy Orange: fiction that acknowledges and examines history's claims on the present but also takes place *in that present*, engaging issues of mass incarceration, gun violence, addiction, and contemporary inequality in its manifold forms. To put it simply, these novels appear less like Morrison's *Beloved* than they do Ellison's *Invisible Man*; or rather, they reimagine the latter after a period in which the former has stood as the paragon of literary excellence. These novels outline new possibilities for the twenty-first-century American novel and a possible way forward for the historical turn that has dominated—and, indeed, defined—the contemporary American literary canon. This is all the more important given recent attacks on activists, educators, journalists, librarians, and scholars dedicated to examining American history and historical injustice. Amid ongoing efforts to sanitize the nation's historical record, these novels are especially powerful for how they narrate both past atrocities and present political realities.

In all, this book presents a new history of twentieth- and twenty-first-century American fiction by examining the authors, texts, and institutions that comprise the contemporary canon and its

INTRODUCTION

overwhelming turn toward the historical past. This year alone, tens of thousands of new novels will be published in English: a few dozen will be lauded in prominent reviews, fewer still will be shortlisted for a major literary prize, and only a handful will survive in cultural memory. Investigating this process of winnowing and its politics, this book maps the newly diverse literary canon and considers how it both sponsors and restricts certain forms of artistic production. In this way, *Writing Backwards* offers both an aesthetic and institutional history of contemporary American fiction, arguing for a new periodization that recognizes just how historical the contemporary has become.

Chapter One

CONTEMPORARY FICTION IN REVERSE

THE RHETORICAL climax of Viet Thanh Nguyen's *The Sympathizer* arrives in its third-to-last chapter. Pushed by torture and interrogation to a breaking point, Nguyen's narrator, a double agent for Vietnamese communist forces, imagines that

> if history's ship had taken a different tack, . . . if my mother had been less of a mother, if my father had gone to save souls in Algeria instead of here, . . . if the Americans hadn't come to save us from ourselves, if we had not bought what they sold, if the Soviets had never called us comrades, if Mao had not sought to do the same, if the Japanese hadn't taught us the superiority of the yellow race, if the French had never sought to civilize us, . . . if the British had defeated the rebels of the new world, if the natives had simply said, Hell no, on first seeing the white man, . . . if the Chinese had never ruled us for a thousand years, . . . if the Buddha had never lived, . . . if Adam and Eve still frolicked in the Garden of Eden, if the dragon lord and the fairy queen had not given birth

to us, . . . if there were no Light and no Word, if Heaven and earth had never parted, if history had never happened, neither as farce nor as tragedy, if the serpent of language had not bitten me, if I had never been born, . . . if you needed no more revisions, and if I saw no more of these visions, please, could you please just let me sleep?[1]

In this single sublime sentence, almost horizonless in its reach, Nguyen unwinds first hundreds, then thousands, of years of history. The passage demonstrates how playing history backwards can both reveal historical causation and alienate it. New possibilities emerge when you consider a series of *what ifs*. If, Nguyen suggests, any one of these events had not occurred, then our protagonist would not be, at this very moment, confessing under duress; he would be spared these visions of the past, he could rest. At the same time, by emphasizing the very conditionality of these events, Nguyen is also stressing their certainty. If *any one* of these things had not happened, then things would be different, but *every one* of them did. When you renarrate history in reverse, the origin is always the present, just as it exists now.

If this is the intellectual climax of *The Sympathizer*, it is motivated by the novel's emotional climax two pages earlier, when the narrator reveals that, long before the action of the book began, he stood by and watched as a fellow communist agent was brutalized during a police interrogation.[2] The scene is horrific to read, and that is the point, its power drawn from the very specificity of Nguyen's narration. But the trope—that the narrative hinges on a traumatic moment in a character's personal history, itself a microcosm for a moment or period in history writ large—is not at all specific to Nguyen. This is true of *The Sympathizer*, yes, and Morrison's *Beloved*, but it is also true of a great many contemporary American novels organized around a journey toward the past, toward some horrific yet formative originary moment.

This chapter examines three novels that take that backwards movement as their very structure: novels, that is, that move in reverse.[3] David Bradley's *The Chaneysville Incident* (1981), Martin Amis's *Time's Arrow* (1991), and Julia Alvarez's *How the García Girls Lost Their Accents* (1991) all begin in the present and work, chapter by chapter, toward the historical past. Like *The Sympathizer*, these novels find their ultimate meaning in the moment furthest back. As Samuel Cohen writes of Don DeLillo's *Underworld* (1997)—another instance of historical fiction in reverse—"along the way, secrets are revealed, connections are found, later events are shown to have had roots in earlier ones, lineages are traced, and history moves backward."[4] Their narratives arrive, in the end, at the very beginning. Yet this chapter is also about what these three novels and the genre to which they belong can tell us about how the American literary field was changing in the 1980s and the early 1990s and how it came to place a premium on narratives of the historical past. *The Chaneysville Incident*, *Time's Arrow*, and *How the García Girls Lost Their Accents* are *examples* of this transformation, in that they are works of historical fiction, but they are also *emblems* of it, in that the logic of a novel that begins in the present and withdraws ever further into the historical past is also the logic of American literature's turn toward history, literally transforming the contemporary novel into a historical one. While the structure of these novels allegorizes the changing literary tastes of the late twentieth century, it is the story of how they came to be—specifically the institutional history of how they were produced, acquired, revised, published, lauded, and canonized *or not*—that illuminates just how those aesthetics changed in the first place.

In the case of Julia Alvarez, the backwards narrative of her debut novel, which retraces the steps of a Dominican American family from the 1980s to the 1950s, also traces a process by which graduate MFA programs and the National Endowment for the Arts incentivized writers, and minoritized writers in particular, to write autobiographical and autoethnographic fiction. After learning to *write what she knows*, Julia Alvarez was then encouraged by her agent and editor to stitch together her various autobiographical short stories into a formally inventive historical novel, modeling what Laura B. McGrath has termed "corporate taste": that is, the way that figures like the literary agent "calibrate their aesthetic judgments to anticipate . . . the demands of publishers and the market."[5] Ultimately, *How the García Girls Lost Their Accents* reads as a kind of *Künstlerroman* in reverse, a story that begins with a portrait of the artist as a grown woman, then narrates her process of becoming a thoroughly ethnicized and historicized subject of "experience." Though scholars have divided Alvarez's oeuvre into two distinct phases, the early "personal novels" and the later "historical novels," this chapter argues that the institutions that shaped Alvarez's career not only motivated that phase change but also worked to collapse the distinction entirely.[6]

For Martin Amis, the story of *Time's Arrow*, published the same year as Alvarez's debut, is the story not of how the author launched his career but of how he transformed it. While the novel follows an American suburbanite back in time to a dark secret buried in World War II, this shift in focus from present to past became, for its author, a secret to literary success. *Time's Arrow* propelled Amis toward greater visibility, increased prestige, a new American agent, and a near-mythic $800,000 advance. The novel not only established its British author as a "serious" artist but also secured his position as a serious presence in the American literary scene.[7] In both its temporal structure and its status in Amis's career, *Time's Arrow* exemplifies the American literary field's increasing appetite for historicity in the late twentieth century. *Time's Arrow* also emphasizes how the form of historical fiction was changing in this period. Drawing on the stylistic experimentation of his postmodern forebears, while rejecting their distrust of history in favor of a newly earnest attitude, Amis stands in for an array of novelists working to forge a new path for historical fiction in a moment when the novel's status in the larger media ecology was increasingly uncertain.

CONTEMPORARY FICTION IN REVERSE

Yet if we, too, move backwards from the early 1990s to the early 1980s, it becomes clear that these aesthetic shifts were neither inevitable nor universally accepted. As in Alvarez's and Amis's novels, David Bradley's *The Chaneysville Incident* chronicles an individual's journey from contemporary subject to product of history. In Bradley's case, the narrative centers on John Washington, a professor of American history who works to reconstruct a line of historical continuity from Black communities in the late 1970s to Vietnam and the civil rights movement, Jim Crow and the rise of the KKK, and, ultimately, slavery itself. Unlike Alvarez and Amis, however, Bradley creates a narrator-protagonist who does not fit neatly into the category of "victim of history" or "historical perpetrator," but rather embodies the grief of intergenerational trauma in equal measure with the rage that it can inspire. While the narratives of *Time's Arrow* and *The García Girls* create a difficult but ultimately recuperative continuity between contemporary life and the historical past—allowing author, character, and reader alike to commune with history—*The Chaneysville Incident* undermines such catharsis by stressing again and again how little has changed for Black Americans. Studying Bradley's novel alongside its lukewarm (and even sometimes hostile) reception by critics and scholars, this chapter reads *The Chaneysville Incident* as an example of a path not taken by American literary history. Analyzing Bradley's work as an alternative model for American literature's relation to the past clarifies both how notions of literary value changed in the late twentieth century and what those changes have effectively foreclosed.

Though the backwards historical novel may not be the most commonly produced genre of historical fiction, its careful study provides a foundation for understanding the other texts, authors, and genres taken up in this book. Divergent as the plots of these three novels are, they each narrate historical trauma and forced migration. Over the course of their reversed narratives, they also transform their protagonists into heightened (or, in the case of Amis, distorted) versions of the identity categories their authors have been sorted into by the contemporary literary marketplace. By the end of these novels, Bradley's Black historian adopts the perspective of his enslaved ancestors, Alvarez's Dominican narrator ventriloquizes a generation of victims of the Trujillo regime, and Amis's white male protagonist becomes the white male perpetrator par excellence. Reading historical novels of the Holocaust, immigration, and enslavement alongside and against one another emphasizes how authors of all races have been canonized for translating questions of identity into a historical register, but also how the rewards for such efforts have not been distributed equally.

WHY ISN'T *THE CHANEYSVILLE INCIDENT* MORE BELOVED?

In the 1980s, two novels that fictionalized the history of American slavery and its legacies in the present were published by Black authors whose curricula vitae looked remarkably alike. Both authors had studied literature as undergraduates and graduate students at elite universities; both wrote book reviews for newspapers of record; both taught literature and creative writing at prestigious institutions within an hour or two of New York City; and both had worked as editors at top publishing houses downtown. One of these authors, of course, was Toni Morrison. The other was David Bradley. Simply switch out the names Howard, Cornell, *New York Times*, SUNY, Rutgers, and Random House on Morrison's resume for UPenn, King's College, *Washington Post*, Temple, and J. B. Lippincott, and you will have Bradley's.[8] But the resemblances run deeper still to the novels themselves. Both *Beloved* and *The Chaneysville Incident* are about young people who escape enslavement and choose death over recapture, about their descendants struggling to uncover that lost family history, and about a larger national history that the authors suggest "we must reexperience in order to understand."[9] Their receptions, too, were similar—at least initially. Both novels received glowing reviews in the Black press and scathing ones from white conservatives (Bradley's was lauded in *Essence* and the *New York Amsterdam News* but labeled "white-baiting" in the *New York Times*).[10] Both were honored by literary prizes (*Chaneysville* edged out Donald Barthelme's *Sixty Stories* and Marilynne Robinson's *Housekeeping* to win the 1982 PEN/Faulkner Award for Fiction). Both were selected for major book clubs (Bradley's novel, which had a first printing of 25,000 copies, was selected as a Book-of-the-Month Club alternate selection, "a rare publishing accomplishment for any black writer").[11] And, as early forecasts indicated, both seemed bound for entry into the African American literary canon (critics likened *Chaneysville* to Alex Haley's *Roots* and the work of James Baldwin, even going so far as to call it "the best novel about the black experience in America since Ellison's 'Invisible Man'").[12]

Yet this is where the comparisons end. Forty years later, *Beloved* stands at the very center of the contemporary American literary canon, and *The Chaneysville Incident*, though not forgotten, is read far, far less. The Open Syllabus Project reports that Bradley's novel has appeared on more than fifty university syllabi, no small feat considering the millions of other novels with which it is competing. By contrast, however, Morrison's *Beloved* has appeared on just under 3,800.[13] These statistics resemble those for scholarly attention, as measured by citations in the Modern Language Association's International Bibliography. There, we find twenty-six entries devoted to *The Chaneysville Incident* and more than a thousand to *Beloved*.[14] To be fair, comparing the long-term reception and relative institutionalization of *any* contemporary novel to Morrison's masterwork is a fool's errand. But the question remains: what accounts for the vast disparity in attention between these two novels and novelists? Why has Bradley— "often considered," one critic wrote in 1983, "'*the* Black American Writer' of the 1980s"[15]—largely fallen away in literary history? Why, in other words, isn't *The Chaneysville Incident* more beloved?

Perhaps it is because, as Missy Dehn Kubitschek has argued, "Bradley simply got there too soon for the rest of us."[16] Perhaps *The Chaneysville Incident* was simply ahead of its time, a half-decade too early for the larger turn toward history that Morrison's novel came to metonymize, if not also inaugurate. Yet the early 1980s were banner years for the publication, reception, and theorization of historical fiction. Alice Walker's *The Color Purple* (1982) and Charles Johnson's *Oxherding Tale* (1982) were published. Thomas Keneally's *Schindler's Ark* (discussed in chapter 2) was republished in the United States as *Schindler's List* (1982). The shortlists of major literary prizes were populated with works of historical fiction.[17] Stephen Greenblatt first used the term "New Historicism," in his introduction to *The Power of Forms in the English Renaissance*.[18] And Fredric Jameson attended the 1982 MLA convention at the Bonaventure Hotel that would feature so prominently in his 1984 essay on "Postmodernism," where he argued that "there no longer [seems] to be any organic relationship between the American history we learn from schoolbooks and the lived experience . . . of our own everyday life."[19]

By this last measure in particular—fiction's capacity for drawing connections between contemporary lived experience and American history—*The Chaneysville Incident* is extraordinarily successful.[20] The novel follows John Washington, a Black professor of Revolution-era American history, as he examines the troubled history of his own Pennsylvania town after the mysterious death of his father. While the structure of the novel is both linear and forward-moving—Bradley's chapter headings are modeled after the research notecards that Washington uses, running from March 3 to March 12, 1979—the book's story moves in reverse. That is, Washington's investigations lead him increasingly further back in the historical record, from the present-day politics of the town to his brother's experience as a Black soldier in Vietnam, on to the discrimination his father faced under Jim Crow, and ultimately to his ancestors' harrowing attempt to escape enslavement. In this way, *Chaneysville* is what Ashraf Rushdy has called a "palimpsest narrative," a novel in which a Black protagonist is "forced to adopt a bitemporal perspective that shows the continuity and discontinuities from the period of slavery."[21] Yet it is also a novel that theorizes the role that fiction itself can play in uncovering historical continuity.

In the first half of *The Chaneysville Incident*, Bradley emphasizes his protagonist's uncompromising faith in facts and figures. As the book progresses, however, Washington is repeatedly confronted with the reality that, though "there was no shortage of facts . . . there were, it seemed, too many gaps" in the archive (146). These gaps, he asserts, "never can be filled, for they are larger than data, larger than deduction" (49). The problem, Bradley's protagonist discovers in the end, is not historiographical, but *creative*: "I could follow a fact through shifts and twists of history. . . . But I could not imagine. And if you cannot imagine, you can discover only cold facts, and more cold facts; you will never know the truth" (146–47). Ultimately, the climax of Bradley's novel comes as Washington decides to move beyond facts into fiction, narrating his own speculative account of the horrific "incident"—the failed escape—that gives the book its name. Practicing, three decades *avant la lettre*, what Saidiya Hartman has described as "critical fabulation," Washington transforms from historian to historical novelist.[22]

On its face, *The Chaneysville Incident* may appear as a case study of "historiographic metafiction," postmodern novels that trouble the "textuality" of the historical record and "problematize the very possibility of historical knowledge."[23] In historiographic metafiction, and in postmodern historical fiction more broadly, "there is no reconciliation" between fact and fiction, "just unresolved contradiction," emphasized through an aesthetics of "radical provisionality, intertextuality, and . . . fragmentation."[24] In Bradley's novel, by contrast, these features are not the means and ends of historical fiction, but rather the very conditions it seeks to repair. The "textuality" and "fragmentation" of history, figured in Washington's array of carefully collated notecards, are ultimately abandoned for the truth that his fictionalizing makes possible in the end. *The Chaneysville Incident* argues that "historical knowledge," hard-won though it may be, can be achieved only if—like its protagonist—the novel's readers come to see fiction as producing rather than problematizing it. This, the recuperative power of historical reconstruction, is what the majority of the modest number of scholars who have studied *Chaneysville* have focused on, and what aligns the novel so well with the protocols surrounding historical fiction's central place in the American literary canon.[25]

Yet this is also the grounds upon which Bradley's novel has been harshly criticized. *The Chaneysville Incident*, argued many of its earliest readers and critics, is simply *too historical*—but what exactly is meant by this merits closer scrutiny. "Bradley is trying to do something very similar to what Alex Haley did in 'Roots,'" charged a review in the *Hartford Courant*, but "too many of the dialogues read like essays on black history. It's understandable that Bradley needs to get this historical material across, but it could have been done in a more creative way."[26] Likewise, a review in the *Chicago Tribune* found fault with Bradley and his narrator's "cold, academic, somewhat pontifical style," claiming that *The Chaneysville Incident* is "a novel about history, rather than a historical novel." For this reviewer, the problem with the novel was not just that it makes its theories of historiography explicit—unlike, say, *Beloved*'s evocative but elliptical theory of "rememory"—but also that it is more interested in narrating historical *thinking* than historical *experience*. "Many of the sensational events in the novel are *unfelt* and thus intellectualized," the review concludes, and as such, "the novel [is] lacking in compassion."[27] That is, Bradley's expository mode effectively blocks the far more sought-after empathetic mode. "Too much of it is thinly disguised history," writes yet another critic, "rather than *deeply felt*, imaginatively transformed *experience.*"[28] What these early readers desired but did not find in Bradley's novel, it seems, was the opportunity to commiserate.

This is a difficult task for a novel whose protagonist—even Bradley admits—is "most of the time . . . an unlikeable person," and not just because he is an academic.[29] Critics and scholars alike have described John as "violently sexist, angry, and resentful," in sum "the most unlovable point-of-view character to emerge in modern African-American literature."[30] Whereas the protagonists of *Beloved* are victims of physical, psychological, and sexual violence—and therefore prime targets for the readerly fellow feeling just described—*Chaneysville*'s central character repels that empathetic gaze. John is arrogant and insensitive, but his most damning flaw is the cruelty he directs at Judith, his white girlfriend and his main interlocutor throughout the novel. In one passage, John confesses to Judith that he raped a white woman on the day of his brother's funeral (75). While some early readers decried Bradley's "problematic treatment of women" in the novel, scholars have since argued that this critique goes too far in conflating the author with his central character.[31] It also reveals the tendency of several key literary institutions to conflate contemporary authors, especially racialized ones, and their historical protagonists. As we shall see in Julia Alvarez's early career, the impulse to collapse the distinction between author and narrator has been an operative protocol in institutions ranging from major publishers and MFA programs to the National Endowment for the Arts.

Yet, beyond all of this, it seems the central reason why Bradley's historical novel is so peripheral to the contemporary American canon is that it is not historical enough. While critics have taken issue with *Chaneysville*'s digressive and essayistic forays into historical writing (i.e., "a novel about history, rather than a historical novel"), they have also lamented how much of the novel takes place in the years just before the book's publication: "for the more distant the past, the clearer we see and the more intensely we feel with the characters."[32] Even as John's investigations take him deeper and deeper into the history of the region and the nation, Bradley's narration remains resolutely in the very near past: March 3 to March 12, 1979. While this decision may foreclose certain empathetic and experiential avenues, it also enhances the novel's ability to directly critique the present. In one passage, as John and Judith are discussing life in 1832, John argues that "if there's one thing a white man hates more than a free n——r, it's a free n——r who isn't on welfare and who pays his rent on time and goes to a big church and has a good job and sends his kids to a decent school." When Judith corrects him, saying "You mean 'hated,'" John quickly counters: "I mean what I said. 'Hates.' It's true now and it was true then, only then it was easier to see" (338). As this passage demonstrates, Bradley's novel is as interested in "the little assumptions and presumptions that go with dormant racism or well-meaning liberalism" as it is in the history of enslavement (66).[33] As John himself puts it, while a great many historians, particularly white historians, may believe that slavery and its aftereffects have "long ago come to rest," "somewhere here with us, in the very air we breathe, all that whipping and chaining and raping and starving and branding and maiming and castrating and lynching and murdering—*all of it*—is still going on" (213).

There is a great deal of pathos in this interminable sentence, which emphasizes both the horrors of the past and, in its list of gerunds, how those horrors persist still. But there is also a great deal of anger. In a series of interviews just after *Chaneysville* was published, Bradley commented on the place of anger in Black writing and Black politics in the 1980s. After praising Haley's *Roots* for dispelling the "feeling in publishing [that] you couldn't sell books on black people to anybody but other blacks and white liberals," Bradley adds that Haley, "a nice middle-class man writing about his middle-class family," may be too reader-friendly in the end.[34] Comparing Haley to an earlier generation of Black writers, Bradley claims that while the novels of Richard Wright and James Baldwin were "accusations, polemical books. . . . Now it's changed like 'Roots' to positive things."³⁵ In the post–civil rights period, Bradley argues, "We're not supposed to be mad any more. We're supposed to get beyond that. I understand that. But sometimes it's hard not to be mad."³⁶ Both the novel's sense of outrage and the target of that outrage—namely, the present—help to explain why *The Chaneysville Incident* was less than warmly embraced by critics in the early 1980s and since. While one *New York Times* reviewer reassured the paper's readers that John's "bitterness toward white people is softened by his eventual reconciliation with the long-suffering Judith," this softened reconciliation is precisely what the novel works relentlessly, if at times also rancorously, to resist.³⁷

Here it is important to note that Bradley's earliest drafts of *The Chaneysville Incident* were set entirely in the nineteenth century, focusing exclusively on the historical incident in its title, and that he added the contemporary frame and the character of John Washington only later on.³⁸ In the final account, it is this decision that sets *The Chaneysville Incident* apart from so much of the historical fiction that has followed it over the last five decades, both because it sharpens the novel's political critiques, which might otherwise be blunted by historical distance, and because by arriving at its imaginative encounter with history only in its conclusion, it also forecloses the reader's desire for empathy, intimacy, and reconciliation. Holding the reader and readerly compassion at arm's length, the novel argues that we must do more than investigate or imagine the past if we are to resolve its legacies in the present. In this way, *The Chaneysville Incident* rejects the interpretive logic that has come to dominate the American literary field by asserting that recovering history is not the same as recuperating it. While both the novel and its reception emphasize that, in the early 1980s, the protocols for writing and reading historical fiction were still coalescing, they also emphasize just how much those protocols have calcified in the period since.

CONTEMPORARY FICTION IN REVERSE

MAKING THE BEST OF
THE WORST PLACE AT THE WORST TIME

"I moved forward, out of the blackest sleep, to find myself surrounded by *doctors* . . . American doctors."[39] So reads the first line of Martin Amis's 1991 novel *Time's Arrow*. Or rather, the last line, as in Amis's novel, the arrow of time, moving ever forward, has been reversed. Taking place in a world where people wash dishes before they eat and answer questions before they are asked, *Time's Arrow* narrates the life story of American doctor Tod Friendly from the moment of his death to the day of his birth more than seven decades earlier. The first half of the novel reads as a comedy of contemporary life set in "washing-line and mailbox America, innocuous America, in affable, melting-pot, primary-colour, You're-okay-I'm-okay *America*." "My name," the narrator declares, "of course, is Tod Friendly"—as if it could be anything else (14). Here we follow a white, male, middle-aged, upper-middle-class protagonist as he goes on dates, falls in love, carries on affairs, and experiences breakups —only backwards. Tod Friendly begins his relationships by moving *in*, having terrible fights, slowly falling *into* love, and then moving *out*, before a period of enchanting first dates that culminate with Friendly acting as if he has never met his former lover, because he hasn't. The story reads like a John Updike novel in reverse: *Redux Rabbit*.

Alongside Friendly's love life, *Time's Arrow* also narrates the better part of the twentieth century: from the early 1990s into the Reagan era, back to the Vietnam War, the JFK assassination, and so on.[40] Throughout this backwards chronicle, the narrative voice drips with a blend of historical irony and Amis's characteristically sardonic style in passages that recount how "industry is coming to the city. Gas is cheap. . . . People all have jobs now, at the steel mill and the auto plant [and they have] really got to grips with their environmental problems" (57). Yet this twentieth-century gallows nostalgia is also tempered by "the sense of starting out on a terrible journey, towards a terrible secret," a secret leading to "the worst man in the worst place at the worst time" (12). As the reader quickly comes to understand, Amis's average American is not who he says he is. Before he was Tod Friendly he was John Young; before that, Hamilton de Souza; and before that, Odilo Unverdorben, a Nazi death camp doctor. Both the protagonist and his name work to miniaturize a half-century of history: from Unverdorben, German for "untainted," to "Tod Friendly," properly pronounced and properly reversed as "Friendly *Tod*," or "Friendly Death." The "terrible secret" at the center of Friendly's name and life, at the very heart of the century, is, of course, the Holocaust and World War II.

It is perhaps unsurprising, then, that critical accounts of *Time's Arrow* have focused their attention almost exclusively on the novel's time in Auschwitz. One group of critics argues that, in the backwards world of Amis's novel, the logic of cause and effect is reversed, and with it the logic of morality.[41] In this world, giving candy to a baby looks like stealing, and a sniper's bullets work to heal. To the naive narrator (often described as Friendly's soul), postwar America is both alienating and full of destruction, while the Nazi regime is ordered, logical, and morally legible. As one early review of the novel put it, from this "warped vantage point, Auschwitz is a culmination, the one place where the world makes sense."[42] In this way, the narrative structure of *Time's Arrow* "produces a moral inversion" that resembles, even reenacts, the disturbingly self-assured logic of the perpetrators of the Holocaust (and, in particular, their medical establishment), performing reverse narration as "a form of moral critique."[43]

Another group claims that the novel in reverse demands greater participation from the reader, an experience that resensitizes her to the horrors of the Holocaust.[44] An action as simple as making and eating a meal requires the reader to reverse, reassemble, and replay its component parts in order to make sense of it. Seymour Chatman likens this to the process of "figuring out a metaphor," where "what we actually read in the book" functions as a *vehicle* for "the underlying or 'real' event" analogous to its *tenor*. The reader acts as a kind of unwilling collaborator, entering the novel's revival of Auschwitz as a participant, stripped of previous exposures by the backwards narration's estranging lens and forced to attend to its horrific details anew. In an interview just after the novel was published, Amis acknowledged this aspect of *Time's Arrow*, declaring that "the reader supplies the truth" of Auschwitz: "you present it as a miracle, but the reader is supplying all the tragedy.... [They're] meeting it as if for the first time, even though we know that this is all much-covered territory."[45] Still more critics contend that the novel stands as a wishful unwriting of Nazi atrocities and a cautionary tale that draws together the Holocaust of the 1940s with the threat of nuclear holocaust in the 1980s.[46]

Yet all of these accounts read *Time's Arrow* as a work fundamentally *about* the Holocaust. The chapters that take place in the 1940s act as the punchline to the novel's dark comedy, the climax that structures the rest and imbues it with meaning. When Amis's narrator ultimately arrives at Auschwitz, he tells us (in a nod to Primo Levi) that "*Hier ist kein warum*. Here there is no why," but it is here that provides, somewhat ironically, the motivation, the *why*, for nearly all of the novel's readers (128). What then are we to make of the rest of *Time's Arrow*, more than a third of which passes before Tod Friendly changes his identity and, with it, the novel's genre? After all, the novel spends more of its time in Massachusetts than in Auschwitz, and the reader is more than halfway through the book when Friendly finally "set[s] sail . . . in the summer of 1948—for Europe, and for war" (107). Critics have described the novel's early chapters as "our preparation for the Auschwitz section," but what would a reading look like that avoids, even momentarily, the backwards-historical telos of the Holocaust and the interpretive telos that it provides?[47]

The answer, in large part, is a comedy of contemporary American life in the tradition of John Updike. This is somewhat unsurprising given Amis's enduring interest in the American author, especially in the years leading up to *Time's Arrow*.⁴⁸ For Amis, what is captivating about Updike's writing is its very contemporaneity. Though Updike's novels are "crammed with allusive topicalities" that "in a few years' time . . . will probably read like a Ben Jonson comedy," this presentism—Amis argues—is precisely what recommends them.⁴⁹ "What Joyce did for the residents of Dublin," Amis wrote in the *Observer* in 1987, "Updike recklessly offered to do for the dreamy dentists and Byronic building-contractors of 'Tarbox,'" the fictional Massachusetts town where Updike's novel *Couples* takes place.⁵⁰ Like Updike, Amis sets his early chapters "in the avenues of Wellport," his very own fictional Massachusetts town (17). Instead of Rabbit Angstrom, Amis opts for Tod Friendly, his own self-loathing, aging male protagonist. The plot, too, is Updikean, not only in its lengthy discussions of suburban life and home improvement but also in its relentless anatomizing of adult romance: "One thing led to another—actually it was more like the other way round" (56).⁵¹

Recovering these early chapters allows us to better understand *Time's Arrow* in its totality, not as an ambivalent example of genre fiction—*either* a historical novel with a comedic preface *or* a comedy of contemporary life with a dark historical conclusion—but instead as a novel about that very generic shift. The reader watches helplessly as a Cape Cod gerontologist becomes a Nazi war criminal and the names of fictional characters and settings are slowly replaced by the proper nouns of a historical survey, from Friendly's Wellport to Eichmann's Solingen. But, horrific though it may be, isn't this the very pleasure promised by the novel? As Chatman notes, few if any readers in 1991 were likely to make this journey unawares, given the book's robust promotion and the blurb on its back cover.⁵² Isn't the backwards roller coaster from "now" to "then," precisely the thrill that first drew readers to Amis's novel, and draws them still? As *Time's Arrow* travels from postwar America to Nazi Germany, it moves not only backwards in time but also across genres, narrating the slide from one generic register to the next and exchanging one currency of cultural capital for another. *Time's Arrow*, in other words, is a contemporary novel that transforms itself into a historical one, trading the prestige of contemporaneity for the prestige of historicity.

From this vantage, *Time's Arrow* can be read as both an example and an emblem of this book's larger literary-historical argument, with the genre transformation at the heart of Amis's novel standing in for the tectonic shift that has occurred in the contemporary American literary canon. The logic of a novel that withdraws from the present and travels into the historical past is also the logic of the American literary field reorganizing itself to increasingly value fictions of history. The backwards chronology of *Time's Arrow* both exemplifies, and literalizes in miniature, the evolution of literary taste in the decade prior to its publication. Amis seems a particularly compelling author to consider in this context, as both his fiction and its reception fall neatly across the fulcrum of *Time's Arrow*. Five of Amis's previous six novels take place in the present (with the sixth set in the near future), and the author's insistent contemporaneity is what comprised the better part of his early career cachet. While Amis described these works as his "record of what it was like to be alive at this time, in this world," critics called them "smears taken from a social body relentlessly reduced to its own cell tissue," novels "incensed by money; in a rage with pornography, confidence, sex, success, failure."[53] Indeed, Amis's early career jeremiads of contemporary life are what established him as "one of the brashest voices" in contemporary fiction, "the Mick Jagger of the literary world."[54]

With *Time's Arrow*, however, Amis's first foray into the historical past, Britain's bad boy suddenly made good—and, what's more, he made a splash across the Atlantic. In the *Washington Post*, Charles Trueheart praised "the author's expanding moral purpose and tightening narrative control," calling *Time's Arrow* "further evidence that Amis is no longer the knockabout of his famous youth."[55] As one critic notes, "a sense was starting to develop that Martin Amis had sustained and developed his stylistic and structural brilliance while moving into a new area of seriousness and responsibility."[56] Importantly, this move toward history came with a wealth of newfound prestige and a much wider audience. Within a month of its publication, *Time's Arrow* was shortlisted for the Booker Prize.[57] In the years that followed, Amis would trade out his British literary agent for the American Andrew Wylie, dubbed "The Jackal," in part for negotiating an $800,000 advance for the author's next novel.[58] (Amis also left his then-wife for the American writer, Isabel Fonseca, and fled to New York for a series of cosmetic dental surgeries. As the *New Yorker* put it, "American agent, American woman, American *dentist*": Amis had "gone over to the other side.")[59] That novel, *The Information* (1995), is largely about "the pressures facing the successful novelist in the mid-1990s," following two rival writers as they themselves switch out agents, negotiate advances, and travel from "flop" to "sleeper" to "smash in the United States": *literally*, too, as the book's entire third section takes place on "the eight-city tour. New York, Washington, Miami, Chicago, Denver, Los Angeles, Boston, New York again."[60]

Nine months after the publication of *Time's Arrow*, Amis published his first work since the release of the novel and his very first piece in the *New Yorker* magazine, a June 1992 short story titled—fittingly—"Career Move." The story narrates the struggles and successes of two contemporary writers in a comically reversed world of popularity and prestige: Alistair, a tortured screenwriter working to place his science fiction script, "Offensive from Quasar 13," in the rarified pages of *LM*, or *Little Magazine*; Luke, the writer of blockbuster sonnets, whose agent informs him that his recent "Eclogue by a Five-Barred Gate" is doing very well domestically. The satire of "Career Move" is so spot-on it seems almost irresponsible not to quote it at least briefly: "Luke parked his Chevrolet Celebrity in the fifth floor of the studio car park and rode down in the elevator with two minor executives in tracksuits who were discussing the latest records broken by ' 'Tis he whose yesterevening's high disdain.'" "[They're] doing a sequel to ' 'Tis,'" says one. "Actually it's a prequel . . . they're calling it ' 'Twas.' "[61]

Though the comedy of "Career Move" relies on exaggeration, it also captures, however ironically, Amis's own soaring reputation and rising fortunes in the early 1990s. To put Amis in his own terms, *Time's Arrow* emerged as a novel that was able to garner both the warm critical reception of "Quasar 13" and the cold hard returns of "Eclogue by a Five-Barred Gate," a work that paired the pyrotechnics of formal experimentation with the growing prestige of historicity. In an interview soon after the novel's release, Amis described *Time's Arrow* as a moment of departure in his career: "Although I didn't become a different kind of writer I certainly felt that I was playing on a different keyboard. . . . I was writing about the past for the first time. I was writing about a historical event for the first time."[62] And though *Time's Arrow* was Amis's first historical novel, it would not be his last: the author's *House of Meetings* (2003) recounts its protagonist's postwar experiences in a Soviet gulag; *The Pregnant Widow* (2010) is set in Italy in 1970; and, most notably, *The Zone of Interest* (2014) stages a return to the Auschwitz setting of *Time's Arrow*.

In both its temporal structure and its status as a pivot point in Amis's larger career, *Time's Arrow* exemplifies the evolving literary field of the 1980s and early 1990s, as well as its increasing taste for historicity. But apart from the growing prestige of historical fiction, the novel also points to several factors that motivated this massive historical turn. First and foremost, *Time's Arrow* manifests the particular historical consciousness of a generation of novelists born just before, during, or just after the Second World War. For these authors, the writing of historical fiction—and, in particular, the writing of historical fiction about World War II—represents neither a return to wartime jingoism nor a postmodern "problematizing" of historical knowledge as such, but rather a complex nostalgia for a time of epic struggle and horrific yet clarifying atrocity. World War II stands as an origin myth for all that they have lived through, a cosmology for the contemporary world. Just after *Time's Arrow* was published, Amis described the war as "the central event of the twentieth century, the culminating event of history."⁶³ For Amis, the "firebreak of 1945" was also a dividing line that separated the generation of writers like his father, Kingsley Amis, and his own: "They lived in one kind of world, then they lived in another kind of world," Amis writes, "and they didn't tell us what the difference was like."⁶⁴

As a work of historical fiction, *Time's Arrow* expresses the desire to understand that divide, literalizing it—and perhaps satisfying it—through the novel's backwards narrative structure. As Chatman points out, reverse narration can operate only in movement: a single moment or event is, in and of itself, neither forward nor backward, but static.⁶⁵ That said, Amis's novel is less defined by the historical periods it moves through, than by that historical movement itself: the act of returning to history. As Richard Menke puts it, "*Time's Arrow* depicts a world in which, instead of one thing leading to another, everything leads to one thing: the past."⁶⁶ Amis's narrator writes that Friendly is "travelling towards his secret. . . . It will be bad. . . . But I will know one thing about it (and at least the certainty brings comfort): I *will* know *how* bad the secret is" (72–73). Here Amis voices a sincere longing for historical knowledge, one that is markedly opposed to the knowing skepticism with which postmodern fiction approached that same possibility. Moreover, Amis's novel offers not only the *desire* for history but also its *experience*: mediated, to be sure, by a postmodern narrative conceit, but altogether uncontaminated (we might say, *Unverdorben*) by postmodern cynicism. The form of *Time's Arrow* may be ironic, in other words, but its function is not.

In this way, Amis's novel manifests a complex relationship to its postmodern antecedents that characterizes the better part of literary fiction in the late twentieth century. Linda Hutcheon argues that literary postmodernism can be defined by how it "effects two simultaneous moves. It reinstalls historical contexts as significant and even determining," while it also "problematizes the entire notion of historical knowledge."⁶⁷ As *Time's Arrow* makes clear, however, while late twentieth-century literary fiction inherited postmodernism's fascinations with history and formal experimentation, it also outgrew and even actively rejected literary postmodernism's "second move," using fiction as a means of connecting with history rather than calling that very connection into question. Critical accounts of *Time's Arrow* have been quick to point out the novel's debt to Kurt Vonnegut, as has Amis himself, who cites, in the novel's preface-like "Afterword," a certain "famous" paragraph from Vonnegut's *Slaughterhouse Five*—the one in which Billy Pilgrim watches a wartime propaganda film in reverse—as a source of inspiration.[68] Yet the difference between the two authors' uses of backwards narration is instructive. While Vonnegut's passage represents a fantasy of undoing the war, removing bullets from bodies and returning their raw metals to the earth, Amis's novel is a fantasy of revisiting it, rewinding the war not *out of* history but *into* literary experience. After all, Billy Pilgrim is unstuck in time; Tod Friendly is stuck inescapably to it.

For writers in the late twentieth century, the novel was not simply one of many media trying to render the historical past in an authentic and ethical manner, but rather *the one* that could properly achieve that goal. As Amis's "Career Move" makes clear, novelists in the 1980s and 1990s understood themselves to be in conversation with and, crucially, *in competition with* other, more popular forms of entertainment. There the exaggerated comedy of film and television studios producing hugely popular and multimillion-dollar-grossing *literature* is also, of course, the realist tragedy of those very studios running fiction out of town. Likewise, the narrator of *Time's Arrow* laments his serious disappointment in contemporary reading habits, Tod Friendly's preference for tabloid journalism over more literary fare: "Appropriately, it is the garbage people who bring me my reading matter.... There is a bookcase in the living-room. Beyond its dusty glass, the dusty spines, all standing to attention. But no. Instead, LOVE LIFE ON PLUTO. I AM ZSA ZSA GABOR SAYS MONKEY. SIAMESE QUINS!" (20). Kathleen Fitzpatrick has deftly described the novel's enduring "anxiety of obsolescence," elucidating the process by which postmodern novelists in particular have converted "a concern about the possibilities for the novel's future into fodder for its continuance, representing and interpreting the functions of the media that appear to threaten [them] with obsolescence in the manner that will best support the novel's claims to edification, humanism, and individuality."[69] Yet while Amis's work may point to a similar anxiety, it manifests an altogether different competitive strategy.

Rather than appropriate competing media, *Time's Arrow* withdraws into a historical past where they no longer exist. "Last week they came and took away my color TV," the narrator reports. "They gave me a black-and-white one. I made on the deal" (98). For Amis, the move backward is not only a move away from the encroaching entertainments of contemporary life but also a move toward the authority, prestige, and cultural capital that history affords. After all, one can easily imagine that Amis looks back more fondly on the historical novel that won him both a Booker Prize nomination and an $800,000 advance than he does on *Saturn 3*, the science fiction screenplay he wrote a decade earlier, which he describes as "a terrible piece of shit," and which garnered only a Golden Raspberry Award for Worst Picture.[70] In this light, it comes as little surprise that American fiction's turn toward history in the 1980s and 1990s also represents a turn away from the technologies that threatened it during that same period.[71] In retrospect, it appears that contemporary fiction's historical turn worked not only to shore up the novel's privileged position as an intellectually serious and morally profound cultural form, but also to ensure its multimedia marketability. Considering the box office and award success of the pipeline from historical fiction to film in this same period, one wonders whether the novel's withdrawal from the present is not a kind of triumph masquerading as retreat. Historicity not only replaces contemporaneity as the literary field's local currency of cultural prestige but also becomes its chief export: "They're doing a sequel to ''Tis.' Actually it's a prequel. They're calling it ''Twas!'"

HOW THE GARCÍA GIRLS *GOT* THEIR ACCENTS

Reflecting on *Time's Arrow* in a March 1992 interview in the *Bloomsbury Review*, Martin Amis suddenly began to ponder the arc of his career, calling it "a funny kind of evolutionary process." Whereas time in *Time's Arrow* runs backward, the protagonist *devolving* throughout in a kind of un-bildungsroman, in the pages of the *Bloomsbury Review* Amis sketches a far more conventional portrait of the artist: "You start out in your early twenties with what you know is your own consciousness. Then later, you know about a peer group. Later yet, you know about a city and a society. Then later, you know about other cities and other countries and their societies. Then, willy-nilly, you have a sense of living on a planet. . . . Then perhaps you become interested in the past."[72] As the writer grows, Amis suggests, so too does the scale of his work: maturing from near-autobiography and local narratives of contemporary life, to international, global, and—ultimately—historical consciousness. It is a fair, even prescient, description of Amis's own writing life and the arc that it would follow in the decades to come. It also describes, given the context of American fiction's larger turn toward history, the trajectory of a great many American novelists writing in the 1980s and 1990s. Yet Amis bows out of singularity in the interview, conceding uniqueness even with regard to his backwards structure: "I really rather believe everything's been done before. . . . And indeed, with *Time's Arrow*, every day people tell me of another ten writers who have done basically the same thing."[73] Still, one imagines Amis might have been at least a little surprised to find, not five pages later, in the very same issue of the *Bloomsbury Review*, a profile of Julia Alvarez and her own historical novel in reverse, *How the García Girls Lost Their Accents* (1991).[74]

Published just three months after *Time's Arrow* in the fall of 1991, Alvarez's *How the García Girls Lost Their Accents* was hailed by the *Bloomsbury*'s reviewer as an "extraordinary first novel" that gives its readers "intimate knowledge of [Alvarez's] narrators, the four García girls ... moving backwards through careers, loves, children, and the neuroses of middle-class immigrant existence."[75] Comprising fifteen interconnected short stories and organized in three sections titled "1989–1972," "1970–1960," and "1960–1956," the novel narrates the lives of the four García sisters from their adulthood and adolescence as Dominican American immigrants to their childhood experience in Rafael Trujillo's Dominican Republic. As it follows each woman's love life, education, and last days under the island's autocratic regime, Alvarez's novel moonwalks through a variety of literary genres, blending tropes of autofiction, romance, the campus novel, the immigrant family saga, and historical fiction.[76] As its title suggests, *How the García Girls Lost Their Accents* is also a kind of bildungsroman that narrates (albeit in reverse) the maturation, socialization, and Americanization of Carla, Sandra, Yolanda, and Sofía García. Combining formal experimentation with a realist portrayal of midcentury migration, Alvarez's debut has been described by critics as the novel that "officially launched [a] new movement of Latina writers" in the late 1980s and early 1990s, with Alvarez herself as the "progenitor of [that] movement."[77] And though the novel's importance in the growing recognition of Latinx literature in the United States has been thoroughly documented by critics, a closer examination of *How the García Girls Lost Their Accents* (and its slant rhyme with Amis's own historical novel in reverse) illuminates not only Alvarez's pride of place but also the figures and institutions of the literary field that shaped her career, as well as the careers of a great many minoritized writers of historical fiction.

Just as the commentator in the *Bloomsbury Review* focused on how Alvarez's novel depicts "the neuroses of middle-class immigrant existence," so too have critical accounts of *How the García Girls Lost Their Accents* worked to highlight the novel's meditations on issues of conflicted identity. Alvarez's work has been read variously as an effort to identify and reconcile multiple, hybrid, liminal, and border-crossing senses of self.[78] Whether she is regarded in the final account as a

Latina autobiographer, a bilingual novelist, or a refugee writer, Alvarez generally, and *The García Girls* in particular, are read "almost exclusively . . . to reproduce arguments about race and gender identity negotiation and to bear the burden of representation that comes with such discussions."[79] Nearly all of these readings make much of the similarities between Alvarez and the third García sister, who narrates or is focalized in more than half of the novel's fifteen vignettes and is called variously Yolanda, Jolinda, Yo, Joe, Joey, and Yoyo. (Indeed, there seem to be as many close readings of Yolanda's numerous nicknames as there are names themselves.) And while many critics have described Yolanda as Alvarez's "alter ego" of sorts, picking up on the latter's impulse toward metafiction, few if any have commented on the novel's narration of Yolanda's time in undergraduate and MFA writing workshops, focusing instead (as with Amis) on the backwards novel's conclusion in the historical past.[80] Recentering the novel's many scenes of writing instruction, however, not only reveals Alvarez's own development as a novelist, but recasts *The García Girls* as a kind of *Künstlerroman*—or, rather, an *un-Künstlerroman*: not the story of a character transforming into an artist, in other words, but the portrayal of a contemporary Dominican American writer as she becomes a fully ethnicized and historicized subject.

Yolanda is introduced to the reader of *The Garcia Girls* as both a writer and a teacher of writing. Though the early chapters of the novel focus largely on her romantic misadventures and her later efforts to "undo [and] unravel John, Brad, Steven, Rudy, and start over," Yolanda's love life is couched always in the language of literature (63). From the "handsome, greying professor" (47)—chair of the comparative literature department where Yolanda is "one of the more popular instructors" (49)—to Rudy Elmenhurst, the paramour of Yolanda's undergraduate creative writing workshop, the male cast of the novel's early dalliances with romance writing work to emphasize the second term far more than the first. Early on in "The Rudy

Elmenhurst Story"—the final chapter in the novel's opening section and the first to be narrated in the first person—Yolanda declares that she wants to explore her relationship with Rudy "by picking it apart the way we learned to do to each other's poems and stories in the English class" where they first met (88). In this way, the "story" of Yolanda's romance with Rudy also narrates her evolution from alienated undergraduate writing student to confident adult writer.

As that story begins, we find Yolanda in her first English literature course, a transfer student at a small American liberal arts college. This mirrors Alvarez's own experience transferring from the then single-sex Connecticut College to co-ed Middlebury College, where she studied English and creative writing, graduating summa cum laude in 1971.[81] Caught between the students' "knowing, ironic looks" and the professor "stumbling over my name and smiling falsely at me," Yolanda feels "profoundly out of place," an "intruder upon the sanctuary of English majors" (88–89). This sanctuary, where Yolanda finds herself unschooled in the "obscure works of literature" that her peers seem to know, where even her pencil anglicizes her name ("the company had substituted the Americanized, southernized *Jolinda*"), is, of course, the undergraduate creative writing workshop (88, 90). It is there that Yolanda becomes infatuated with the only other foreign student in the class, the confident, overprivileged, and thoroughly blond Austrian Rudy Elmenhurst, who stands in for the white, Western literary traditions that she is likewise courting.

As they compose their fitting first assignment, "a love poem in the form of a sonnet," Yolanda and Rudy come together romantically even as they clash creatively (91). After turning in her own sonnet, rigid in its construction and "sublimated" in its *eros*, Yolanda begins helping Rudy, who has not written a single iamb but has acquired a leisurely extension (94). Alvarez writes: "We spent most of the weekend together, writing [the sonnet], actually me writing down lines and crossing them off when they didn't scan or rhyme, and Rudy coming up with the ideas ... explain[ing] all the word plays and double meanings" (93). The contrast Alvarez draws is all too clear: Yolanda is both eager and gifted when it comes to the technical aspects of English literary form, but utterly naive with regard to its content. She knows *how* to write, but not *what* to write. "It seemed to me not only that the world was full of English majors," Yolanda recounts, "but of people with a lot more experience than I had. For the hundredth time, I cursed my immigrant origins. If only I too had been born in Connecticut or Virginia, I too would understand" (94). Yolanda's writing is not at all lacking in technical skill, but instead in the *experience* to apply it to, experience she mistakenly searches for in Connecticut or Virginia rather than in her own Dominican origins.

"The Rudy Elmenhurst Story" ends in an epilogue, set "five years later," when Yolanda is "in grad school in upstate New York," no longer the "profoundly out of place" undergraduate but "a poet, a bohemian," and an MFA writer (102). This, too, resembles Alvarez, who, two years after graduating from Middlebury, began a graduate degree in creative writing at Syracuse University. In the novel version, Rudy reappears with an expensive bottle of wine in a clumsy attempt to rekindle their romance. The newly mature Yolanda rejects his advances but keeps and drinks the wine: "I held the bottle up to my mouth and drew a long messy swallow, as if I were some decadent wild woman who had just dismissed an unsatisfactory lover" (103). The simile here, in the chapter's final sentence, points up Yolanda's development throughout "The Rudy Elmenhurst Story": she is no longer "the lover" but the "wild woman" writer; neither the vehicle nor tenor of metaphor but its author. Thus, the epilogue that brings the story and the novel's first section to a close works as a kind of prologue for the novel itself.

Yolanda evolves from a naive yet ambitious student of literature to a newly wise writer of fiction. "The Rudy Elmenhurst Story" is, of course, just that: a story, one that the Yolanda of its epilogue might submit to her MFA workshop. Indeed, one way of reading the episodic, generically fluid, story cycle structure of the novel is as the product of Alvarez's own experience in various institutions of creative writing. Given Alvarez's time at Syracuse, and given that she workshopped portions of the novel at the prestigious Bread Loaf Writers' Conference in Vermont, to whose director Alvarez dedicates the novel, it is perhaps unsurprising that the various vignettes of *The García Girls* would most resemble the workshop's favored form.[82] Yet another way to understand the genre experimentation of *The García Girls* is as a record of Alvarez's own false starts and attempts to "find her voice" as a fiction writer, much like her metaliterary alter ego.

Trained in the English canon and its rarefied forms but gifted now with a sense of the value of her own experience, Yolanda comes to see literature not as a cloistered space, "reserved for deep feelings and lofty sentiments," but as a venue for narrating her personal and familial history (93). Alvarez's use of first-person narration in this chapter only emphasizes what her reader already knows: Yolanda has found her voice in the creative writing program, turning now to *write what she knows*. It is altogether unsurprising then that the novel moves immediately from "The Rudy Elmenhurst Story" to "A Regular Revolution," a story set in the Dominican Republic in the 1960s, the first step on its journey away from the contemporary United States and into the Caribbean historical past: retreating, in other words, from "Connecticut or Virginia" and the desire for what those settings represent and moving backward toward the protagonist's—and the author's—"immigrant origins."[83]

In the chapters that follow, Alvarez narrates Yolanda's process of unbecoming in a backwards montage of her education. As Alvarez moves in reverse through scene after scene of literary instruction, her reader comes to understand that the school, and in particular the English classroom, is the answer to the question posed in the novel's title: that is, how did the García girls lose their accents? In "A Regular Revolution," Yolanda goes from college back to boarding school, where—like Alvarez, who attended the prestigious Abbot Academy that later merged with Phillips Academy Andover—she finds herself alienated from "the cream of the American crop" to whom her family name and history "smacked of evil and mystery" (108). In "Daughter of Invention," we find Yolanda now in primary school, nervously writing a speech at the invitation of her English teacher and concerned about her delivery as "she still had a slight accent" (141). In each episode, the more Yolanda works to assimilate, taking "root in the language" of her new American home, the more Alvarez alludes to—in the context of her backwards narration, we might say *foreshadows*—"*la situación* back home" and the troubled history toward which the novel is heading (141, 171–72).

As Yolanda drafts her speech for assembly, inspired by the liberating free verse of Walt Whitman, her father is plagued by nightmares that pull him "back to those awful days and long nights," and the "secret fear [that] they had not gotten away after all; the SIM"—Trujillo's secret police—"had come for them at last" (139). When Yolanda ultimately finishes her speech, her eyes welling because "she finally sounded like herself in English," these twinned trajectories converge (143). Yolanda delivers the address to her father who, fresh from reading news of Trujillo in a Dominican paper, interprets her Whitmanesque language as an insubordinate and therefore dangerous affront to her teachers, and rips up the speech. "Daughters of Invention" therefore functions as the meeting point of the novel's seemingly competing temporal vectors: one, leading forward, that narrates Yolanda's education as a writer; the other, leading back, that tracks the family history that she will ultimately write about.

As the novel's final section makes clear, however, these two vectors are not competing, but converging. In "The Blood of the Conquistadores," the opening of the novel's "1956–1960" section and the story that reviewers and critics alike regard as the climax of *The García Girls*, Alvarez recounts the family's last tense days in the Dominican Republic.[84] Dispensing altogether with the romance and humor that define the novel's early chapters, Alvarez's writing in "Conquistadores" resembles that of a historical thriller more than anything else.

With the sudden arrival of armed SIM agents at the Garcías' doorstep, Yolanda's father rushes to the secret panel in his bedroom closet, and *The García Girls* hastens similarly into its own hidden compartment of genre. Nestled in the back of this romantic comedy of contemporary life, this immigrant bildungsroman of the 1960s and 1970s, is a 1950s Cold War spy thriller that looks less like Sandra Cisneros than Tom Clancy or John le Carré.

Yet if the climax of a traditional *Künstlerroman* sees its protagonist finally become an artist, where does "The Blood of the Conquistadores" leave Yolanda at the conclusion of Alvarez's narratively reversed *un-Künstlerroman*? Her central appearance in the chapter is in an anecdote, relayed by the narrator, about a previous close call with the secret police: "This must be serious like the time Yoyo told their neighbor . . . a made-up story about Papi having a gun, a story which turned out to be true because Papi did really have a hidden gun for some reason. The nursemaid Milagros told on Yoyo telling . . . that story, and her parents hit her very hard with a belt in the bathroom, with the shower on so no one could hear her screams" (198). And with this Yolanda's journey in the novel is complete: with her capacity for fiction so dangerous that it must be silenced and punished, she is no longer the writer of stories but the subject of them. The portrait of the artist as an adult woman has become the chronicle of a helpless child at the mercy of her parents and her island's troubled history.

To put this all another way, one wonders how the narrator of *Time's Arrow* might describe the plot of *How the García Girls Lost Their Accents*, which—among other revisions—would have to be called *How the García Girls Got Their Accents*. It might go something like this: a Dominican American writer visits the island as a foreigner then returns to the United States and, over the course of two hundred pages *forgets* how to write, *develops* an accent, *loses* her Americanness, and *becomes* a Dominican citizen, transforming from a vaguely ahistorical contemporary woman into a deeply and authentically historical subject. As Raphael Dalleo and Elena Machado Sáez explain, *The*

García Girls "appears to depict a loss of voice for Yolanda or at least a submerging of her individual voice as we move forward in time," yet "it is a paradoxical loss because the plot's reverse chronology means that the novel begins with Yolanda's story being told in the third person and ends with her speaking directly to us in the first."[85] Throughout the novel, white Americans hurl slurs at the four sisters, yelling at them to "go back to where you came from!" (171). But while the sisters and the novel's readers may balk at these casual displays of bigotry, that is to some extent what the García girls and *The García Girls* do throughout the structure of the book's reverse narration. This is also, incidentally, the experience of Alvarez herself, who both returned to her family's homeland to write part of the novel and used the writing process "to connect deeply not only with my characters, but with the Dominican Republic." As Alvarez put it in one interview, in the process of writing *The García Girls*, "I had to become a Latin American again."[86]

Ironically, this process of becoming Latin American was sponsored by the largest public funding body for creative writing in the United States: the National Endowment for the Arts (NEA). Yet Alvarez credits her 1987 NEA grant not only with making her first novel possible, but also with making her feel "as if I was now included among the storytellers and poets of my new country!"[87] The endowment regularly boasts about its "outstanding track record of nurturing talented writers early in their careers," but were it not for a number of changes made within the organization, it is possible that Alvarez—and a generation of minoritized writers of historical fiction—may not have been so sponsored.[88] Until the early 1970s, applicants had to be nominated "by an established writer" in order to be considered for an NEA Literature Fellowship, a process that presumably privileged well-connected, which is to say white and male, writers. Between the mid-1970s and the early 1980s, however, this process was superseded by an "open application policy" at the same time that the organization was making structural changes to both its grant committees and its grantees.[89] A March 1979 report on the NEA by the House Appropriations Committee included a number of recommendations "on the question of minority representation" within the organization, advocating for "selecting minority individuals who have a definite identification with disadvantaged groups."[90] This led to the appointment of writers such as Toni Morrison to the Literature Program advisory panel, where she served from 1980 to 1987.[91] It also, in its desire to identify "a definite identification" between applicants and "disadvantaged groups," resulted in a wealth of historical fiction by minoritized writers funded by the NEA.

In a 2006 pamphlet on the fellowships, the organization lauds its own "anonymous process in which the sole criterion for review is artistic excellence" but asks (albeit rhetorically) how it is nevertheless possible to "ensure the diversity of the group of writers to whom we give grants." While the pamphlet credits the diversity and annual rotation of its panel of judges, a more telling answer comes on the previous page. There, Amy Stolls, an "NEA Literature Specialist" who later served as the organization's director of literary arts, describes her own selection process: "When the language sings, you can find yourself in a civil war or a morning routine. . . . On [one] particular afternoon, we were led to . . . an old Jewish woman who, after fifty years . . . whispered for the first time the circumstances of her horrific capture during the Holocaust." As is clear from these examples, it is the language of historical atrocity more than the recounting of "a morning routine" that most stands out in this process. "We ended the story with our hands over our hearts . . . and a visceral desire to say to everyone in the office *read this!*" she continues. "Then we wanted to know who this writer was."[92]

Yet surely the members of the selection committee already knew, to some extent, who the writer was, or at least to which "disadvantaged group," she might belong. In this way, ethnicized history—whether of the Holocaust, the Trujillo regime, or the antebellum plantation—appears to work as a kind of proxy for the NEA's selection of a diverse array of fellowship recipients: an anonymous submission process circumvented by a work's all-too-telling historical setting. No wonder then that that same pamphlet also prominently features Ishmael Reed, who used his NEA fellowship to "conduct research and write [his] fourth novel, *Flight to Canada*"; Cristina Garcia, whose grant helped her finish *Monkey Hunting*, "a book about a 19th-century Chinese farmer in colonial Cuba"; and Oscar Hijuelos, who was selected while working on his own historical novel, *The Mambo Kings Play Songs of Love*. Moreover, it mentions a number of similar NEA grantees, including Leslie Marmon Silko three years before *Ceremony* was published; Charles Johnson two years before *Oxherding Tale*; Alice Walker two years before *The Color Purple*; Louise Erdrich in the year leading up to the publication of *Love Medicine*; and Jeffrey Eugenides in the years before *Middlesex*.[93]

Following Alvarez's early career from the institutions that trained and sponsored her to those that published and promoted her, it becomes clear that what Machado Sáez has called "the aesthetic value of otherness" was an operative force in the late twentieth-century American literary field.[94] Machado Sáez explains how "the institutional realities of the publishing market" have worked to incentivize Caribbean diasporic writers like Alvarez to produce historical fiction over and above other genres—and the evolution of Alvarez's first novel bears this out.[95] When Alvarez began to write *The García Girls*, she imagined it as a loose collection of short stories, not as a novel. When her agent, Susan Bergholz—then the premier literary agent for Latinx writers, representing Ana Castillo, Sandra Cisneros, and Denise Chávez, among others—sent Alvarez's manuscript to editor Shannon Ravenel at Algonquin Books, however, Ravenel commented that "there's a bigger story here you're trying to tell."[96] As the manuscript had already been rejected by a number of publishers, Alvarez took this advice to heart.[97] "Once I started to view it that way," Alvarez later recalled, "I saw that there was a bigger story than the individual chapters."[98] Notice here how the discourse of scale mediates questions of value: not a collection of *little* stories, but a *big* story, worthy of a novel and worth taking a chance on a debut Dominican American novelist. This is an example of what McGrath calls "corporate taste" in action, as agents "subject the literary fiction they represent to the logic of the marketplace through a developmental strategy carefully calibrated to corporate interests."[99] In this case, Bergholz and Ravenel worked "through their 'fixes'" to Alvarez's manuscript as "administrators of market logic," a logic that sees a novel as more profitable than a collection of short stories, and a "bigger" historical narrative as more marketable than a tale of modern romance.[100]

By all accounts, these strategies were highly successful. *How the García Girls Lost Their Accents* "was an immediate success," and "sales of the book exceeded Alvarez's wildest expectations." The novel went on to win the 1991 PEN Oakland/Josephine Miles Award, and it was selected as a Notable Book by the American Library Association.[101] While early reviews of *The García Girls* were almost exclusively positive, few if any commented on the novel's formal experimentation (unlike Amis's own historical novel in reverse). They focused instead, as the *New York Times* did, on the novel's portrayal of "the threshold experience of the new immigrant, where the past is not yet a memory and the future remains an anxious dream."[102] Like the private deliberations of the NEA selection committee, these public comments testify to Machado Sáez's claim that "the mainstream market's demands for the genre" of historical fiction work to "position the writer as cultural informant and cultural object."[103]

We catch a glimpse of this in *The García Girls*, as Alvarez describes the interactions between Yolanda and Rudy Elmenhurst's parents. When Rudy tells his parents that he is "seeing 'a Spanish girl,'" they remark that it "should be interesting for him to find out about people from other cultures." Reflecting on this, Yolanda remarks that "it bothered me that they should treat me like a geography lesson for their son. But I didn't have the vocabulary back then to explain even to myself what annoyed me about their remark" (98). In this instance, Alvarez invites her readers to side with Yolanda against the Elmenhursts, criticizing them for instrumentalizing her as part of the education of their white, well-educated, upper-class son.[104] And yet, given Alvarez's complex relationship to the American literary marketplace and its white readers, it is easy to imagine multiple institutional contexts within which readers of this scene are positioned far closer to the Elmenhursts than to Yolanda herself.[105] That is, even as they identify in opposition to the Elmenhursts' culturally consumerist gaze, readers can and are even welcomed to approach *The García Girls* "like a geography lesson"—and a history lesson as well. While the Elmenhursts insult Yolanda by commenting on her "'accentless' English," a range of American literary institutions have celebrated Alvarez precisely for providing readers with a pedagogically useful account of how the García girls *got* those accents (100).

Given this early success, it is little wonder that Alvarez has spent the better part of the last three decades writing historical fiction. Alvarez's second novel, *In the Time of the Butterflies* (1994)—similarly about, and narrated by, four sisters under the Trujillo regime—moves even further into the historical past, beginning in the mid-1940s and ending in 1960, the year of "The Blood of the Conquistadores." Whereas *The García Girls* becomes a historical novel over time, *In the Time of the Butterflies* declares, from its very title, that it is (as the first words after its copyright information suggest) a "work of fiction . . . based on historical facts." The novel—which narrates the radicalization, rebellion, and ultimate execution of the nonfictional Mirabal sisters—was met with even greater praise than Alvarez's first novel, criticized, if at all, for not being historical enough.[106] Ultimately, *In the Time of the Butterflies* propelled Alvarez to national recognition, appearing not only in the pages of *Vanity Fair* but also among the list of finalists for that year's National Book Critics' Circle Award.[107] According to Alvarez, "The ink of *Butterflies* was barely dry," when she "began work on [another] historical novel."[108]

Alvarez has since written a number of other historical novels about the Dominican Republic, including: *¡Yo!* (1997), a semihistorical prequel/sequel to *The García Girls*; *In the Name of Salomé* (2000), which narrates the converging stories of a Dominican exile turned Vassar professor in the 1960s and her mother, the nineteenth-century Dominican poet Salomé Ureña; *Before We Were Free* (2002), a young adult novel about a cousin of the García girls who stays behind under Trujillo's regime; and *Saving the World* (2006), which bounces between a contemporary novelist volunteering at an AIDS clinic and a nonfictional nineteenth-century rectoress who led an expedition of orphans working as live-carrier smallpox vaccines. For these novels, Alvarez has received the Hispanic Heritage Award in Literature, the F. Scott Fitzgerald Award for Outstanding Achievement in American Literature, and, in 2013, the National Medal of Arts, awarded by President Obama. Despite the many accolades that Alvarez's historical fiction has garnered, she is most often cited (by reviewers and critics alike) as a prominent and canonical "Latina novelist" (or "Ethnic novelist," in the idiom of the 1990s) rather than as a gifted and prolific "historical novelist." Yet the arc of her career and the literary institutions it has passed through offer an account of why this might be, and how—in the late twentieth century—the latter came to define the former.

By way of conclusion, let us turn to one final artifact from Alvarez's career, a poem from *Homecoming*, her first collection of published poetry, that indexes not only that career itself but also the larger literary-historical phenomena that have shaped it:

> Let's make a modern primer for our kids:
> A is for Auschwitz; B for Biafra;
> Chile; Dachau; El Salvador; F is
> the Falklands; Grenada; Hiroshima
> stands for H; Northern Ireland for I;
> J is for Jonestown; K for Korea;

CONTEMPORARY FICTION IN REVERSE

> L for massacres in Lidice; My Lai;
> N, Nicaragua; O, Okinawa;
> P is the Persian Gulf and Qatar, Q;
> Rwanda; Sarajevo—this year's hell;
> T is Treblinka and Uganda U;
> Vietnam and Wounded Knee. What's left to spell?
> An X to name the countless disappeared
> when they are dust in Yemen or Zaire.[109]

Here Alvarez offers not only a world map of modern historical trauma, but an alphabet from which countless historical narratives might be composed. Notably, it begins with the Holocaust and World War II, the single most reproduced historical setting in the literary fiction of the last seventy years (and the subject of chapter 2). The very point of Alvarez's alphabet, however, seems to be the equivalence and interchangeability that its non-chronological listing implies: crucially "A is for Auschwitz" *just as* "B [is] for Biafra."[110] We might also imagine this as a "primer" in literary prestige, with each letter, like each García sister, "competing . . . for the most haunted past" (217). Moreover, by calling the poem "a primer," Alvarez points to its pedagogical utility. To borrow from Yolanda, the poem is a history lesson in the guise of a "geography lesson." What we have here are chapters in a textbook—or, better still, books on a syllabus—for a course on twentieth-century history or, it seems, "the novel after 1945." Finally, what we find in the journey from Auschwitz to Zaire is a canon: a canon of world-historical events, and a challenge issued to a generation of writers to narrate them. Martin Amis and Thomas Keneally and countless others have traced out "A"; Isabel Allende's written "C," Ronyoung Kim "K"; and scores since have reinscribed "V"; but there are still several "left to spell." Somewhat surprisingly, Alvarez has given "D" to Dachau and not the Dominican Republic, though that very choice suggests that the alphabet itself can be multiplied, made endless, limited only by a lack of curiosity and research.

CONTEMPORARY FICTION IN REVERSE

As a collection, *Homecoming* itself works as a kind of miniature of Alvarez's early career. Its early poems, in a cycle called "Housekeeping," are largely unconcerned with the author's Dominican heritage and instead revolve around familial and romantic relationships and the realities of everyday life. Then there are a series of poems that recount "reckless" time spent "at a mountaintop writers' conference," presumably the Bread Loaf Writers' Conference in Ripton, Vermont. There Alvarez was encouraged "during workshops" by "writers whose bestsellers had made them rich" and "warned . . . against giving our characters / our own predictable, excessive lives." As she drives away at the end of the retreat, Alvarez writes: "My manuscript / of stories lay beside me . . . and as I reached the summit, / that spot renowned for sacrifice and vision, / I wondered what else I had to offer / besides my own excessive character?"[111] This is the question answered to some extent by Alvarez's first novel, and definitively by her historical fiction that followed it. It is also the question answered by her "primer" poem, which—as the description of Sarajevo as "this year's hell" indicates—was not published as part of the collection when it was first released in 1984 by independent publisher Grove Press. Rather, it was added in 1996, when the volume was reprinted by a Penguin imprint, after the success of *How the García Girls Lost Their Accents* and *In the Time of the Butterflies*, Alvarez's first two histories of the Dominican Republic. By then, it seems, Alvarez had found a language all her own, in an alphabet she shared.

Chapter Two

THE MAKING OF THE GREATEST GENERATION

All wars are fought twice, the first time on the battlefield, the second time in memory.
— Viet Thanh Nguyen, *Nothing Ever Dies*

WAR MEDALS

IN A 2018 interview with the *Dallas Morning News*, Luis Alberto Urrea was asked how he came to write *The House of Broken Angels*, his much-lauded novel about an extended Mexican American family. "I never intended to write this book," Urrea responded, explaining that he had actually been "working on a World War II epic for a while." An ambitious choice for a prominent American novelist, given that in the first two decades of the twenty-first century alone, more than two dozen finalists and winners for the National Book Award, the Pulitzer Prize, and the National Book Critics Circle Award were set partly or entirely during the war, including novels by Michael Chabon, Jeffrey Eugenides, Joyce Carol Oates, Philip Roth, and William T. Vollman.[1] Despite the abiding sense of artistic seriousness attached to the period, Urrea found that his own war novel in progress was, among his closest confidants, something of an object of comedy. "The joke amongst my loved ones is that the readers are going to get that book when it comes out, and say, 'Where are the

Mexicans?'"² Though half a million Latinx service members served in the U.S. Armed Forces during the war, for Urrea, there was something about the genre of the "World War II epic" that could not quite accommodate them.³ At least for the time being, Urrea explained, "I put the World War II epic aside."⁴

In the seventy years between 1950 and 2020, the shortlists for the National Book Award, the National Book Critics Circle Award, and the Pulitzer Prize included 140 novels set to some extent in the 1940s and more than eighty that take place during the war itself.⁵ Given that even an appearance on the shortlist of a major literary prize means that a work of fiction is more likely to be read, taught in university classrooms, and studied by scholars, the fact that nearly a third of all historical novels to be honored by these awards in the last seven decades are novels of the 1940s represents a truly remarkable concentration of literary prestige.⁶ Indeed, from the mid-twentieth century to the present, World War II stands as the single most prized, most consecrated, and most canonized historical setting in American literature.⁷ While the enduring cultural cachet of the war is remarkable in its own right, it also sheds light on who, in particular, is most celebrated for memorializing it, and what types of narratives are most prized or overlooked. As the list of authors just mentioned makes abundantly clear, the consecrating force of the 1940s has not been distributed equally: fifty-seven of the eighty-one prize finalists set during World War II (70 percent) were written by men, and seventy-two of them (89 percent) were by white writers. Given how lauded fiction of the war has been, and given how much the canonization of minoritized writers has revolved around historical fiction, it is remarkable just how rarely writers of color have been prized for fictionalizing World War II.

Even the exceptions to this are telling. In Toni Morrison's *Song of Solomon* (1977), which won the National Book Critics Circle Award, the war is never narrated directly, though one character protests before

THE MAKING OF THE GREATEST GENERATION

a roomful of Black veterans that "you can join the 332nd [airborne] if you want to and shoot down a thousand German planes all by yourself and land in Hitler's backyard and whip him with your own hands, but you never going to have four stars on your shirt front, or even three."[8] In Alice Walker's *The Color Purple* (1982), which won both the Pulitzer Prize and the National Book Award, the war is mentioned only in the final chapters, when the protagonist, Celie, speculates as to where the Army will send her enlisted sons.[9] Though over 900,000 Black soldiers served in the U.S. Army during World War II, comprising 11 percent of all Army inductions, in both novels the war is waged outside the narrative, with Black soldiers and civilians described merely as figures of disregard or disappearance.[10] Later, when Celie tries to find out whether a ship her sister was aboard has been sunk by a German mine, she laments that has heard "nothing [from] the department of defense. It's a big war. So much going on. One ship lost feel like nothing, I guess. Plus, colored don't count to those people."[11] There is a sense in which these two passages, about overlooking Black men for medals and not counting Black women at all, reflect not only the whiteness of the war's public memory but also the canon of literary fiction that preserves it.

This chapter is about that memory and that canon, and how they have sustained one another over the last seven decades. In that time, narratives of the 1940s, and of the war in particular, have pervaded nearly every genre, medium, and echelon of American culture, from bestselling novels, blockbuster films, and popular nonfiction to TV miniseries and videogame franchises. All of this is to say that the literary field has never existed in a vacuum, insulated from other cultural forms, nor has literary fiction—the small subset within that vast field of writing for which awards like the Pulitzer matter most—ever been cloistered completely from the stories that sell. Yet, though prizewinning fiction has no special purchase on World War II, World War II does exert a powerful force on literary prizes and, by extension, the literary canon that they help to draft. If award shortlists inscribe the aesthetic and thematic preoccupations of the writers, critics, and scholars who comprise their juries, they also signal *which* writers, and *which groups* of writers, those judges deem best suited to tell a particular story and, in this case, enlist in a particular history.

The pages that follow chronicle the evolving aesthetics of World War II historical fiction, reading white writers elevated by major literary prizes alongside writers of color who were overlooked by those same awards but nonetheless challenged the dominant aesthetics of their moment as well as the cultural memory of the war that they propped up. Rejecting both the ironic tone and the obsession with bureaucracy that defined prizewinning war novels of the 1960s and 1970s—such as those by Joseph Heller, Kurt Vonnegut, and Thomas Pynchon—Leslie Marmon Silko's *Ceremony* (1977) works to *localize* both the war and its memory, grounding them in the culture, landscape, and traditions of the Laguna Pueblo people. Drawing on modernist aesthetics to memorialize the Indigenous soldiers who fought and died in "the white people's war," Silko's novel offers a counterpoint to postmodernism's manipulation and mistrust of the historical record.[12] In the 1980s and 1990s, as the cultural primacy of World War II was contested by writers who located the ethos of the nation not in the so-called *good war* but in the Civil War and Vietnam, literary fiction contributed to the manufacturing of the "greatest generation" mythology, which viewed the war with newfound reverence. While many racialized writers avoided the war as a fictional setting altogether—evoking the atrocities of the 1940s only as a cultural touchstone for representing the atrocities of, say, the 1860s—Ronyoung Kim challenged the lionizing of World War II in public memory with her historical debut, *Clay Walls* (1987). Chronicling two generations of Korean immigrants in Los Angeles, the novel recognizes Korean American participation in the war effort as well as the prejudice that thwarted it. Kim not only critiques nostalgic narratives of wartime

FIGURE 2.3 Joseph Cornell, *Untitled (To Marguerite Blachas)*, 1939–1940. Book containing several small objects, magazine clippings, fabric, and synthetic hair.
Museo Nacional Centro de Arte Reina Sofía, Madrid. © Joseph Cornell Estate / VAGA at Artist Rights Society (ARS) / Copyright Visual Arts-CARCC (2023).

perspective, familiarity and prestige with novelty."[66] After several decades of the war's proliferation in literary fiction, these writers must collect and exhibit novel archives of the period—traveling, in at least Chabon's case, to the very ends of the world—in order to generate some originality within the most prestigious setting in contemporary American literature. And this strategy has proved fabulously successful. In their citations of *All the Light We Cannot See*, the judges of the Pulitzer Prize and the National Book Award make special mention of the novel's *intricacy* ("imaginative and intricate"; "sweeping . . . intricately interlocking"), with the latter commending how Doerr's "larger themes of loss and isolation play out upon characters' fixations with radio waves, locksmithing, gemology, and shell collecting." "Part historical fiction, part fable, part cabinet of curiosities," the judges conclude, *"All the Light We Cannot See* builds its own rare and fabulous world."[67]

Like Cornell's box constructions, these novels thematize practices of collection, but they also weave those practices into their very form. Chabon, Doerr, Egan, and Foer fill their fictional *Wunderkammern* not only with miniaturizations and obscure fascinations but also with literary and artistic cameos, song lyrics, set pieces, and a parade of metatexts: from Chabon's comic-within-the-novel, *The Escapist*, to Foer's letters, flowcharts, and "Book of Recurrent Antecedents" (196–97). The resemblance to Cornell is not only evident in *Everything Is Illuminated*—"the book itself is illuminated," Foer said in one interview, "with images, and colors, and stories within stories"[68]—but also in Foer's career, which began with his first book, *A Convergence of Birds* (2001), an edited collection of "Original Fiction and Poetry Inspired by Joseph Cornell."[69] According to Petra Rau, in contemporary novels of World War II, intertextual allusion, the use of photographs, and "self-consciously 'periscopic' storytelling" all serve to "caution us against reading the past in any straightforward way."[70] By contrast, these novels draw on an aesthetic of assemblage to furnish readers with a stable sense of historicity. Just as in their acknowledgments sections, where history books and university archives are cited explicitly (an increasingly common practice among writers of historical fiction), the novels themselves model collection not to trouble historical experience but to make "reading the past" possible in the first place.[71] This manifests even at the level of the sentence in these novels, dominated as they are by the use of litany and epic catalogue. In the 1980s, for Thomas Keneally and his hero Oskar Schindler, "the list is life," a catalogue of real people to be saved or memorialized. In the twenty-first-century, listing after *Schindler* means assembling "the spines of hundreds of books; a birdcage; beetles in matchboxes; an electric mousetrap; . . . jars of miscellaneous connectors; [and] a hundred more things [one] cannot identity" in order to bring history itself to life.[72]

What is most curious about these tropes and techniques is not why they have proliferated but how they have traveled across various writers and groups of writers as a kind of ethnic aesthetic. On the one hand, miniaturization, assemblage, and litany appear to be common in the first decade of the twenty-first century among Jewish writers narrating both the war and the Holocaust. *Kavalier & Clay* and *Everything Is Illuminated* are prime examples of this, as is Philip Roth's counterfactual historical novel of the 1940s, *The Plot Against America* (2004), whose central image is a collection of rare postage stamps.[73] On the other hand, these same aesthetics are common among other white writers such as Doerr and Egan, whose World War II novels published in the 2010s make only glancing mention of the Holocaust. As I argue in the introduction, the racial and ethnic politics of the American literary field have shifted considerably over the last five decades, effectively whitening Jewish writers to the point that their status as "ethnic writers" became uncertain. As such, it is not entirely clear whether what we are seeing is the *appropriation* of techniques common in Jewish American historical fiction or the *coalescing* of a common white aesthetic.

From the latter vantage, listing in these novels appears not only as a technique for generating historicity by way of particularity but perhaps also as a gesture that uses particularity itself to overcompensate for a certain self-consciousness about being "generically white." In *Playing in the Dark*, Morrison reads "images of impenetrable whiteness" in the works of canonical white American writers, arguing that "whiteness, alone, is mute, meaningless, unfathomable, pointless, frozen, veiled, curtained, dreaded, senseless, implacable."[74] Likewise, these novels are littered with images of "unfathomable" and unexamined whiteness. The Antarctic setting of Chabon's wartime sequences is a place where "there was nothing to be seen in any direction," save the icy, "lupine mountains," akin to "piles of giant bones" (443–44). In *All the Light We Cannot See*, Doerr stresses the whiteness of his characters rather than his setting. The novel's two protagonists are

Marie-Laure *LeBlanc*, rendered colorblind by her degenerating vision (44), and Werner Pfennig, a German teenager with hair so white it "stops people in their tracks": "Snowy, milky, chalky. A color that is the absence of color" (24). Reading these passages alongside Morrison suggests that their desolate landscapes and pallid figures can perhaps be read as unconscious emanations of white anxiety: figures of the mountainous complexities of working as a white writer, within a largely white historical genre, in a literary field that has grown significantly less white. Yet if whiteness in these novels is cast as "the absence of color," it is in their cast of characters that people of color are more or less absent.

Despite taking place largely in 1940s New York City, *Kavalier & Clay* features almost no characters of color, save the racialized caricatures of the sidekicks who accompany the Escapist, a.k.a. "Tom Mayflower": "Omar was once the slave of a sultan in Africa; Miss Plum Blossom had toiled for years in the teeming dark sweatshops of Macao" (134). Across town, the racialized characters in Egan's *Manhattan Beach* (all of whom are Black) are minor figures whose primary role is to assist the novel's white protagonists: Marle, Anna's diving sidekick, spends the novel "holding her lifeline" (327); and Milda, Dexter Styles's housekeeper, always leaves a pot of coffee despite never actually appearing. Similarly, despite taking place in wartime Germany and France, *All the Light We Cannot See* registers ethnic difference only peripherally and recognizes the Holocaust only at its margins: German radio vilifies "hook-nosed department-store owners" (39); trains pass in the distance, and Werner reflects that "always the trains move to the east" (277); and, in one scene, he shares a brief elevator ride with an older Jewish woman, who says nothing and continues her ascent. In other words, for all their specificity—their tireless production of particularity at the level of plot, theme, and sentence—these novels appear particularly anxious when it comes to racial and ethnic specificity. If, as Morrison claims, "the subject of the dream is the dreamer," then the unspoken subject of these prizewinning World War II novels is their abiding connection between the 1940s and whiteness.[75] In the context of the literary field's ever-growing recognition of racially minoritized writers, especially for works of historical fiction, World War II appears as a kind of last outpost—akin to Chabon's Antarctic station—for narratives of white heroism, valor, and innocence.

Given this, it seems fitting that the protagonists of each of these novels—Chabon's Kavalier and Clay, Doerr's Werner and Marie-Laure, Egan's Anna, and Foer's Jonathan—are young people. In one light, this seems like an expression of the historical distance felt by these second- and third-generation authors, the way that, even as they tell these stories, they remember (or long to remember) hearing them from their parents or grandparents.[76] But the focus on adolescence—and, in particular, the figure of the disabled or vulnerable young adult—also embodies these writers' investment in a certain idea of innocence. From Marie-Laure's fading vision, to the bout with polio that leaves Sam Clay "with the legs of a delicate boy" (4), to Anna's disabled sister and her many colleagues declared "4-F" (or physically unfit for military service), these novels continually use youth and disability as telling details to denote their characters' blamelessness.[77] And nearly all are rendered blameless, not just the American soldiers described by Egan as "beautiful kids . . . innocents," but those they are fighting as well (415).

When Chabon's Joe Kavalier finally comes face to face with a German soldier in combat, that soldier, a conscripted geologist, is described as "a peaceful and scholarly man who had always deplored violence" (464). Likewise, in *All the Light We Cannot See*, Werner is a well-trained Nazi soldier, but one whose nerdy fascination with radio technology casts him as redeemable—and in the end, when he uses his knowledge of broadcasting to rescue Marie-Laure from another Nazi soldier, redeemed. But this asks the reader to overlook the fact that, for much of the novel, Werner uses his technological expertise to help locate small pockets of resisters across Europe, freedom fighters that Werner's comrades summarily execute. Moreover, neither Chabon nor Doerr remarks upon the continuity between these remediable science-minded Nazis and the race science and technologized extermination that fueled the Holocaust. At the end of *All the Light We Cannot See*, Werner's sister laments "what the war did to dreamers," but there is little regret or recrimination—on her part, or on Doerr's— for what those dreamers did during the war (506). This is perhaps best emblematized in *Everything Is Illuminated*, when the protagonist's Ukrainian tour guide admits to giving up his Jewish best friend to the Nazis in order to save himself, adding, "I am not a bad person. . . . I am a good person who has lived in a bad time" (227); in a letter, his grandson beseeches Foer's alter ego to "*forgive us, and . . . make us better than we are. Make us good*" (145).[78] And, indeed, Foer does. Ultimately, though some of these novels offer poignant narratives of the Holocaust and its intergenerational traumas, all of them couch whiteness in cabinets of curiosity and eccentricity, ignoring minoritized subjects while absolving their white characters, no matter how compromised they may be. There is no such thing as absolute evil in these novels, nor even the banality of evil, only good people in difficult situations. Everything is illuminated; everyone is recuperated.

PRIZED POSSESSIONS

In stark contrast to the novels just described, Julie Otsuka's *When the Emperor Was Divine*, which narrates a Japanese American family's expulsion from their Berkeley home and incarceration in the deserts of Utah, recriminates wartime America and its public memory by reversing these very same techniques.[79] Unlike in Chabon's and Doerr's novels, the war in Otsuka's book (inspired by her own family's experience of Japanese American incarceration) takes place entirely within the barren landscape of the western United States.[80] Like its setting, both the object world of the novel and its prose are notably evacuated of particularity. The family's home and their possessions are described by Otsuka only as they are being hastily packed away: "Upstairs, in the boy's room, [the woman] unpinned the One World One War map of the world from the wall and folded it neatly along the crease lines. She wrapped up his stamp collection. . . . She pulled out the *Joe Palooka* comic books from under his bed. . . . The rest of his things she put into boxes and carried into the sunroom" (7). Rather than assembling these Americanized images of innocence in an overstuffed sentence-long list, Otsuka compartmentalizes them, as if she, too, is packing them for safekeeping. On the next page, Otsuka tucks away the family's heirlooms in an em dash: "Everything else—the china, the crystal, the set of ivory chopsticks her mother had sent to her fifteen years ago from Kagoshima on her wedding day—she put into boxes" (8). Notably, the "things [the family] could take with them: bedding and linen, forks, spoons, plates, bowls, cups, clothes," are drained of detail entirely (9).

Unlike in Foer's novel, where "everything, down to the last and smallest detail, was made extraordinary" (161), Otsuka has been explicit in interviews that, despite her intensive research process, she "didn't want to weigh down the novel with historical details": "The backdrop—the awfulness of the war, of the internment—speaks for itself, I think. There's no need to accentuate it. If anything, I wanted to tone it down."[81] Indeed, almost every aspect of the novel is without accent, from its spare prose and unnamed characters ("The boy. The girl. Their mother" [50]), to its plot and setting. Chabon's Antarctic tundra is icy, silent. Otsuka's desert, though similarly blanched, is filled with "scorched white earth . . . stretching all the way to the edge of the horizon" (23). The "white glare of the desert" is "blinding" (48), and the "white and chalky" dust "made your skin burn . . . made your nose bleed . . . made your eyes sting. It took your voice away" (64). Whereas the industrious particularizing of Doerr and the rest works to endow whiteness with specificity, in this novel, Otsuka's disciplined avoidance of detail emphasizes the dehumanizing and departicularizing white gaze aimed at Japanese Americans during the war. In one particularly poignant moment, the boy writes his name—never mentioned in the novel—in the pale dust that has settled on a table in the camp. "By morning," Otsuka writes, "his name was gone" (64).

For the reader of Otsuka's historical novel, this insistent vacuousness is all the more powerful for how it turns historical details to a political purpose by withholding them entirely. The texture of historicity, a great part of the genre's pleasure, is largely removed from the novel and replaced with narration of a historical episode that is all the more distressing for its deprivation. When the family is finally released from the camp and allowed to return home, Otsuka returns to the period details—like the *Joe Palooka* comics—that one might expect in historical fiction of the 1940s. Whereas in the novel's early chapters, Otsuka described the family's possessions in the idiom of their being packed away, at the end of novel, Otsuka mentions these periodizing objects only to record what has been lost or stolen. "At the end of the hall, in the room where she had locked up our most valuable things—the View-Master, the Electrolux, our collection of old *Dime Detectives*, the wedding china that she had set out only on Sundays (*Why didn't we use those dishes every day of the week?* she would later ask)—there was hardly anything left at all" (111). In this passage, Otsuka revisits her earlier technique of storing objects in em dashes, only to violate it. The slide viewer, vacuum, and comics are conjured, and with specificity, so that their theft can be more fully felt. The family's dinnerware has disappeared from the locked room, and all that is left in its place—in room and em dash both—is regret that they did not make better use of it before. As the mother and her two children settle back into their Berkeley neighborhood, they begin to find their lost possessions in the windows of their white neighbors' houses: "Wasn't that our mother's Electrolux Mrs. Leahy was pushing back and forth across her living room floor? Didn't the Gilroys' mohair sofa look awfully familiar? Hadn't we seen that rolltop desk in Mr. Thigpen's library somewhere before?" (123). Here again Otsuka strategically deploys period detail to deepen the reader's sense of what her characters have lost.

Inverting the very techniques that dominate the World War II novel of the early twenty-first century, *When the Emperor Was Divine* takes up some of the same critiques as *Ceremony* and *Clay Walls*. Highlighting the contradiction at the heart of Silko's and Kim's novels, Otsuka has asserted that "the story of what happened to the Japanese-Americans during WWII is an important one, a story that needs to be told, especially since it took place right here, in America, during a time when we were supposedly fighting for democracy and freedom overseas."[82] This comment underscores two tensions explored in the novel: first, between the nation's rhetoric and its actions during the war; and second, between the history of the period and the cultural narratives that have congealed around it. Like *Ceremony* and *Clay Walls*, *When the Emperor Was Divine* represents an effort to reintegrate the history of racialized Americans into the thoroughly whitened public memory of the war. Though her characters claim that "all we wanted to do, now that we were back in the world, was forget," Otsuka's novel represents an effort to remember what has been conveniently forgotten by the myth of the greatest generation (133).

Critics of the novel have noted how its unnamed characters appear to invite identification with its central family by readers of all races and backgrounds. Had Otsuka concluded *When the Emperor Was Divine* one chapter earlier, with the image of the family searching for their mother's beloved rosebush "in some stranger's backyard," hoping that it was still somehow "blossoming madly, wildly, pressing one perfect red flower after another out into the late afternoon light," this reading might be persuasive (139). The beauty of this last image and the lyricism of the line that renders it, both withheld for much of the novel, hold out the possibility of an ending that, if not entirely rosy, offers some redemption. This calls to mind the oft-quoted passage from the chapter "How to Tell a True War Story" in Tim O'Brien's *The Things They Carried*, in which O'Brien writes that, "if at the end of a war story you feel uplifted, or you feel that some small bit of rectitude has been salvaged from the larger waste, then you have been made the victim of a very old and terrible lie."[83] Wary of this same impulse toward uplift, Otsuka's final chapter, "Confession," trades redemption for outrage, and upends readerly identification entirely.

The novel's evacuated third-person narrative shifts to the embittered first-person voice of the family's father, offering up a sardonic admission of guilt: "I admit it. . . . It was me. I did it. I poisoned your reservoirs. . . . I planted sticks of dynamite alongside your railroads. . . . I spied on your airfields. I spied on your naval yards. I spied on your neighbors. I spied on you" (140). Like the last section of Kim's *Clay Walls*, Otsuka's closing monologue can be understood as taking ownership of its own perspective, only here that voice, according to Josephine Park, is "twisted by a perverse desire to claim the wild array of crimes for which [the father] has been incarcerated." In this way, Park argues, the ending of *When the Emperor Was Divine* "provides a literary mode of resistance that works by enticing and then finally blocking readerly identification."[84] Tina Chen claims that the use of direct address in the father's narrative implicates the reader, "insisting that the reader occupy the much more uncomfortable position of someone complicit in perpetrating the injustice experienced by Japanese Americans during World War II."[85] Unlike the efforts toward universalizing absolution in Doerr's or Foer's novels, Otsuka's closing chapter restores the specificity of identity in order to tell "a True War Story" in the end.

A year after *The Amazing Adventures of Kavalier & Clay* won the Pulitzer Prize and W. G. Sebald's *Austerlitz* won the National Book Critics Circle Award, *When the Emperor Was Divine* appeared on the shortlists for neither prize nor that of the National Book Award. Twenty years later, however, Otsuka's novel did win the Children's Literature Association's Phoenix Award, which recognizes "a book for children first published twenty years earlier that did not win a major award at the time of its publication but which, from the perspective of time, is deemed worthy of special attention."[86] Setting aside the assumption that Otsuka's book is somehow "for children"—especially ironic, given how it complicates the abiding adolescence of so much twenty-first-century World War II fiction—it is worth considering what, exactly, it means for a prize to honor a novel "from the perspective of time." After all, this is precisely what literary awards are best at.

Critics of prizes such as the Pulitzer or the National Book Award, among which we can count a fair few literary scholars, will tell you that their imprimatur is no guarantee of aesthetic quality. As the shortlisted and snubbed novels discussed in this chapter can certainly attest, literary prizes do not always get it right, and they often get it wrong. The silver or gold medallion imprinted on a book's front cover may indicate that it was once well received, at least by some, but that stamp cannot ensure that a work will stand the test of time. Books that are still being read, taught, and written about decades later were woefully underappreciated in their moment; prizewinning novels from just a few years ago are already barely remembered. Yet, for historians of literature, this is perhaps the greatest strength of the prize: its record of what was valued—aesthetically, thematically, generically—if only by some, if only for a moment. Longevity produces a certain kind of literary-historical knowledge, as does ephemerality. In this case, both are useful.

Over the course of a half century in which historical fiction has represented the majority, and at times the *vast* majority, of the literature consecrated by major awards, World War II has stood reliably as the most prized period in history. And while it may be tempting for the literary critic to view this enormous concentration of literary prestige around a single fictional setting as a kind of monument to the prize's poor taste, for the literary scholar, it offers a viewfinder through which to observe the evolving aesthetics of American fiction over the last seven decades. The enduring prominence of World War II fiction testifies not only to how much has changed during that time—the ways in which irony gave way to sincerity, which gave way in turn to an amalgamation of the two—but also to how much has not. Despite the increasing recognition of racially and ethnically minoritized writers within the prize economy, and despite the fact that the overwhelming majority of that recognition is focused on works of historical fiction, the literary imagination of World War II remains about as white as it has ever been.

This matters for a number of reasons, not least because the prize, by consecrating fictions of the historical past, also works to elevate the very histories that they inscribe. Moreover, literary awards do not just record cultural valuation; they also mediate it. The repeated consecration of a given period or event does not just denote a shared sense of its artistic seriousness, it also signals to readers, publishers, agents, and authors what is considered ambitious, praiseworthy, and *literary* in the first place. While, as this book argues, the genre of historical fiction has proved both deeply capacious and reliably prestigious for writers of all races, the genre of World War II fiction demonstrates just how segregated the newly inclusive literary field remains.

Chapter Three

COLSON WHITEHEAD'S HISTORY OF THE UNITED STATES

PICKING A GENRE

SINCE THE publication of his first novel in 1999, Colson Whitehead has become one of the most lauded, prized, taught, and studied American novelists writing today. Winner of the National Book Award, two-time winner of the Pulitzer Prize (the only writer apart from William Faulkner and John Updike to accomplish this), recipient of a MacArthur "genius grant" and the nearly-as-lucrative honor of Oprah's Book Club, among the youngest writers to receive the Library of Congress Lifetime Achievement Award, and the most contemporary novelist included in the *Norton Anthology of African American Literature*, Whitehead stands at the very center of the contemporary American canon. According to critics and scholars alike, part of what makes Whitehead so singular is his ability to write across a vast array of literary and mass-cultural forms: detective and encyclopedic fiction (*The Intuitionist*, 1999; *John Henry Days*, 2001), contemporary satire and the bildungsroman (*Apex Hides the Hurt*, 2006; *Sag Harbor*, 2009), postapocalyptic zombie fiction (*Zone

One, 2011), the meta–slave narrative (*The Underground Railroad*, 2016), historical fiction (*The Nickel Boys*, 2019), and the heist novel (*Harlem Shuffle*, 2021).

Whitehead's play with genre is so well-known and so self-conscious that he has even joked about it publicly in the pages of the *New York Times*. Before the release of his zombie novel, *Zone One*, Whitehead published an essay titled "Picking a Genre," in which he describes his artistic process. "If you're anything like me, figuring out what to write next can be a real hassle. . . . To make things easier, I modified my dartboard a few years ago. Now, when I'm overwhelmed by the untold stories out there, I head down to the basement, throw a dart and see where it lands. Try it for yourself!" What follows is a list of targets on that dartboard, both a catalogue and a sendup of the genres that characterize contemporary American fiction, ranging from the "Encyclopedic" novel for the "postmodern, or postmodern-curious," to the "Ethnic Bildungsroman," "Little Known Historical Fact," and "Southern Novel of Black Misery."[1] Here Whitehead is satirizing not only his own career but also the phenomenon that critics such as Andrew Hoberek, Theodore Martin, and Jeremy Rosen have called the contemporary "genre turn": that is, the spate of literary novelists in recent years who have drawn on the "frameworks" of mass-market genres. By now, the set of these "literary genre writers" is familiar—Margaret Atwood, Michael Chabon, Jennifer Egan, Kazuo Ishiguro, Cormac McCarthy, and Viet Thanh Nguyen—as is the array of those genres themselves: detective, dystopian, fantasy, Western, and postapocalyptic fiction.[2] One of the central aims of this book, however, is to document the process by which historical fiction, despite its mass-market popularity and its "déclassé" status for much of the twentieth century, has been left off that list.[3] After all, every one of the writers just mentioned has published a historical novel, and in some cases several.

While Whitehead's own oeuvre represents a veritable catalogue of genres, it also chronicles nearly two hundred years of American history.⁴ If we rearrange his novels not by publication date but loosely by their historical settings, we end up following Whitehead from the slave narrative and folklore of the nineteenth century (*The Underground Railroad* and *John Henry Days*) to the hard-boiled civil rights noir and ethnic bildungsroman of the mid- and late twentieth century (*The Intuitionist*, *Harlem Shuffle*, *The Nickel Boys*, and *Sag Harbor*). From this vantage, it seems clear that Whitehead is not only a writer of genre fiction, but a prolific writer of one genre in particular: historical fiction. Yet this is somehow not what critics mean when they say that these literary novelists have "turned to genre." Writing historical fiction is not what makes them "genre writers," but rather what makes their work "literary" in the first place.

The historical survey course that Whitehead's body of work represents therefore offers insight not only into one of the most important twenty-first-century novelists but also into the larger structures of the contemporary literary field that Whitehead's career indexes. Reading *The Intuitionist* as an academic satire that is both a product and an allegory of the campus canon wars of the 1980s and 1990s, this chapter argues that Whitehead's first book dramatizes contemporaneous debates over literary canon reformation in a formally inventive (and Intuitionist-influenced) historical novel. Situating the novel in the context of Whitehead's undergraduate years at Harvard University thus provides a new rubric for *The Intuitionist* as well as a historical account of the institutional forces that motivated American literature's significant historical turn. Moving from the author's first novel to his more recent successes, this investigation then turns to *The Underground Railroad* as a case study in twenty-first-century historical fiction, and in particular the hypercanonical genre of the meta–slave narrative. Focusing closely on the novel's allusive and performative relationship to the genre it participates in, this chapter argues that *The Underground Railroad* embodies both the recent history and the present limits of contemporary narratives of slavery. Finally, this chapter examines *The Nickel Boys* and *Harlem Shuffle* as more recent additions to Whitehead's single-author syllabus of American history, and it argues that the novels both exemplify the field-specific forces that have encouraged Whitehead's canonization and emphasize the inadequacies of an aesthetic program that relies on historical analogy as its chief method of political intervention. If *The Intuitionist* offers us a glimpse at the academic and aesthetic debates that launched the historical turn, Whitehead's career since then stands as a testament to the ways in which that period and its logics have reshaped American literature.

INTUITIONIST HISTORY

Published in 1999, *The Intuitionist* narrates the investigations of Lila Mae Watson, a municipal elevator inspector in a thinly veiled version of New York. As the novel opens, the city is in crisis, torn asunder by the upcoming election for chair of the Elevator Inspectors Guild and the rival theoretical camps that the two candidates represent. On one side, we have the Empiricists, long dominant in the world of elevator inspection, invested in observable facts, and marked by methodological and social conservatism. On the other, we have the Intuitionists, the upstart underdogs of elevator maintenance, who believe in "communicating with the elevator on a nonmaterial basis," and boast (somewhat inexplicably) of "a 10 percent higher accuracy rate."[5] Lila Mae Watson is not only a devout Intuitionist but also the first Black woman inspector in the biz. To make matters even more interesting, the Fanny Briggs Building—the high-profile skyscraper named after an enslaved woman who taught herself to read, and the building for which Lila Mae is responsible—has just suffered a catastrophic accident: an elevator in complete free fall.

Critical accounts of *The Intuitionist* have read it variously as "a wry postmodern *noir*," a "racial protest novel" with a "gothic sensibility, and a "not-quite-steampunk, alternative history of the future."[6] Yet while many scholars have commented on the novel's historical themes, nearly all have stopped short of calling it a (capital-H, capital-N) Historical Novel, preferring instead to read it—as an early *Time* magazine review did—as "the freshest racial allegory since Ralph Ellison's *The Invisible Man*."[7] One reason why critics may prefer to read the novel as a kind of allegory seems to be the lack of consensus as to *when*, exactly, *The Intuitionist* takes place. The novel is set, Lauren Berlant states definitively, "around 1964."[8] Or, at least, in "something like 1960s New York."[9] Well, "1950's or 60's."[10] Either that, or it's "'40s-ish New York," or "before . . . the 1940s," or "during the Harlem Renaissance."[11] To summarize, *The Intuitionist* is a novel of "the early twentieth century," the "post–civil rights era," and "some unspecified mid-twentieth-century milieu."[12] No wonder, then, that critics read the novel as an "allegory," a "historical fantasia" set in "an alternative reality."[13] In Whitehead's world, history works differently.

At first glance, *The Intuitionist* seems an easy target for Fredric Jameson's well-known critique of contemporary historical fiction: namely, that it traffics in "stylistic connotation . . . and pseudohistorical depth, in which the history of aesthetic styles displaces 'real' history." Not the historical moment, in other words, but its aesthetic trappings; not the 1950s, but what Jameson calls "1950s-ness."[14] Whitehead's novel is littered with periodizing references to fashion ("fedoraed men" and "torpedo bras"), popular culture ("big band music" and "stickball"), technology ("new watches equipped with . . . radium dials," an "icebox" and "milk bottle"), and historical referents: we're told that one of Lila Mae's professors had "been in the war" (99)—though not *which* war—and we catch a brief glimpse of Martin Luther King Jr. (248). Jameson's notion of "stylistic connotation" seems to run aground on *The Intuitionist*, a novel that—as critical confusion makes clear—connotes '50s-ness, '60s-ness, and '20s–'30s–'40s-ness all at once. While the temporal indeterminacy of Whitehead's novel has led critics to read it as a portrait of "an alternative reality," what *The Intuitionist* ultimately represents is an alternative *history* of our own. Looking only at the usual clues, the novel's setting seems muddled, indecipherable. Yet, as in any great detective novel, the answer is hiding in plain sight. In its first paragraphs, Whitehead announces precisely *when The Intuitionist* takes place.

In the novel's opening scene, as Lila Mae first inspects the doomed Fanny Briggs elevator, the building's superintendent asks, "You aren't one of those voodoo inspectors, are you? Don't need to see anything, you just feel it, right?" (7). When Lila Mae corrects him, saying that she practices Intuitionism rather than "voodoo," the super adds: "I haven't ever seen a woman elevator inspector before, let alone a colored one, but I guess they teach you all the same tricks" (8). This is the first of many instances in the novel where Lila Mae and the rest of *The Intuitionist*'s Black cast are referred to as "colored." What is more, she is the first "colored" woman in her field. Here Whitehead offers an alternative, but no less historically grounded, method of periodization. *The Intuitionist* takes place in the time of burgeoning integration, the time of "colored," a term that Whitehead half-jokingly claims in a later essay "lasted 82.3 years."[15]

Whitehead further emphasizes this synchronicity on the level of the novel's form by narrating the action of *The Intuitionist* in the perpetual present and collapsing multiple decades into a single novel temporality. What may seem like a playful pastiche of period styles is in fact a deadly serious historiographical claim: the novel nods to the Harlem Renaissance and the civil rights movement and the decades in between because that was precisely the period of so many African American "firsts." In this way, *The Intuitionist* operates on a clear historical timeline, albeit one with a different structure than historical fiction as it is traditionally understood. Abandoning specific dates and coherent decade aesthetics, Whitehead offers an alternative to what we can think of as historical fiction's latent "Empiricism": that is, an *Intuitionist* historical novel.

COLSON WHITEHEAD'S HISTORY OF THE UNITED STATES

But in order to fully appreciate just what kind of historical novel this is, and how it frustrates existing accounts of the genre, we first need to go back in time ourselves—not to the period of desegregation in which it takes place, but to another, far more animating context for *The Intuitionist*: the campus culture wars of the 1980s and early 1990s. At the risk of adding still one more genre to Whitehead's dartboard, I submit that *The Intuitionist* is, in large part, an academic satire: a campus novel and archival thriller shaped by Whitehead's years at Harvard and the canon wars that marked them. For as much as the present action of the novel narrates Lila Mae's investigation of the Fanny Briggs elevator crash, that investigation itself hinges on the prominent theorists, ideological debates, and institutional histories of the academy—the elevator academy. The world of *The Intuitionist* may read as an "alternative reality" to some, but I posit that it is likely all too familiar to the scholars and students who hold it in their hands. As readers, we learn of "the early days of passenger-response criticism" (5). We hear of "Erlich," the "mad" French theorist, who "never gets invited to conferences" and whose "monographs wilt on the shelves" (229). We even meet Ben Urich, a young writer desperate to publish in *Lift*, the leading professional journal, but willing to place his article in "one of the smaller elevator newsletters who don't pay as well and have a smaller circulation" (72).

Whitehead's mirror-image academy is best captured in one early passage, when the narrator describes Lila Mae's colleague, Chuck, who harbors a passion for an overlooked corner of the profession, the field of escalator studies:

> Escalator safety has never received its due respect. . . . But Chuck can live with the obscurity and disrespect and occasional migraines. Specialization means job security, and there's a nationwide lack of escalator professors in the Institutes, so Chuck figures he's a shoo-in for a teaching job. And once he's in there, drawing a bead on

tenure, he can branch out from escalators and teach whatever he wants. He probably even has his dream syllabus tucked in his pocket at this very moment, scratched on a cheap napkin. A general survey course on the history of hydraulic elevators. . . . Or hypothetical elevators; hypothetical elevator studies is bound to come back into vogue again, now that the furor has died down. Chuck's assured Lila Mae that even though he is a staunch Empiricist, he'll throw in the Intuitionist counterarguments where necessary. His students should be acquainted with the entire body of elevator knowledge, not just the canon. (21)

As this last line makes clear, the battle between the Empiricists and the Intuitionists is being waged not only in municipal elections but also on the syllabus itself, much like the 1980s culture wars which displaced national political debate onto the English department and the substance of what was taught there.[16]

On the right, the group of conservative thinkers branded as "The Traditionalists" argued that the preservation of the Western—largely white and male—literary canon was essential to the project of national education. William Bennett claimed it was the university's responsibility to uphold the "legacy" of the Western tradition currently being undermined by "respect for diversity."[17] Allan Bloom's *The Closing of the American Mind*—published in 1987, the year Whitehead entered Harvard—decried in even stronger terms multiculturalism's "demagogic intention . . . to force students to recognize that . . . Western ways are not better."[18] Focusing on contemporary prize culture in particular, Carol Iannone's 1991 essay "Literature by Quota" contended that a "new order" ruled by the "democratic dictatorship of mediocrity" had taken over the nation's major literary awards, transforming them into "less a recognition of literary achievement than some official act of reparation."[19]

Responding in part to the rise of Black and ethnic studies curricula that grew from student activism in the 1960s and '70s, the

Traditionalists' sneering at "diversity" and "reparation" appears now as little more than a racially coded backlash couched in the language of academic debate. In this way, the Traditionalists are not unlike our very own Empiricists, who label their intellectual rivals as "swamis, voodoo men, juju heads, [and] witch doctors" (57). Sounding as much like Bennett or Bloom as he does more contemporary conservatives, the leader of the Empiricist party—the aptly named Frank Chancre (pron. *canker*)—advocates for tradition in the key of racist dog whistle: "sometimes the old ways are the best ways. Why hold truck with the uppity and newfangled when Empiricism has always been the steering light of reason? Just like it was in our fathers' day, and our fathers' fathers.' Today's [accident] is just the kind of unfortunate mishap that can happen when you kowtow to the latest fashions" (27). *Make Elevators Great Again.*

Meanwhile on the left, the Multiculturalists and New Historicists pushed not only for a diversification of the curriculum but also for an end to the practices of reading in isolation that they saw as a kind of ethical failure. From Jameson's commandment at the start of the decade—*Always Historicize!*—to the New Historicist approaches that largely defined it, a surge of literary scholarship worked to "combat empty formalism by pulling historical considerations to the center stage of literary analysis."[20] Joseph North has recently described this period as the beginning of the "historicist/contextualist paradigm" in literary studies, a program that prizes historicity over aesthetics, celebrates "the opening up of the canon," and dominates the discipline to this day.[21]

For all of the disagreement between the right's ethnicized traditionalism and the left's multiculturalist revisionism, both sides had one thing in common. Whether literature served as a testament to racial and national preeminence within a global meritocracy or worked instead to identify and redress systems of inequality, both sides mobilized it against what they described as a contemporary culture of forgetting. Central to the arguments of Bennett and the like was the idea that "students [simply cannot] understand their society without studying its intellectual legacy. If their past is hidden from them, they will become aliens in their own culture, strangers in their own land."[22] Likewise, Henry Louis Gates Jr. argued in his book *Loose Canons* (1992) that

> this is one case where we've got to borrow a leaf from the right, which is exemplarily aware of the role of education in the reproduction of values. We must engage in this sort of canon deformation precisely because Mr. Bennett is correct: the teaching of literature *is* the teaching of values; . . . it has become . . . the teaching of an aesthetic and political order, in which no women or people of color were ever able to discover the reflection or representation of their images, or hear the resonances of their cultural voices.[23]

This agreement—perhaps the only one between Bennett and Gates—is crucial to understanding the origins of American literature's historical turn. Given that the two sides of the canon wars were united in their desire for a renewed historical consciousness (however variously defined), it comes as little surprise that, as literature became the central battleground of political debate, historical fiction arose as the dominant—and, indeed, ideal—literary genre to mediate that debate.

After all, what better way for the left to dispute the critique that literary multiculturalism was both erasing history and sacrificing quality than to prize, study, and teach a new canon of novels deeply concerned with the historical past and therefore imbued with the authority that its historicity affords? John Guillory has argued that "a syllabus of study always enacts a negotiation between *historical* works and *modern* works" and that "obviously in order to 'open' [the literary] canon, one would have to *modernize* it, to displace the preponderance of works from earlier to later."[24] But while this seems obvious, it is not entirely accurate. Certainly, in order to diversify the list of authors taught in the university English classroom, it is necessary to devote greater attention to periods in which marginalized writers had at least a modicum of access to the means of literary production. That said, what better way to mitigate this necessary modernization than by canonizing minoritized authors almost exclusively for the writing of historical fiction? Morrison's *Beloved*, for example, may have been published in 1987, but it is also, in a manner of speaking, a novel of the nineteenth century. In this way, the institutions of literary studies in the 1980s and early 1990s—torn between competing impulses to simultaneously modernize and historicize—were able to both have and eat their cake by baking heirloom recipes.

For Whitehead, these battles in the culture wars were not merely part of some vague historical background but raging in front of him on the Harvard campus, where he studied from 1987 to 1991. Even a quick glance at the archives of the *Harvard Crimson* bears this out, as headlines drawn from just a few weeks in Whitehead's junior year demonstrate: harsh critiques and impassioned defenses of political correctness ("'Politically Correct' Thought Control," "Two Views on PC Ideology"); a campus controversy over the public hanging of a Confederate flag ("The Flag Is Harassment"); debates over affirmative action and faculty hiring ("Affirmative Action Debated," "Educators Urge Women, Minority Role Models"); even Harvard's own African American "first" ("Obama Named New Law Review President").[25] That said, the tense campus climate was nowhere more apparent than in the English and African American studies departments where Whitehead took most of his classes.

In the editorial pages of the *Crimson*, English majors decried the department's core curriculum, which they saw as overly Western, white, and male.[26] We hear an echo of this in *The Intuitionist*—an echo, perhaps, of Whitehead's own experience—as Lila Mae begins her course of study.

She learned plenty her first semester at the Institute for Vertical Transport. She learned about the animals in the Roman coliseums hoisted to their cheering deaths on rope-tackle elevators powered by slaves, learned about Villayer's "flying chair," a simple . . . counterweight concoction described in a love letter from Napoleon I to his wife, the Archduchess Marie Louise. . . . She read about Elisha Graves Otis [and] the cities he enabled through his glorious invention. . . . The rise of safety regulation, safety device innovations, the search for a national standard. She was learning about Empiricism but didn't know it yet. (44–45)

Notice here the Institute's insistence on elevator studies' Western European roots, the pioneering "innovations" of white Americans, and the development of Bennett-esque "national standards." Before Lila Mae is exposed to the iconoclastic and liberatory curriculum of Intuitionism, she is steeped in an Empiricist tradition so naturalized that it is effectively invisible.

For students like Lila Mae, there is but one refuge beyond the ivied gates of the Institute for Vertical Transport: Intuitionist House, "the international headquarters of Intuitionism," and the unofficial clubhouse of like-minded elevator undergraduates (54). (Later on, Intuitionist House is also a literal refuge for Lila Mae, who hides out there while on the run from Johnny Shush's muscle.) This is where "the gathering magic of the time" coalesces: "From the continent come foreign scholars of the art," lectures are held, cocktails consumed, and "grand parties celebrating the publication of the latest Intuitionist tract" (55) are thrown. For literary-minded Black students at Harvard in the 1980s and 1990s, there was likewise one place to be: not the 117 Second Avenue headquarters of Intuitionism, but the 31 Inman Street home to the Dark Room Collective. Founded by Thomas Sayers Ellis and Sharan Strange in 1987, after the two former Harvard students attended the funeral of James Baldwin, the Dark Room Collective was a place for undergraduates and community members alike to "connect with and honor other still-living Black writers," whom the aspiring writers dubbed their "living literary ancestors."[27] Just as the novel's community of Intuitionists only grows after the death of its founding thinker, so too did the Dark Room Collective spring to life in the wake of Baldwin's passing. In its first two seasons at 31 Inman, the collective hosted readings by Derek Walcott, Alice Walker, Ntozake Shange, Yusef Komunyakaa, Samuel Delany, Toni Cade Bambara, John Edgar Wideman, Elizabeth Alexander, Randall Kenan, and Trey Ellis, among dozens of others.[28] This list of luminaries is matched only by the list of the organization's undergraduate and young alumni members, including Strange ('81), Janice Lowe ('87), Carl Phillips ('81), Tracy K. Smith ('94), Kevin Young ('92), and Whitehead himself, who went by Chipp at the time.[29]

Young and Whitehead's close friendship also energized the revival of Harvard's then-dormant literary magazine, *Diaspora: The Journal of Black Thought & Culture*, where Young served as an editor-in-chief and Whitehead as a fiction editor and contributor. One of Whitehead's first published works of fiction, the moody and surprisingly un-genrefied short story "Sylvia's Crime," appeared in *Diaspora*.[30] In his editorial preface to the Fall 1989–Winter 1990 issue Young emphasizes the importance of thinking beyond the bounds of Harvard itself: "It is restricting, and slightly dangerous, to think only in terms of a university that does not even serve the needs of its own African-American students, whether in hiring Black faculty, or in supporting an undergraduate department in African-American Studies."[31] In interviews, Whitehead has described moving beyond Harvard's core curriculum in those years, taking classes in both English and African American studies that focused more on contemporary literature and far more on Black authors. "In sophomore English, reading Jane Austen all the time, you think that's what literature is," Whitehead said before adding, "the canon is not all that it's cracked up to be—there's a lot more out there."[32]

Just as Lila Mae discovers the work of James Fulton and his theory of Intuitionism, Whitehead himself found writers and thinkers that transformed him. Indeed, Whitehead's reading as an undergraduate makes itself apparent throughout *The Intuitionist*, which alludes to many of the authors he first encountered at Harvard and still counts among his greatest influences. The metacanonical novel is littered with citations, from Lila Mae's resemblance to Oedipa Maas of Thomas Pynchon's *The Crying of Lot 49* and her favorite lunch spot in "the Metzger building" (20) to the Intuitionist society's chief counsel, Mr. Jameson, and lead advisor, Mr. Reed—that is, Ishmael Reed, who taught as a visiting professor at Harvard in 1987, and whom Whitehead regularly cites as a particularly important influence and an "overlooked" and "groundbreaking voice in black fiction."[33] (In a 2021 *New Yorker* profile of Reed, published in the same issue as an excerpt from *Harlem Shuffle*, Whitehead explains how he first came to the novelist's work as an undergraduate by following Pynchon's call in *Gravity's Rainbow* to "check out Ishmael Reed.")[34] Even the Fanny Briggs building, the site of the novel's inciting elevator crash, bears the traces of Whitehead's Harvard syllabi, located as it is at "125 Walker," a nod to the author of *The Color Purple* and a neighbor to what is perhaps the most famous street address in African American literature: 124 Bluestone Road (1–2).

In fact, in the spring of his junior year, as Whitehead was enrolled in Harvard's "Introduction to African American Literature" course, Toni Morrison visited campus to give a series of lectures that would ultimately become *Playing in the Dark*, her now-canonical book of essays on American literature's racial imaginary.[35] In the lectures, Morrison reveals what she calls the "abiding ... Africanist presence" in the work of writers like Poe, James, O'Connor, and Hemingway, staging an intervention in contemporary literary studies by way of a return to American literary history.[36] Ultimately Morrison both advocates and exemplifies a new wave of scholarship committed to excavating Black history from the American literary canon. As

Morrison herself put it that spring at Harvard, "Criticism of this type will show how . . . narrative is used in the construction of a history and a context for whites by positing history-lessness and context-lessness for blacks."[37]

Regardless of whether Whitehead was in the room, Morrison's call for a renewed investment in Black literary history would have appeared all the more pressing to students of African American literature at Harvard, in light of the fact that the university's "Afro-American Studies" department was in the midst of an existential crisis.[38] Like the elevator institute's courses on Intuitionism—which Whitehead tells us "were always . . . full" despite being relegated to "the dingy recesses of the course catalog" and even dingier classrooms (59)—Afro-American Studies at Harvard in 1990 enjoyed a wealth of student interest but little institutional support.[39] Descriptions of these two institutional programs are practically interchangeable: Whitehead notes how far Intuitionism has come in "two decades," "continuing to stubbornly prosper even after Institute administrations reversed themselves, offered classes on the new science and even bestowed large (although not well-situated) offices upon its intrepid instructors" (53–54). Likewise at Harvard where, in the two decades since the department's 1969 establishment, Afro-American Studies had become both soundly institutionalized and institutionally unsupported. Hardly a month passed in Whitehead's last semesters when the department's ever-dwindling faculty was not making campus news. In Whitehead's final year, when "Afro-Am" was poised to retain only a single tenured professor, student protesters occupied campus buildings, marched through football games, and appealed to the Cambridge City Council for support. According to intrepid student reporter Rebecca L. Walkowitz, as demonstrations escalated, the administration swung into action, extending a handful of offers, including one to Henry Louis Gates Jr.[40] As the *Crimson*'s headline—"Can He Save Afro-Am?"—suggests, Gates's acceptance was big news at Harvard. Asked to comment on the announcement, Toni

Morrison offered that the union of Gates and Harvard was "a perfect marriage."[41]

Here it is helpful to return to Gates not only because his impending arrival at Harvard would have caught the interest of "Afro-Am" student Colson Whitehead, but also because his writing from this period includes a somewhat surprising intertext for *The Intuitionist*. Published in the March 1990 issue of the *New York Times Book Review*, and again in 1992 as the opening chapter of *Loose Canons*, "Canon Confidential" was Gates's own attempt to recompose the canon wars in the key of detective noir. In brief, the story follows private detective Sam Slade as he tries to uncover the forces that destine works either for posterity or for the pulp mill. Like *The Intuitionist*, Gates's academic satire is littered with cameos: Helen Vendler has Slade bounced from the Harvard Club; Jacques Barzun holds him up with a .38; and Harold Bloom, who has a "rap sheet longer than a three-part *New Yorker* profile," is wanted for multiple murders, chief among them T. S. Eliot's.[42] Eventually, Slade confronts the figure behind the entire canon cabal, described as a small, old man in an "enormous . . . leather chair." "Don't [you] understand how big this thing is," he says. "We've got people all over. . . . We've got the daily reviewers. . . . the literature profs at your colleges. . . . the guys who edit the anthologies—Norton, Oxford, you name it—they all work for us."[43] In the end, he even buys off Slade, offering him his very own spot in the canon, and the opportunity to be "deconstructed, reconstructed and historicized in *PMLA*."[44]

The arc of "Canon Confidential" offers a stark contrast to Whitehead's own canon noir. Unlike Sam Slade, whose struggle for the truth leads him into the heart of a vast literary conspiracy, Lila Mae's investigations return her, again and again, to the university and its history. As *The Intuitionist* builds toward a close, Lila Mae draws repeatedly on her scholarly training as she works to track down the lost papers of Intuitionism's founding theorist, the late James Fulton. Performing what can only be described as archival research, Lila Mae scours institutional documents, deciphers manuscript marginalia, and pores over old issues of *Lift*. Piecing together the gaps in Fulton's biography, Lila Mae ultimately discovers a startling secret: James Fulton, institute professor and Intuitionist thinker, was in fact a Black man passing for white. Just as Morrison argues of literary history in *Playing in the Dark*, here the elevator's own history of innovation harbors an overlooked but "abiding . . . Africanist presence." In the shadow of this knowledge, which Whitehead describes as "reconnoting" all that Lila Mae has ever been taught, Fulton's description of "[a] race . . . . stirred by dreaming . . . *this dream of uplift*" accrues a far deeper meaning (186).

Confronted with this new perspective on history, Lila Mae begins "teaching herself how to read" all over again (186). Realizing that the archive can only take her so far—its dates and facts the last vestiges of her Empiricist education—Lila Mae returns to the Fanny Briggs Building in an effort to commune firsthand with history. From the very start of the novel, the high-rise figures as what Morrison has elsewhere called a "site of memory,"[45] taking its name from an enslaved woman who, like Lila Mae, "taught herself how to read" (12). Its lobby features a grand historical mural that is as ambitious as it is selective: jumping quickly from "the infamous sale of the island" to a "nice set-piece [*sic*]" on the Revolution (47). However, Whitehead tells us, "the painting ended there. . . . Judging from the amount of wall space that remained . . . the mural would have to [become] even more brief in its chronicle. . . . Either the painter had misjudged how much space he had or the intervening years weren't that compelling to him. Just the broad strokes, please" (48). In this way, the Fanny Briggs Building stands as a towering symbol of the losses and omissions etched into its very design.

And it is here that Whitehead stages the climax of the novel, an extended demonstration of Intuitionism. As Lila Mae begins her "reenactment" of the building's catastrophic elevator crash, she "shuts [everything] out," "closes her eyes," and "reaches out into the darkness" (226). Whitehead writes:

This is the wrong darkness. It is the darkness of this day and this time and this elevator and Lila Mae needs that further-back darkness, the one she encountered on her first visit to Fanny Briggs. . . . She imagines her hand extending out to the unyielding solidity of that dead elevator's walls, the way the inner paneling embraced her hand's curves. . . . It is a slow curtain dropping before this day's darkness. There. . . . She watches the sure and untroubled ascent of Number Eleven. The genies appear on cue, dragging themselves from the wings. The genie of velocity, the genie of the hoisting motor's brute exertions, the red cone genie of the selector as it ticks off the entity's progress through the shaft, the amber nonagon genie of the grip shoes as they skip frictionless up T-rails. All of them energetic and fastidious, describing seamless verticality to Lila Mae in her mind's own tongue. They zigzag and circle, hop from foot to foot. . . . They gyrate . . . and reenact without omission. (226)

The first and most obvious thing to say about this passage is that it is likely the most beautiful description of an elevator in all of English literature. Moving beyond the archive and its documentary evidence, Lila Mae reconstructs the past by communing with it firsthand—literally firsthand. Unlike the Empiricists who "imagined elevators from [an] . . . inherently alien point of view," here "reenactment" is a tactile experience, an empathic one (62). Clearly, Whitehead's protagonist has not only taught herself "how to read," but how to *close read*, deconstructing the elevator's passage and examining its previously overlooked constituent parts. Dredging the past from the darkness that obscures it, Lila Mae transcends the lobby mural fourteen floors below, discovering a history "without omission."[46]

I want to return now to the idea with which I began: namely, that Whitehead's novel represents a kind of Intuitionist historical fiction, set in the desegregation of the midcentury but structured according to the logics of the canon wars at that century's close. Bearing the traces of the multiculturalist and New Historicist programs that marked Whitehead's development as a thinker and writer, *The Intuitionist* works to reenact history and resurrect figures like Lila Mae Watson, James Fulton, and Fanny Briggs—not from "an alien point of view," but from a new perspective using novel techniques. As Whitehead puts it in his final pages, "Intuitionism is communication. That simple. Communication with what is not-you" (241). The novel's third-person narration appears to take this advice to heart as well, evolving from the Empiricist-inflected omniscience of the book's early chapters to its heavily focalized, increasingly "close" conclusion.

In its rejection of empiricist principles, *The Intuitionist* frustrates previous accounts of historical fiction in ways that are representative of the genre writ large at the turn of the twenty-first century. Georg Lukács has argued that the protagonist of the historical novel must be a "middling" figure, "never heroic" but thrust into a decisive moment of historical transition.[47] By contrast, Whitehead's protagonist is not at all "middling" but exceptional: the first Black woman to break into her field and a rising hero of new theoretical methods. Moreover, though Whitehead's portrait of desegregation depicts just such a transition, the novel's indeterminate setting undermines the idea of neat historical breaks, pointing up the uneven and often illusory qualities of progress. While Jameson has derided contemporary historical fiction for what he calls its "'nostalgia' art language" and its "random cannibalization of . . . the styles of the past," Whitehead interleaves a range of period styles in part to critique such nostalgia as a weapon of conservatism seeking to revert to the time of "our fathers . . . and our fathers' fathers."[48] If the novel appears to abandon what Jameson has described as "the American history we learn from schoolbooks," that is because Whitehead is arguing that we need better schoolbooks.[49] *The Intuitionist* takes its cues from Henry Louis Gates, "deforming" canonical history in order to recuperate the "resonances of . . . cultural voices" previously unheard. The novel literalizes, *narrativizes*, Morrison's arguments from *Playing in the Dark*, not only recognizing the historically invisible but drafting a new history that centralizes them. As one character says of Fulton: "What he made, this elevator, colored people made that. It's ours" (139).

Whitehead's novel is both historiographical and metafictional, but not in the ways that Linda Hutcheon and Amy Elias have described.[50] For Hutcheon, postmodern historical fiction points up the "textual" nature of history, stressing that the past is fundamentally unstable and inaccessible. As Elias puts it: "postmodern literature . . . seems hyperconsciously aware that the drive to write and know history may be a futile endeavor, at worst an imperialist drive to control the past, at most a Hollywood-inspired move to profit from history's . . . simulation."[51] In *The Intuitionist*, however, the drive to "write and know history" is not at all futile, but central to Whitehead's recuperative project. For that project to succeed, history cannot remain forever inaccessible. Like his protagonist, Whitehead has to reach out through "that further-back darkness" in order to lay hands on the "unyielding solidity" of the past. In the final pages of *The Intuitionist*, Lila Mae returns to "her alma mater, the Institute for Vertical Transport" (230). Yet this time she arrives not as a student but as a scholar of Intuitionism, drawing on her training to fill in the gaps in the historical record and sitting down to write Fulton's lost third volume herself. If the bulk of the novel is consumed with the process of her education and the scholarly debates that shaped it, its conclusion finds Whitehead's protagonist—like Whitehead himself—renewing a tradition of Black authors and academics by writing historical fiction.

And yet, there is something somewhat deflationary about *The Intuitionist*'s conclusion. In a fittingly noirish twist, the mystery of the Fanny Briggs elevator crash runs all the way to the top, to Arbo and United, the rival manufacturing corporations that Lila Mae learns are "the real players here" (207). "Did you think this was all about philosophy? Who's the better man—Intuitionism or Empiricism?" one character asks. "No one really gives a crap about that. Arbo and United are the guys who make the things. That's what really matters" (208). While true to its genre roots, this moment—the novel's "Forget it, Jake" reveal—also casts *The Intuitionist*'s central intellectual debate as somehow provincial, somehow naive. The battle over the canon of elevator studies is less a frontline conflict than a rearguard action of an increasingly irrelevant corps of institute professors. This is precisely Guillory's conclusion about the 1990s canon wars: namely, that "it has proven to be much easier to quarrel about the content of the curriculum than to confront the implications of a fully emergent professional-managerial class" that cares little for literature.[52]

But what about Lila Mae, taking up the mantle of her revolutionary forebears and writing a new chapter in a liberatory volume? Throughout the novel Fulton's work is figured as a "doctrine of transcendence," both a theory and a methodology for a "perfect elevator that will lift him"—and countless others—into a new era (241). Like the canonical Black thinkers to whom Whitehead alludes throughout the novel, many of whom he crossed paths with as a young writer at Harvard, Fulton and his utopian thinking are less a telos than a passing of a torch. "He's thought it through as far as he can see," Whitehead tells us. "It will be up to someone else to execute the plan" (252). The end of the novel does not find Lila Mae working to "execute the plan," however, so much as "nailing Fulton's voice . . . filling in the interstitial parts that Fulton didn't have time to finish up" (254). The language here is ambiguous, as is the project itself: equal parts ventriloquism and imagination, recovery and intervention. While both this project and the novel that centers it are invested in the speculative possibilities of a materially different future, their method for arriving at that future is, somewhat ironically, archival. Fulton's black box is the novel's Maltese falcon, a richly symbolic MacGuffin that drives protagonist and reader alike but ultimately distracts from the central object of interest.[53] *The Intuitionist* hinges on an investigation and a final discovery, yes, but not of a device with which to reimagine the future, rather a prehistory with which to renarrate the present. When the guard at the Fanny Briggs building tells Lila Mae that he "thought you guys were all finished with Number Eleven," she counters that "It's never finished" (224). The work continues, to be sure, but for Lila Mae—and Whitehead himself—moving forward means writing backward into the past.

THE INSTITUTIONALIST

Whitehead is less a writer of characters than a writer of worlds. As Madhu Dubey argues, "a hallmark of Colson Whitehead's fiction—and the source of its distinctive power—is its strategy of building elaborate narrative worlds based on the logic of literalizing metaphor."[54] This is because his novels are deeply invested in the structures, institutions, and forms of labor that these elaborate worlds make visible in our own. Though *The Intuitionist* bears the traces of Whitehead's years at university—and that university's fraught debates over race, historiography, and the uses of literature—so too do all of Whitehead's novels. In this way, the most common typo in my students' essays on Whitehead, the misspelling of the title of his first novel, is also a brilliantly apt description of him as an author: *The Institutionalist*.

Scholars have written much about how *John Henry Days*, the author's transhistorical and encyclopedic second novel, develops *The Intuitionist*'s interest in lost archives and competing historiographies but they have made little of how the novel extends *The Intuitionist*'s engagement with the institutional politics of historical memory.[55] As "a sophomore in college," J. Sutter, the novel's journalist-cum-PR-"junketeer" protagonist, embeds himself in "the Afro-Am Department" and the classroom of fictional former Black Panther and "visiting lecturer" Toure Nkumreh (324). Widely admired by his undergraduate and graduate students alike, Nkumreh, who describes himself as "the last member of the Black Power Traveling All-Stars," calls to mind the language applied to Harvard's own "Afro-Am" department in a two-page spread in *Vibe* magazine, published just a few years after Whitehead's graduation (325). Accompanying a photograph that includes Gates, Cornel West, Kwame Anthony Appiah, and Evelyn Brooks Higgenbotham, the caption cautions that the U.S. Olympic basketball squad "may have trouble keeping the title Dream Team from Harvard University's Department of Afro-American Studies."[56] As in *The Intuitionist*, J.'s undergraduate department looks much like Whitehead's: popular yet institutionally unsupported; championed by student protesters (including J. himself), who "enlisted in the takeover of the Dean's Office"; even led by a department chair who looks conspicuously like Werner Sollors (326–27). Like Lila Mae, whose time at the Institute is largely solitary, and whose potential mentor is largely absent, J.'s undergraduate experience is marked by an inability to find community.

If *The Intuitionist*'s institute is a contentious place, riven by debate over racialized theories of knowledge, and the college in *John Henry Days* a lonesome place, where meaningful connections are difficult to forge, then the university of *Apex Hides the Hurt* is one where power begets power and "diversity" runs cover for the status quo. In keeping with the plot of the novel—which follows a "nomenclature consultant" hired to devise a new name for a town founded by formerly enslaved people—the prestigious university the protagonist attends is one where names matter.[57] In fact, while the protagonist remains wryly *unnamed* throughout, we are told early on: "He was a Quincy Man, and it turned out the firm had been founded by Quincy men. The name meant something. He fit right in" (28–29). Despite the assurance that "Quincy was a name that . . . opened doors," the protagonist of *Apex*, as in Whitehead's first three novels, does not *fit right in*, either at the school or the firm to which it grants him access (71). Quincy is a place where "the sons and daughters of the famous . . . were anointed anew, for now they had two royal titles, one from the circumstance of their birth and the second from the four-year galvanizing process that occurred behind those ivy walls" (69). Though Whitehead concedes that it is also a place where "the sons and daughters of the working class" could prepare to ascend to the middle, his description of Quincy stresses the centrality of the sons of "presidents of foreign countries," the "great-grandsons of presidents," and "those who wanted to be president one day" (69). For the protagonist, whose entrée to Quincy comes via the conference he attends for "African American Leaders of Tomorrow," the university is alienating to say the least. Though Whitehead tells us dryly that "Quincy believed in diversity," he quickly notes that the protagonist "never bought into the Quincy mystique" (70).

In a novel that deeply satirizes racial capitalism and its twenty-first-century program of incorporated multiculturalism, the very idea of a diverse Quincy is fatally undermined. After all, the brand of "multicultural adhesive bandages" that gives the novel its title does not promise that "the deep psychic wounds of history" can be recuperated, but rather that they "could be covered."[58] Apex doesn't *heal* the hurt, that is, but hides it: "It erased. Huzzah" (90). Likewise, Quincy's commitment to diversity is as nominal and lackluster as a sentence that follows "Huzzah" with a full stop rather than an exclamation point. Albie Winthrop—whose family both named Quincy's library and *renamed* the novel's largely Black town after themselves—tells the protagonist that "it doesn't matter where you come from, once you walk into those ivy halls, you're in the brotherhood." But he is also quick to note who deviates from the unmarked, yet assumed, identity of a "Quincy man": "I go back to visit and I can't help but say, Golly, look at how it's changed! You got all kinds of people, from all over the world. . . . But even in my day, there was that spirit. . . . Had a black fella lived in my dorm. There were only five or six, but you have to understand the times" (80). In the same conversation, Albie sighs and asks, perhaps a little too genuinely: "No, you can't stop progress, can you?" (82). The central theme of *Apex* is not the battle between racialized traditionalism and multicultural progress as in *The Intuitionist*, but rather the idea that representational progress alone, whether in the form of a newly inclusive Ivy League (both "Winthrop" and "Quincy" are dormitories at Harvard[59]) or a newly diverse product line, is paltry progress after all: "crayon boxes of the melanin spectrum" that "serve diversity," while also acting as "perfect camouflage" for existing structures of power (89).

Even *Sag Harbor*, the author's autobiographical historical novel about a Black enclave in the Hamptons in the 1980s, digresses to consider how the family patriarch's years among "a handful of young black men infiltrating the big-time Northeast schools" figure as a kind of origin story:

> Brothers from Brooklyn, Harlem, huddling together as the Massachusetts winters, the New Hampshire winters, took a bite out of their asses. What were they doing getting Ivy League educations? They weren't supposed to be there. They hung tight with the five or six other black guys in their school, drank beer with the fix or six black guys the next school over. Dated the five or six black ladies at the genteel women's college the next town over, and the other schools on the black network, road-tripping to the big dance that weekend at B.U. or Smith, or up to Montreal, where from all accounts some crazy racial utopia existed, integration of the sort that'd get you lynched in half the south. My father met my mother during that time, on the New England black-college circuit. So that's where all this begins, maybe.[60]

Benji's father, like the unnamed consultant, and J. Sutter, and Lila Mae, attempts to negotiate the complex position of being an institutional outsider at an insider institution.[61] In a 2021 interview coinciding with the publication of *Harlem Shuffle*, the critic Laura Miller suggested that the "abiding theme" of Whitehead's work is, well, work—a proposition that Whitehead appeared to confirm: "Weird jobs. Yes . . . 'weird job' has been my shorthand for a while, though

I've never actually said it out loud."[62] While the elevator inspectors, nomenclature consultants, and junketeers in Whitehead's novels certainly support this idea, the fact that each of these "weird" workers is the product of an elite education in which they are one of only "a handful of young black [students]" is also unmistakably central to his oeuvre.

Yet Whitehead's widespread focus on institutional life is not just an autobiographical allusion to his time at Harvard or simply an allegory for the role of an increasingly renowned Black author in a largely white literary field, but also a call to examine how such flawed institutions structure connections to the historical past. Reflecting on his parents' years "on the New England black-college circuit" allows Benji to commune with a historical moment where integration, lynching, and "some crazy racial utopia" are all immediate, and yet also mediated by the university. "That's where all this begins," too, for the protagonist of *Apex*, who first learns, on the quad across from Winthrop Library, to mistrust a rebranded *belief in diversity*, regarding it as little more than a coverup for "the deep psychic wounds of history." For J. Sutter, the university's neglected "Afro-Am" department and its apathetic mentor figures may be imperfect, but they are also a link to the generation of Black radicals who came before him. Elsewhere in the novel Whitehead narrates the rivalry between two early twentieth-century scholars of John Henry, one Black and one white, dramatizing how the challenge of "convincing the department of the worth of . . . research" into Black history is an institutional problem with enormous historiographical stakes (157).[63] As in *The Intuitionist*, most of these novels feature some form of archival research, and all—including *Apex*, which is set in the historical present—locate their central conflict, mystery, or trauma in the historical past. Cameron Leader-Picone argues that Whitehead's characters exist "within the wake of substantial societal changes from which they feel somewhat distant," and that the author "emphasizes his generation's contradictory relationship with the civil rights era."[64]

COLSON WHITEHEAD'S HISTORY OF THE UNITED STATES

Nearly all of Whitehead's novels engage these "substantial societal changes" via the university, evincing a similarly "contradictory relationship" with an era of institutional changes that is crucial to both the author's personal history and to his understanding of history writ large. An Institutionalist indeed.

LIVING HISTORY

While Whitehead's first five novels garnered considerable recognition and prestige, his 2016 foray into the hypercanonical genre of the meta–slave narrative marks a turning point in his career. Lauded by critics and scholars alike, *The Underground Railroad* won both the National Book Award and the Pulitzer Prize, was selected for Oprah's Book Club, and was adapted for television by Barry Jenkins, the Academy Award–winning director of *Moonlight* (2016). In an August 2016 interview on *CBS This Morning*, itself a measure of the novel's mass-market attention, Whitehead explained that "the response [to the book] has been just so different and new."[65] As some readers have pointed out, it is more than a little ironic that an author who once lampooned the ubiquity of the "Southern Novel of Black Misery" can now count his own experiment in that quadrant of the genre "dartboard" as a literary blockbuster.[66] This may be ironic, but it is not particularly surprising, given Whitehead's manifest fascination with the racial politics of American historical memory and the institutions of higher education that preserve and manage it. Moreover, given the centrality of contemporary narratives of slavery in university English departments, the fact that Whitehead spent much of the five years between *Zone One* and *The Underground Railroad* teaching in those departments at the University of Wyoming, Princeton, SUNY Purchase, and Wesleyan, among others, is similarly noteworthy.[67]

Though six books and sixteen years passed between the publications of *The Intuitionist* and *The Underground Railroad*, Whitehead's two novels appear as fraternal twins—or perhaps two halves of a literary slant rhyme—that illuminate the trajectory of the author's career as well as the evolution of the literary field that has canonized him. Both novels narrate the lives of Black women on the run; both blend historicity and fabulation to amend the historical record of the United States; and both rely on anachronism, and the temporally indeterminate settings it produces, to critique the idea of progress. Yet if Whitehead's first novel offers us a glimpse at the canon wars that partly launched the historical turn in American literature, *The Underground Railroad* figures as a testament to the ways in which that period and its logics have reshaped the contemporary literary field. In the nearly three decades since Morrison's and Gates's (and countless others') calls for a revised literary canon that revives the lost histories of people of color, historical fiction by minoritized writers emerged as the exception to, but has become more or less the rule in, the contemporary American canon.

In this context, the meta–slave narrative—arguably the most prestigious American literary genre of the last half century—stands as a shining example of the aesthetic, political, and pedagogical potential of historical fiction and its subgenres. In recent years, however, scholars have called into question both the centrality and the significance of contemporary narratives of slavery. Stephen Best has critiqued the "primacy [of slavery] in black critical thought" and the "unassailable truth that the slave past provides a ready prism for apprehending the black political present."[68] Aida Levy-Hussen has likewise worked "to interrogate the premise that reexperiencing historical pain is transformative and necessary" and investigate "how therapeutic reading's claim to moral urgency may inadvertently produce rote habits of canon construction and interpretation, blinding us to contemporaneous works of African American fiction that expressly disavow an orientation toward the past."[69]

While Best and Levy-Hussen might read *The Underground Railroad*'s tremendous reception as still more evidence of the phenomena they describe, the novel itself appears markedly aware of both the legacy and the limits of the meta–slave narrative genre.[70] Like *The Intuitionist*, Whitehead's contemporary narrative of slavery nods to its literary forebears, many of which the author first encountered as an undergraduate. Whitehead cites his reading of Harriet Jacobs's autobiography during his junior year as "the inspiration for the North Carolina chapter" of the novel, in which his protagonist, Cora, seeks refuge from her captors by hiding away in an attic.[71] As with Jacobs, Cora's "only source of light and air was a hole in the wall that faced the street"—a hole, Whitehead adds, that was "carved from the inside, the work of a previous occupant . . . [Cora] wondered where the person was now."[72] Yet though the novel alludes throughout to non-fictional slave narratives of the nineteenth century, its main intertexts are the meta–slave narratives of the late twentieth century, chief among them Reed's *Flight to Canada* (1976) and Morrison's *Beloved* (1987). Cora's main companion in the novel is Caesar, a man who Whitehead tells us was born into slavery on the farm of one "Mrs. Garner" (49). In this way, Whitehead inscribes in the central character nearly the entire history of the slave narrative in English: his first name drawn from the protagonist of Aphra Behn's *Oroonoko* (1688), his last from the "Sweet Home men" of Morrison's novel, published three centuries later.

Although it is altogether unsurprising that Morrison's novel would loom large in the mind of any writer approaching the meta–slave narrative genre, Whitehead's attention to *Beloved* is nonetheless remarkable. Though the novel does not appear in the acknowledgements section of *The Underground Railroad*, it sat above Whitehead's writing desk, alongside works by historians Eric Foner and Edward Baptist (which do appear), as Whitehead wrote the book.[73] In interviews, Whitehead has likewise referred back to Morrison: "You have to do your own thing, right? Morrison already wrote *Beloved*; you're not going to compete with that."[74] Even Whitehead's longtime friend Kevin Young has praised *The Underground Railroad* in distinctly Morrisonian terms: "Reading the book, I thought, he's written his 'Beloved.'"[75] Taken together, these allusions—both within the pages of Whitehead's novel and without—suggest that thirty years after *Beloved*, the literary genre that it metonymizes now stands overshadowed, and indeed overdetermined, by it. To put it simply, Whitehead's continual citation suggests that to some extent one can no longer write meta–slave narratives, only (pardoning the inelegance) meta–meta–slave narratives.

Even the tremendous suffering that *The Underground Railroad* narrates appears citational, less the reimagining of horrific historical violence than the evocation of a generic trope. In the novel's early and more realist chapters, before the introduction of its literalized underground railway network, Cora and the others enslaved on the Randall plantation are exposed to countless unspeakable horrors that remain, in Whitehead's account, both uncounted and unspoken: "travesties so routine and familiar that they were a kind of weather . . . so imaginative in their monstrousness that the mind refused to accommodate them" (15). Cora hears gruesome "stories from the southern half" of the plantation—divided, as the nation soon would be, into relativized systems of racial violence and subjection—that "were chilling, in magnitude if not in particulars" (44). Even Cora's rape by a group of enslaved men is elided between sentences, as is the punishment of one of the perpetrators, who escapes and is captured soon after: "Cora would have said it served him right, had his punishment not made her shiver to think about" (21).

On the one hand, Whitehead's elision of these "particulars" appears as a kind of rebuttal to what Levy-Hussen has called the "*masochistic fantasy intrinsic to the contemporary narrative of slavery,*" the idea that "the desire for liberation is inextricably entwined with a desire for the reenactment of punishment and pain."[76] On the other, the "shiver"-inducing yet amorphous "monstrousness" of the Randall plantation, can be read as a return to the style of nineteenth-century slave narratives that—Morrison argues in "The Site of Memory"—draw a "veil" over "the more sordid details of [slaves'] experience" in order "to make it palatable to those who were in a position to alleviate it."[77] For twenty-first-century readers acquainted with the horrific particulars recounted by twentieth-century historians and historical novelists alike, Whitehead's violent evocations read as just that: evocative, even allusive, rather than immediate. Even in the novel's few, and brief, scenes of graphic violence—the torture and murder of Big Anthony, for example, or the execution of an escaped enslaved person in North Carolina—the discourse of performance *and reperformance* pervades: both events are described as spectacles that take place "onstage" for the cruel "instruction" of a Black audience, or the bloodthirsty pleasure of a white one (46, 159). Calling to mind Saidiya Hartman's claims that overly familiarized scenes of anti-Black violence are often couched in "theatrical language" that serves to "reinforce the spectacular character of black suffering," in *The Underground Railroad*, atrocity is almost always narrated in the idiom of reenactment.[78]

The most compelling scenes in the novel do not occur underground, as it were, but in the "squat limestone building" in South Carolina where Cora works as a reenactor in the "Living History" division of the "Museum of Natural Wonders" (108–109). The purpose of the museum, its white director, Mr. Fields, explains to Cora, is to educate the white citizens of South Carolina about the history of their "young nation": "Like a railroad, the museum permitted them to see the rest of the country beyond their small experience. . . . And to see its people. 'People like you'" (109). In reality, the museum appears less like the railroad that names the novel than it does the historical mural in *The Intuitionist*'s Fanny Briggs building. From "Plymouth rock" to the Boston Tea Party, the museum professes to "illuminate the American experience . . . the truth of the historic encounter," but it is structured exclusively by white, Western, and colonial narratives of the nation and its past (115–16). In order to make this history, in all its inaccuracy, come to life, Cora works as one of "three actors, or types as [Mr. Fields] referred to them," in a trio of exhibits: "Scenes from Darkest Africa," "Life on the Slave Ship," and "Typical Day on the Plantation" (110). In these scenes, the novel reincarnates what Zora Neale Hurston called, in her 1950 essay "What White Publishers Won't Print," "The American Museum of Unnatural History." This "intangible" cultural structure, Hurston writes, is built on the assumption that "all non-Anglo-Saxons are uncomplicated stereotypes . . . lay figures mounted in the museum where all take them in at a glance. They are made of bent wires without insides at all." "The whole museum," Hurston claims, "is dedicated to the convenient 'typical'. . . . [and] the folklore of 'reversion to type.'"[79]

Dubey outlines how Whitehead's museum of types evokes the "living human displays of slavery" that emerged in late nineteenth-century exhibitions, as well as the "numerous museum exhibits, historical reenactments, plantation tours, monuments, roadside markers, and freedom trails" that served to "museumize" the history of enslavement in (and since) the 1990s.[80] In 1993, even the Disney corporation sought to join the chorus of reenactors, proposing a three-thousand-acre theme park in Virginia dedicated to "painful, disturbing, and agonizing" aspects of American history, including enslavement. "This is not a Pollyanna view of America," announced senior vice president Bob Weis. "We want to make you feel what it was like to be a slave or what it was like to escape through the underground railroad."[81] Unlike in Disney's failed project, however, in Whitehead's novel the only ones who feel the pain of history are the reenactors themselves. Lee Konstantinou has argued that unlike "a run-of-the-mill postmodern simulacrum," the "point" of the Museum of Natural Wonders is "to highlight how the Museum unambiguously falsifies slavery."[82] And while this is certainly correct—Cora remarks, while working at the museum, that "truth was a changing display in a shop window, manipulated by hands when you weren't looking" (116)—it overlooks a central aspect of the episode and a large part of its "point": Cora's experience of reifying the museum's distorted historical narratives.

In each of the three "scenes" that she performs, Cora encounters the reality, not of "official" accounts of the past, but of her interpellation by them in the present. In "Scenes from Darkest Africa," Cora is asked to reenact a life that she has never known. Under the "peaked thatch roof" and amid the "assorted tools, gourds, and shells"—all, presumably, taken by force, as Cora's grandmother Ajarry was—Cora is "reminded" only of "the buzzards that chewed the flesh of the plantation dead when they were put on display" (109–10). On the "frigate's deck" of "Life on the Slave Ship," Cora reckons with the fact that, while the museum's "whites were made of plaster, wire, and paint," as a Black woman she is coerced into repeatedly reperforming the trauma of slavery (110, 115). Though "Typical Day on the Plantation" replaces the nightmare of the novel's Randall plantation with the pastoral fantasy of work at a "spinning wheel," Whitehead suggests that both the motivations for and the effects of Mr. Fields's historical fiction are no less pernicious. Fields's desire to instrumentalize the Black women around him is not unlike the Randalls' as he wishes "that he could fit an entire field of cotton in the display and had the budget for a dozen actors to work it" (110). For Cora, playing the role that she once lived is both physically and psychologically damaging: "Typical Day's wardrobe . . . was made of coarse, authentic negro cloth. She burned with shame twice a day when she stripped and got into her costume" (110). The scene may be fabricated, in other words, but the pain and shame are no less "authentic."

As much as the scene exposes the sadism of the white institution, it also reflects a self-consciousness on Whitehead's part about how he, too, may be instrumentalizing Cora. Whitehead's Museum of Natural Wonders both literalizes and critiques what Levy-Hussen describes as "the role of pain in [literary] fantasies of historical repair," the idea that "feeling historical pain is a requisite component of [that] pain's alleviation."[83] While the "therapeutic reading" of "black literary studies' historical turn" suggests that Cora's fictive simulation is necessary in order to heal, Whitehead suggests here that slavery's reenactment—unavoidably mediated by a racialized marketplace and white spectators "bang[ing] on the glass"—can be injurious to the individual as well as to the collective (111).[84] If Morrison's concept of "rememory" has worked since the 1980s to bring the atrocities of American slavery back to life and into national consciousness, Whitehead's "Living History" claims three decades later that their continual reviving is not unequivocally productive, especially when pressed into the service of specious narratives of progress. "In the fields," Whitehead writes, Cora "was ever under the merciless eye of the overseer or boss. 'Bend your backs!' 'Work that row!' ... Her recent installation in the exhibition returned her to the furrows of Georgia, the dumb, open-jawed stares of the patrons stealing her back to a state of display" (125).

The Underground Railroad is both an inventive example of the meta–slave narrative and a fictional interrogation of that genre's present "state of display."[85] To some extent, this echoes Levy-Hussen's claim that the institutionalization of the meta–slave narrative over the last several decades has led to a pervasive affect of "boredom" in the genre. "Decades after the invention of such insurgent art and scholarship, justice and liberation remain frustratingly deferred," Levy-Hussen argues. "For a growing number of black writers and African Americanist critics," then, "boredom brings to view a mode of literary and scholarly engagement that confronts us with the limits of [the genre's] agency—and the limits of our own, as readers, writers, and critics." In this light, Whitehead's highly reflexive relationship to the meta–slave narrative in this novel, as well as the "Living History" set piece at its center, may appear as "bored repetitions" that dramatize "the genre's tragic ineffectuality, its inability to compel the radical change it desires."[86]

For Cora, the most effective mode of resistance is to disrupt the chronology of the historical script she is given, following instead a reversed "progression from Plantation to Slave Ship to Darkest Africa [that] generated a soothing logic." This "unwinding of America,"

Whitehead explains, "never failed to cast her into a river of calm, the simple theater becoming more than theater, a genuine refuge" (125). Likewise, Whitehead himself works to disrupt normative historical narratives in and through the novel, to varying degrees of success. As in *The Intuitionist*, the setting of *The Underground Railroad* is temporally complex; it blends and juxtaposes historical referents from the Fugitive Slave Law of the Antebellum and the 1921 Black Wall Street massacre in Tulsa, to the Tuskegee syphilis study and programs of forced sterilization that continued into the mid-1970s. The climax of the novel even alludes to the uniquely (and shamefully) American phenomenon of contemporary mass shootings, particularly the 2015 Charleston church massacre that took the lives of nine African American worshippers. Yet while the multiple periodizing details of *The Intuitionist* place the novel in a temporally indeterminate period of desegregation, these historical allusions, in the context of *The Underground Railroad*'s far more stable antebellum setting, appear far more akin to the anachronisms of Ishmael Reed's *Flight to Canada*.

In Reed's self-described "neo-slave narrative," runaway slaves literally take flight aboard Air Canada jetliners heading north, abolitionist poems are xeroxed, and Abraham Lincoln is assassinated live on satellite television. These jarring moments recur with such frequency in Reed's book—a novel as interested in Nixon's administration as it is in Lincoln's—that Elias has suggested that "the novel may actually be set in the late twentieth century," with the anachronism emerging counterintuitively from "the antebellum features of the text." In *Flight to Canada*, Elias argues, "the time of slavery, in many ways, is now."[87] Whereas Reed's anachronisms function primarily as tethers to the present, however, Whitehead's seem instead to gather multiple pasts under the rubric of the history of slavery. Unlike other twenty-first-century meta–slave narratives, such as Edward P. Jones's *The Known World* (2003) and Yaa Gyasi's *Homegoing* (2016, discussed in chapter 4), Whitehead's novel does not so much trace the legacies of slavery across multiple generations as it does collapse those legacies into the time of slavery itself, in effect sequestering more recent and ongoing injustices in a more distant historical moment.

While Reed's and Gyasi's protagonists find a kind of freedom eventually, either in Canada or in the generations to come, Whitehead's Cora never reaches "The North," even in the novel's final section which bears that ambiguous title. By contrast, *The Underground Railroad* closes with Cora heading not north but west, a deviation from the genre's geographic and thematic telos and a suggestion that Cora's "northern fantasy" is ultimately just that (171). Though American slave narratives, in both their nineteenth- and twentieth-century formulations, have also functioned as narratives of liberation, *The Underground Railroad*, for all its movement across space and time, never fully departs from the context of slavery. On its face this reads as a reiteration of Whitehead's argument in *The Intuitionist* that narratives of neat historical progress are often illusory and always more complicated than they appear. But it also underlines the suspicion that, unlike Cora hitching her wagon to the promise of California, Whitehead is not entirely sure where to go next. As much as *The Underground Railroad* evokes the history of contemporary American fiction's most prestigious genre, it also points up, often self-consciously, the limits of that genre at present. If, after Douglass and Jacobs and Reed and Morrison, the literary history of American slavery can only ever function as allusive, metafictional, and self-referential reenactment, then despite the genre's commercial and critical success—or perhaps because of it—*The Underground Railroad* may figure as both "Whitehead's *Beloved*" and (to borrow from Best) "the epitaph to the *Beloved* moment" (72).

ALWAYS ALREADY PAST

In July 2019 Whitehead's seventh novel, *The Nickel Boys*, was published to great acclaim. Months before the book, which went on to become both a bestseller and a prizewinner, was released, the publisher's promotional copy hailed the novel as a sequel of sorts, the next chapter in an ambitious historical survey: "In this bravura follow-up to the Pulitzer Prize and National Book Award–winning #1 *New York Times* bestseller *The Underground Railroad*, Colson Whitehead brilliantly dramatizes another strand of American history through the story of two boys sentenced to a hellish reform school in Jim Crow–era Florida. . . . *The Nickel Boys* is a devastating, driven narrative that showcases a great American novelist writing at the height of his powers."[88] The week before *The Nickel Boys* was published, Whitehead was similarly lauded on the cover of *Time* magazine as "America's Storyteller" and "one of the greatest [writers] of his generation," particularly for his gifts in "mining the past."[89] At this point, the equation of literary greatness with "mining the past," the idea that a novelist's "powers" are best showcased in reenactments of a "devastating" history, will come as little surprise. Yet Whitehead's historical "follow-up" to *The Underground Railroad* in *The Nickel Boys* and its own sequel of sorts in *Harlem Shuffle* demonstrate both a continuation of the field-specific forces that have encouraged Whitehead's canonization and the limitations of an aesthetic program that relies on historical analogy as its chief instrument of political intervention.

While each chapter of *The Underground Railroad* begins with an advertisement for an escaped enslaved person, which Whitehead culled from a collection at the University of North Carolina at Greensboro, *The Nickel Boys* takes this archival impulse still further.[90] As Whitehead writes in the novel's acknowledgments, the book is "inspired by the story of the Dozier School for Boys in Marianna, Florida," a so-called reform school where, over the course of the twentieth century, countless children were imprisoned and tortured, and scores were killed and buried in unmarked graves. Like the newspaper fragment on Margaret Garner that inspired Morrison's *Beloved*, it was "exhaustive reporting" in the *Tampa Bay Times* that first piqued Whitehead's interest in the school and its story.[91] The work that that story became metonymizes the racial apartheid of the American criminal justice system in a kind of nightmarish campus novel, following two teenage boys, Elwood Curtis and Jack Turner, incarcerated at Nickel Academy in the mid-1960s.

Like *The Intuitionist*, *The Nickel Boys* is set in the period of ongoing desegregation, but unlike the academic satire that Whitehead published exactly twenty years earlier, his more recent novel avoids temporal indeterminacy—the productive uncertainty of its exact setting in time—in favor of a more direct and more didactic approach. Whereas Martin Luther King Jr. makes only a brief appearance in *The Intuitionist*—when "Lila Mae notices a photograph . . . a head shot of the famous reverend . . . who is so loud down South" (248)—both King and his public speeches are fixtures in *The Nickel Boys*, beginning with the opening line of chapter 1. There the reader is introduced to Elwood and the novel's historical setting by learning that he received "the best gift of his life on Christmas Day 1962": a vinyl LP of *Martin Luther King at Zion Hill*. Elwood idolizes King and his comrades in the struggle for civil rights, which Whitehead emphasizes in a particularly confounding early passage:

> *Life*'s photo essays conveyed [Elwood] to the front lines, to bus boycotts in Baton Rouge, to counter sit-ins in Greensboro, where young people not much older than him took up the movement. They were beaten with metal bars, blasted by fire hoses, spat on by white housewives with angry faces, and frozen by the camera in tableaus of noble resistance. The tiny details were a wonder: how the young men's ties remained straight black arrows in the whirl of violence, how the curves of the young women's perfect hairdos floated against the squares of their protest signs. Glamorous somehow, even when the blood flowed down their faces. Young knights taking the fight to dragons. Elwood was slight-shouldered, skinny as a pigeon, . . . but he wanted to enlist. He had no choice. (22)

In many ways, this passage—devoid as it is of anachronism and prolepsis and Whitehead's other favored techniques for manipulating historical time—could not be clearer. The images in Elwood's *Life* magazine form a familiar montage of civil rights era heroism and nonviolent resistance in the face of violent white supremacy. Surely, these "tableaus" of the period are well known to nearly all of Whitehead's readers, even the middle and high school-age students for whom *The Nickel Boys* seems at least partly intended.[92] The confusion here is rather an issue of tone. In a historical novel about the lives of young Black men in the early 1960s, based on a horrifyingly *nonfictional* historical episode, what are we to make of Whitehead's descriptions of these "noble," "perfect," "glamorous," and altogether "knight"-like heroes of the movement? "Frozen" as they are in these well-circulated images, one wonders if the lionizing point of view in this passage is the product of the character's youthful idealism, or the author's public memory of the period? Does the hagiography here belong to Elwood, or to Whitehead?

The desire "to enlist" in this moment in history, shared presumably by character, author, and reader alike, is both the primary affect of *The Nickel Boys* and its central site of confusion. In interviews, Whitehead has repeatedly explained that, after the 2014 police killings of Michael Brown and Eric Garner, and especially after the 2016 election of Donald Trump, the subject of the Dozier school felt increasingly urgent to him, so much so that he set aside the project he was then working on (the manuscript that would eventually become *Harlem Shuffle*) in order to write *The Nickel Boys*. "The book . . . seemed relevant, just to make sense of where we are as a country," said Whitehead. "I think we've regressed and I think a lot of normal people and artists are trying to make sense of this moment."[93] This is the paradoxical logic of the American literary field's turn toward history: to make sense of *this moment*, Whitehead travels more than a half century into the past. The novel does not target the broken institutions that contributed to Brown's and Garner's deaths but rather transmutes them into proxies from a previous period. The only White House depicted is Nickel's "White House," the campus shed where boys are beaten, tortured, and even killed (66). Allusions to Ellison's *Invisible Man* are everywhere, from the novel's Battle Royal boxing match to Elwood painting houses an optic shade of "Dixie White" (92). But to what end? Elwood pores over Baldwin's *Notes of a Native Son*, but Baldwin's razor-sharp critique of contemporary politics is removed and replaced with arguments made by way of historical analogy. *The Nickel Boys* engages the present only by enlisting in the past, making a prosthesis of literary and political history. This is not to say that Whitehead's latest works of historical fiction are apolitical, but rather that they favor a politics of indirection.

Just as in *The Underground Railroad*, where the reenactment of slavery is self-consciously interrogated within the historical novel of slavery, in *The Nickel Boys* Whitehead is reflexive about the efficacy of writing as a form of political intervention. While *The Underground Railroad* critiques the pernicious reperformance of the past in the Museum of Natural Wonders, *The Nickel Boys* reminds readers just how profitable stories like those can be. Nickel Academy makes money by laundering governmental support and by farming out its child prisoners, but its greatest source of revenue seems to come from its status as a publisher. "Nickel's printing press did all the publishing for the government of Florida, from the tax regulations to the building codes to the parking tickets," Whitehead writes, calling "the construction of the printing plant . . . a bona fide success by any measure" (51, 76). With this detail, the novel appears to question whether the boys' labor—and, by extension, their stories—are being used to shore up the very powers that oppress them.

Reviewers and scholars alike have described how *The Nickel Boys* is, at its core, "a debate between Elwood's optimism and Turner's resignation."[94] And while this is an apt description of the novel's plot, it overlooks how that very debate is undermined by the novel's structure. Much of the book is taken up with Elwood and Turner's conversations about how best to resist the ravages of the institution, and whether Elwood "had outwitted Nickel because he got along and kept out of trouble" or whether, "in fact," that means "he had been ruined" by it (155–56). This debate comes to a head as Elwood reflects in the novel's closing chapters on King's praise of *"our capacity to suffer"* and the ability to nonetheless *"love"* one's oppressors: "Elwood shook his head. What a thing to ask. What an impossible thing" (172–73). When Whitehead finally reveals that, as the two boys make their escape, Elwood is murdered, the debate, it seems, is settled. The novel's retrospective narration is not the account of Elwood the triumphant optimist, but his ventriloquizing by Turner, the cynic who survives and takes his name as a kind of memorial.

While the implicit claim of this conclusion seems clear enough, it is the structure of this revelation that offers the greatest insight into Whitehead's forays into history. Crucially, we learn of Elwood's death only at the very end of *The Nickel Boys*. In other words, the central "debate" of the novel (at least according to critics) has been settled from its very first words. The possibilities held out by Elwood's narration have been foreclosed from the start. What is more, this device is not unique to *Nickel*. In *The Underground Railroad*, we learn of Caesar's death at the hands of a bloodthirsty white mob chapters later, only after his fate has already been sealed; in the penultimate chapter we discover that Cora's mother, Mabel, did not in fact escape the Randall plantation but died of a snakebite in a swamp on its outskirts. In moments like these, Whitehead's twist endings create something like the opposite effect of dramatic and historical irony. Rather than confirm that readers know something that the characters do not, these reveals point up that the readerly hope for a recuperative history are misplaced. This technique heightens the pathos of historical pain, but it also emphasizes the limits of historical fiction as a means of addressing the challenges of the present. History may provide a clear analogy, but Whitehead's historical fiction reminds us that only looking backwards means that the crucial moment of action—the chance to free Caesar, save Mabel, rescue Elwood, and abolish Nickel—will always have already passed. The novel's reader is always a step behind. The moment to "enlist" or intervene is always already over.

As if to stress this still further, Whitehead's eighth novel, *Harlem Shuffle*—published in the summer of 2021, one year after protests against anti-Black police violence swept the United States and the world—is in part "set against a backdrop of the 1964 Harlem race riots."[95] While the novel is the author's first foray into the genres of crime fiction and the heist thriller, with its focus on elite institutions, weird jobs, and the racial history of the United States, *Harlem Shuffle* sits comfortably on the shelf of Whitehead's other novels. The book follows Ray Carney, a furniture salesman who also works as a front for the novel's seedier characters. Whitehead himself has described Carney as a "liminal figure" and "a middle man between the straight and crooked worlds," adding that "all sort of meanings began to accrue to the idea of the fence, and I went with it."[96] The book is fun, fast-paced, and nearly impossible to put down, and yet the question remains whether its historical setting is more than mere "backdrop." That is, it is not entirely clear whether *Harlem Shuffle* engages the racial violence and ensuing activism of the mid-1960s as an apt analogy for the early 2020s, or whether the novel's historical setting is itself a kind of "fence," running cover for the author's "having fun with [the] kind of genre I've liked since I was little."[97] In fact, in one of Whitehead's earliest pieces of published work—a review essay on the films *Shaft* and *Action Jackson* for the Harvard journal *Diaspora*—the budding author praises *Shaft* as a product of "black political movements of the sixties, with all [their] hope and anger," one that ultimately "challenges the status quo": "The end of *Shaft* is open, implying that the fight to stave off white domination does not end. . . . The credits roll and we see Shaft walking off into the night, but there is no conclusion to the struggle."[98]

As with the *Shaft* franchise, Whitehead's *Harlem Shuffle* became a series. By the time the novel was published, Whitehead was "already 200 pages into the [sequel]," *Crook Manifesto* (2023), which follows Ray Carney into the 1970s.[99] Though it remains to be seen how Whitehead's relationship to historical struggle will develop, it appears that there is no end in sight to the historical survey that his career represents. Far from the end of his career, Whitehead still has a lot of writing left to do, a great many more darts to throw. Yet, as one of the most celebrated novelists of the twenty-first century and as a central figure in American literature's pervasive historical turn, Whitehead appears—at least for the time being—to have found his bull's-eye.

Chapter Four

READING THE FAMILY TREE

> *Kunta lay awake thinking how so many things—indeed, nearly everything they had learned—all tied together. The past . . . with the present, the present with the future, the dead with the living and those yet to be born.*
> —Alex Haley, *Roots: The Saga of an American Family*

GENEALOGY AND GENRE

What does it mean to begin a novel with a family tree? What claims does it make about the narrative that follows and its relation to the historical past? What work does it do for readers, and what work, in turn, does it ask of them? Louise Erdrich's now-canonical debut novel, *Love Medicine* (1984), which chronicles three generations of Ojibwe families from the 1930s to the 1980s, begins with such a family tree. Likewise, Cristina García's *Dreaming in Cuban* (1992) and Rosario Ferré's *The House on the Lagoon* (1995)—both multigenerational family sagas, both debut novels, both shortlisted for the National Book Award—open with the same device. Add to this Yaa Gyasi's debut novel, *Homegoing* (2016), a similarly ambitious family saga that garnered a seven-figure advance and won awards from the National Book Foundation, the National Book Critics Circle, and the Center for Fiction; and, more recently, Namwali Serpell's debut novel, *The Old Drift* (2019), winner of the Arthur C. Clarke Award and placed on "best of" lists by *The New York Times*, NPR, and *The Atlantic*, among many others.[1] Even this small sample reveals quite a bit about both the genre of the family tree novel and its position in the contemporary American literary field.

First, and most obviously, these are novels that derive their narrative structures from the heuristic of the heteronormative family and its rhythm of marriages, births, and deaths.[2] These family sagas are likewise sweeping in their historical scope, inspiring what Julia Creet has called "the genealogical sublime" by following three, four, seven, or (in the case of *Homegoing*) nine generations across anywhere between five decades and three centuries.[3] As a result, each novel is marked by a process of selection and exclusion, choosing one narrative path to follow through the family tree but nodding visually to other, untold stories. As you might suspect of any book that begins with a detailed diagram, the family tree novel is also insistently structural, replete with section and chapter breaks, subtitles that identify narrators, settings, and moments in time. Moreover, though the genre of multigenerational historical fiction has been taken up by everyone from Gabriel García Márquez to William Faulkner, Virginia Woolf and Thomas Mann, the array of novels just mentioned—by Ojibwe, Cuban, Puerto Rican, Ghanaian, and Zambian authors—suggests that, over the last several decades, the genre has been especially common among racialized and ethnicized writers, and women writers in particular. That these debut novels have all been consecrated by the cultural organizations most central to contemporary canon formation signals that the ambitious historical scope of the multigenerational family saga is one way that novelists now announce their talent, one way that literary institutions identify such talent, or both.

The family trees that open these novels operate as both textual and paratextual devices, visualizing the narrative that follows, but also organizing it for writers, categorizing it for critics, and summarizing it for readers. Yaa Gyasi "didn't really outline" *Homegoing* before she began to write it, but she did make a family tree of its characters and

READING THE FAMILY TREE

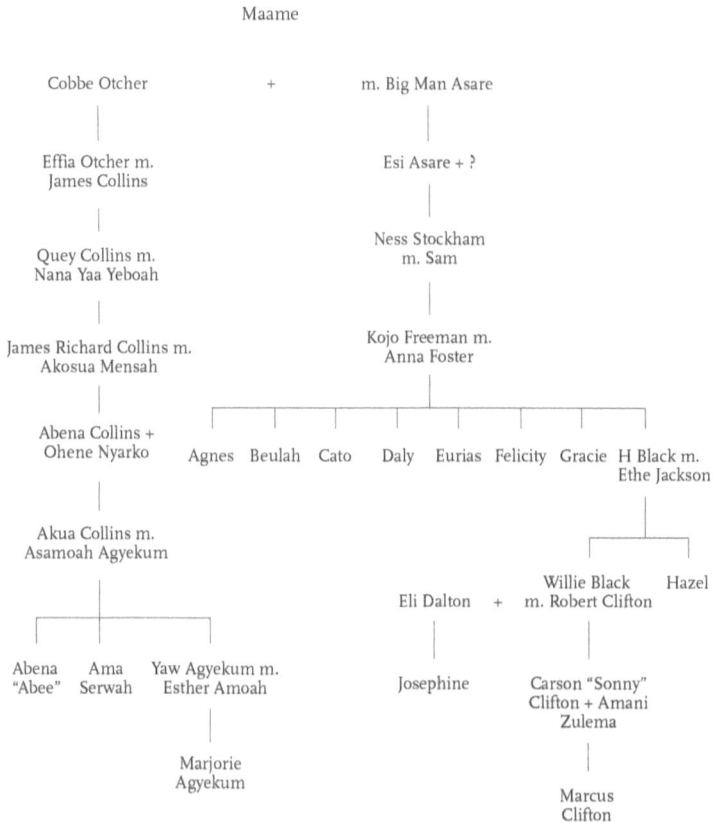

FIGURE 4.1 Family tree from Yaa Gyasi's *Homegoing* (2016).
"Family Tree" from *Homegoing: A Novel* by Yaa Gyasi, copyright © 2016 by YNG Books, Inc.. Used by permission of Alfred A. Knopf, an imprint of the Knopf Doubleday Publishing Group, a division of Penguin Random House LLC. All rights reserved.

hang it on the wall above her desk.[4] In an early review of the novel, the critic Ron Charles declares that "the speed with which Gyasi sweeps across the decades isn't confusing so much as dazzling," but mentions parenthetically that "the family tree at the front of the book is an invaluable reader's crutch."[5] Likewise, Kimberly N. Parker, author of the "Teacher's Guide" that Penguin Random House released alongside the novel, suggests that "bookmarking the family tree allows for frequent reference as students read the text," adding that "teachers might spend time studying it" with their classes.[6] In each of these cases, the family tree not only works on behalf of a given figure in the literary field, but it also reveals their assumptions about what, exactly, multigenerational historical fiction is: epic, ambitious, "dazzling," pedagogical.

This chapter investigates Gyasi's *Homegoing* as a fascinating case study of the contemporary family tree novel, comparing it with Min Jin Lee's *Pachinko* (2017) to demonstrate how it represents the wider genre, and contrasting it with Margaret Wilkerson Sexton's *A Kind of Freedom* (2017) to interrogate that genre's imaginative limits. Reading these exemplary and exceptional works, I argue that the multigenerational family saga has become one of the most celebrated genres of contemporary fiction precisely because it appeals to the "interpretive strategies" shared by institutions as seemingly disparate as the university English department and the middlebrow book club.[7] Given its recent focus on historically marginalized groups, the genre's twenty-first-century manifestations are particularly appealing to the empathetic and pedagogical reading practices that now dominate both the seminar room and the living room. In both venues, *reading to learn* and *reading to feel* have become increasingly intertwined, and multigenerational historical fiction allows amply for both. Part of what makes a text like *Homegoing* so attractive to instructors of literature and history courses alike is how the novel both narrativizes and personalizes such a wide swath of historical time in a single text. Yet if one of the novel's greatest strengths is its ability to trace the afterlives of transatlantic slavery across several centuries, I propose that this comes, somewhat ironically, at the cost of its characters, who serve as stand-ins for key moments in African and African American history. The question that *Homegoing* provokes—by way of its vast plot, ambitious character system, and even its individual paragraphs—is whether chronicling "something that stretched so far back" ultimately stretches the limits of what can be felt at all.[8] If literary fiction not only works to memorialize the stories of the past but also dilates to encompass an entire survey course of history, it can ultimately undermine the very empathy that many claim it is uniquely capable of producing.

As *Homegoing* hastens from descendant to descendant without looking back, the novel produces a feeling of loss directed at those whose stories have been disregarded by the historical record, even as it subsumes those stories in a larger narrative of intergenerational progress. Though Gyasi's chronicle begins in the colonialism of the mid-eighteenth century, it ends—despite its 2016 publication—amid the Obama-era optimism of the early twenty-first, a choice that celebrates personal and political struggles while also sequestering them firmly in the historical past. By contrast, Sexton's *A Kind of Freedom*, which narrates the lives of three generations in a Black family in New Orleans from 1945 to 2010, not only challenges Gyasi's long arc of progress through its cyclical narrative structure but also pushes against the boundaries of the genre by historicizing the near past with equal intensity and political force. In these novels, whether history is a narrative of incremental improvement or a never-ending cycle of injustice is as much a question of politics as literary form.

The end of this chapter turns from the multigenerational family saga to empathetic reading itself, questioning (as Namwali Serpell and others have) whether that interpretive strategy has become "a distraction or a palliative" for readers, divorced from any clear "imperative to take action." As Serpell puts it, "systemic change," of the kind that multigenerational historical fiction is particularly adept at narrating, "needs deliberation, yes, but we've deliberated much of this already."[9] Ultimately, the multigenerational family saga represents the apotheosis of American literature's turn toward the historical past, exemplifying its pedagogical, political, and affective imperatives to amplify the historically voiceless. But it also typifies the limits of contemporary literature's fixation on historical fiction, chief among them the increasingly imperceptible disconnect between knowledge of the past and action in the present.

■ ■ ■

Although the genre is common in contemporary American literature, multigenerational historical fiction is not particularly contemporary. An article in the June 1928 issue of *PMLA*, titled "The Genealogical Novel, a New Genre," announced the growing prominence of fiction that "affords a panorama of several generations" rather than "dealing, as the biographical novel usually does, with a single hero." The rise of this genre, the critic A. E. Zucker argued, was "a direct result of the widespread discussion of Evolution during the third quarter of the nineteenth century" and "connected especially with the publication of Darwin's *Origin of Species* in 1859."[10] Zucker cites (among other examples) Thomas Mann's *Buddenbrooks: The Decline of a Family* (1901) and John Galsworthy's *The Forsyte Saga* (1922), as have a number of scholarly accounts of this genre. In twentieth- and twenty-first-century literary studies, multigenerational historical fiction is something like the genre with a thousand faces—or, at least, half a dozen names, including the "chronicle novel," the "narrative of community," and the *Familienroman* or family novel.[11]

Buddenbrooks is a particularly illustrative example of the genre in its early twentieth-century form. The novel, which chronicles four generations in a bourgeois German family from the mid-1830s to the 1870s, is a self-conscious work of historical fiction (in its opening chapters, one character can be heard "reading Walter Scott's *Waverley* aloud") as well as a key influence for William Faulkner's own multigenerational family sagas of the American South.[12] And yet, over the course of its seven hundred pages, *Buddenbrooks* is far more interested in the vicissitudes of the eponymous family's fortunes than it is in the stuff of history. Napoleon is mentioned briefly, as is Felice Orsini's plot to kill him; the Great Fire of Hamburg burns in the distant background, and the revolution of 1848 is ignited for a single chapter; wars begin and end, and the reader hears little of them.[13] Mann's preference for family history over history writ large is made particularly clear when, after several pages detailing Elizabeth Buddenbrook on her deathbed, her doctors pause for a moment "on the landing to talk about other things—politics, the shocks and upheavals of the war just ended," and indeed barely mentioned before now (543).

Even as the title of *protagonist* is passed down from generation to generation, Mann encourages the reader to see each character as but a temporary occupant of that role. As Johann Buddenbrook—or, rather, Johann Jr., the second character in the novel with that name— tells his daughter Antonie: "We are not born . . . to pursue our own small personal happiness, for we are not separate, independent, self-subsisting individuals, but links in a chain; and it is inconceivable that we would be what we are without those who have preceded us and shown us the path that they themselves have scrupulously trod . . . following a venerable and trustworthy tradition" (144). Throughout the novel, Mann symbolizes both that history and the family's reverence for it in a "heavy gilt-edged notebook" that contains the Buddenbrooks' "extensive genealogy," catalogued in "tidy entries" alongside "certificates of citizenship . . . insurance policies, poems of congratulation, and requests to serve as a godparent" (53–54). Like the family saga it metonymizes, the ornate volume functions as a kind of archive for the bourgeois values of accumulation, convention, and high self-regard. Mann details how "each writer had picked up where his predecessor had left off, instinctively adopting the same stately, unexaggerated chronicle style, which in its very discretion spoke all the more nobly of a family's respect for itself, its traditions and history" (154).

As with all the genres discussed in this book, a proper history of the multigenerational family saga would require a monograph of its own. Tracing the family resemblances between the various "links in the chain" of this genre—from Mann and Galsworthy, to Woolf and

Faulkner, and on to García Márquez and Allende—would be fascinating. But genealogy is the subject of this chapter, not its strict method. Given that, let us jump a few branches on the family tree to the moment when the *decline* of Mann's title, and the genre as a whole, was flipped on its head. That moment was the 1976 publication of Alex Haley's novel *Roots: The Saga of an American Family* and its adaptation to broadcast television one year later. These were national events, which provoked a "popular awakening," by both scholars and the wider public, to the power and promise of genealogy.[14] Haley's *Roots* narrates seven generations in a family, from the iconic Kunta Kinte all the way to the author himself. Along the way, the novel not only ignited a national conversation about the history of American slavery, it also transformed the family saga and its place in the literary field. After *Roots*—for the novel stands as a clear dividing line in the literary history of this genre—multigenerational historical fiction began to focus increasingly on historical events, not as mere background but as central to the narrative.[15] Moreover, the family tree novel became largely the domain of racially and ethnically minoritized writers, who traced ambitious tales of immigration, assimilation, progress, and uplift rather than the decline and disgrace of the genre's (primarily) white and male authors in the first half of the twentieth century.[16] Whereas the genre was previously invested in linearity, continuity, and the bourgeois "illusion of causality," trauma was now its central theme, breaks and gaps its key devices.[17] Characters became figures of absence, speaking on behalf of history's voiceless, fictional embodiments of the forgotten or misremembered. Drawing the family tree became a revisionist and even recuperative endeavor.

If Zucker is correct in claiming that the "genealogical novel" of the nineteenth and early twentieth century was "a new type of fiction ruled by science," then perhaps the most obvious explanation for the resurgence of the genealogical novel over the last several decades is the growing cultural visibility of scientific advancements in the field of genomics, as evidenced by the rise of corporations like 23andMe and popular programs like *Finding Your Roots with Henry Louis Gates, Jr.*[18] Though these developments in science have contributed to a global "genealogy boom," they have also revealed how genealogy itself is "a mode of knowing that effaces huge numbers of persons because of their gender, class, or race." It is, to quote Jerome de Groot, "a science of erasure" that, for example, "know[s] more about nineteenth-century criminals than [it does] about women and slaves."[19] This is the lacuna that the contemporary multigenerational family saga addresses directly, especially when taken up by women writers and minoritized writers, drawing inspiration from genealogical models insofar as it works to correct them. Though the audience for such research is large (it is one of the most searched topics online), and though the demographics of that audience ("mostly white women, 55 and older") overlap significantly with readers of literary fiction, the popularity and prestige attached to the family saga genre is as much a product of specific literary institutions as it is scientific innovation and broad cultural interest.[20]

The multigenerational family saga has become particularly central to the contemporary American literary canon in large part because it fulfills many of the pedagogical objectives of contemporary literary study. To borrow a common phrase from teachers of literature, the family tree novel *teaches well*. Whereas the genre formerly insulated its central families from capital-H history, key events and periods are now at the forefront. This is particularly useful for classroom teachers, at both the secondary school and university levels, looking "to entertain and to teach, to simplify and to complicate, to make history both palatable and challenging."[21] As previous chapters have argued, this focus on literature's ability to transmit historical knowledge has much to do with the rise of New Historicism as a scholarly methodology, which is itself a response to the marginalization of literary studies within the late twentieth-century university. "By drawing connections between literature and its social contexts," Timothy

Aubry argues, "New Historicism was implicitly drawing connections between English departments and *their* social context, thus seeking to establish the relevance of what they taught to other political and economic spheres."[22] Multigenerational historical fiction fulfills the earnest pedagogical imperative to *trace the longer histories* of certain phenomena, while also responding to institutional pressures to cover more (history and literary history) with less (financial support, class time, space on the syllabus). The same is true across the quad, where history teachers (and educators in other disciplines) are drawing on historical fiction to "set the scene" and "stimulate initial interest in a topic," as well as to "give a more human shape to individuals and cultures badly underrepresented in the historical record."[23]

Beyond the genre's ability to function as a kind of single-serving historical survey, the family tree novel also satisfies the expectation that literary studies can and should furnish "an affective investment in the lives of social others."[24] Elena Machado Sáez argues that this "ethical imperative" is only intensified for minoritized writers of historical fiction, for whom "the struggle to imagine an ethical pedagogical relationship between reader and author is encoded"—within the novels themselves—"in the depictions of student-teacher encounters."[25] This does much to explain the proliferation of teachers, students, and scenes of instruction in Gyasi's *Homegoing* and Lee's *Pachinko* discussed later on. Of course, the opportunities presented by these novels to empathize with the historically marginalized also explain their tremendous uptake by university instructors. According to the Open Syllabus Project, *Roots* has appeared on nearly 200 university syllabi, *Middlesex* on more than 350, and *Dreaming in Cuban* on 470. *Love Medicine* has featured on nearly 800 university syllabi, far more than, say, Cormac McCarthy's *Blood Meridian* (401 syllabi) or Marilynne Robinson's *Housekeeping* (196), two canonical novels from the same period. In the years since its publication, *Homegoing* has appeared on more than 110 university syllabi and been selected for campus-wide "Common Reads" programs at more than a dozen public and private institutions, including the Community College of Baltimore County, Connecticut College, Grinnell, Rutgers, Stanford, and the University of South Alabama.[26] As Machado Sáez makes clear, higher education's embrace of the multigenerational family saga genre, or any genre for that matter, has "market currency in the publishing field" because of "the centrality of the classroom to the publishing economy."[27] Publishers know, perhaps best of all, that a great portion of the readership for literary fiction consists of students; therefore what teachers teach can ultimately influence what gets published in the first place.

The pedagogical and affective affordances of the family saga novel are similarly well suited to the contemporary book club. As Beth Driscoll explains, "book clubs have some overlap with universities in terms of their reading material" because they are thoroughly "middle-class institutions, part of a package of values that includes education and self-improvement."[28] Not unlike university English departments, book clubs and their members are under pressure (self-imposed, in this case) to make their activities enriching. Yet the desire to learn and the desire to feel are not opposed, but commingled, in the contemporary book club. Though its readers are "eager to acquire cultural capital," Driscoll argues, "its central goal is emotional engagement," "encourag[ing] people to read for empathy."[29] Aubry agrees, adding that these informal institutions work to "mediate encounters across racial and cultural boundaries," wherein difference serves "not to preclude but to intensify [readers'] experience of identification."[30] No wonder, then, that when Now Read This, the book club cosponsored by the *PBS NewsHour* and the *New York Times*, selected *Pachinko* in July 2018, its published "Discussion Questions" invited readers to engage the novel both as learners (Question 7: "Did you know much about the Japanese occupation of Korea from 1910 through the end of World War II before reading this book?") and as empaths ("10. Which character throughout the four generations do you identify with most, and why?").[31]

As Driscoll notes, "publishers' attempts to specifically court the book club market are increasingly visible," including "free reading group guides" published online, like the ones that Grand Central Publishing and Penguin Random House released for *Pachinko* and *Homegoing*, respectively.[32] Dissimilar as these literary institutions may first appear, the contemporary book club and the university English department are both driven by a shared set of priorities that have encouraged the publication, prestige, and canonization of the multigenerational family saga. Publishers have appealed directly to these readerly expectations in their marketing strategies, as have critics in their early reviews. An edition of *Pachinko* features Caroline Kennedy's "Remarks from the Martha's Vineyard Book Festival," which praises both how the novel "illuminates the systemic discrimination suffered by three generations of a Korean family in Japan," and the way its characters "made me look differently at people in my own daily life."[33] Likewise, reviews of *Homegoing* lauded how the novel offers both "a panoramic view and an empathetic entry point into . . . the effects of slavery and colonialism."[34] Despite these grand pronouncements, the pages that follow will argue that the contemporary literary field's twin imperatives to historicize and empathize can, if pushed too far, result in a failure to do either.

MINOR HISTORIES

The first two chapters of Yaa Gyasi's *Homegoing* are ostensibly about disunion. In these paired openings, we meet Effia and Esi, two half-sisters living on the Gold Coast in the mid–eighteenth century, whose separation—one wedded to a white slaver in the chapel of the Cape Coast Castle, the other kidnapped and dragged through the castle's Door of No Return—sets the action of the book in motion. And yet, for as much as the novel and its opening chapter are concerned with this divergence, and how it cleaves the family in two for generations to come, *Homegoing* is ultimately invested in multiple forms of union. Its first chapter focuses in large part on Effia's literal union, a kind of marriage plot in miniature that culminates in her wedding to James Collins, tying Effia's family tree to the history of the British slave trade in West Africa. Of course, Effia is also wedded structurally in the novel to Esi, who lies shackled in the dungeon of the very castle where Effia sleeps. In these first chapters, Gyasi repeatedly emphasizes the mirrored—which is to say both linked and inverted—fates of the two sisters, from the way their social positions are literalized by the topography of the castle, to the "black stone pendant" given to each sister by their mother, Maame.

While Effia's necklace, given to her on her wedding day, is passed down through six generations of the family, Esi's lies buried in the castle's dungeon as she is dragged onto a slave ship bound for the United States. For the rest of the novel, Gyasi draws on the image of the pendant—both its presence and felt absence—as a visual metaphor of the ties that bind the two halves of the family over the course of several centuries. The necklace comes to symbolize the unity of the novel's family tree in two ways: horizontally, as a representation of the two halves' shared lineage; and vertically, as an image of continuity across the generations. In this way, the pendant metonymizes the governing narrative grammar of the multigenerational family saga as a genre: namely, that "history may not repeat itself, but it often rhymes." Moreover, as the reader of *Homegoing* follows the black stone pendant through chapters that alternate between the African and African American sides of the family tree, her reading itself becomes an act of producing these same continuities.

But though Gyasi's novel opens with a marriage, *Homegoing*'s most operative union is the wedding of family history and history writ large. As the novel proceeds, it becomes clear that Gyasi's family tree serves mainly as a kind of scaffold onto which an entire survey course of African and African American history is grafted. Effia's and Esi's chapters are vehicles for the history of the eighteenth-century slave trade, as is James's for the Anglo-Ashanti War of the 1820s; Kojo's chapter narrates (as Frederick Douglass does) the Baltimore shipyards of the mid-nineteenth century, while H's tracks the horrors of convict leasing at that century's end; Akua's takes up the Ashanti uprising at the turn of the twentieth century, as Willie's treats the poetry and racial passing of the Harlem Renaissance; Yaw's chapter chronicles Ghanaian independence, Sonny's the fight for civil rights, and so on. Indeed, Gyasi often links familial and historical events so closely that they are almost inextricable: a century after Effia's wedding to the slave trade via James Collins, Kojo and Anna are married "on the morning the Fugitive Slave Act passed" (123).

Homegoing appears less like a traditional historical novel—whose major historical events arrive, as Lukács outlines, at the climax of the narrative—than a collection of New Historicist anecdotes.[35] Aubry's description of the anecdote as device ("the rhetorical strategy for which the New Historicists are most famous") reads as much like a sketch of the scholarship of Stephen Greenblatt or Catherine Gallagher as it does the chapters of Gyasi's novel: "they invariably begin . . . by narrating an obscure historical episode culled from the archive, generally circumscribed enough in scope to conform to the Aristotelian unities, before using the episode to illuminate a broader set of historical issues." The union of Kojo and Anna, for example, illustrates the threat to both individual safety and family stability posed by the Fugitive Slave Act. When Anna (who is born free) is *unlawfully* kidnapped into slavery, the family anecdote performs what Aubry describes as a "synecdochal function" for both *de jure* violence and the *de facto* violence for which it runs cover.[36]

In large part, this stylistic resemblance has to do with Gyasi's extensive research process for the novel. Keeping with a growing trend among contemporary historical novelists, Gyasi's acknowledgments section cites a dozen or so scholarly works on African and African American history (304–5). In interviews, Gyasi appears sensitive to the possibility that *Homegoing* might "feel stifled by research": "I didn't want to become obsessed with trying to find out what color of shoes people would be wearing in the 18th century. . . . I wanted the research to feel atmospheric, really backgrounded, as though it was *informing* the characters' lives but not *crushing* them."[37] Yet these goals are somewhat in tension with Gyasi's research process, which, without crushing her characters, certainly shaped them:

> I wrote probably the first two chapters without any kind of outline or anything. Then I made a family tree that I put on my wall, which had the characters' names, if I knew them, their gender, if I knew it, the time period in which the bulk of each chapter took place, and just one thing that was happening historically or politically in the background of that time period. So, I would take something like the beginning of cocoa farming in Ghana or the Great Migration and use it as my entry point to do research. I wrote chronologically, so at the beginning of every chapter, I would stop, take a look at the family tree, get a couple of books, and read until I felt like my imagination was sparked enough to get going.[38]

The family tree, then, works as a guide not only for *Homegoing*'s readers but for its author as well. Moreover, this description of Gyasi's writing process emphasizes the tension between the branches of that tree and their historical backdrops. Despite the author's efforts to the contrary, "the background" is actually the "entry point" for imagination, with each character performing a similar "synecdochal function" for the "one thing that was happening historically." Gyasi has stressed that she "never wanted a chapter to be *about* the Fugitive Slave Act or the Great Migration," but rather, "this chapter is about Kojo, this chapter is about Willy."[39] And while this is further supported by *Homegoing*'s family tree, a testament to the novel's focus on its characters and the historically disregarded persons they emblematize, it is also in tension with the fact that each character functions as a kind of historical emblem, a single figure through which a period or event is metonymized. After all, this is the novel's key pedagogical affordance.

Like Whitehead's cheeky allusions to Ishmael Reed and Thomas Pynchon in *The Intuitionist*, Gyasi's characters also nod self-consciously to literary history. The "intricate scars on [Ness's] bare shoulders," for example, which are "shaped like a man hugging her from behind," and likened to "the ghost of her past made seeable," call to mind the chokecherry tree on Sethe's back and Paul D's embrace of it in the early chapters of *Beloved* (73–74).[40] Likewise, Kojo works at ship caulking in Baltimore's Chesapeake Bay, a few decades after, though allusively alongside, Frederick Douglass. Two generations later, after Willie's father dies of black lung—"coughing . . . as though some invisible man were behind him . . . choking him"—she migrates north from Alabama to Harlem, and Gyasi's writing evokes Ellison's own iconic descriptions of first arriving in the city (204). There, Willie befriends a Langston Hughes–like poet, attempts to break into the jazz scene best described by Zora Neale Hurston, and, in a scene that echoes Nella Larsen, momentarily misrecognizes her husband, who is passing as white. Willie names her son Carson, but he goes by "Sonny," fittingly, given that both the nickname and the chapter that focalizes him borrow heavily from James Baldwin.[41]

Much like Edmund Blackadder or Forrest Gump, the novel's central family is uncannily present at key moments in history, and the novel itself is uncannily allusive to key texts in the African and African American literary traditions. In order to accomplish this, Gyasi must at times move briskly—at the pace of Billy Joel's "We Didn't Start the Fire"—across historical time. Unlike Haley's *Roots*, which subjects the reader to the painful slowness of time passing, *Homegoing* hops lithely from period to period. Whereas Haley's research process (the subject of that book's final chapters) is focused on searching through the archives for his own family history, the goal of Gyasi's research—and perhaps her novel—is context itself.[42] This shift in attention has elicited some criticism from both scholars and critics.

Lisa Ze Winters has argued that "history is at once the *raison d'être* for the novel and something that happens to and around the characters, a series of events to which the characters must somehow adapt rather than an active force that demands their participation and attention."[43] Likewise, Laura Miller has derided what she calls *Homegoing*'s "demographic imperatives," suggesting that Sonny's experiences, for example, "feel less like the emanations of a coherent personality than like boxes that must be checked to make sure that Sonny represents a generation of black men."[44] Walton Muyumba has critiqued Gyasi's characters as "barely disguised invocations" of John Henry, Solomon Northup, and Clare Kendry, claiming that in *Homegoing*, "black American experience [becomes] narrowed, flattened into something especially recognizable to white readers."[45]

Though these critiques of the novel are not unfounded, one wonders to what extent this "flattening" is unavoidable, given *Homegoing*'s ambitious project of historical recovery. While the verticality of the novel's family tree emphasizes the vast scope of its plot, that tree's horizontality illustrates what Alex Woloch would call its "character-system," how it "apportion[s] attention to different characters who jostle for limited space within the same fictive universe."[46] As the reader travels down the family tree over the course of the novel, she can only ever follow a single branch, as Gyasi selects it alone, and not the others, to narrate. "This," Gyasi's historian and educator character, Yaw, tells us, "is the problem of history. . . . So when you study history, you must always ask yourself, Whose story am I missing? Whose voice was suppressed so that this voice could come forth?" (226–27). And yet, even as Gyasi thematizes how individuals come to be disregarded by the historical record, at times her novel, finite as novels are, cannot help but reenact that same suppression.

Nowhere is this more apparent than in Kojo's chapter, where Gyasi introduces the character's eight children through the metaphor of the alphabet: "Agnes, Beulah, Cato, Daly, Eurias, Felicity, and Gracie. It seemed like he and Anna were going to have one child for every letter of the alphabet.... Now everyone in the house called the new baby 'H,' as a placeholder until it came out and brought its name along with it" (114–15). Although the tragedy of this chapter's *story* is Anna's enslavement and the loss this represents for her family, the tragedy of its *discourse* is that only H will get a chapter of his own, while his seven siblings are left as "placeholders" for stories left untold. In one particularly striking passage, Gyasi performs this on the level of the paragraph by progressively compressing the space afforded to Kojo's alphabet of children:

> [Kojo] studied his children, the few hours of every night that he got to see them before they went to bed or every morning before he went off to the docks. Agnes was the helper. He'd never known a kinder, gentler spirit. Not Anna and certainly not his world-weary mother. Beulah was a beauty, but she didn't know it yet. Cato was soft for a boy, and [Kojo] tried every day to put a little grit into him. Daly was a fighter and Eurias was too often his target. Felicity was so shy she wouldn't tell you her own name if you asked her, and Gracie was a round ball of love. (115)

Notice how three sentences are devoted to Agnes and her kindness, then a single line to Beulah's beauty and Cato's sensitivity. By the end of the passage, the descriptions of Daly and Eurias share a sentence, as do those of Felicity and Gracie, the former too chagrined to speak or act at all, the latter reduced from the status of character to that of a vague affective shape. Of course, these are the exigencies of attempting to introduce and individualize seven characters in the finite space of a single paragraph. Yet this passage also emphasizes in miniature the costs of Gyasi's attempt to do the same with *fourteen protagonists* in the finite space of a single novel.

While the multigenerational historical novel is often praised for its capaciousness, it is as invested as any realist novel in the strict apportioning of attention to some characters over others—perhaps even more so, given that even its major characters are destined, in a generation or two, to be made minor after all. In the opening pages of *Pachinko*, Lee introduces Sunja, one of the novel's protagonists, in the context of her mother's previous three children, all unnamed and all lost in a single paragraph: "Yangjin gave birth to Sunja, her fourth child and the only girl, and the child thrived; after she turned three, the parents were able to sleep through the night without checking the pallet repeatedly to see if the small form lying beside them was still breathing."[47] Gyasi's progressive compression of character is here reversed by Lee, as Sunja overtakes her late siblings not only in the story but also in the discourse, with this unfurling sentence announcing the start of her narrative arc. According to Woloch, this "tension between the one and the many" embodies the "two contradictory generic achievements" of realist fiction: "depth psychology and social expansiveness, depicting the interior life of a singular consciousness and casting a wide narrative gaze over a complex social universe."[48] This paradox is only further heightened in a work of historical fiction explicitly dedicated to the recovery of the historically marginalized, and it is nowhere more stark than when that novel is a multigenerational family saga devoted, by definition, to the many. *Homegoing* pushes this generic logic to the limit, by casting its characters as emblems of lost histories to such an extent that they become, at least for some readers, flattened, instrumentalized, and press-ganged into historical metonymy. The irony of this is hard to overstate. In her attempt to recognize more and more of the historically voiceless, Gyasi has written a novel whose characters can speak only insofar as they ventriloquize major moments, well-known periods, and literary canonical figures.

When I teach *Homegoing*, my students often report that, despite their best efforts and much to their dismay, they become increasingly apathetic readers as the novel goes on. They invest heavily in learning the details of Effia's and Esi's lives and likewise invest emotionally in the pathos of their stories. By the end of the novel, however, they find they are simply not capable of the same investment. Unlike, say, Haley's *Roots*, which devotes hundreds of pages to Kunta Kinte's story and compresses the discursive space of his descendants, Gyasi is rigorously egalitarian in doling out discursive space, with each character focalized for almost exactly twenty pages. Despite the author's conscious efforts to make her characters "all feel equally weighted," the novel's reader cannot distribute her own affective resources as democratically.[49] One review of *Homegoing* points out that "each chapter must immediately introduce a new setting and new characters making fresh claims on our engagement," and concludes that "it's no criticism of the latter chapters to say that the earlier ones are particularly haunting."[50] But perhaps these comments are more related than they first appear. Perhaps the earlier chapters are more engaging precisely because their narrative and affective claims are, well, fresher. Even on the scale of a single text, it seems, readerly attention and empathy are finite resources.

When asked why *Pachinko*'s narrative perspective switches between so many characters, "rather than focusing on one person's experience," Lee explains that because "history so often fails to represent all of us," "I wanted the narrator to be sympathetic to every character's plight."[51] But at what point does the authorial impulse to empathize or sympathize with *every* character—made possible by a genre where such capaciousness is coded into its very DNA—actually result in a loss of readerly identification? In Gyasi's original conception of *Homegoing*, the novel consisted only of the earliest two chapters (focusing on Effia and Esi) and the most contemporary (Marjorie and Marcus).[52] For some readers, however, this may still be the operative experience of the novel: the beginning's ancestral roots, the end's contemporary inheritances, and the middle's necessary passage from one to the other. According to one critic, "as the narrated events grow ever more horrifying and the cruelty becomes unbearable" in *Homegoing*'s middle chapters, "the rapid pace of the narrative comes as a merciful relief to the reader who can comfort herself with the fact that for herself at least it will soon be over."⁵³ But the "merciful relief" of emotional divestment that the novel's (and the genre's) "rapid pace" affords would seem directly at odds with not only its author's intentions but also the institutions that have most contributed to its central place in the contemporary canon. With its inherently diffuse character system, the multigenerational family saga holds out the promise of both a more democratized historical record and a more empathetic encounter with that history. The obverse of this is that the genre's ambitious historical breadth may come at the cost of the depth of its characters, as well as its readers' sustained engagement with them. When the multigenerational genre is stretched far enough, one cannot see the branches for the family tree.

THE LONG MORAL ARC

Who—or what—is the protagonist of *Homegoing*? It is not an easy question, given that all of Gyasi's central characters eventually disappear from the action of the novel.⁵⁴ When asked in an interview if she wished she could "revisit some of these characters" as *Homegoing* progresses, Gyasi replied, simply, "not really . . . because, again, I had that long arc in mind."⁵⁵ In other words, the protagonist in the service of whom each of Gyasi's fourteen focalized characters is compressed and then abandoned, the cause for which the voices of minor characters like Felicity and Gracie are overlooked, is both the family tree and the "long arc" of history that it indexes. While the multigenerational family saga is a kind of leviathan genre composed of miniature marriage plots and bildungsromans, each of these are nested in a larger structure wherein (as one critic wrote of *Buddenbrooks*) "the family is the real hero of the book."⁵⁶ Just as in the bildungsroman, where "the hero's progress is facilitated through a series of interactions" with characters who "stand for particular states of mind, or psychological modes, that the protagonist interacts with and transcends," in the family saga this process is played out across and *by way of* successive generations.⁵⁷ Although *Homegoing* is often discussed as a novel of contemporary African migration, as Brian Yothers rightly points out, only one of its fourteen main characters is actually an immigrant; thus, the there-to-here narrative of migration stretches beyond any individual character's experience, unfolding instead over the course of multiple generations.⁵⁸ Though it is often harrowing, this process is presented as largely positive. If the superstructure of *Buddenbrooks* is one of deterioration and failure—the novel's subtitle is, after all, *The Decline of a Family*—the overarching plot of *Homegoing*, and a great many contemporary family sagas by writers of color, is one of mobility, advancement, and ascent. The novel's protagonist is progress itself.

Of course, Gyasi's passing mention of the "long arc" that she had "in mind" when writing the novel betrays this. However consciously, the phrase evokes Martin Luther King Jr.'s adage that "the arc of the moral universe is long, but it bends toward justice," and perhaps still more, Barack Obama's adoption of it as a kind of mantra for his presidency. (Obama not only drew on the quotation as a common refrain in his speeches, he also had it woven into a rug in the Oval Office.)⁵⁹ In its twenty-first-century reincarnations, the bromide seeks to emphasize the triumph of postwar liberalism, the steady improvement that is at once persistent and passive, inevitable and indefinitely deferred. The moral arc bends, we are told, but who or what is bending it—and how? The same logic pervades *Homegoing* and its insistently linear plot. Unlike the high modernist blending of past and present, unlike Morrison's or Nguyen's modernist-influenced convolution of periods, which are themselves haunted by the specters of history, Gyasi's chronology moves in only one direction (echoing another triumphal Obama slogan): forward. Unlike Sexton's *A Kind of Freedom*, which we will turn to in a moment, *Homegoing*'s chapters continually ask the reader to *wait and see*, to keep reading as its characters suffer under the hope that their children may lead better, freer lives.

At one point in the novel, Abena's father comes upon her in tears and asks why she is crying. "'The plants have all died, and I could have helped them,'" she answers, "between sobs." To this Abena's father responds, "then next time bring more water, but don't cry for this time" (144–45). This is, to some extent, the narrative and affective gambit of *Homegoing*, asking the reader to defer passing judgment—on the family, on the novel, and on the history it recounts—until it has arrived at its conclusion. As Gyasi herself puts it, "the long arc of the book . . . the accumulation of all of the chapters was more important to me than the individual chapters."[60] The end of the "long arc"—where the characters, particularly the *last* characters, end up—is what matters most, legitimizing both the stories and the suffering that come before.

The idea that the conclusion is what gives a story its meaning is not unique to Gyasi or her chosen genre. Shakespeare tells us that "*La fin couronne les oeuvres*."[61] Peter Brooks tells us that "the end writes the beginning and shapes the middle."[62] But in contemporary iterations of the multigenerational family saga, the end acquires still greater importance, as it not only provides closure to the chronicle of an individual family but also proffers a coherent shape to history and its moral arc. "We often love grand, sweeping, multigenerational narratives," Michelle Wright claims, "for providing us with a sense of clarity, for affording us the sensation of standing outside space and time so that we may fully comprehend the long, complicated, and awesome journey our ancestors made across the centuries."[63] As readers, we have the privilege of historical irony, knowing what is going to happen, which is to say what *has happened*, in a way that the characters, particularly the ones most removed in historical and genealogical time, do not. A number of family sagas incorporate this irony, and the pleasure it affords, by paying particular attention to scenes of formal instruction, especially in the final generations. That is, in both senses of the word, *the end* of a great many multigenerational historical novels lies in education.

Take the close of *Buddenbrooks*, for example, which finds young Hanno Buddenbrook in a primary school classroom, dreading every minute. Asked by his teacher to recite a bit of Latin, Hanno reluctantly accepts, bungling the attempt despite cheating off a friend's notes. "You have dragged beauty through the dust," his schoolmaster chides, "you have behaved like a Vandal" (704). One chapter later, Hanno dies of typhoid fever and *the decline of a family* is complete. While, for Mann, Hanno's scholastic failure typifies the family's descent, for more contemporary novelists, the opposite is true: progress means that the highest branches of their family trees are stocked with star students. "We have to think of his education as an investment," the elder generations in *Pachinko* decide for Noa, the boy who proudly declares that he "could read books all day and do nothing else."[64] Noa goes on to study English literature at Waseda University, where, "ravenous for good books," "he read through Dickens, Thackeray, Hardy, Austen, and Trollope . . . then fell in love with Tolstoy."[65] This syllabus, devised by Lee for Noa, provides a kind of generic bibliography for *Pachinko*, populated as it is by authors of marriage plots, bildungsromans, historical novels, and family sagas. To the extent that it places *Pachinko* in conversation with these classics, this reading list is also metacanonical, both affirming and amending this all-white list of literary greats.

Homegoing's final chapters likewise feature characters en route to the honor roll, and allusions to a changing canon. When we first meet Marjorie—who, like Gyasi herself, was born in Ghana and moved to Alabama at a young age—she is working her way through high school and its library: "By senior year, she had read almost everything on the south wall of the school's library, at least a thousand books, and she was working her way through the north wall" (270–71). Whereas Whitehead's *The Intuitionist* allegorizes the canon wars that marked his time at Harvard in the early 1990s, Gyasi dramatizes how those same debates over literary multiculturalism are still playing out at the secondary school level decades later. At the start of the chapter, Marjorie is nose-deep in *Lord of the Flies*, she has just checked out *Middlemarch* from the library, and she is anxiously looking forward to her *Great Gatsby*–themed prom. In other words, whether her high school experience most resembles an island of adolescent rage, a study of provincial life, or a bacchanal of romantic ambition, it is couched decidedly in the themes and tropes of a largely white canon. That is, until her English teacher, Mrs. Pinkston, "one of two black teachers in a school that served almost two thousand students," approaches her at lunch to ask what she thinks of Golding's novel. When Marjorie replies that she likes the book, her teacher pushes further: "'But do you love it? Do you feel it inside of you?' Marjorie shook her head. She didn't know what it meant to feel a book inside of her, but she didn't want to tell her English teacher that" (270).

By the end of the chapter, Marjorie puts down *Middlemarch*, and picks up her pen. Encouraged by Mrs. Pinkston, Marjorie writes a poem that both recognizes her two homelands and acknowledges the parts of her heritage that are lost to history. "Split the Castle open, / find me, find you," Marjorie begins, performing her work before the school's two thousand students, and revising Langston Hughes's iconic "I, too" as "We, two," a pithy miniaturization of the novel itself (282). Whereas Hanno Buddenbrook bungles his recitation and is silenced by his teacher, Marjorie is lauded for finding her voice, creating something she can truly "feel inside." In its final chapters, *Homegoing* performs—in a high school auditorium, no less—precisely the virtues that attract so many secondary school and university educators to it: literature's ability to make diverse histories available to empathy, and the power of that empathy in turn to energize a new generation of readers and writers.

If each of Gyasi's characters metonymizes a given period—H, Reconstruction; Willie, the Harlem Renaissance—then Marjorie and

Marcus (the novel's final focalizer) suggest, somewhat paradoxically, that education is the end of history. Or, rather, that after suffering and enduring and overcoming it, *learning* history represents an end in itself. Six generations after Effia and Esi are torn asunder by the violence of colonialism, Marjorie and Marcus become friends while both are living in northern California and studying at Stanford—the former pursuing a degree in African and African American literature, the latter a PhD in sociology. The university thus provides a spatial bookend to the Fanteland village in which the novel begins. There the bonds of family, community, and culture held the two sides of Maame's family together; here the institution, its myth of meritocracy, and its structures of knowledge do the same work. Learning the horrors of the past and also the vocabulary with which to render them, *Homegoing* suggests, is where family history finds its natural conclusion. The long moral arc bends and bends, but for Gyasi where it stops is Stanford.

This is not entirely surprising, given that Stanford is where Gyasi, herself the daughter of a literature professor, "first heard the word 'diaspora'" and won a research grant that would both send her to Ghana and launch what would become her first novel.[66] *Homegoing*'s history—which is to say, both the development of the novel and the development of its historical narrative—is inflected by the institutions that sponsored it. The same is true for *Pachinko*, which Lee also began thinking about as an undergraduate at Yale University. It was there, Lee explains, that she first "learned about the Korean-Japanese people . . . as a history major and as an immigrant," who was "curious" about both the Korean diaspora and "the compelling stories of individuals who struggled to face historical catastrophes."[67] (Lee graduated from Yale in 1990, a year before Colson Whitehead graduated from Harvard.) In this way, Lee, Gyasi, and their prizewinning novels appear as prime examples of the phenomenon, described by Claire Grossman, Juliana Spahr, and Stephanie

Young, in which authors "with an elite degree (Ivy League, Stanford, University of Chicago)" are far more likely (nine times more likely, in fact) to win a literary prize than those without one. For minoritized writers, this correlation is even more pronounced. "In the contemporary moment," they argue, "serious literature is more or less written by graduates of elite institutions, often to be read in educational or education-adjacent settings."[68]

That said, this book argues that contemporary American fiction is deemed more or less "serious" not simply because of its author's curriculum vitae but more precisely as a result of the shared political and aesthetic priorities of academic and literary institutions. The twin promises of the multigenerational family saga genre—to cultivate empathy with historically marginalized individuals *qua* individuals and to narrate vast swaths of history in the *longue durée*—are prized by university English departments, campus "Common Reads" programs, literary awards organizations, and "education-adjacent" book clubs alike. And yet, while these radically different scales of attention appear to pose little problem for such disparate interpretive communities, their juxtaposition does create a tension that is registered in the works themselves—a tension described, not coincidentally, as a problem of academic discipline. In Lee's novel, Noa is walking out of a seminar on George Eliot when he meets Akiko, "a Sociology major" and "the radical beauty on campus" (277). As the two fall in love, their relationship metonymizes *Pachinko*'s own "interdisciplinary" approach to history, a fusion of the sociologist's impulse toward "collect[ing] pieces of data" and the literary scholar's interests in narrative, characterization, and individual experience (299).

Likewise, at the end of *Homegoing*, Marcus's and Marjorie's academic projects figure transparently as metatexts for the novel itself. As Marcus works toward a PhD in sociology, he is frustrated by the inextricability of historical phenomena: "the deeper into the research he got, the bigger the project got. How could he talk about

Great-Grandpa H's story without also talking about his grandma Willie and the millions of other black people who had migrated north, fleeing Jim Crow? And if he mentioned the Great Migration, he'd have to talk about the cities that took that flock in," and so on, tracing the trajectory of the latter half of the novel, from convict leasing to the "war on drugs" (289). Gyasi has commented that she shares both "Marcus' frustration" that "you can never capture the fullness of history in a single novel," as well as his "desire" to "get as close as possible."[69] When Marcus asks Marjorie how she came to study African and African American literature, she responds, echoing Mrs. Pinkston and her ethos of literary representation, that "those were the books that she could feel inside of her." "It was one thing to research something," Marcus concludes, "another thing to have lived it. To have felt it. How could he explain to Marjorie that what he wanted to capture with his project was the feeling of time, of having been a part of something that stretched so far back" (295). For Gyasi's fictional descendants, as with Lee's, the challenge of understanding historical injustices and their contemporary effects is transfigured into the challenge of choosing a major. Ultimately, both *Homegoing* and *Pachinko* comprise a kind of joint thesis in literature and sociology that toggles back and forth between each discipline's preferred scale of inquiry. This reflects each author's liberal arts education, but it also betrays an uncertainty as to how best to render "compelling stories of individuals" (Lee) amid "the fullness of history" (Gyasi).

The last chapter of *Homegoing* takes place at the turn of the twenty-first century, when Marjorie and Marcus not only reunite and therefore reconnect the long-separated halves of the family but also return to Cape Coast Castle together. This last sequence parallels the end of Haley's *Roots*, which follows the author-narrator as he returns to the Gambian village of Juffure (where Kunta Kinte was born) and comes to the "staggering awareness . . . that *if* any black American could be so blessed as I had been to know only a few ancestral clues . . .

then [they might be] able to locate some wizened old black *griot* whose narrative could reveal the black American's ancestral clan."⁷⁰ But if the tantalizing fantasy held out by Haley is the prospect of the recovering *of history*, the promise of the end of Gyasi's novel is the therapeutic recovery *from history*. In *Homegoing*'s final lines, Gyasi writes that Marjorie "lifted the stone [pendant] from her neck, and placed it around Marcus's. 'Welcome home,'" she says, before they splash one another and swim, laughing, back "toward the shore" (300).

Gyasi describes her own visit to the castle—a week or so before Barack Obama's historic trip there in 2009—as "a healing moment," in which she was "thinking a lot about the way we try to heal ourselves and heal these wounds that stretch for centuries."⁷¹ Obama, too, focused on the recuperative in his remarks at the castle, emphasizing that while "on the one hand this place was a place of profound sadness; on the other hand, it is . . . where the journey of much of the African American experience began." Capturing not only the "postracial" optimism of his early years in office but also the sense of progress that *Homegoing*'s historical narrative emphasizes, Obama concluded: "to be able to come back here in celebration . . . of the extraordinary progress that we've made because of the courage of so many, black and white, to abolish slavery and ultimately win civil rights for all people, I think is a source of hope. It reminds us that as bad as history can be, it's also possible to overcome."⁷² In retrospect, this triumphal declaration appears premature at best.

In contrast to both Obama's and Gyasi's narratives of progress, Saidiya Hartman's description of her own journey to Cape Coast Castle in *Lose Your Mother* acknowledges both "the hope . . . that return could resolve the old dilemmas, make a victory out of defeat, and engender a new order," as well as "the disappointment . . . that there is no going back to a former condition. Loss remakes you. Return is as much about the world to which you no longer belong as it is about the one in which you have yet to make a home."⁷³ Like Gyasi,

Hartman recognizes how the present is shaped by the traumas of history, but unlike Gyasi, she also recognizes that "healing" cannot take place while fresh wounds are being inflicted: "I, too, live in the time of slavery, by which I mean I am living in the future created by it. It is the ongoing crisis of citizenship. . . . If slavery feels proximate rather than remote . . . this has everything to do with our own dark times."[74] While *Homegoing* is decidedly *about* "the future created" by slavery, it ultimately—and quite deliberately—avoids the darkness of recent history, choosing instead to focus on Marjorie and Marcus's shining return to Ghana. "Everything was brilliant here, even the ground," Gyasi writes. "Sunlight bounced off of the sand, making it shimmer. Sand like diamonds in the once gold coast" (297).

This is where and when *Homegoing*'s three centuries of history come to a hopeful close. In this way, both the novel and genre it represents point to the promise, and the central problem, of American literature's overwhelming historical turn. Though a generation of minoritized writers has been canonized for excavating previously disregarded histories, and though a generation of teachers and readers has drawn on those writers' work to keep the memory of the past alive, does all this historicism come at the cost of engaging meaningfully with the present? As Machado Sáez has argued persuasively, the sizable "academic market" for contemporary fiction is "oriented toward the commodification of literary representations of resistance, equating resistance with a progressive ideology of contextualization."[75] This desire for contextualization—and, in particular, the misunderstanding of contextualization *as a form of resistance*—has worked, on the scale of both individual educators and educational institutions, to elevate the multigenerational family saga as a central genre of contemporary fiction. Yet this is a pedagogy that attempts to alchemize historical knowledge into contemporary political action. As Yaw, Gyasi's teacher-historian figure, puts it, "if you point the people's eye to the future, they might not see what is being done to hurt them in the present" (238). The same is true if one looks only backward.

ROUND AND ROUND

"At some point, long after we are gone, there will be stories about our time, too," Yaa Gyasi offered in an interview the week *Homegoing* was published.[76] Not ten days later in another interview, Gyasi provided one such story, in which her twelve-year-old brother "had the police called on him by our new neighbors while riding his bike on a nearby lot": "This is the tame version of this too common story of black boys in America. In the other version my brother dies."[77] Despite how autobiographical the later sections of her novel are, neither version of this encounter with police ended up in *Homegoing*. Instead, the novel touches on contemporary police violence and mass incarceration only by way of historical analogy. By contrast, Margaret Wilkerson Sexton explains that part of the inspiration for her own debut novel was the story of her dear cousin, who "went to jail for the first time" in 2012, the same year Sexton herself was "sworn into the bar to practice law." Both "haunted and curious" about the distance between these "parallel" lives, Sexton started researching and writing about Black families in New Orleans throughout the twentieth century.[78] The result is *A Kind of Freedom*, a multigenerational historical novel that follows one such family from World War II to the War on Drugs and the aftermath of Hurricane Katrina.

Like Gyasi, Sexton is a graduate of elite schools (studying creative writing at Dartmouth College and law at UC Berkeley) and her semi-autobiographical debut received considerable acclaim (winning the First Novelist Award from the Black Caucus of the American Library Association; appearing on the longlist for the National Book Award, as well as annual best-of lists from the *New York Times*, *San Francisco Chronicle*, *Ebony*, and the *BBC*). Sexton's publisher even listed *Homegoing* as a "comp" for the novel, a "comparable" or "comparison title" used to predict a book's sales and guide its marketing.[79] Despite these similarities, what sets *A Kind of Freedom* apart from the majority of multigenerational historical novels, and *Homegoing* in particular, is the novel's cyclical structure. Rather than plow ever forward through linear historical time, Sexton runs her three settings on a kind of continual loop, subverting the easy correlation between narrative progress and political progress.

The novel opens in the Seventh Ward of New Orleans in 1944. Evelyn, a young nursing student following in the footsteps of her father and grandfather, both doctors, meets and falls in love with Renard, the youngest in a family of twelve, who is hoping to become a doctor himself. For Evelyn and Renard, as well as for Sexton, these careers in medicine are both the means toward, and the emblems of, upward mobility.[80] By contrast, the ongoing war effort and the opportunities for advancement that it may or may not afford Black soldiers are far more uncertain. Echoing Black activists of the 1940s and their "Double V," or double victory, campaign against fascism abroad and racism at home, Sexton's characters (much like Leslie Marmon Silko's in chapter 2) see enlistment as a viable, if tenuous, pathway to full citizenship.[81] Evelyn's sister's boyfriend proclaims that "maybe when we exercise our duty this country will start to exercise theirs." Put off by this naive optimism, Evelyn's father points out how life for Black soldiers is warped by segregation, reminding the young men that "the likelihood is you won't be flying planes or healing the sick over there," but "serving meals, cleaning quarters, digging graves." To this, Evelyn's father adds the example of a local man who lost his leg while serving as "a mail clerk in France" only to be denied a job at the local post office, despite his superlative marks on the entrance exam and preferential hiring for veterans. Though Renard initially agrees, lamenting the nation's "hypocrisy" and its call to "sacrifice our lives just to come back still not quite American," he is ultimately persuaded to enlist (37–38). "They said they would pay for my schooling," Renard tells Evelyn, wondering aloud "if this is our ticket to full manhood in this country. Maybe if not for me, for my children" (112).

A dozen pages later, however, Sexton undermines Renard's (and perhaps also the reader's) hope for progress by leaping ahead to the lives of those very children in the fall of 1986. From the very first lines of this second section, which focalizes Renard and Evelyn's daughter Jackie, it becomes clear that the longer arc of *A Kind of Freedom* bends in a different direction than *Homegoing*: "Jackie didn't blame [her husband] for leaving her; mostly she just worried she would get a call one morning that he had been arrested inside some crack den, or outside it, stealing to support the habit. He was by no means a thief, but Jackie had learned the hard way that life could drag disgrace out of you" (41). As in the novel's 1940s chapters, its 1980s chapters point up that "disgrace" is less a problem of individual choice than it is the product of systemic racism. Indeed, Sexton draws a bright, straight line from Reagan's "tax cuts and spending bans" to everybody's knowing "somebody who was standing in the unemployment line" to an epidemic of drug addiction in New Orleans's Black community and the devastating criminalization of that addiction (54). This includes Jackie's husband, Terry, a two-time valedictorian, who begins self-medicating with drugs after he is laid off from his job at the Department of Veterans Affairs. That Reagan, a central spokesman of the greatest-generation mythos, was also a chief architect of near-annual proposals to cut the VA's budget only strengthens Renard's earlier charge of "hypocrisy." That both Renard and Terry pursue social mobility under the illusory auspices of national service, and are both punished for it, only further emphasizes the "cruel optimism" and historical irony at the heart of *A Kind of Freedom*.[82] By the end of Jackie's section, when Terry, motivated by his love for their newborn son, promises to put an end to his cycle of rehab and relapse, reader and character alike are eager to believe him. All the more devastating, then, when on the very next page Sexton lurches forward yet again; this time, to the summer of 2010, opening on Jackie and Terry's son, T. C., in his mid-twenties and about to be released from the Orleans Parish Prison, incarcerated for the misdemeanor possession of marijuana.

In his *New York Times* review of *A Kind of Freedom*, Jesse McCarthy writes that "Sexton pursues [the] family's history in a downward spiral," but this is less a dead metaphor of decline than it is a deft description of the novel's cyclical structure.[83] Sexton circles back again and again, revolving through her three historical settings, demonstrating both the traumatic legacies of the past in the present (as Gyasi does) and the power of the present to act as a kind of clarifying solvent to the idealism of that past. In several moments, Sexton draws on this structure in the service of a particularly dispiriting irony that works both ways in historical time: forward, as when we learn that "T. C. didn't remember meeting his father" (64) on the page after Terry promises to make good on his son's behalf; and backward, as when we realize that Evelyn's brother has died years earlier of a drug overdose, only to find him "playing cops and robbers" a few pages later and four decades before (91, 98–99).

In an interview with the For Colored Girls Book Club, Sexton explains that her use of these "parallel timelines" demonstrates "how little, despite popular belief, has changed, though we've made significant progress. There are some strands of history that just weave themselves into the present over and over."[84] One such "strand" that Sexton emphasizes in the novel is the continuity of racist policing and racial disparities in the American criminal justice system. In 1944, Renard and Evelyn are accosted by a police officer, "clutching the baton at the side of his waist," simply for walking in a city park (33). Four decades later, in 1986, Jackie and Terry witness a young man violently assaulted by two cops as he pleads his innocence (144). Nearly twenty-five years later, in the summer of 2010, T. C. feels "his heart tense" when a police car passes him in a restaurant parking lot, hopeful that "the most they would do was throw him up against the car, search his empty pants' pockets, and slap him up for their lost time" (73). In moments like these, *A Kind of Freedom* offers an essential revision to the well-worn adage that those who fail to learn from history are doomed to repeat it. This unyielding repetition of anti-Black racism and violence, Sexton makes clear, is precisely what those who learn from history *must learn*. The choice of the novel's three historical

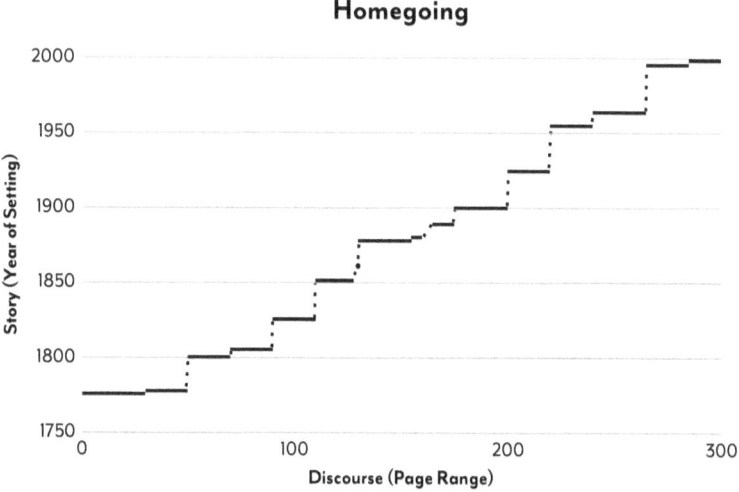

FIGURE 4.2 Historical setting and narrative time in Yaa Gyasi's *Homegoing* (2016).

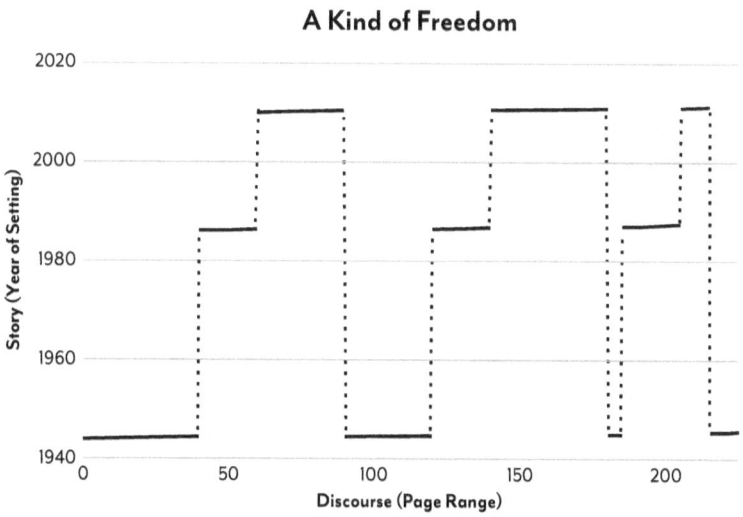

FIGURE 4.3 Historical setting and narrative time in Margaret Wilkerson Sexton's *A Kind of Freedom* (2017).

settings further undermines the idea of neat historical progress, skipping over the civil rights era and the election of the first Black president entirely. Whereas Obama and his optimism are a kind of absent presence in the final chapters of *Homegoing*, in *A Kind of Freedom* they are played for sardonic irony. Speaking with Evelyn after getting out of jail, T. C. smiles while boasting that he "was able to vote for Obama." "That's it now though, huh?" Evelyn replies, marking the limits of that milestone which, in a novel published in 2017, rings somewhat hollow (92).

Sexton gives shape to this structural inequality by focusing on the built environment of New Orleans. Like the novel's central family, the spaces they inhabit narrate a steady intergenerational decline. In the 1940s chapters, Sexton pays particularly close attention to the ornate details of Evelyn's family home: "its wood frame with sky-blue trim, the baskets of fresh watered ferns adorning its porch, the pansies and petunias on either side of the long, winding driveway." In these descriptions, Sexton draws a small curtain "*guarding* the window on the side of the front door," and two pages later, "a large palm tree [that] *guarded* the corner of their property," as if the house itself is under threat from invisible forces without (15–17, emphasis added). A generation later, Jackie is forced from a home with a lawn "as fresh as first-day-of-school hair-cuts"—a middle-class simile if ever there was one—to an apartment in the "housing projects . . . covered in graffiti and littered with trash." In an allusion to the opening of Richard Wright's *Native Son* and its billboard blaring "YOU CAN'T WIN," Sexton describes the billboards that "dotted every corner: Nancy Reagan leaning into a black child's face, bold white letters above her head. JUST SAY NO" (42).[85] By 2010, even the projects have been "gutted" and "razed" in the wake of Hurricane Katrina (69). While city officials move quickly to replace "vacant storefronts" with new and "pricey" restaurants where T. C. "had no business even reading the menus" (76), he and his mother are fresh from "three years in a [FEMA] trailer," underserved and overlooked by the federal government's "Road Home" program (86). From a stately home in the Seventh Ward to the "Stately Grove" housing projects to abandoned flood-ravaged lots, the novel's architecture belies the arc of progress that its historical trajectory might suggest (41).

In a literary genre long partial to narratives of familial decline, *A Kind of Freedom* is made all the more heartrending by the perpetual belief—on the part of Sexton's characters and her readers—that things will get better. After Terry promises to get clean, Jackie wakes "with a new resolve . . . as if she'd been shown a reel from their future . . . and in it they were impenetrable to threat" (133). Later, when T. C. is pulled over by the police with a backpack full of marijuana, Sexton ends the tense episode on a cliffhanger, with "T. C. just wait[ing] for a miracle to kick in" (184). But in the end, T. C.'s and Jackie's lives are impenetrable only in their imaginations: Terry relapses and leaves; T. C. is sent away for three more years in prison.

In a kind of epilogue to the novel, Sexton returns one final time to winter 1945 and Renard's homecoming from service overseas. As Evelyn's father predicted, and as Renard himself had feared, his time in the military is marked by segregation, inequality, and even racist violence—a grim portent of what is to come and what, in the novel, has already occurred. The night before Evelyn and Renard's wedding, her parents give them a key to "a two-bedroom old shotgun house down the block . . . a perfect starter house" for the new couple; though, as readers are well aware, this also marks the start of their move from the Seventh Ward to FEMA trailers (225). The next day, Renard—with eyes "so hopeful, so impossibly hopeful"—slides a ring onto Evelyn's finger and Evelyn "squeals" with delight, imagining that "their lives lay out uncharted before them" (228). The dramatic irony in these final lines is nearly unbearable, as readers confront the irreconcilability of the couple's optimism and its inevitable ends. Sexton has described the "false sense of hope" that attends this moment, as well her desire to "demonstrate on a visceral level what it would feel like to be in the circumstances that inhibit my characters' lives."[86]

Throughout *A Kind of Freedom*, Sexton leverages the reader's expectation that narrative and political progress will travel together only to frustrate that expectation, evoking the very disappointment that plagues her characters. As if to emphasize these deflated hopes still further, even the novel's family tree structure withers over time: Evelyn, one of three children, gives birth to two daughters, Sybil and Jackie, whose only child, T. C., fathers a single son. Likewise, the novel's title holds out the possibility of "freedom," qualifies it, and ultimately ironizes it as the story unfolds: the phrase appears only once in the novel, as a disillusioned T. C. reflects from prison that "everybody knew it was better to adjust to the kind of freedom available on the inside" (211–12). Sexton's novel may be bleak at times, but it also offers a necessary corrective to the multigenerational family saga's narratives of incremental advancement. In this way, *A Kind of Freedom* embodies what McCarthy has described as "the urgent appeal" of contemporary activists to reject the "racial politics that . . . reached its apogee in both the persona and policy offers of Obama's presidency": namely, the "rose-tinted conception of politics as the transactional but egalitarian rule of the demos by the best and the brightest"—a conception reified in Gyasi's rosy final chapters.[87]

If one of the family tree novel's chief pedagogical affordances is its ability to represent crucial moments of historical transition, then perhaps it is Sexton's disavowal of transition, her commitment to repetition, that accounts for the novel's ambivalent institutional reception. Though both *Homegoing* and *A Kind of Freedom* were nominated for and received several awards, Gyasi's multigenerational historical novel has been embraced far more by readers, book clubs, and educators. As of this writing, *Homegoing* has received more than forty times as many reviews on Goodreads.com as *A Kind of Freedom*, and more than fifty times as many ratings, one indicator of readership and readerly engagement.[88] According to Open Syllabus, *Homegoing* has appeared on more than 110 university syllabi, while *A Kind of Freedom* has been included only once (perhaps on mine).[89] This is likely also the result of the difference in the two novels' publishers—*Homegoing* was published by Big Five giant Penguin Random House, *A Kind of Freedom* by the independent Counterpoint Press—and the vast disparity in their budgets for marketing and promotion. Yet that, too, points up which kinds of multigenerational sagas are seen as most marketable.

When a reviewer writes that "*A Kind of Freedom* challenges, illuminates, and inspires," it stresses the pedagogical mission that subtends so much of the canonization of historical fiction by minoritized writers.[90] Yet this program not only comes at the cost of engaging critically with the recent past as much as distant history, as in *Homegoing*, it also elevates readerly empathy as an end unto itself. As Driscoll makes clear, in the contemporary book club, "emotional engagement trumps social engagement" and books are positioned as "tools to transform the lives of readers, with the implicit promise that this will lead to social change."[91] On the other hand, in an essay titled "The Banality of Empathy," published in the *New York Review of Books*, Namwali Serpell argues that "empathy is, in a word, selfish." Despite its lofty intentions, "the idea that [readers] can and ought to use art to inhabit others, especially the marginalized" can all too easily lead to the "relishing of suffering by those who are safe from it" and become "an emotional palliative that distracts us from real inequities."[92]

These concerns are all the more acute in the case of multigenerational historical fiction, which, despite its deftness at chronicling historical injustice, frequently stops short of narrating recent historical events. This is often the formal and indeed political limit of the genre. Looking over "the family tree of the Buddenbrooks [that] had been plotted out with parentheses, rubrics, and clearly ordered dates," little Hanno finds his own name "at the very end," and, "with great yet somehow thoughtless and mechanical care, he [draws] two neat, lovely horizontal lines across the bottom"; when his irate father asks what he could have possibly been thinking, Hanno replies, "I thought . . . I thought . . . there wouldn't be anything more" (509–10). A century later, in another novel about *the decline of a family*, Evelyn asks, "That's it now though, huh?" But *A Kind of Freedom* succeeds in fictionalizing and historicizing 2010 as if it were as significant as 1986 or 1945. If the multigenerational family saga pushes the form of the historical novel to its very limit, stretching its temporal boundaries so as to hold multiple centuries in their grasp, the next chapter takes up almost the opposite problem: not vastness, but nearness, in the historical novel of the very recent past.

Chapter Five

THE RISE OF THE RECENT HISTORICAL NOVEL

ON MARCH 13, 2020, just two days after the World Health Organization declared the novel coronavirus a pandemic, writer and *New Yorker* staffer Hannah Seidlitz took to social media to express their fears. "What I'm really most afraid of that's incubating in my neighbors' homes," Seidlitz wrote on Twitter, "is the next character-driven, pulitzer shoo-in pandemic novel. it's a race to the finish and I know you're all . . . type-type-typing away. absolute scavengers, all of you. yeah I'm on page 27, so what."[1] And Seidlitz wasn't alone. Four days later, when there were still fewer than ten thousand documented cases in the United States, the writer Sloane Crosley published an essay in the books section of the *New York Times* titled "Someday, We'll Look Back on All of This and Write a Novel." "What happens," Crosley wondered, "when every writer on the planet starts taking notes on the same subject?"[2] What happens, apparently, is precisely what Seidlitz and Crosley expected. Within the first two years of the pandemic, a number of novels set during the crisis were published, including Jodi Picoult's *Wish You Were Here* (2021), Gary Shteyngart's *Our Country Friends* (2021), Isabel Allende's *Violeta* (2022), Ian

McEwan's *Lessons* (2022), and Anne Tyler's *French Braid* (2022), among many others. These novels, Alexandra Alter wrote in a February 2022 analysis of "the Pandemic Plot," "seek to capture the texture of daily life in the Covid era: the corrosive effect of isolation, the tedium and monotony of lockdowns and quarantines, the strain on relationships, the way the virus changed casual interactions and ripped some families apart and brought others together." "Given how much the virus has dominated our lives," Alter concluded, "a flood of pandemic fiction is perhaps inevitable."[3]

This chapter is about these writers' shared sense of expectation and inevitability, about the relation between the front page and the books section, and about the notion that contemporary novelists not only *can* but *will* and *should* transcribe the events of recent history into literary fiction. Two years into an ongoing pandemic, Alter's comments about writers attempting to "capture the texture of daily life *in the Covid era*" betray a historical self-consciousness—the sense that one is living in a period that *we are going to read about in history books one day*—that these pandemic novels share. That's because these novels, and the others discussed in this chapter, are less interested in fictionalizing the present than they are in using fiction to cast the recent past as historical with a capital H. The other chapters in this book examine genres of historical fiction alongside the literary institutions that have helped to canonize them: the World War II novel and the literary prize, for example, or the multigenerational family saga and the middlebrow book club. This chapter considers how the prestige of, and demand for, historical fiction has grown so pronounced that the twenty-four-hour news cycle has been conscripted as a literary institution in its own right.

In *The Antinomies of Realism* (2013), Fredric Jameson acknowledges that "the historical novel has never been so popular nor so abundantly produced as at the present time," but he objects that "what seems to survive at best are a host of names and an endless warehouse of images," "Harlequin 'histories,' in which a romantic tale is played out against this or that costume setting." "What kind of History," he asks, "can the contemporary historical novel then be expected to 'make appear?'"[4] This is an important question, the answer to which reveals not only the status of historical fiction in the contemporary literary market, but also—as that market's chief commodity—the status of the novel writ large. If American fiction's pronounced turn toward the past is in part what defines the novel after postmodernism's grip has slackened, then both the shape of that turn and its historical imagination are of paramount importance to readers of contemporary American literature. With that in mind, this chapter takes up a literary phenomenon centrally invested in the very near-term process of making historical memory, arguing that amid contemporary American fiction's fascination with history a new literary subgenre has taken root: the recent historical novel.

Though it goes without saying that fiction set in the recent historical past has been written long before the turn of the twenty-first century, in the last two decades, an array of novels has coalesced around a set of increasingly common conventions that demand scholarly attention. The genre includes novels that fictionalize:

- the events of 9/11 and its aftermath: Don DeLillo's *Falling Man* (2007), Laila Halaby's *Once in a Promised Land* (2007), Mohsin Hamid's *The Reluctant Fundamentalist* (2007), Porochista Khakpour's *The Last Illusion* (2014), Jarett Kobek's *Atta* (2011), Jay McInerney's *The Good Life* (2006), Claire Messud's *The Emperor's Children* (2006), H. M. Naqvi's *Home Boy* (2009), Thomas Pynchon's *Bleeding Edge* (2013), and Amy Waldman's *The Submission* (2011);
- the 2003–2011 phase of the war in Iraq: Sinan Antoon's *The Corpse Washer* (2013), Ben Fountain's *Billy Lynn's Long Halftime Walk* (2012), Matt Gallagher's *Youngblood* (2016), Phil Klay's

Redeployment (2014), and Kevin Powers's *The Yellow Birds* (2012);
- the 2008 financial crisis: Jade Chang's *The Wangs vs. The World* (2016), Lucy Corin's *Swank Hotel* (2021), John Lanchester's *Capital* (2012), and Imbolo Mbue's *Behold the Dreamers* (2016);
- recent natural disasters: Dimitry Elias Legér's *God Loves Haiti* (2015) and Jesmyn Ward's *Salvage the Bones* (2011);
- international terrorism: Karan Mahajan's *The Association of Small Bombs* (2016) and Rebecca Makkai's *The Great Believers* (2018);
- the Second Sudanese Civil War: Dave Eggers's *What Is the What* (2006);
- the Columbine massacre: Wally Lamb's *The Hour I First Believed* (2008);
- the 1999 WTO protests: Sunil Yapa's *Your Heart Is a Muscle the Size of a Fist* (2016);
- the early career, election, and inauguration of Barack Obama: Chimamanda Ngozi Adichie's *Americanah* (2013), Nawaaz Ahmed's *Radiant Fugitives* (2021), Michael Chabon's *Telegraph Avenue* (2012), and Salman Rushdie's *The Golden House* (2017);
- and the presidency of Donald Trump: Barbara Kingsolver's *Unsheltered* (2018), Jonathan Lethem's *The Feral Detective* (2018), Lauren Oyler's *Fake Accounts* (2021), and Gary Shteyngart's *Lake Success* (2018).[5]

Diverse as this incomplete and ever-growing list is, its works all share a common temporal setting: the very recent past. Though Walter Scott first imagined the historical novel in English as a tale "of the last generation"—defined concisely by *Waverley*'s subtitle, *'Tis Sixty Years Since*—these historical novels all take place less than a dozen years in the past.[6] This means that they are ineligible for the Walter Scott Prize for Historical Fiction, awarded to novels "of exceptional quality" whose "storyline must have taken place at least

60 years ago."[7] Moreover, it means that these historical novels of the very recent past are not counted as such in James F. English's analysis of fictional setting in more than 1,700 novels. English argues that "the field of anglophone fiction has undergone a radical retemporalization" since the 1980s: while popular fiction continues to favor setting novels in the temporal present, literary fiction has turned dramatically—and so far irreversibly—toward the historical past.[8] By counting as "historical" only those works that are "predominantly set more than twenty years prior to publication," however, English significantly undercounts the amount, and variety, of historical fiction that has been produced over the last several decades.[9] From 2000 to 2019, major American literary prizes shortlisted novels that take place within that twenty-year window nearly fifty times, accounting for 29 percent of all historical fiction shortlisted for the Pulitzer Prize, the National Book Award, and the National Book Critics Circle Award.

What delimits the recency of the novels listed here is not some precise quantity (*'Tis Five or Ten—but Not Fifteen—Years Since*), but the particular form of historicity that this narrow gap belies. Despite the pronounced pastness of their settings, these novels are not—and cannot be—"period pieces," as the historical events that structure them have not yet congealed into a coherent and legible period. By contrast, these works occupy a historiographical middle distance between event and period, specific date and stylized decade: after Kent State but before "the Seventies," between Iran-Contra and "Eighties Style."[10] This is what distinguishes the recent historical novel from the historical narratives described by Nicholas Dames: those that, like *Vanity Fair* and *Middlemarch* and *The People vs. O.J. Simpson*, represent "a shift back two, three, or four decades, into the youth of the writers themselves," thriving not only on the "evocation of a vanished era," but also on the tension "between nostalgia . . . and identification, the recognition of how much of that past unhappily persists."[11] Dames's arguments apply far better to Ben Lerner's

The Topeka School (2019)—set in the late 1990s, littered with references to Tupac and Windows 95, and interested in the prehistory of a certain Trumpian white masculinity—than they do his previous two novels, *Leaving the Atocha Station* (2011) and *10:04* (2014).[12] Yet the recent historical novel, devoid of nostalgia not yet developed, shorn of the historical novel's "different haircuts and outfits" and peculiar "quality of light," stands as historical fiction nonetheless, invested as it is in documenting the process by which history is made.[13]

Thus far, however, these novels have been mistaken less often for historical fiction than they have for works of contemporary realism, set in the present alongside "current events." After all, novels take time to write and edit, publish and distribute: a novelist may aim to set her work in the present but find herself pushed into the past by the realities of the publishing industry. Subject to this inevitable lag time, isn't every work of realist fiction relegated to a kind of recent history?[14] Perhaps, but there are few people more attuned to the vicissitudes of the publishing process and the strategies one might use to circumvent them than novelists themselves. This is why so many writers of contemporary realism are loath to include specific dates and names (whether of celebrities, or brands, or songs on the radio) and why so many historical novelists love to: these details place a novel in historical time. Scott himself, in an attempt to distinguish *Waverley* from what he called a "Tale of the Times," wrote that the latter is not so much a historical portrait as "a dashing sketch of the fashionable world, a few anecdotes of private scandal *thinly veiled.*"[15] A novel set in the present, in other words, must always be set in the indefinite present, its details legible enough to be contemporary, "veiled" enough to avoid becoming antiquated prematurely. Scott, on the other hand, is committed to "fixing ... the date of my story Sixty Years before this present," just as these writers are to attaching their own novels to particular dates and events in the recent past.[16] Their recency may set them apart from the historical novel as it is traditionally understood, but it does not disqualify them *tout court* as "historical narratives," defined by Gérard Genette as any narrative "explicitly placed (even by only one date) in a historical past, even a very recent one."[17]

In an attempt to outline the contours of this genre, this chapter draws on three novels all set in the very near past: Ben Lerner's *Leaving the Atocha Station* and *10:04*, and Ruth Ozeki's *A Tale for the Time Being* (2013).[18] In focusing on these three works, I do not contend that they are either the first or the finest of their kind, only that they are particularly representative and self-reflexive examples of this emerging genre. Grounded in catastrophe, mediated by the news, and marked by a particularly ambivalent politics, these novels reveal not only the contradictions at the heart of contemporary historical consciousness but also the crucial oversights in literary criticism's approach to narratives of the past. They have emerged from what Linda Hutcheon called "historiographic metafiction" in 1989, what Jameson called "postmodernist 'nostalgia' art" in 1991, and what Amy Elias called "metahistorical romance" in 2001—yet they are distinct from all three.[19] Recruiting the "world-historical" event of the classical historical novel (as per Lukács) and repurposing the self-conscious mediation of that genre's postmodern transformations, the recent historical novel positions itself in the pivotal space between literary fiction and contemporary journalism.

By fictionalizing the crises of recent history before they become fully historical, the genre represents both an acceleration of the novel's historical imagination and a decelerating double take at the modern news cycle. In this way, the recent historical novel stands as the paradigmatic form of historical fiction in the age of CNN. Amid contemporary journalism's near-constant proliferation of events and American literature's decisive turn toward history, recent historical fiction reasserts the novel's relevance while at the same time profiting from the prestige of historicity. It offers its readers the pleasure of witnessing the events of their lives become the stuff of literature and history. Yet it also threatens—far more than traditional historical fiction—to foreclose possibilities for the future, since that very pleasure is derived from a kind of teleology of the present. Although its climaxes are drawn from the crises that mark the contemporary, its denouements deliver only what was and what is. Nevertheless, the recent historical novel appears as a significant genre of contemporary fiction, not only because of its recent and rapid rise, but also due to its complex relation to the larger phenomena this book documents. In the context of the overwhelming prestige attached to historical fiction, and in particular historical fiction by minoritized writers, the recent historical novel can be understood as a method of further mining the past for fiction and as a means for white writers to elevate their work beyond mere topicality by communing with history. The genre exemplifies both the limits of historical fiction as a contemporary literary mode, and the extent to which that mode has reshaped the American literary field.

CATASTROPHE AS PUNCTUATION

Jameson has criticized contemporary historical fiction for conjuring the past by way of "stylistic connotation . . . a new connotation of 'pastness' and pseudohistorical depth, in which the history of aesthetic styles displaces 'real' history." Not the historical moment, then, but its aesthetic trappings; not the 1950s, but "1950s-ness."[20] The recent historical novel, however, precisely because of its recency, cannot rely on a convenient aesthetic warehouse of retro fashions, antiquated technologies, and musical golden oldies. Instead, it declares its pastness by attaching itself to particular historical events. While it is possible to describe a work of historical fiction as taking place in some amorphous "Sixties," the recent historical novel's dependence on the event will always fix it precisely on this or that day, in this or that year. It is Ben Lerner's narration of the Madrid train bombings that sets *Leaving the Atocha Station*—his debut novel about a young American poet on a fellowship in Spain—firmly in the months leading up to, and just after, March 2004. Similarly, Lerner's novel *10:04*—about another young writer, in this case trying to make good on an outlandish second-book advance—would likely be mistaken for a narrative set in the present were it not for the twin hurricanes, Irene and Sandy, that bookend the novel, setting it squarely between 2011 and 2012. The same can be said about Ruth Ozeki's *A Tale for the Time Being*, divided as it is into alternating chapters between the diary of a Japanese teenager named Naoko and a novelist named Ruth who finds Naoko's diary on a beach in western Canada, believing it to have washed up after the 2011 Tōhoku earthquake and tsunami.

Early on in *10:04*, Lerner's narrator describes the feel of New York City as it prepares for the fast-approaching Hurricane Irene, writing that it was "something like the feel of a childhood snow day . . . when the snow seemed like a technology for defeating time" (20). For the reader, however, something like the opposite effect occurs. The storm's nonfictional, precisely datable, eventness cements rather than "defeats" historical time in the novel. Had Lerner rendered the hurricane as a thinly veiled *fictional version* of Irene, the novel might be read as set in a kind of amorphous present, *in the time of superstorms*. By naming the storm and thus attaching the novel to it, *10:04* is cast into a defined historical past, albeit a very recent one. This commitment to the nonfictional event is at the heart of Lerner's work, and he has made that commitment explicit in interviews, declaring that fiction should not be understood as "an escape from reality but . . . a technology for making contact with reality."[21] The same is true for Ozeki, who, in an interview with the *New York Times*, explained that she had been working on *A Tale for the Time Being* since 2006, but when "the earthquake and tsunami hit" in 2011, "I realized that the book I had just written was irrelevant. . . . I just threw away half [of it]."[22] What she added in its place was the tsunami itself.

In this way, the hybrid genre of recent historical fiction benefits from an exchange of cultural capital between its constituent parts. In the context of "the pervasive recasting of [the literary field] around the past," the work gains prestige from being historical just as it gains relevance from being recent.[23] Novelists like Lerner and Ozeki push toward the boundary between fiction and the "real" by way of the collision between fictional storylines and nonfictional events. This move furnishes the novels with a certain authenticity, despite the fact that it threatens their very fictionality.[24] Whereas more historically distant and more thoroughly historicized events such as World War II seem today, because of their incessant fictionalization, more like the stuff of fiction, the events of recent history work, perhaps ironically, to wrest a novel out of the fictional world and into reality. Early on in *10:04*, just after the episode depicting Hurricane Irene, Lerner reprints the iconic Paul Klee image from Walter Benjamin's "Theses on the Philosophy of History" with the caption: "The storm irresistibly propels him into the future to which his back is turned" (25). As the pun makes all too clear, it is Lerner's own fictionalization of Hurricane Irene that propels his novel into contact with history as well as philosophies like Benjamin's. Moreover, just as the work is elevated by its contact with capital-H history, the events narrated within gain currency *as history* by virtue of their being featured in a historical novel: a phenomenon that reveals the genre's agency not only to represent, but also to amend the historical record in fiction. Contemporary fiction functions as both a currency by which historicity is measured and the process through which it accrues.

As these examples also make clear, the events that define recent historical fiction are almost always catastrophic: natural disasters, terrorist attacks, political assassinations, and violent revolutions.[25] This is not to suggest, as Jean-Luc Nancy has, that the nature of catastrophe has fundamentally changed in recent history, but rather to argue that fictionalizations of that recent history—as opposed to fictionalizations of more distant periods—rely on catastrophe as their chief convention.[26] Just as the writer of a "period piece" or "costume drama" makes her name with renderings of historically accurate dialogue or garb, the novelist of recent history hits her stride in rich descriptions of destruction and emergency. The narrator of *Leaving the Atocha Station* wanders through the streets of Madrid for about a hundred pages "until I arrived at what they call a scene of mayhem" (117). Moreover, and as the etymology of the term *catastrophe* suggests, these disasters often represent the structural climax of the novels in which they appear. Here the resemblance to Lukács's historical novel and its plotting of the "world-historical" event or "collision" is most recognizable.[27] For Lukács, it is the task of the historical novelist to create "a plot in which these significant situations become necessary, organic parts of a much broader and richer total action . . . a plot which is so contrived that its own inner logic impels it towards such situations because they provide its real fulfillment."[28] The genre of recent historical fiction reimagines history as something akin to a disaster film, wherein both the structure of narrative and its ultimate meaning are drawn from catastrophe. Like a disaster film, the novel spends its first two-thirds erecting what Lukács would call "a broad picture of the times"—the architecture of the tower, the decks of the *Titanic*—before introducing a cataclysmic threat to that structure, precisely "when the action is nearing its climax"—inferno, iceberg.[29] Within this structure, the world-historical crisis or catastrophe represents both the impetus to write, and the traumatic event the novelist must write her way through.

At one point in *10:04*, Lerner's narrator, a thinly fictionalized version of Lerner himself,[30] gives a lecture about how he became a writer: "In the story I've been telling myself lately, I became a poet, or became interested in becoming a poet, on January twenty-eighth, 1986. . . . Like most Americans who were alive at that time, I have a clear memory of watching the space shuttle *Challenger* disintegrate seventy-three seconds into flight" (110). Yet for the protagonist (as well as for Lerner, who confirms this anecdote in interviews), it is not the disaster itself that inspired him to write, but its powerful transformation into language. For him the decisive moment was not the explosion of the *Challenger* but Ronald Reagan's presidential address, written by speechwriter Peggy Noonan, later that evening:

> The meaning of the words was nothing compared to that first experience of poetic measure—how I felt simultaneously comforted and stirred by the rhythm and knew that all across America those rhythms were working in millions of other bodies too. Let me allow the preposterousness of what I'm saying to sink in: I think I became a poet because of Ronald Reagan and Peggy Noonan. The way they used poetic language to integrate a terrible event and its image back into a framework of meaning. (112)

The call to write and the character of that writing is marked by a shared experience of disaster. If we accept Lukács's claim that "what matters" in a historical novel "is that we should reexperience the social and human motives which led men to think, feel and act just as they did in historical reality," then the recent historical novel suggests that recent history is a period defined by insistent states of emergency.[31] World-historical catastrophe punctuates both narrative time and historical time: a particularly useful function in an age of forever wars and "slow death" threats like climate change.[32] Without it, the protagonist would continue merely living, the story merely continuing, events merely proliferating without any definitive rupture to structure the flow. It is the crises in the second half of the terms "post-9/11," "post-Katrina," "post-Fukushima," and "post-Covid" that produce the *post*-ness of the first half. Cataclysm is what allows the novelist, critic, historian, and reader to mark the passage of historical time. To borrow from Wallace Stevens, catastrophes in the recent historical novel have functioned just as the lights in the harbor do in "The Idea of Order at Key West": they have "Mastered the night and portioned out the sea, / Fixing emblazoned zones and fiery poles, / Arranging, deepening, enchanting night."[33]

NEWS MEMORY AND "THE FIRST ROUGH DRAFT OF HISTORY"

In the bildungsroman, the key events of a character's youth are often colored by a narrator's mature retrospection. In the detective novel, the central crime is almost always narrated in the criminal's vernacular of confession or the investigator's vernacular of detection. Likewise, in recent historical fiction, the news and its narratives mediate the novel's most significant moments.[34] In all of the texts under discussion in this chapter, narration of the central historical event is synonymous and simultaneous with narration of its media coverage. Ozeki's novel includes several lengthy passages describing the destruction in Japan, narrated not through the character of Naoko, who lives there and is perhaps present at the disaster, but the character of Ruth, who watches from her computer screen thousands of miles away: "Every few hours, another horrifying piece of footage would break, and she would play it over and over, studying the wave as it surged over the tops of the seawalls, carrying ships down city streets, picking up cars and trucks and depositing them on the roofs of buildings" (112–13). As Hurricane Irene bears down on New York, Lerner writes that "from a million media, most of them handheld, awareness of the storm seeped into the city, entering the architecture and . . . inflecting traffic patterns. . . . The city was becoming one organism, constituting itself in relation to a threat viewable from space" (17). Lerner's style in this passage is particularly reminiscent of Don DeLillo's *White Noise* (1985) and its fascination with mediations of disaster and Baudrillardian simulacra—the latter a favorite preoccupation of postmodern fiction, and postmodern historical fiction in particular.[35]

Yet while postmodern histories approach mediation most often with a sense of curiosity, sublimity, or playfulness, contemporary novelists like Ozeki and Lerner engage it with what I have been calling *new historical sincerity*. As Adam Kelly has described it, the "New

Sincerity" in literature is both a rejection and an extension of postmodern styles—a literary teenager that, for all its rebellion, cannot fully escape the family resemblance.[36] As in the work of novelists described in previous chapters, writers of recent historical fiction use many of the same techniques of defamiliarization that mark the postmodern historical novel—from Lerner's metanarratives and embedded photography, to Ozeki's dueling narrators and experimental typography—in order to pursue a longing for the past with renewed sincerity, effectively *refamiliarizing* the reader with recent history. For Lerner and Ozeki, however, a sincere belief in the novel's capacity to mediate history is not necessarily a positive thing. Whereas the postmodern historical novel used fiction to trouble the concept of mediation, the recent historical novel seems altogether troubled by it.

What Lerner's and Ozeki's novels are narrating in passages like these is the contemporary phenomenon—not of news *mediating* experience—but of news *constituting* experience entirely.[37] Amid twenty-four-hour news and handheld computing, the media coverage of a historical event *is* its lived experience for the vast majority of people on the planet.[38] True to their postmodern forebears, these novels include a host of instances in which media representation distorts historical memory or supplants it entirely. Yet what was once cause for DeLillo's bemusement and Pynchon's jest now occasions sincere dismay. After the bombs go off in Madrid, Lerner's narrator writes: "I considered walking back to Atocha, but instead I opened *El País* in another window and the *Guardian* in a third. I sat smoking and refreshing the home pages and watching the numbers change. I could feel the newspaper accounts modifying or replacing my memory of what I'd seen; was there a word for that feeling?" (119).

Similarly troubled, Ozeki's narrator laments how coverage all too quickly moves on from Fukushima to an uprising in Libya and a tornado in Missouri: "What is the half-life of information? Does its rate of decay correlate with the medium that conveys it? . . . Does [it] correlate with the decay of our attention? Is the Internet a kind of temporal gyre, sucking up stories, like geodrift, into its orbit? What is its gyre memory? How do we measure the half-life of its drift . . . the garbage patch of history and time?" (113–14). The allusion to Yeats's "The Second Coming" in this passage works to underline Ozeki's sense that contemporary "centers" of attention, taken up and discarded ambivalently by news media, "cannot hold." Moreover, the succession of questions in both texts points to a deep uncertainty about the limits of historical experience in the context of contemporary media saturation. In this sense, mediation smacks less of simulacrum than of a particularly contemporary form of realism.

But what, then, distinguishes "recent history" from "news" in these novels? In the early 1940s, the journalist Alan Barth wrote in the *New Republic* that the news is "the first rough draft of history"—an iconic phrase, printed only a few years after Ezra Pound's own iconic claim that "Literature is news that stays news."[39] Recent historical fiction falls somewhere between news and literature: on the one hand, it attempts to revise journalism's "rough draft" and refocus its increasingly fleeting attention on the events of the recent past; on the other, it is deeply uncertain about the historical significance of those very events in a way that the likes of Walter Scott never had to be. Seen in this light, the recent historical novel appears less like the canonical historical novel than it does the New Journalism or, perhaps less obviously, the popular twentieth-century publishing phenomenon of "Instant Books."[40] Described as the perfect "marriage of the worlds of journalism and mass marketing," "Instant Books" were wildly popular paperback accounts of recent historical events that were rushed to press immediately after the events themselves. Beginning in the 1940s and continuing into the 1970s, publishers like Pocket Books and Bantam released titles on the death of Franklin Roosevelt, the bombing of Hiroshima, and the assassination of John F. Kennedy, weeks—and in some cases, only days—after the events they depicted.[41] Not only did these books sell tremendously—in the order of hundreds of thousands of copies in their first weeks on sale—they also helped to shape the public memory of the events they narrated. At the height of their popularity, Bantam alone produced up to three such "Instant Books" (or "Extras," as they called them) each year, "as events warranted."[42] Though these books were almost exclusively nonfiction and not novels, the "Instant Book" phenomenon provides a kind of precedent for the recent historical novel and the middle space between journalism and book publishing that it occupies.

Just as the "Instant Book" turned to the events of newspapers—which Benedict Anderson famously called "one-day best-sellers"—to create actual bestsellers, the recent historical novel narrates its central events only after they have been narrated by multimedia news platforms like CNN.[43] Although it seems difficult to imagine a recent historical novel narrating a catastrophe that *did not* originally enter the culture via cable or live-streamed news, the genre's temporal logic is something like the reverse of news media's commitment to the "live."[44] Rather than artificially maintaining a sense of ongoing "presence" or topicality of the given crisis, these novels work to shore up the distance between the event and its narration: its pastness, its historicity. To this end, Lerner and Ozeki draw on what we might think of as the *news memory* of their readers in an effort to combat the fragile and amnesiac historical memory that the news itself creates. As each novel approaches its climactic event, its author creates a particular kind of dramatic irony, using significant dates (March 2004) and place names (Atocha Station) last encountered while scrolling through the morning news or watching *PBS NewsHour* before dinner. When Lerner's narrator visits Madrid's Atocha metro station for the first time in the novel, only thirty pages before the bombing, the reader experiences an uncanny sense of déjà vu: the peculiar mingling of half-remembered news coverage with the vague sense of foreboding that its prolepsis somewhat ironically occasions (89). *Where do I know that name from? What happened on that date? Is this where it happened?* In moments like these, the reader of the recent historical novel is forced to confront the gaps in her own historical memory, reproduced here in the form of a dramatic irony that is available only to those who remember the dates and details. The news and the particular type of historical memory that it creates mediate not only the protagonist's encounter with catastrophe and the form of the novel, but the reader's experience of the novel as well.

In her essay on the "Pandemic Plot," Alter writes that the seemingly unavoidable "flood of pandemic fiction" is also a "necessary" one: "unlike the fire hose of news coverage about Covid, which can leave readers feeling numb and overwhelmed, fiction can provide a way to process the emotional upheaval of the past two years."[45] Alter's particularly liquid diction is worth parsing. Incessant news coverage, pouring in from multiple channels—phone, laptop, radio, television—is ultimately overwhelming, and it therefore needs to be "processed" by other cultural forms. The sheer volume pumped out by contemporary news platforms can, Alter suggests, be countered to some extent by the novel's comparative slowness and deliberation. Simply put, these things take longer to read (and to write) and, as such, they provide a sustained experience of focused attention. Funneling the deluge of the news into literary fiction, Alter argues, is not only salutary but "necessary." The result of this process, however, is a "flood." The proliferation of historical events that the news creates is matched by a similar proliferation of recent historical fiction. In this way, the institutions of contemporary news not only motivate the composition and canonization of historical fiction, they also shape its form.

THE PAST PERFECT TENSE

Elias argues that, while the historical romance "signals a longing for the past—not a longing for a past simpler time or a past simpler culture, but for *the past itself* as a situating, grounding foundation for knowledge and truth," writers of postmodern historical fiction "seem not to be able to take this longing seriously or even to acknowledge it without irony."⁴⁶ By contrast, the recent historical novel works, with a renewed historical sincerity, to repurpose the aesthetics of postmodern historical fiction for wholly unironic ends. As the novelist-narrator of Lerner's *10:04* tells his agent in the opening scene, his goal for his next project is to "work [his] way from irony to sincerity in the sinking city, a would-be Whitman of the vulnerable grid" (4). The longing for a stable sense of the past as a "situating, grounding foundation for knowledge" is no longer the subject of parody, but an object of renewed desire.

Yet this presents a problem for the would-be novelist of recent history, since recent history is by definition partly unwritten, mostly unfinished, and entirely unstable. One is reminded of the German novelist Lion Feuchtwanger's quip that "in portraying contemporary circumstances I am discomforted by a lack of perspective; it is a scent which evaporates because you cannot close the bottle."⁴⁷ Maurice Halbwachs makes a similar, and similarly playful, remark in *The Collective Memory*, joking about "the character in the farce who exclaims, 'Today the Hundred Years War begins!'"⁴⁸ The point in both cases is clear: a certain historical distance is required to properly narrate the events of the past. Rather than wait patiently for the requisite—and indeed arbitrary—amount of historical distance, however, the recent historical novel produces it internally by way of structural juxtaposition.

A Tale for the Time Being, *10:04*, and *Leaving the Atocha Station* all fictionalize periods of recent history, but each novel also situates that recent history in the context of a relatively more distant historical period or event. This functions as a kind of structural version of the grammatical past perfect tense, a novelistic syntax that links the events of the near past to historical moments that predate them. For as much as Lerner points up the events of 2004 that establish the temporal setting of *Leaving the Atocha Station*—the first throes of the so-called War on Terror, the 11-M Bombings—he also works hard throughout the novel to point back to a wider historical context, focusing particularly on the reign of Francisco Franco. At one point, Lerner's poet-narrator, Adam, is embarrassed by an introduction at a reading that casts his work as "intensely political and reminiscent of a Spanish poet I'd never heard of, only instead of protesting Franco, it took on the United States of Bush" (36). Despite Adam's discomfort with the comparison, Lerner spreads such moments of historical juxtaposition throughout *Atocha*. Likewise in *10:04*, Lerner's first descriptions of Hurricane Irene come immediately after a trill of reflections on historical tragedies including the *Challenger* disaster and the September 11th attacks (11–17). One page in particular features a photograph of Christa McAuliffe, followed by an excerpt from Ronald Reagan's speech on the *Challenger* explosion, followed immediately by a sentence—"An unusually large cyclonic system with a warm core was approaching New York"—announcing the onset of Hurricane Irene (16). This sequence of juxtapositions makes an argument about the history to which it points: despite the recency of the latest event, it is no less historical than the others that precede it.

In *A Tale for the Time Being*, Ozeki takes this principle of structural past-perfectness still further. Descriptions of the Fukushima disaster and its aftereffects are interwoven throughout the novel with meditations on 9/11 and World War II. Naoko writes at one point that she needs "to back up a little, to September 11, in order to really explain this properly." This is because "September 11 is like a sharp knife slicing through time. It changed everything" (265). As with Lerner's allusions to 9/11, Ozeki's suggestion that the story of recent history would not be complete or "proper" without the "sharp knife" of earlier events cuts both ways. It poses the question of whether the 2011 Japanese tsunami "slices through time" as deeply as the 2001 attacks on the United States. But the novel seems to answer that question, by way of its structure, in the affirmative. As the novel progresses, Ozeki's historical juxtapositions travel further into the past and further into the territory of canonized history. As Naoko learns about "Haruki #1," her great-uncle, who died while serving as a kamikaze pilot in World War II, excerpts from Haruki's diary become a recurring feature. In the other half of the novel, narrated by the novelist Ruth, the connection between more recent and more distant periods is made even more explicit. Commenting on the fact that Ruth's family is Japanese and her husband Oliver's family is German, she posits that "their marriage was like this, an axial alliance—her people interned, his firebombed in Stuttgart—a small accidental consequence of a war fought before either of them was born. 'We're by-products of the mid-twentieth century,' Oliver said. 'Who isn't?'" replies Ruth (32).

Just as the play-within-a-play works to shore up, by comparison, the reality of the drama in which it figures, the event-before-the-event of the recent historical novel bolsters the historicity of its own central action. By equating structurally the events it looks back to and the events it narrates at its close, the novel of recent history insists on a kind of historical equivalency. But, as with any metatheatrical device, the balance of the recent historical novel's past-perfect structure is precarious and can easily tip from shoring up the novel's construction of the past into threatening it entirely. Rebecca Makkai's *The Great Believers*, for example, is structured according to precisely this type of historical comparison. In alternating chapters, Makkai's novel juxtaposes the 1985–1992 period of the AIDS crisis in Chicago with the 2015 terrorist attacks in Paris. In the 1980s sections of the novel, Makkai is explicitly interested in which disasters are given wide attention and which are overlooked. Like *10:04*, *The Great Believers* narrates the news-mediated revelation of the *Challenger* explosion, only this time to make the point that while Reagan "weeps with the nation," canceling his State of the Union address in light of a "handful of dead astronauts," he is "too busy" to "address the disaster" of "thirteen thousand dead gay men."[49] While the comparison here underscores the historical significance of the AIDS crisis, it also underscores (albeit unintentionally) how much more significant that crisis is than the recent historical events with which Makkai closes the novel. As the sound of sirens—"far too many, for far too long"—moves the protagonist of the 2015 sections "to the living room to watch the news," she tries to reimagine the attacks happening across the city as if she were "hearing about something on the far side of the world."[50] Yet this imaginative distancing only emphasizes what the reader of the novel already intuits: the juxtaposition of recent history with further-back periods can foreclose feelings of equivalence just as often as it produces them.

THE AMBIVALENCE OF HERE AND NOW

"It is no accident," Lukács writes, "that this new type of novel"—that is, the classical historical novel—"arose in England."[51] According to Lukács, the literary aesthetics and the national politics of eighteenth-century England colluded to produce it. For Benedict Anderson, writing twenty years later, it is the novel more generally that stands as an instrument and indicator of national consciousness. The feeling of simultaneity, the temporal "meanwhile" it creates, provides, as does the newspaper, "the technical means for 're-presenting' the *kind* of imagined community that is the nation."[52] Fredric Jameson, writing thirty years after Anderson, argues that the historical novel, in one sense, "confirms our obscure suspicion . . . that all great historical novelists must in one way or another harbor conservative sympathies, and have a deep ontological investment in the old ways of life in the process of being destroyed by the new order." After all, the genre "has so often been marshaled to serve political ends, of which nationalism is only the most obvious."[53] More than a half-century of criticism points to the unmistakable nationalism of the historical novel, a claim that seems at odds with much of the historical fiction described in this book. Given that, it is worth considering the attitude of the recent historical novel toward the concept of the nation.

Anderson argues in *Imagined Communities* that both the novel and the newspaper furnish "the presentation of simultaneity . . . a complex gloss upon the word 'meanwhile'" that is essential to the construction of national consciousness.[54] Like the assumed simultaneity of the novel's various subplots, the "inclusion and juxtaposition" of various news stories in the daily paper "implies the refraction of even 'world events' into a specific imagined [community] of vernacular readers"—namely, the nation.[55] The recent historical novel, positioned somewhere between novel and newspaper, seems as if it should double down on Anderson's claim, providing an *especially imaginative* example of thinking the nation. Yet Lerner and Ozeki each produce phenomena of simultaneity in their novels that, contra Anderson, actually undermine the status of the nation, crafting intranational and transnational "meanwhiles" that subvert rather than strengthen that particular imagined community.

In the context of contemporary news platforms and their global reach, the events of recent history are—to borrow from Rebecca L. Walkowitz—"born translated."[56] While Anderson suggests that the logic of the newspaper's juxtapositions is a logic of national interest, the structural logic of Ozeki's *A Tale for the Time Being* is precisely extranational. Not only does Ruth find out almost instantaneously about the tsunami and reactor meltdown threatening Japan, but the juxtaposition of Ruth's narrative with the novel's other narrator, Naoko, also creates a discursive "meanwhile" between Canada (where Ruth is), Japan (where Naoko is), and the United States (where part of the novel takes place, where it was partly written and first published, and where Ozeki claims dual citizenship with Canada). Throughout *Leaving the Atocha Station*, Lerner's narrator wanders Madrid, reads *The New York Times* online, and watches cable news coverage of "contractors firing on Iraqi civilians" (103). Therefore, it comes as little surprise that the bombings at Atocha station are narrated in a similarly transnational assemblage of perspectives: "Surprised at how much time had passed, I opened a browser, called up the *New York Times*, and clicked on the giant headline. The article described the helicopters I could hear above me" (118). Though I do not mean to suggest that Adam's nationality—nor Lerner's or Ozeki's, for that matter—has somehow been dissolved by contemporary news, it is clear that journalism's national interest, described by Anderson, has been supplanted by something far more global, a shift that these novels dramatize in both form and content.

Their media circulation notwithstanding, the central events of these novels are themselves "born translated" as a result of their particularly transnational vernacular of catastrophe. A bomb in a metro station requires little translation to reverberate far beyond national borders. An attack in Madrid, or Paris, or some other capital or its suburb, is often read as an "attack on the West," rather than a strictly national affair. In this way, the lexicon of contemporary terrorism stands as a revision of the adage long embraced by environmentalists and other activists: *act locally, stream globally*. Though obviously less intentional, climate change's own vocabulary of disaster—drought, flood, tsunami, cyclone—functions similarly as a *lingua franca* of the contemporary historical event. Events like the earthquake and tsunami in *A Tale for the Time Being* are not just legible internationally, they also remind us that an imagined community can do little to insulate one from a global food shortage or nuclear contamination. Naoko's diary washes ashore a continent away; one wonders what else is radiating from nation to nation.

Rather than subvert this sense of imagined simultaneity by exceeding national borders, Lerner's *10:04* creates alternative "meanwhiles" from within. In his extended narration of Hurricane Sandy, Lerner points up what Hartmut Rosa would call contemporary "desynchronization" and what historian Harry Harootunian has termed "noncontemporaneous contemporaneity": the coexistence of multiple temporalities—multiple "contemporaries"—in the same contemporaneous historical moment.⁵⁷ Lerner writes:

> We never lost power. Another historical storm had failed to arrive, as though we lived outside of history or were falling out of time. Except it *had arrived, just not for us*. Subway and traffic tunnels in lower Manhattan had filled with water. . . . Power and water were knocked out below Thirty-ninth Street and in Red Hook, Coney Island, the Rockaways, much of Staten Island. Hospitals were being evacuated after backup generators failed; newborn babies and patients recovering from heart surgery were carried gingerly down flights of stairs and placed in ambulances that rushed them uptown, where the storm had never happened. Houses up and down the coast had been obliterated, flooded, soon a neighborhood in Queens would burn. Emergency workers were fishing out the bodies of those who had drowned during the surge; who knew how many of the homeless had perished? (230–31, emphasis added)

Like Ozeki's *A Tale for the Time Being*, Lerner's description of catastrophe stresses a complex simultaneity that juxtaposes distance and alienation from the effects of disaster with narrative closeness and emphasized copresence. As the narrator of *10:04* walks through New York in the aftermath of the storm, he remarks that "Trying to remember the bustling uptown neighborhoods we'd left an hour or two ago . . . was like trying to recall a different epoch" (235). "Brooklyn was illuminated across the river," he continues, "sparkling in a different era" (238). Even the cover of the novel—an aerial photograph of New York after Hurricane Sandy that contrasts such "sparkling" districts with their darker neighbors—posits a sense of simultaneity that disaggregates national consciousness. Though the three novels under consideration here can all be considered, in one sense, American, the recent historical novel is by no means a strictly American phenomenon.⁵⁸ In fact, quite the opposite: through their complex intranational and transnational focalization of catastrophes that are themselves "born translated," writers like Lerner and Ozeki use recent history as a means of questioning the very category of the nation in contemporary historical consciousness.

This ambivalence on the part of the recent historical novel with regard to the nation is matched by a commensurate ambivalence about the genre's politics of historical representation. If, as Jameson suggests, the historical novel must always "harbor conservative sympathies," what are the politics of fictionalizing recent history? As Rosa helpfully reminds us, "the very labels 'progressive' vs. 'conservative'" manifest "a temporal index" whereby progressive politics seeks to accelerate the "historical movement" of progress, and conservative politics stand as "'reactionary' in opposing the forces of change and acceleration."[59] The left looking to the future, the right to the past: one need only consider Barack Obama's 2012 campaign slogan ("Forward") alongside Donald Trump's in 2016 ("Make America Great Again"). In the contemporary context of "social acceleration," however, Rosa argues that "progressives" ironically "tend to sympathize with the advocates of deceleration (stressing locality, political control of the economy, democratic negotiation, environmental protection, etc.), whereas 'conservatives' have become strong defenders of the need for further acceleration (embracing new technologies, rapid markets, and fast administrative decision-making)."[60] As I have already argued, the recent historical novel's second pass at journalism's "rough draft" of history does indeed seem to be an effort toward deceleration, combating the acceleration of historical event-making brought on by the modern news media. At the same time, one could easily read the genre's speedy historicism as a symptom of, rather than a treatment for, that very phenomenon. Rosa claims that in an "acceleration society," the "*intra-* rather than *inter*-generational" scale of social change is "mirrored" in a language of contingency and "temporary markers": "People speak of *working* (for the time being) *as a baker* rather than *being a baker . . . going to the Methodist Church* rather than *being a*

Methodist, voting Republican rather than *being a Republican*, and so on."⁶¹ Likewise, Lerner's titles (*Leaving the Atocha Station*, the minutely defined *10:04*), and Ozeki's (*A Tale For the Time Being*) present a similar discourse of contingency.

After these novels narrate the events of recent history, they end by effectively delivering their protagonists, as well as their readers, back to the present. With the recent past now marked through writing as a bounded and closed period of history, the political present seems as open as Feuchtwanger's metaphorical bottle of perfume. Whereas the reader of the classical historical novel encountered war, revolution, and vast change as a kind of "prehistory of the present," the reader of the recent historical novel is left to evaluate not only the transformative power (or lack thereof) of recent events, but also her own political power (or lack thereof) to make change in the present.⁶² Take, as just one example, the sequence in *10:04* wherein Lerner's narrator opens his home to an Occupy Wall Street protester, offering a hot shower and a home-cooked meal to the man living in a tent in Zuccotti Park (44–49). Though intermittent protests continued for years after Occupy's original protest in 2011, by 2014, when Lerner's novel was first published, the main action of the Zuccotti Park demonstration had already ended. Lerner's reader is therefore forced to confront the question of the extent to which the recent historical events alluded to in his novel can really be said to be a kind of prehistory of the present. What, in other words, did this event actually change? Everything? Anything? In *Leaving the Atocha Station*, Lerner dramatizes this very question in the scene in which Adam participates in a panel on "Literature Now"— that is, literature in the wake of the 11-M bombings—almost immediately after the bombings themselves (161–75). The scene's skepticism with regard to the power of "the event," combined with the novel's own sincerity in inscribing and institutionalizing that power, stands as a perfect crystallization of this very ambivalence.

The recent historical novel therefore gives the lie to Lukács's claim that though "the present is obscure, the past reveals clear outlines."⁶³

THE RISE OF THE RECENT HISTORICAL NOVEL

Whereas the central "collisions" of the traditional historical novel—and the past-perfect events of the recent historical novel—are significant, transformative, and historically canonical, the recent events at the heart of this genre are marked by ambivalence. Despite the recent historical novel's seemingly progressive intentions, its very recency does not allow—or cannot produce—any broader narratives about history. Its reader cannot yet know whether this or that was the decisive moment of change, or simply a historical red herring. As one character in *The Great Believers* puts it, "I hate that we have to live in the middle of history."[64] Another question the genre poses is whether the reappearance in fiction of a CNN-style "multiday story" impresses the significance of this or that particular historical event, or whether it belies that event's very *insignificance*, plucked as it is from a larger series of stories.[65] Moreover, by stressing the narrative conclusion of the recent past, writers like Lerner and Ozeki inadvertently emphasize the political and historical uncertainty of the near future. (How will climate change *end*?[66]) Though this may, in fact, be part of the authors' project, it also lays bare the extent to which these contemporary writers can or cannot motivate political change. On the one hand, the recent historical novelist works to "open" the present and future by revealing more clearly the recent past; on the other, she seems able only to "process" or "retell," but never to intervene—always a step behind catastrophe, ever ready with her pen.

This ambivalence is only further compounded by the particular forms of narrative satisfaction that the genre creates. Part of the pleasure of recent historical fiction comes from something akin to posttraumatic exposure therapy, wherein the reader can once again experience a world-historical catastrophe, only this time without the surprise of its occurrence and the uncertainty of its unfolding. This pleasure is made possible by the genre's deployment of historical irony as dramatic irony. As readers, we know in advance the boundaries of Hurricane Sandy's destruction and that it will not ultimately destroy New York. We know that the people having breakfast at

Windows on the World are doomed, and that the raid on the compound in Abbottabad will result in Osama Bin Laden's death. The rest of the pleasure of the recent historical comes, somewhat ironically, when the catastrophic event actually occurs: the storm making landfall, the bombs going off, the planes hitting the towers, but crucially *on cue, as we knew they would*, confirming our historical knowledge and establishing a fleeting moment of historical predictability. Rick Altman describes the satisfaction of genre as a temporary escape from cultural norms followed by a pleasurable return: "The greater the wrong, the greater the pleasure taken in righting it. The greater the chaos, the greater the pleasure of restoring order."[67] In this case, however, the pleasure of order comes from the predictable chaos of historical catastrophe. The genre offers its readers a far less revolutionary, far more conservative reward than its authors might care to admit. Catharsis comes when things turn out *just as they should*; which is to say, *just as they did*; which is to say, *just as they are now*.

THE WHITENESS OF THE POST-X NOVEL

The recent historical novel affords its readers not only the narrative satisfaction of historical telos, but also the particularly contemporary pleasure of self-recognition. Unlike the traditional historical novel, which begs the question of who one *might have been* or what one *might have done* in a particular historical moment, this genre asks its readers only: *where were you?* Novelists like Lerner and Ozeki are invested in a kind of generational self-documentation—the historical equivalent of their own autofiction—that gratifies by way of the pleasant surprise that the reader's memories of recent events are now the stuff of history and, what is more, literary history. While neither this collision of personal and historical memory, nor its recounting, is particularly new, the acceleration of this process of identification seems to be. Just as twenty-four-hour news assures viewers that there is

THE RISE OF THE RECENT HISTORICAL NOVEL

always an event happening somewhere, the recent historical novel promises yet another event to remember, and to remember oneself through. The sublime experience of seeing one's life become history, however, becomes itself almost parodic in a period of ever-proliferating markers and memories. *Where were you when JFK was shot?* or *Where were you when the Wall came down?* becomes *Where were you when the levees broke, when Lehman folded,* or *when the first lockdown began?* At the same time, the reader is also invited to imagine recent history, qua history, being looked back upon from the future. The genre represents another result of what Mark Currie has argued is an "enhanced ... faculty [for] the anticipation of retrospection," a phenomenon brought on by "an enormous technological apparatus of archiving machines" through which "the contemporary world increasingly experiences the present, both personally and collectively, as the object of a future memory."[68]

Yet this imagined future audience provokes the question of how exactly these books will age—of how, that is, recent historical novels like Lerner's and Ozeki's will be read when the history they retell is no longer recent. If the genre itself is to a certain extent historically specific, one wonders to what extent the phenomenology of reading described here is as well. On the one hand, if the historical events at the core of these novels are regarded as pivotal in another decade—or regarded at all in two or three—it may be in part because of the historiographical work done by these novels and others inspired by them. As the last half-century of historical fiction teaches us, historical interest in a given period or event tends to accrete. (Take, as just one example of this, chapter 2's discussion of the historical fiction of World War II.) While fiction's power to resuscitate and reclaim lost histories is often commented upon, its ability to preserve and promote certain histories is equally significant.

On the other hand, if these novels are successful in shoring up the historical significance of the events they narrate, they run the risk of being subsumed by them. Rather than a novel of recent history, *A Tale for the Time Being* would become just another "Fukushima novel," *10:04* another novel of 2010s climate change. In this way, the wider lens of historicism's historical distance ironically collapses the distance between event and retelling that the recent historical novel both requires and implies. Just as these works are misread now as being set in the amorphous present ("contemporary fiction about current events"), they may be misread in the future as more about the "when" they describe than when and how they describe it. To some extent, this is already the case with Lerner's *Leaving the Atocha Station*, a novel that, within a decade of its publication, appeared to have less to do with "recent history" than with "the post-9/11 War on Terror." It is not hard to imagine Lerner's novel on the syllabus of some university course with that very title, but it is also easy to see how that association stands to erase the inherent gradation of that post-ness and the multiple periods therein. Historical distance, it seems, may obscure more than it reveals in the case of the recent historical novel, a literary genre whose recency is fundamental to its production as well as its reception.

This points up a certain deictic quality—Recent *to whom*? Recently *from when*?—at the heart of both the genre and "the contemporary" itself. Theodore Martin, among others, has noted the "historically imprecise and temporally indeterminate" quality of the contemporary as a literary period that "doesn't so much delimit history as drift across it."[69] Because of this, Martin argues, "the contemporary has its problems": "it is a periodizing term that doesn't exactly periodize; a measure of history that fails to designate a specific literary or historical period."[70] For all it shares with the contemporary, the recent historical novel may be as much a manifestation of those problems as a possible way of addressing them. The genre's preoccupation with the catastrophes of recent history resembles literary criticism's own efforts to periodize the present (e.g., post-2001 or post-2008). Both focus on discrete events as a way of marking off a period metonymically. Nevertheless, like the recent historical novel, a literary history founded in a string of events may be both more concretely historical and more ephemeral, undermined as each event is by the fact of the larger string. Seen in this light, reading a work as a "novel of recent history" as opposed to a "9/11 novel" may be more deictic, more "temporally indeterminate," but it may also be more accurate and historically specific. By focusing on contemporary American literature's shifts in form and the literary market's allocations of prestige rather than the historical events these phenomena follow, we may yet arrive at a more coherent literary history of the present.

With this in mind, yet another way of understanding the rise of the recent historical novel is as a result of the turn toward history that this book documents. The market for contemporary literary fiction has become so deeply invested in historicity as a commodity that turning to recent events may be a way of mining for more material. The proliferation of historical fiction is so ubiquitous that, only a few years after a world-historical event, readers, critics, and even novelists look around and ask, "Who will write *The Great Post-X Novel*?" In the case of the Covid-19 pandemic, that question was being asked after only days. Describing Joseph O'Neill's *Netherland* (2008) as "the post-September 11 novel we [had] hoped for," Zadie Smith wondered: "Were there calls in 1915, for the Lusitania novel? In 1985, was the Bhopal novel keenly anticipated? It's as if, by an act of collective prayer, we have willed it into existence."[71] My argument here is that perhaps both the artistic impetus for the "post-X novel," as well as the critical ambivalence with regard to whether it has yet been achieved, are part of the same literary-historical phenomenon. This explains, in part, the apparent contradictions of the recent historical novel: the descendant of postmodernism's formal play and ironic cynicism, raised with renewed sincerity in a time where history cannot be fully distrusted if it is to stand as the very currency of literary prestige.

At the same time, the fictionalization of the recent past becomes still more complicated when one considers the implicit racial politics of the genre. While this book has documented how the increasing representation of minoritized writers within the literary canon has occurred almost exclusively in the genre of historical fiction, the ever-growing list of recent historical novels is populated largely by white authors. Writing about the 9/11 novel in particular, Jay N. Shelat has described the "enduring whiteness" of the genre as it has been constructed thus far by literary critics, noting that 88 percent of writers taken up in recent scholarly monographs on 9/11 literature are white.[72] And yet, taking into consideration the demographics of the larger genre of recent historical fiction, to which the 9/11 novel belongs, this whiteness endures still further. Indeed, Ozeki may be one of the rare exceptions that proves the rule of Chabon, Eggers, Fountain, Kingsolver, Lerner, Lethem, Makkai, Messud, McInerney, Oyler, Powers, Pynchon, Shteyngart, and Waldman, among other white American novelists working in this genre. Amid the overwhelming literary prestige attached to fiction of the historical past, and given the many ways that the writing and reception of that historical fiction has been racialized by several key literary institutions, the preponderance of white novelists turning to recent history takes on a new hue. In this context, fictionalizing the catastrophes of yesteryear may appear as an appropriately serious and weighty topic, albeit one that is more available to white writers than, say, a novel about enslavement, internment, or immigration. Chronicling the near past, in other words, may be a way of claiming some of the aesthetic prestige of history while avoiding the periods and topics most central to the American literary field's larger turn toward the historical past.

It is also a way for white writers to differentiate their work from that of other contemporary white novelists—Jonathan Franzen comes quickly to mind—invested in the realist cataloguing of the twenty-first-century lives and social climates of middle- and upper-middle-class white Americans.[73] In a 2021 interview with Merve Emre, Franzen derided the idea of writing about the Trump administration or other recent political crises: "I'm such a partisan of the novel, I don't want it subordinated to anything. I do not want to be the little dog yapping after the garbage truck of history."⁷⁴ And yet, one reason these novelists may be interested in such a chase is to elevate their fiction as somehow more serious, more ambitious. Perhaps they think it better to spend their time trailing behind the garbage truck of history than to focus solely on the middle-aged white suburbanite taking out his trash.

Jess Row has described Franzen's fiction as the "apotheosis" of a literary form of "white flight," yet the genre of recent historical fiction is, to some extent, similarly consumed with what Row calls the "fantasy of deracination."⁷⁵ While the white novelists just mentioned are invested in narrating the catastrophes of recent history, their mostly white characters are also largely insulated from them. The insistent mediation of events via news coverage is also a marker of just how far away those events are. (Recall Makkai's narrator learning of the terrorist attacks across the city from her as if she were "hearing about something on the far side of the world.")⁷⁶ Here again DeLillo's *White Noise* comes to mind. When the novel's white narrator, the college professor Jack Gladney, is trying to reassure his wife that a toxic spill will not affect them, he cites their class and implicitly (always implicitly) their race: "Nothing is going to happen. . . . These things happen to poor people who live in exposed areas. Society is set up in such a way that it's the poor and the uneducated who suffer the main impact of natural and man-made disasters. People in low-lying areas get the floods, people in shanties get the hurricanes and tornados. I'm a college professor. Did you ever see a college professor rowing a boat down his own street in one of those TV floods?"⁷⁷ DeLillo's protagonist mistakenly believes that his race and class will protect him from history's catastrophes, a belief that largely proves true in Lerner's novels.

Hurricane Sandy "fail[s] to arrive" in *10:04*, at least for the narrator and those closest to him: "it had arrived, just not for us" (230). For the Black family at the center of Jesmyn Ward's *Salvage the Bones*, however, Hurricane Katrina is "a storm so great and black the Greeks would say it was harnessed to dragons . . . the murderous mother who cut us to the bone but left us alive, left us naked and bewildered as wrinkled newborn babies, as blind puppies, as sun-starved newly hatched baby snakes."[78] If the diction here—epic in its violence and pathos and allusion—seems a far cry from that of the passages cited so far in this chapter, perhaps that is because *Salvage the Bones* is an effort to "tell the story of Katrina" as it was experienced by those for whom the flood was literal, or even mythological, rather than a metaphor for news coverage. If, as Shelat argues, the "enduring whiteness" of 9/11 fiction "detrimentally flattens and skews our understandings of the attacks," then the dominant (though not exclusive) whiteness of recent historical fiction may have the same pernicious effect on the cultural memory of recent history writ large.[79]

At its core, the genre represents not the postmodern "crisis in historicity" that Jameson pointed to at the end of the last century, but a newly mounted and newly sincere response to it in this one.[80] The central characters of Lerner's and Ozeki's novels express a deep longing to commune with history. When Hurricane Sandy fails to impact Lerner's narrator in any meaningful way, "as though we lived outside of history or were falling out of time," he actively seeks it out (230). The narrator of *Atocha* imagines the jealousy on the part of his friends were he to die in another metro bombing, describing "their amazement and maybe envy at the death I had made for myself, how I'd been contacted by History" (150). In *A Tale for the Time Being*, Ozeki dramatizes this desire for history through the division and juxtaposition of her two narrators: a brilliant structural metaphor that questions the ability of the recent historical past to communicate with the contemporary present and the present's ability to make sense of what that past has to say. The same can even be said of the title *10:04*, which alludes to the 1985 film *Back to the Future* and the exact time of night when lightning strikes the courthouse clock tower, propelling Marty McFly—and the historical lessons he's learned—back to the present. According to Elias, postmodern historical fiction used "avant-gardist styles [to] force readers to think about history in new ways."[81] Turning this claim on its head, it seems that recent historical fiction is using those same styles to think about the near past with a reinvigorated belief in its ability to be both comprehended and retold. In other words, thinking in old ways about new history.

CODA

EXCAVATING THE PRESENT

THIS BOOK is about a large and diverse group of writers who have turned to historical fiction as a way of both memorializing the past and intervening in the present. It is also about a sea change in the American literary field, and in particular the institutions that comprise the literary canon, which have lauded that backwards glance as the single most ambitious, important, and *literary* move a writer can make. These include creative writing programs, literary agents, and funding bodies that have encouraged contemporary authors to write heightened, ethnicized, and historicized versions of themselves; major literary awards that have prized historical fiction above all other genres and concentrated that prestige in a handful of historical settings; literary scholars who have placed the work of historical recovery at the very heart of their method; university English departments and middlebrow book clubs that have celebrated narratives that stretch across generations; and even news platforms, which have been drafted into literary service in order to elevate the events of the recent past to the status of history. While the writers that these institutions have consecrated are incredibly diverse—indeed, equating diversity with history has been a central, if unintended, outcome of these institutional shifts—both the genres and the politics of their writing have been largely consistent. The World War II novel, the meta–slave narrative, the multigenerational family saga, immigrant fiction, and the recent historical novel all work to nuance the historical record and address the inequities that it both records and promotes.

This transformation of the American literary field has been, in many ways, a salutary one. It has led to a dazzling wealth of historical narratives and novel forms in which to narrate them. It has also fostered the careers of a new generation of American writers and contributed to the formation of a literary canon that is markedly more inclusive than it has ever been. More important still, it has helped to reshape American historical consciousness. As historians have recognized for at least a half century, our understanding of the historical past is inseparable from the structure of the stories we tell about it. The long-refuted assumption that "the difference between 'history' and 'fiction' resides in the fact that the historian 'finds' his stories, whereas the fiction writer 'invents' his" overlooks both the historian's commitment to narrative tropes and the historical novelist's commitment to factual research.[1] As the writers examined in this book have demonstrated, fiction is a powerful technology for producing historical knowledge. Historical fiction shapes our collective memory, personifies key events and periods, reveals the deeper roots of contemporary crises, unsettles neat chronologies, challenges the historical record, exposes its lies and lacunae, recovers disregarded stories, and conjures others to stand in for those that have been lost entirely. Not only meditating on the past but simulating an encounter with it, historical fiction turns its reader into a kind of time machine.

We are living in a golden age of historical fiction, but also a period in which the understanding it promotes is being increasingly policed. When I began writing this book, I was fascinated by how the culture and canon wars of the 1980s and 1990s had impacted the central institutions of American literature. Now that I have reached the end of this project, I am struck by just how much that moment offers a kind of prologue to our own. Decades after the publication of John Guillory's *Cultural Capital* (1993), ferocious debates over which books are taught, and how, have not only resurfaced but intensified. The political proxy wars that once focused largely on university English departments have now spread to new and alarming cultural fronts. As I write these pages, many of the novels and ideas discussed in this book have already been targeted by pundits, banned by local school boards, and outlawed by state legislators. I have little doubt that more will follow. In *Cultural Capital*, Guillory argued that both sides of the canon debate in the late twentieth century were overlooking the more important "crisis" of the "long-term decline" in literature's perceived value.[2] While the cultural centrality of literature and the institutional structures of literary study have been continually threatened in the years since, these renewed attacks on literary fiction and its historical thinking only testify to their potential power in contemporary life.

At the same time, the sustained assault on narratives of history also emphasizes their political limits. Although it may be comforting to imagine that these efforts to stymie literary culture and sanitize the historical record will someday *be judged harshly by history*, that way of thinking only highlights how thoroughly retrospection, and the anticipation of it, have come to frame contemporary politics. Understanding the past is a necessary but ultimately insufficient condition for effecting change in the present. Over the last five decades, a number of literary institutions have inadvertently encouraged the belief that history can act as the central staging ground for issues of contemporary injustice and inequality. In this period, the political potential of the novel was not so much replaced by archival, empathetic, and pedagogical imperatives as it was reconstituted so that those priorities became essentially interchangeable. Given fiction's extraordinary capacity to resuscitate the past, these institutions have at times mistaken historical recovery for a form of historical redress.

CODA

In the early 1990s, Toni Morrison argued that the American literary canon had assisted in "the construction of a history and a context for whites by positing history-lessness and context-lessness for blacks."[3] In the decades since then, a generation of Black, Asian American, Latinx, and Indigenous writers has marshaled historical fiction as a means of rectifying this disparity, and a range of cultural organizations has consecrated those writers for doing so. As a result, that disparity has effectively been flipped on its head. Writers of color have been canonized almost exclusively for providing history and context, while white writers make up the vast majority of those celebrated for writing about the present. Although it is certainly not lost on historical novelists—or the teachers and readers who study them—that historical fiction is always to some extent about the time in which it is written rather than set, in recent years writers have used their fiction to point out the limits of that analogizing structure, as well as how it is applied to minoritized writers in particular. As *The Underground Railroad* makes clear, when the only job in town is historical reenactment, representing the past can seem more like containment than a means of getting free. As the narrator of *The Sympathizer* puts it, "the talent you cannot *not* use . . . that is a hazard, I must confess."[4]

In the last several years, however, there has emerged a small but countervailing force to the wave of historical fiction celebrated by the American literary field. These are novels that bear the thematic and aesthetic traces discussed in the previous chapters of this book, but also ones that directly address the present by way of narratives that are set expressly *in* that present. Jesmyn Ward's *Sing, Unburied, Sing* (2017), Valeria Luiselli's *Lost Children Archive* (2019), and Tommy Orange's *There There* (2018) allude to both history and historical fiction, but they train their focus squarely on the crises of the contemporary moment, including mass incarceration, racialized policing, drug addiction, gun violence, and child separation at the southern border of the United States.[5] In this way, these novels work to excavate the present, bringing the contemporary to light with the very same tools that have been used to uncover the past.

Ward's *Sing, Unburied, Sing* is a kind of odyssey, following a mother and her two children as they travel from Mississippi's nonfictional Parchman Prison to their home in the fictional town of Bois Sauvage. As in *Beloved*, there are ghosts that haunt the living, but Ward's main interest is how her characters carry "the weight of history" in the twenty-first-century American South.[6] Rather than set her novel in the Parchman of the past, where inmates were "tortured and beaten like slaves,"[7] Ward trains her attention on "the stabbings and the hangings and the overdoses and the beatings" that still occur today (95). Given the sheer scale of mass incarceration in the United States, the paucity of literary fiction addressing the phenomenon is startling. Ward takes up this issue and a host of other contemporary inequities directly. What is more, that directness is woven into the novel's very form: *Sing, Unburied, Sing* is not just set in the present but narrated throughout in the present tense. In her closing pages, Ward compresses the novel's bitemporal vision—the way it regards the past with one eye always on the present—in a fitting final image: a tree whose branches are "full with ghosts" (282). As Ward ventriloquizes their stories in line after unpunctuated line, she makes a point to note "the clothes they wear: rags and breeches, T-shirts and tignons, fedoras and hoodies." United across time in both this image and its syntax, "their eyes close and then open as one" (283). It's a fitting end to a novel that chronicles "past, present, and future all at once" (186).

The better part of Valeria Luiselli's *Lost Children Archive*—or, at least, the better part of the novel that is not composed of photographs, maps, and other archival material—is also narrated in the present tense.[8] Moreover, like Ward's novel, Luiselli's is narrated by a mother and her young son and also concerns a family road trip, only this time the journey is from New York to Arizona, motivated by two documentary sound projects. The mother, who narrates the first half of the novel, is producing a "documentary about the children's crisis at the border" (20). Her husband, meanwhile, is working on what he calls an "inventory of echoes" of the Apache tribes: "travel[ing] through some of the same spaces where Geronimo and his people, in the past, once moved . . . trying to capture their past presence in the world . . . by sampling any echoes that still reverberate of them" (21, 141). While the novel is concerned with how the past informs the present, its unwavering focus remains on the contemporary United States. Though *Lost Children Archive* resembles recent historical fiction, fixated as it is on how the news mediates catastrophe, here the aim is to ground the novel in a deliberately ambiguous and ongoing present. "From what I can gather by listening to the radio and fishing for news online," the woman narrates, "the situation [at the border] is becoming graver by the day" (63). Eventually her children start to combine and confuse the stories of contemporary migrant children and historical Apaches, as does the narrator herself: "the more I listen to the stories [my husband] tells about this country's past, the more it seems like he's talking about the present" (133). Despite its interest in this historical continuity, that's precisely what Luiselli's novel is talking about as well.

Like his own documentarian character, Orange endeavors in *There There* "to bring something new to the vision of the Native experience:" namely, the contemporary "Urban Indian story" (40). Though the novel opens with an epic and essayistic prologue that draws together moments in Indigenous American history, *There There* takes place almost exclusively in the twenty-first century and in "the city [that] made us new" (8). Like Ward and Luiselli, Orange's novel is highly allusive: Acosta, Baldwin, Baudelaire, Brecht, Faulkner, Fitzgerald, Hemingway, and Kesey all make appearances, as does Louise Erdrich, who one character notes is his grandmother's "favorite author" (20). Yet as with the other metacanonical writers in this book, Orange's allusions, and his allusion to Erdrich in particular, are both a gesture of deference to his literary forebears and an expression of his desire to forge a new path. Given that nearly all of the Indigenous writers recognized by major American literary prizes have been honored for works of historical fiction, Orange's explicit goal in *There There* is to find a way out of the "double bind" described succinctly by one of his characters, a former graduate student of Indigenous literature:

> The problem with Indigenous art in general is that it's stuck in the past. The catch, or the double bind, about the whole thing is this: If it isn't pulling from tradition, how is it Indigenous? And if it is stuck in tradition, in the past, how can it be relevant to other Indigenous people living now, how can it be modern? So to get close to but keep enough distance from tradition, in order to be recognizably Native and modern-sounding, is a small kind of miracle. (77)

Orange's novel attempts and largely achieves such a miracle by nodding to Indigenous history, but moving beyond it to contemporary issues of poverty, addiction, gun violence, and technological mediation.[9] To be sure, the novel does not resolve these issues or the "double bind" that plagues Indigenous writers. Nevertheless, *There There* succeeds in making it new by making it *now*.

Taken together, these three novels represent an alternative possibility for contemporary fiction's engagement with the past. Ward, Luiselli, and Orange metabolize the historical into their narrative form—itself archival, citational, and metacanonical—but they nevertheless resist historical setting. Of course, one of the consequences of literary fiction's overwhelming turn toward the historical past over the last five decades is that the present itself has sometimes faded from view. The imperatives to uncover, explore, experience, feel with, and learn from history—and the incentives for writers, particularly racially and ethnically minoritized writers, to make these things possible in their fiction—have at times displaced the urgent questions of contemporary life in favor of their historical antecedents.

CODA

While it is impossible to predict whether these authors' alternative aesthetic will take further hold, their future prospects suggest that historical fiction may yet persist as American literature's most consecrated form. Orange has asserted that his current project is a kind of sequel to *There There*, which will not only "pick up the lives of the original characters . . . but will also deal heavily with the early history of Indian boarding schools." "The historic part of the book will be much more extensive" than in *There There*, chronicling the history of these institutions in the years before and during the Spanish flu pandemic of the early twentieth century.[10] While Luiselli has not yet announced the topic of her next work of fiction, Ward's *Let Us Descend* (2023) is "a reimagining of American slavery. . . . a journey from the rice fields of the Carolinas to the slave markets of New Orleans and into the fearsome heart of a Louisiana sugar plantation."[11] If the past several years are any indication, we are likely to see many more novels like these in bookstore windows and starred reviews, on award shortlists, scholarly panels, and university syllabi. At least among the institutions that comprise the American literary canon, the past isn't dead, it isn't even past.

NOTES

INTRODUCTION

1. Toni Morrison, *Beloved* (New York: Vintage, 1987); hereafter cited parenthetically.
2. As of December 2022, Morrison's novel has appeared on more than 2,700 university literature syllabi (Open Syllabus Project) and in more than 1,000 scholarly articles and books (MLA International Bibliography). Nearly thirty new scholarly articles or book chapters on *Beloved* are added to the Modern Language Association's International Bibliography each year, outstripping even its nearest rivals by a significant margin. For a thorough analysis of scholarly responses to *Beloved*, see Timothy Aubry, *Guilty Aesthetic Pleasures* (Cambridge, MA: Harvard University Press, 2018), ch. 5.
3. Given the slipperiness of "contemporary fiction" as an aesthetic description or periodizing concept, Theodore Martin has argued that "there simply is no paradigmatic contemporary novel" because "the phrase indexes exactly zero intrinsic concerns, forms, or features—except perhaps for the vague metacritical sense that these are the novels that literature scholars today feel they are supposed to have read." Theodore Martin, "Contemporary, Inc." *Representations* 142, no. 1 (2018): 137. On the problem of "contemporary literature" as such, see also Theodore Martin, *Contemporary Drift: Genre, Historicism, and the Problem of the Present* (New York: Columbia University Press, 2017).

INTRODUCTION

4. This is a common figure in the historical fiction of the late twentieth and early twenty-first centuries. Georg Lukács has argued that the protagonist of a historical novel should be a "middling" figure, who is placed atop the fault lines between conflicting historical or political forces. By contrast, the protagonists in many of the novels discussed here function as proxies for the reader: figures who do not embody the *experience* of history so much as its *discovery*. Georg Lukács, *The Historical Novel*, trans. Hannah and Stanley Mitchell (Lincoln: University of Nebraska Press, 1983), 33.
5. On the novel's relationship to institutions of higher education, and a reading of the figure of "Schoolteacher," see Mark McGurl, *The Program Era: Postwar Fiction and the Rise of Creative Writing* (Cambridge, MA: Harvard University Press, 2009), 346–57.
6. James Baldwin was shortlisted for *Giovanni's Room* in 1956; Ishmael Reed for *Mumbo Jumbo* in 1973; Morrison herself for *Sula* in 1975; and David Bradley for *The Chaneysville Incident* in 1983. Alice Walker, who won the 1983 National Book Award for *The Color Purple*, became the first African American woman and only the second Black novelist to do so.
7. While the language of "minoritized," "racialized," and/or "ethnicized" writers is somewhat clunky, I favor these terms over their more colloquial counterparts ("minority," "racial," "ethnic") as a way of recognizing the historical and social construction of these identity categories.
8. As of December 2022, Open Syllabus had aggregated more than 310,000 syllabi for English literature courses at American universities. Among the twenty novels published after 1945 that appear most on these syllabi, fourteen are works of historical fiction. What is more, the top ten most-taught works of historical fiction published after 1945 appear on university literature syllabi over 50 percent more than the top ten most-taught other novels. "Open Syllabus Explorer," Open Syllabus.
9. Between 1950 and 1979, 234 novels were shortlisted for the National Book Award, the Pulitzer Prize, and the National Book Critics Circle Award. Of these, 126 (54 percent) were works of historical fiction. In the 1980s, eighty out of 120 shortlisted novels (67 percent) were works of historical fiction. In the first decade of the twenty-first century, eighty-nine works of historical fiction (80 percent) were shortlisted. Between 2000 and 2019, 164 of the 223 novels shortlisted for these prizes (74 percent) were works of historical fiction.
10. Among the works shortlisted for a major American prize, thirty of the fifty most-cited texts are works of historical fiction. On average, historical fiction accrues 50 percent more citations per year than novels set in the present, and of the fifty texts that have accrued the highest number of citations per year, thirty-nine are works of historical fiction. "MLA International Bibliography," Modern Language

INTRODUCTION

Association. For a fascinating study of literary canon formation that uses this metric, see J. D. Porter, "Popularity/Prestige," *Literary Lab*, Pamphlet 17 (2018).

11. For more on the primacy of historical fiction in contemporary African American literature, see Aida Levy-Hussen, *How to Read African American Literature: Post-Civil Rights Fiction and the Task of Interpretation* (New York: New York University Press, 2016). See also Stephen Best, *None Like Us: Blackness, Belonging, Aesthetic Life* (Durham, NC: Duke University Press, 2018), especially ch. 2; and Michael DeRell Hill, *The Ethics of Swagger: Prizewinning African American Novels, 1977–1993* (Columbus: Ohio State University Press, 2013). For an account of historical fiction's pride of place in contemporary literature of the Caribbean diaspora, see Elena Machado Sáez, *Market Aesthetics: The Purchase of the Past in Caribbean Diasporic Fiction* (Charlottesville: University of Virginia Press, 2015).

12. Richard Jean So, *Redlining Culture: A Data History of Racial Inequality and Postwar Fiction* (New York: Columbia University Press, 2020).

13. On the concept of "literary enfranchisement," see Josh Lambert, *The Literary Mafia: Jews, Publishing, and Postwar American Literature* (New Haven, CT: Yale University Press, 2022), 7–8.

14. Samuel Cohen, *After the End of History: American Fiction in the 1990s* (Iowa City: University of Iowa Press, 2009), 27; Fredric Jameson, *The Antinomies of Realism* (London: Verso, 2013), 259; Jameson, *Postmodernism, Or, The Cultural Logic of Late Capitalism* (Durham, NC: Duke University Press, 1991), 22. On the relation between historiography and historical fiction, see Linda Hutcheon, *A Poetics of Postmodernism: History, Theory, Fiction* (New York: Routledge, 1988), and Amy J. Elias, *Sublime Desire: History and Post-1960s Fiction* (Baltimore: Johns Hopkins University Press, 2001).

15. For more on this, see chapter 1.

16. On the controversy surrounding *Beloved* and the 1987–1988 prize season, see James F. English, *The Economy of Prestige: Prizes, Awards, and the Circulation of Cultural Value* (Cambridge, MA: Harvard University Press, 2009), 237–46. On the conservative backlash to *Beloved*, see Bryan M. Santin, *Postwar American Fiction and the Rise of Modern Conservatism: A Literary History, 1945–2008* (Cambridge: Cambridge University Press, 2021), ch. 5.

17. Stephen Greenblatt, *Shakespearean Negotiations: The Circulation of Social Energy in Renaissance England* (Berkeley: University of California Press, 1988), 1.

18. Hilton Als, "Toni Morrison and the Ghosts in the House," *New Yorker*, October 27, 2003, www.newyorker.com/magazine/2003/10/27/ghosts-in-the-house.

19. See Evan Brier, "Unliterary History: Toni Morrison, *The Black Book*, and 'Real Black Publishing,'" *American Literature* 94, no. 4 (2022): 651–76.

20. Attributing the initial success of her first novel to university English departments and the advent of Black studies curricula, Morrison proclaimed, "it was the

INTRODUCTION

academic community that gave 'The Bluest Eye' its life.... People assigned it in class. Students bought the paperback." Als, "Toni Morrison."
21. Toni Morrison, *Playing in the Dark: Whiteness and the Literary Imagination* (New York: Vintage, 1993), 22.
22. Morrison, *Playing in the Dark*, 17.
23. Pierre Bourdieu, *The Rules of Art: Genesis and Structure of the Literary Field*, trans. Susan Emanuel (Stanford, CA: Stanford University Press, 1996), 204.
24. English, *The Economy of Prestige*, 12.
25. On creative writing programs: McGurl, *The Program Era*; Loren Glass, *After the Program Era: The Past, Present, and Future of Creative Writing in the University* (Iowa City: University of Iowa Press, 2017); Kalyan Nadiminti, "The Global Program Era: Contemporary International Fiction in the American Creative Economy," *Novel: A Forum on Fiction* 51, no. 3 (2018): 375–98. On literary agents: Laura B. McGrath, "Literary Agency," *American Literary History* 33, no. 2 (Summer 2021): 350–70. On publishing: Amy Hungerford, *Making Literature Now* (Stanford, CA: Stanford University Press, 2016); Kinohi Nishikawa, *Street Players: Black Pulp Fiction and the Making of a Literary Underground* (Chicago: University of Chicago Press, 2018); Dan N. Sinykin, "The Conglomerate Era: Publishing, Authorship, and Literary Form, 1965–2007," *Contemporary Literature* 58, no. 4 (2017): 462–91; So, *Redlining Culture*; Claire Squires, *Marketing Literature: The Making of Contemporary Writing in Britain* (London: Palgrave, 2007). On internationalization: Rebecca L. Walkowitz, *Born Translated: The Contemporary Novel in an Age of World Literature* (New York: Columbia University Press, 2015). On reading practices: Timothy Aubry, *Reading as Therapy: What Contemporary Fiction Does for Middle-Class Americans* (Iowa City: University of Iowa Press, 2011); Beth Driscoll, *The New Literary Middlebrow: Tastemakers and Reading in the Twenty-First Century* (London: Palgrave Macmillan, 2014); Merve Emre, *Paraliterary: The Making of Bad Readers in Postwar America* (Chicago: University of Chicago Press, 2018). On literary prizes: English, *The Economy of Prestige*; Claire Grossman, Juliana Spahr, and Stephanie Young, "Literature's Vexed Democratization," *American Literary History* 33, no. 2 (Summer 2021): 298–319. On English departments and the canon: John Guillory, *Cultural Capital: The Problem of Literary Canon Formation* (Chicago: University of Chicago Press, 1993); Jodi Melamed, *Represent and Destroy: Rationalizing Violence in the New Racial Capitalism* (Minneapolis: University of Minnesota Press, 2011); Joseph North, *Literary Criticism: A Concise Political History* (Cambridge, MA: Harvard University Press, 2017); Aubry, *Guilty Aesthetic Pleasures*; Porter, "Popularity/Prestige." Outside of literary studies the work of cultural sociologists has offered much, in terms of both methodology and insight, to the study of literary history.

INTRODUCTION

See John B. Thompson, *Merchants of Culture: The Publishing Business in the Twenty-First Century* (London: Polity Press, 2013), and *Book Wars: The Digital Revolution in Publishing* (London: Polity Press, 2021); Clayton Childress, *Under the Cover: The Creation, Production, and Reception of a Novel* (Princeton, NJ: Princeton University Press, 2017); Phillipa K. Chong, *Inside the Critics' Circle: Book Reviewing in Uncertain Times* (Princeton, NJ: Princeton University Press, 2020); and Laura J. Miller, *Reluctant Capitalists: Bookselling and the Culture of Consumption* (Chicago: University of Chicago Press, 2008).

26. I owe both this formulation and the aesthetic thinking that supports it to Seo-Young Chu's theory of science-fictional representation. With Chu's work in mind, we might imagine yet another continuum that organizes works of speculative fiction, which variously narrate the near and far future. Seo-Young Chu, *Do Metaphors Dream of Literal Sleep? A Science-Fictional Theory of Representation* (Cambridge, MA: Harvard University Press, 2010), 6–8.
27. Jameson, *Postmodernism*, 18–20.
28. Jameson, *Antinomies*, 260.
29. Among finalists for major American literary awards, historical settings from the twentieth century appear far more often than those from any other time. For most of the last sixty years, more than 80 percent of all historical novels shortlisted for these prizes were at least partially set in the years between 1900 and 1999. The nineteenth century is the next most prestigious historical setting, appearing in 19 percent of historical novels overall. Only 4 percent of shortlisted novels take place before the year 1800. To put this in perspective, as fictional settings, both the Vietnam War and the early 2000s appear more than the period between the dawn of time and Thomas Jefferson's inauguration.
30. Morrison, *Beloved*, 44.
31. Walter Scott, *Waverley or 'Tis Sixty Years Since* (New York: Penguin, 1985), 33–36. In his iconic introduction, Scott defines *Waverley* as "neither a romance of chivalry, nor a tale of modern manners," as those two genres, "to be interesting, must either refer to antiquity so great as to have become venerable, or . . . must bear a vivid reflection of those scenes which are passing daily before our eyes." By contrast, Scott explains, "my hero will neither have iron on his shoulders, as of yore, nor on the heels of his boots, as is the present fashion of Bond Street."
32. In a study of more than 1,700 anglophone novels, James F. English found that contemporary fiction has undergone "a radical retemporalization" since the 1980s: while popular fiction continues to favor present-day settings, literary fiction favors the historical past. For this investigation, English counted as historical novels those that are "predominantly set more than 20 years prior to

publication." While this methodology is helpful, even essential, for digital humanities research such as English's, it also suggests that a novel published in 2018 and set in the months leading up to 9/11 (such as Ottessa Moshfegh's *My Year of Rest and Relaxation*), or one published in 1961 but set at the end of World War II (such as Joseph Heller's *Catch-22*), takes place in the present. These limit cases suggest that understanding historical fiction requires more than merely counting years. James F. English, "Now, Not Now: Counting Time in Contemporary Fiction Studies," *Modern Language Quarterly* 77, no. 3 (2016): 395–418.

33. See Lukács, *The Historical Novel*, 31. See also, Jameson, *Antinomies*. Jameson argues there that the historical novel "harbor[s] conservative sympathies" (266) and that it "has so often been marshaled to serve political ends, of which nationalism is only the most obvious" (260).

34. The literary-historical phenomenon at the heart of this study extends, without a doubt, beyond the bounds of the United States. Historical fiction is similarly prominent on university syllabi in the United Kingdom and among nominations for international awards like the Booker Prize. Given this, it is not difficult to imagine a similar study that might include historical novels by Chinua Achebe, Margaret Atwood, Pat Barker, Kiran Desai, Amitav Ghosh, Kazuo Ishiguro, Marlon James, Andrea Levy, Hilary Mantel, Ian McEwan, Michael Ondaatje, Arundhati Roy, and Salman Rushdie, among many others. That said, the methodology of this investigation both calls for and rewards a more local approach. Focusing on a single nation broadly defined may be more modest in its scope, but for that very reason it also affords a more precise accounting of the institutional forces that have shaped the literary history of the last several decades.

35. These novels attest to claims that contemporary American fiction is "born translated" into a global publishing system, and increasingly "extraterritorial" in its concerns. Walkowitz, *Born Translated*; Matthew Hart, *Extraterritorial: A Political Geography of Contemporary Fiction* (New York: Columbia University Press, 2020).

36. It is worth considering, however, how even works of speculative fiction in the late twentieth and early twenty-first centuries—Octavia Butler's *Kindred* (1979), Margaret Atwood's *The Handmaid's Tale* (1985), David Mitchell's *Cloud Atlas* (2004), Naomi Alderman's *The Power* (2016), and short fiction such as George Saunders's "Love Letter" (2020), to name just a few—have adopted the logics of historical fiction, explicitly framing their narratives in terms of historical artifacts, archives, and accounts.

37. Perry Anderson, "From Progress to Catastrophe," *London Review of Books* 33, no. 15 (2011): 24–28.

INTRODUCTION

38. Henry James to Sarah Orne Jewett, October 5, 1901, in Ferman Bishop, "Henry James Criticizes *The Tory Lover*," *American Literature* (1955): 263. On the American historical novel, the modernist period, and the phenomenon of historical ignorance, see T. Austin Graham's forthcoming monograph, *The Unknowing of American History: U.S. Historical Fiction and the Varieties of Historical Ignorance*.
39. Elias, *Sublime Desire*, xv, xvii. See also Hutcheon, *A Poetics of Postmodernism*.
40. English, "Now, Not Now," 403, 406–8. See also Jordan Pruett, who demonstrates in his study of twentieth-century bestselling American fiction that, while historical fiction and domestic fiction represented "the most common genres on the [*New York Times*] bestseller list" for most of the twentieth century, "after 1980, these genres were decisively supplanted" by mystery novels and thrillers. Jordan Pruett, "Managed Abundance: A Quantitative History of American Fiction, 1931–2009" (PhD diss., University of Chicago, 2022), 39. Anderson notes that "at the upper ranges of fiction," historical fiction is now "more widespread than it was even at the height of its classical period in the early 19th century." Perry Anderson, "From Progress to Catastrophe."
41. Bourdieu, *The Rules of Art*, 227–31.
42. So, *Redlining Culture*, 4, 29.
43. Eleven of the twenty most-taught novels published since 1945 are by writers of color. From 2000 to 2019, 223 novels were shortlisted for the National Book Award, the Pulitzer Prize, and the National Book Critics Circle Award, of which 80 were by writers of color.
44. Of the eleven most-taught novels by racially minoritized writers to be published since 1945, nine are works of historical fiction. Of the 110 novels by writers of color to be shortlisted for a major American prize from 1980 to 2019, 85 are works of historical fiction. That said, Grossman, Spahr, and Young have demonstrated that prizewinning writers of color are much more likely than their white counterparts to be graduates of elite academic institutions ("Literature's Vexed Democratization," 309–10). This is borne out by the corpus of writers discussed in this book, the vast majority of whom attended elite academic institutions.
45. Elias, *Sublime Desire*, xvii.
46. Lee Konstantinou, *Cool Characters: Irony and American Fiction* (Cambridge, MA: Harvard University Press, 2016); Adam Kelly, "The New Sincerity," in *Postmodern/Postwar—and After: Rethinking American Literature*, ed. Jason Gladstone, Andrew Hoberek, and Daniel Worden (Iowa City: University of Iowa Press, 2016), 197–208. See also Adam Kelly, "David Foster Wallace and the New Sincerity in American Fiction," in *Consider David Foster Wallace: Critical Essays*, ed. David Hering (Los Angeles: Sideshow Media Group Press, 2010), 131–46.

INTRODUCTION

47. Morrison, *Beloved*, 324; Viet Thanh Nguyen, *The Sympathizer* (New York: Grove Press, 2015), 70 (hereafter cited parenthetically).
48. Roderick A. Ferguson, *The Reorder of Things: The University and Its Pedagogies of Minority Difference* (Minneapolis: University of Minnesota Press, 2012), 12.
49. As Sarah Chihaya notes, "It has already become a critical commonplace to begin a discussion of Viet Thanh Nguyen's *The Sympathizer* (2015) by invoking its powerful opening declaration." Sarah Chihaya, "Slips and Slides," *PMLA* 133, no. 2 (2018): 364.
50. Ellison, *Invisible Man*, 3. As the acknowledgments to the novel make clear, Nguyen's homage to *Invisible Man* goes beyond the pages of *The Sympathizer*: his son is named Ellison.
51. For a reading of Nguyen's "intertextual cathexis" in the novel, as well as *The Sympathizer*'s "interethnic imagination," see Caroline Rody, "Between 'I' and 'We': Viet Thanh Nguyen's Interethnic Multitudes," *PMLA* 133, no. 2 (2018): 396–405. See also Rody, *The Interethnic Imagination: Roots and Passages in Contemporary Asian American Fiction* (Oxford: Oxford University Press, 2009).
52. Paul Tran, "Viet Thanh Nguyen: Anger in the Asian American Novel," Asian American Writers Workshop, June 29, 2015, aaww.org/viet-thanh-nguyen-anger-asian-american-novel/. See also Andrew Lam, "Viet Thanh Nguyen in Conversation with Andrew Lam," *Asian American Literature: Discourses & Pedagogies* 9 (2018): 13.
53. Viet Thanh Nguyen, *Nothing Ever Dies: Vietnam and the Memory of War* (Cambridge, MA: Harvard University Press, 2016).
54. On the topic of doubleness and the racist trope of divided loyalty in Asian American literature, see Tina Yih-Ting Chen, *Double Agency: Acts of Impersonation in Asian American Literature and Culture* (Stanford, CA: Stanford University Press, 2005).
55. Viet Thanh Nguyen, "Canon Fodder," *Washington Post*, May 3, 2018.
56. On the connections between Nguyen's career, *The Sympathizer*, and the institutionalization of Asian American literature, see Min Hyoung Song, "Viet Thanh Nguyen and the Scholar–Public Intellectual," *PMLA* 133, no. 2 (2018): 406–12; Timothy K. August, "Spies Like Us: A Professor Undercover in the Literary Marketplace," *Lit: Literature Interpretation Theory* 29, no. 1 (2018): 60–79; and Ben Tran, "The Literary Dubbing of Confession," *PMLA* 133, no. 2 (2018): 417.
57. Mark Chiang, *The Cultural Capital of Asian American Studies: Autonomy and Representation in the University* (New York: New York University Press, 2018), 1.
58. Ferguson, *The Reorder of Things*, 33.
59. Ferguson, *The Reorder of Things*, 32.
60. Ferguson, *The Reorder of Things*, 125. See, e.g., *Aiiieeeee! An Anthology of Asian-American Writers* (1974), which sought to honor Asian American writing

INTRODUCTION

"recovered from seven generations." Frank Chin, et al., "Preface," *Aiiieeeee! An Anthology of Asian American Writers* (Washington, DC: Howard University Press, 1974), xvi.
61. As an undergraduate Nguyen majored in both English and ethnic studies, taking classes in which he not only encountered what his protagonist's professor would call "the best of what was thought and said" but also where he first "discovered Asian American literature" and "found African American literature, from the slave narratives onward." Nguyen, "Canon Fodder."
62. On the "paradoxical set of assumptions" underlying the conservative forces of the so-called canon wars, see Bryan M. Santin, *Postwar American Fiction and the Rise of Modern Conservatism: A Literary History, 1945–2008* (Cambridge: Cambridge University Press, 2021), 187, 198–201. Santin explains that "for Reaganite conservatives, highbrow fiction was somehow both an elitist liberal discourse that betrayed traditional American values *and* a great civilizational barricade against the untutored, racialized masses" (201).
63. Guillory, *Cultural Capital*, 32, 53.
64. H. Aram Veeser, "Introduction," in *The New Historicism*, ed. H. Aram Veeser (London: Routledge, 1989), xii.
65. North, *Literary Criticism*, 105, 1.
66. Amy Hungerford, "On the Period Formerly Known as Contemporary," *American Literary History* 20, no. 1 (2008): 416.
67. Childress, *Under the Cover*, 114. Childress likens the act of "publishing a literary work that is assigned across the country to future generations of students" to winning the "literary lottery." This is why Bourdieu refers to works in the literary canon as "lasting bestsellers." Bourdieu, *The Rules of Art*, 147.
68. Kenneth W. Warren, *What Was African American Literature?* (Cambridge, MA: Harvard University Press, 2011), 42–43.
69. Sandra M. Gilbert and Susa Gubar, *The Madwoman in the Attic: The Woman Writer and the Nineteenth-Century Literary Imagination* (New Haven, CT: Yale University Press, 2020), 59.
70. These include four historical novels by Toni Morrison, Leslie Marmon Silko's *Ceremony* (discussed in chapter 2), and Alice Walker's *The Color Purple*. See Open Syllabus.
71. All but five of the forty-four novels by women shortlisted for a major American award between 2000 and 2009 were works of historical fiction.
72. Lambert, *The Literary Mafia*, 13.
73. Jennifer Glaser, *Borrowed Voices: Writing and Racial Ventriloquism in the Jewish American Imagination* (New Brunswick, NJ: Rutgers University Press, 2016), 94. At times Lambert takes a more critical view, arguing that Jews were "complicit in the U.S. publishing industry's and literary field's misogyny and white

INTRODUCTION

supremacy, and they can be understood to have supported social closure that made it more possible for Jews than for members of many other U.S. minority groups to envision and pursue literary careers for themselves." *The Literary Mafia*, 27.

74. Philip Roth, *The Human Stain* (New York: Vintage International, 2001), 5. Set amid the Clinton impeachment hearings of 1998, Roth's novel embodies many of the features of the "recent historical" novels discussed in chapter 5, including a historical overture that sounds less like 1990s fiction than Dickens's *A Tale of Two Cities*.
75. Roth, *The Human Stain*, 19.
76. Glaser, *Borrowed Voices*, 95. Likewise, Mark McGurl writes that "seen against the forty-year backdrop of the field he has inhabited, [Roth] can seem to figure either as a culturally conservative white male writer, staunchly upholding high modernist literary values, or, as was more plainly the case in the 1960s, as a conspicuously 'ethnic' writer ... who introduces cultural difference into that system." *The Program Era*, 56.
77. Glaser, *Borrowed Voices*, 95.
78. Lisa Lowe, "Canon, Institutionalization, Identity: Contradictions for Asian American Studies," in *The Ethnic Canon: Histories, Institutions, and Interventions*, ed. David Palumbo-Liu (Minneapolis: University of Minnesota Press, 1995), 53.
79. Chiang, *Cultural Capital*, 4–5. On the institutionalization of Black and ethnic studies, see also David Palumbo-Liu, "Introduction," in Palumbo-Liu, *The Ethnic Canon*, 1–27; Lowe, "Canon, Institutionalization, Identity"; Ferguson, *The Reorder of Things*; Melamed, *Represent and Destroy*; and Rolland Murray, "Not Being and Blackness: Percival Everett and the Uncanny Forms of Racial Incorporation," *American Literary History* 29, no. 4 (2017): 726–52.
80. Michael LeMahieu, Angela Naimou, and Viet Thanh Nguyen, "An Interview with Viet Thanh Nguyen," *Contemporary Literature* 58, no. 4 (2017): 449.
81. For a discussion of the "the ways in which writers of Asian descent working and living in the United States are hemmed in by the expectations that an ethnic label bears" (88), and a reading of Nam Le's short story, "Love and Honor and Pity and Pride and Compassion and Sacrifice," see Min Hyoung Song, *The Children of 1965: On Writing, and Not Writing, as an Asian American* (Durham, NC: Duke University Press, 2013), especially ch. 3.
82. Melamed, *Represent and Destroy*, 34.
83. "In order to refashion minority difference as an opportunity for power," Roderick Ferguson writes, hegemonic institutions "construct racism as an increasingly illegible phenomenon in U.S. society, the unfortunate past that was gradually receding" (58). While in the contemporary literary field the historical past has

1. CONTEMPORARY FICTION IN REVERSE

been surging rather than receding for the last five decades, and while novels like *Beloved* and *The Sympathizer* have done much to make the inequities of American society increasingly legible, they have done so almost exclusively by way of historical analogy. As just one example, consider the fact that the contemporary canon now contains a wealth of historical novels of enslavement (discussed further in chapters 3 and 4), while the "novel of mass incarceration" is largely overlooked not only by publishing houses and prize committees but also by university English departments.

84. Guillory, *Cultural Capital*, 30.
85. Guillory, *Cultural Capital*, 6.
86. Alexander Manshel, Laura B. McGrath, and J. D. Porter, "Who Cares about Literary Prizes?" *Public Books*, September 3, 2019, https://www.publicbooks.org/who-cares-about-literary-prizes/.

1. CONTEMPORARY FICTION IN REVERSE

1. Viet Thanh Nguyen, *The Sympathizer* (New York: Grove Press, 2015), 353–54.
2. Nguyen, *The Sympathizer*, 350.
3. For a thorough narratological analysis of Amis's *Time's Arrow* and its temporal structure, as well as a typology of narratives in reverse, see Seymour Chatman, "Backwards," *Narrative* 17, no. 1 (January 2009): 31–55. For an overview of "Retrograde Narratives" and their history, see Ken Ireland, "Peeling the Onion: Outcomes to Origins in Retrograde Narrative," *Journal of Literary Semantics* 39, no. 1 (2010): 29–41.
4. Samuel Cohen, *After the End of History: American Fiction in the 1990s* (Iowa City: University of Iowa Press, 2009), 197. Cohen argues that the backwards structure of the novel "lends a sense not only of causation but also of inevitability to the order in which events happened chronologically" (198).
5. Laura B. McGrath, "Literary Agency," *American Literary History* 33, no. 2 (Summer 2021): 351. As McGrath points out, literary agents "exercise a great deal of control over [authors'] manuscripts" before editors acquire them: "The agent's most significant (and least visible) work occurs in the time between signing a client and selling their book" (357).
6. Raphael Dalleo and Elena Machado Sáez, *The Latino/a Canon and the Emergence of Post-Sixties Literature* (New York: Palgrave Macmillan, 2007), 139.
7. For this reason alone it seems misguided to exclude from a study of American fiction a novel that is set largely in the United States and shaped by American influences, which received considerable attention in the American press and from American literary tastemakers, and which led to further publication in U.S.

1. CONTEMPORARY FICTION IN REVERSE

venues and an eventual move to Brooklyn, simply because the author has an English accent. As readers know well, a novel can mean much *to*—and *as*—American literature regardless of where its author was born, whether Oxford, Akron, or Accra.

8. For more on Bradley's early career, see Michael DeRell Hill, *The Ethics of Swagger: Prizewinning African American Novels, 1977–1993* (Columbus: Ohio State University Press, 2013), 128.
9. Kenneth W. Warren, *What Was African American Literature?* (Cambridge, MA: Harvard University Press, 2011), 102. For these reasons, Warren describes Bradley's novel as "a similar project" to Morrison's *Beloved* (98).
10. See Judith Wilson, "Books." *Essence* 12, no. 4 (August 1981): 22; "Monitor Manuscripts: 'The Chaneysville Incident,'" review of *The Chaneysville Incident*, by David Bradley, *New York Amsterdam News*, August 28, 1982; Vance Bourjaily, "Thirteen Runaway Slaves and David Bradley," review of *The Chaneysville Incident*, by David Bradley, *New York Times*, April 19, 1981; Christopher Lehmann-Haupt, "Books of the Times," review of *The Chaneysville Incident*, by David Bradley, *New York Times*, May 12, 1981.
11. Mary Helen Washington, "Black History: His Story or Hers?," review of *The Chaneysville Incident*, by David Bradley, *Washington Post*, April 12, 1981. See also Edwin McDowell, "'Chaneysville Incident' Wins Faulkner Award," *New York Times*, April 11, 1982.
12. Bruce Allen, "Well-Made Novel Sifts Black History," review of *The Chaneysville Incident*, by David Bradley, *The Christian Science Monitor*, May 20, 1981. See also Ann Charles, "'Chaneysville Incident:' Gripping, Provocative Story," review of *The Chaneysville Incident*, by David Bradley, *New York Amsterdam News*, January 24, 1981; and Art Seidenbaum, "Superior Saga Tracks Heritage from Slave Times," review of *The Chaneysville Incident*, by David Bradley, *Los Angeles Times*, April 8, 1981.
13. "Open Syllabus Explorer," The Open Syllabus Project.
14. "MLA International Bibliography," Modern Language Association.
15. Martha Jablow, "Novelist Has All the Moves," *Philadelphia Daily News*, September 12, 1983 (emphasis added).
16. In her 1996 article, Kubitschek concludes by exploring why Bradley's novel is "not often taught" and "only a few articles have been forthcoming in the fourteen years since publication." Missy Dehn Kubitschek, "'So You Want a History, Do You?': Epistemologies and 'The Chaneysville Incident,'" *Mississippi Quarterly* 49, no. 4 (1996): 773–74.
17. The same year that *Chaneysville* won the PEN/Faulkner, both the National Book Award and the National Book Critics Circle Award went to works of historical fiction.

1. CONTEMPORARY FICTION IN REVERSE

18. Stephen Greenblatt, *The Power of Forms in the English Renaissance* (Ann Arbor: University of Michigan Press, 1982).
19. This passage from the 1984 article is reproduced more or less exactly in Jameson's 1991 book. Fredric Jameson, *Postmodernism, or, The Cultural Logic of Late Capitalism* (Durham, NC: Duke University Press, 1991), 22.
20. David Bradley, *The Chaneysville Incident* (New York: Harper & Row, 1981); hereafter cited parenthetically.
21. Ashraf H. A. Rushdy, *Remembering Generations: Race and Family in Contemporary African American Fiction* (Chapel Hill: University of North Carolina Press, 2001), 5. The protagonist of such palimpsest narratives, Rushdy argues, is often "a contemporary subject whose psychic health, romantic success, and even physical survival depend on an ability to comprehend the role of the past in the production of the present" (33).
22. Saidiya Hartman, "Venus in Two Acts," *Small Axe* 12, no. 2 (2008): 11.
23. Linda Hutcheon, *A Poetics of Postmodernism: History, Theory, Fiction* (New York: Taylor & Francis Group, 1988), 106.
24. Hutcheon, *A Poetics of Postmodernism*, 106, 116.
25. See, e.g., Klaus Ensslen, "Fictionalizing History: David Bradley's *The Chaneysville Incident*," *Callaloo* 35 (1988): 280–96; Kelly Wagers, "Seeing 'From the Far Side of the Hill': Narrative, History, and Understanding in *Kindred* and *The Chaneysville Incident*," *MELUS* 34, no. 1 (2009): 23–45; and Warren, *What Was African American Literature?*
26. Rod Steier, "Trying for Another 'Roots' Saga," review of *The Chaneysville Incident*, by David Bradley, *Hartford Courant*, April 9, 1981.
27. Marge Piercy, "A Historian Obsessed by Ghosts of Past," review of *The Chaneysville Incident*, by David Bradley, *Chicago Tribune*, April 26, 1981 (emphasis added).
28. Thomas Gannon, "The Chaneysville Incident," review of *The Chaneysville Incident* by David Bradley, *America* 144, no. 21 (May 30, 1981): 449 (emphasis added).
29. Kay Bonetti, "David Bradley Interview with Kay Bonetti," American Audio Prose Library, February 1992, https://searchworks.stanford.edu/view/2403852.
30. Kubitschek, "So You Want a History," 760.
31. Mary Helen Washington, "Black History"; Cathy Brigham, "Identity, Masculinity, and Desire in David Bradley's Fiction," *Contemporary Literature* 36, no. 2 (1995): 291. This defense of Bradley's personal politics tends to overlook his public spat with Alice Walker in 1984. See David Bradley, "Novelist Alice Walker Telling the Black Woman's Story," *New York Times*, January 8, 1984; Alice Walker, "The Black Woman's Story," *New York Times*, February 12, 1984.
32. Piercy, "A Historian Obsessed."

1. CONTEMPORARY FICTION IN REVERSE

33. Aida Levy-Hussen argues that "whereas *Beloved* depicts the transmission of traumatic memory within the temporal range of legal slavery and its immediate aftermath, *The Chaneysville Incident* imagines the reach of slavery's postmemorial effects extending into the present." Aida Levy-Hussen, *How to Read African American Literature: Post–Civil Rights Fiction and the Task of Interpretation* (New York: New York University Press, 2016), 30.
34. Howard Kissel, "David Bradley: Writing Beyond the Rage," *Women's Wear Daily* (April 7, 1981), 17.
35. Ali Stanton, "David Bradley's New Book Tells of 13 Slave Martyrs," *New York Amsterdam News*, April 18, 1981.
36. Kissel, "David Bradley," 16.
37. Lehmann-Haupt, "Books of the Times."
38. Wayne Warga, "An English Professor's Historical Tale," *Los Angeles Times*, April 24, 1981.
39. Martin Amis, *Time's Arrow: Or the Nature of the Offence* (New York: Vintage, 1991), 11; hereafter cited parenthetically.
40. In one particularly poignant moment, Amis describes how Kennedy is "flown down from Washington and flung together by the doctors' knives and the sniper's bullets and introduced on to the streets of Dallas [for] a hero's welcome" (90).
41. See, e.g., Mark Currie, *About Time: Narrative, Fiction and the Philosophy of Time* (Edinburgh: Edinburgh University Press, 2007), 101; Richard Menke, "Narrative Reversals and the Thermodynamics of History in Martin Amis's *Time's Arrow*," *MFS: Modern Fiction Studies* 44, no. 4 (1998): 964; James Phelan, *Somebody Telling Somebody Else: A Rhetorical Poetics of Narrative* (Columbus: Ohio State University Press, 2017), 117; Susan Vice, *Holocaust Fiction* (New York: Routledge, 2000), 13. This reading of the novel was not lost on its first readers and reviewers. See also Frank Kermode, "In Reverse," review of *Time's Arrow*, by Martin Amis, *London Review of Books*, September 12, 1991, 11.
42. David Lehman, "From Death to Birth," Review of *Time's Arrow*, by Martin Amis, *New York Times Book Review*, November 17, 1991.
43. Currie, *About Time*, 101.
44. See, e.g., Chatman, "Backwards," 44; Maya Slater, "Problems When Time Moves Backwards: Martin Amis's *Time's Arrow*," *English: The Journal of the English Association* 42, no. 173 (1993): 150; Brian Finney, *Martin Amis* (New York: Routledge, 2008), 57.
45. Anthony DeCurtis, "Britain's Mavericks," *Harper's Bazaar*, November 1991, 146.
46. See John A. Dern, *Martians, Monsters and Madonna: Fiction and Form in the World of Martin Amis* (New York: Peter Lang, 2000), 128; Dermot McCarthy, "The Limits of Irony: The Chronillogical World of Martin Amis' *Time's Arrow*,"

1. CONTEMPORARY FICTION IN REVERSE

War, Literature, and the Arts: An International Journal of the Humanities 11, no. 1 (1999): 315.
47. Vice, *Holocaust Fiction*, 18.
48. See Martin Amis, *The Moronic Inferno, and Other Visits to America* (London: Jonathan Cape, 1986); *Visiting Mrs. Nabokov, and Other Excursions* (London: Jonathan Cape, 1993); "When Amis Met Updike," *The Guardian*, January 31, 2009.
49. Amis, *Moronic Inferno*, 155.
50. Amis, *Visiting*, 52.
51. It is no coincidence that one of the only early readers of Amis's novel to engage seriously with its opening was Updike himself. Reviewing *Time's Arrow* in the pages of the *New Yorker*, Updike praised the novel as "ambitious" and "a work of impressive intensity and virtuosity." Though he gives the "monstrous riddle [at] the center of the twentieth century" its due, Updike also comments on how "the large American section of the novel, which comes first, has a racy freshness of impression that suggests the world of 'Lolita' seen in a crazy inverting mirror." John Updike, "Nobody Gets Away with Everything," *New Yorker*, May 25, 1992, 86–87.
52. Chatman, "Backwards," 49.
53. Christopher Bigsby, *Writers in Conversation: Volume One* (Norwich, UK: Pen & Ink Press, School of English and American Studies, University of East Anglia, 2000), 41; John M. Harrison, "Speeding from Cradle to Grave," *Times Literary Supplement* (September 20, 1991), 21.
54. DeCurtis, "Britain's Mavericks"; Finney, *Martin Amis*, 25.
55. Charles Trueheart, "Through a Mirror, Darkly," Review of *Time's Arrow*, by Martin Amis, *Washington Post*, November 26, 1991.
56. Nicolas Tredell, *The Fiction of Martin Amis* (London: Icon Books, 2000), 127.
57. Amis's appearance on the 1991 shortlist (his first time as a finalist) exemplifies what James F. English calls "capital intraconversion," or the ability of literary prizes to mediate between various forms of social and material value. With *Time's Arrow*, Amis effectively transmuted the symbolic capital of the Holocaust into the literary prestige of the Booker Prize and, ultimately, into the financial capital—as measured in prize money and future sales figures—that that award confers. James F. English, *The Economy of Prestige: Prizes, Awards, and the Circulation of Cultural Value* (Cambridge, MA: Harvard University Press, 2005), 11.
58. For more on this scandal, see Simone Murray, *The Adaptation Industry: The Cultural Economy of Contemporary Literary Adaptation* (New York: Routledge, 2011), 57–62.
59. Joan Acocella, "Martin Amis's 'Experience,'" *New Yorker*, June 19, 2000, 182. For an account of this melodrama, see also Finney, *Martin Amis*, 24–25.

60. Martin Amis, *The Information* (New York: Vintage, 1995), 211, 85, 95.
61. Martin Amis, "Career Move," *New Yorker*, June 29, 1992, 32–35.
62. Bigsby, *Writers*, 41.
63. Carl Bellante and John Bellante, "Unlike Father, Like Son: An Interview with Martin Amis," *Bloomsbury Review* 12, no. 2 (1992): 16.
64. Martin Amis, *Einstein's Monsters* (New York: Harmony Books, 1987), 23.
65. Chatman, "Backwards," 46.
66. Menke, "Narrative Reversals," 973.
67. Hutcheon, *A Poetics of Postmodernism*, 89.
68. Amis, *Time's Arrow*, 175; Kurt Vonnegut, *Slaughterhouse-Five, or The Children's Crusade* (New York: Vintage, 2000), 53–54.
69. Kathleen Fitzpatrick, *The Anxiety of Obsolescence: The American Novel in the Age of Television* (Nashville, TN: Vanderbilt University Press, 2006), 230–31.
70. Bellante, "Unlike Father," 5.
71. On the relation between technology, literary prestige, and historical fiction, see Alexander Manshel, "The Lag: Technology and Fiction in the Twentieth Century," *PMLA* 135, no. 1 (2020): 40–58.
72. Bellante, "Unlike Father," 16.
73. Bellante, "Unlike Father," 4.
74. Julia Alvarez, *How the García Girls Lost Their Accents* (Chapel Hill, NC: Algonquin Books, 2010); hereafter cited parenthetically.
75. Catherine Wiley, "Memory Is Already the Story You Made Up About the Past: An Interview with Julia Alvarez," *Bloomsbury Review* 12, no. 2 (1992): 9.
76. For more on the genre blending and "generic transgression" in Alvarez's novels, see Kelli Lyon Johnson, *Julia Alvarez: Writing a New Place on the Map* (Albuquerque: University of New Mexico Press, 2005); David J. Vazquez, *Triangulations: Narrative Strategies for Navigating Latino Identity* (Minneapolis: University of Minnesota Press, 2011).
77. Elizabeth Coonrod Martínez, "Julia Alvarez: Progenitor of a Movement," *Americas* 59, no. 2 (March–April 2007): 6–13. On the rise of the "Latina novel" in the late 1980s and early 1990s, see also Dalleo and Machado Sáez, *The Latino/a Canon*, and Ellen McCracken, *New Latina Narrative: The Feminine Space of Postmodern Ethnicity* (Tucson: University of Arizona Press, 1999).
78. See, e.g., William Luis, *Dance Between Two Cultures: Latino Caribbean Literature Written in the United States* (Nashville, TN: Vanderbilt University Press, 1997), 266–67; Jacqueline Stefanko, "New Ways of Telling: Latinas' Narratives of Exile and Return," *Frontiers: A Journal of Women Studies* 17, no. 2 (1996): 50–69; Julie Barak, "'Turning and Turning in the Widening Gyre': A Second Coming Into Language in Julia Alvarez's *How the Garcia Girls Lost Their Accents*," *MELUS* 23,

1. CONTEMPORARY FICTION IN REVERSE

no. 1 (March 1998): 159–76; Rosa-Linda Fregoso, "Julia Alvarez, *In the Time of the Butterflies*," in *Reading U.S. Latina Writers: Remapping American Literature*, ed. Alvina E. Quintana (New York: Palgrave Macmillan, 2003): 7–14; and Catherine Romagnolo, *Opening Acts: Narrative Beginnings in Twentieth-Century Feminist Fiction* (Lincoln: University of Nebraska Press, 2015).

79. Sarika Chandra, "Re-Producing a Nationalist Literature in the Age of Globalization: Reading (Im)migration in Julia Alvarez's *How the García Girls Lost Their Accents*," *American Quarterly* 60, no. 3 (September 2008): 839. On Alvarez as autobiographer, see Julia Ortiz-Vilarelle, "Julia Alvarez and the Autobiographical *Antojo*," in *Inhabiting La Patria: Identity, Agency, and Antojo in the Work of Julia Alvarez*, ed. Rebecca L. Harrison and Emily Hipchen (Albany: State University of New York Press, 2013), 21–42. On Alvarez as bilingual novelist, see Jeehyun Lim, *Bilingual Brokers: Race, Literature, and Language as Human Capital* (New York: Fordham University Press, 2017). On Alvarez as refugee writer, see April Shemak, *Asylum Speakers: Caribbean Refugees and Testimonial Discourse* (Philadelphia: Temple University Press, 2010). For masterful accounts of Alvarez's work in the context of the "multicultural" literary marketplace, see also McCracken, and Elena Machado Sáez, *Market Aesthetics: The Purchase of the Past in Caribbean Diasporic Fiction* (Charlottesville: University of Virginia Press, 2015).

80. A notable exception to this is Deborah Thurman's analysis of *¡Yo!*, Alvarez's 1997 sequel to *The García Girls*, which emphasizes the ways in which Alvarez "invokes the institutional power of the creative writing program to promote her own model of multicultural literary politics, a model critical of the market dynamics in which it remains embedded." Deborah Thurman, "Professions of Craft: Program Era Pedagogy in Julia Alvarez's *¡Yo!*," *Arizona Quarterly: A Journal of American Literature, Culture, and Theory* 77, no. 4 (2021): 64.

81. Silvio Sirias, *Julia Alvarez: A Critical Companion* (Westport, CT: Greenwood, 2001), 3.

82. Robert Pack, director of the Bread Loaf Writers' Conference from 1973 to 1995, even earns top billing over Alvarez's own family: "For Bob Pack and, of course, the sisters." As to the short story cycle structure, Mark McGurl makes a similar argument with regard to Sandra Cisneros's *The House on Mango Street* (1984). See *The Program Era: Postwar Fiction and the Rise of Creative Writing* (Cambridge, MA: Harvard University Press, 2009), 339. For more on how "the market and culture of an MFA education informs generational shifts within the US Latinx canon," see Elena Machado Sáez, "Generation MFA: Neoliberalism and the Shifting Cultural Capital of US Latinx Writers," *Latino Studies* 16, no. 3 (2018): 361–83. On short story cycles by Latinx writers, see Long Le-Khac, *Giving Form to an Asian and Latinx America* (Stanford, CA: Stanford University Press, 2020).

1. CONTEMPORARY FICTION IN REVERSE

83. "Throughout her climb to literary fame in the 1990s," Thurman argues, "Alvarez deployed the vocabulary of creative writing pedagogy to critically negotiate the demands of a US publishing market hungry for Latinx literature—and a US cultural sphere eager to categorize and commodify ethnic difference." Thus, "alignment with the MFA equipped Alvarez to effectively relitigate the dominant modes of reception for 1990s Latinx fiction." Thurman, "Professions of Craft," 62.
84. Like the wealth of Amis criticism that focuses nearly exclusively on *Time's Arrow*'s time in Auschwitz, nearly all accounts of *The García Girls* include a substantial reading of "The Blood of the Conquistadores." Despite the chapter's dazzling shifts in free indirect discourse, however, and its play with the tropes of the spy genre, its meditations on the experience of exile are what have most captured the interest of critics.
85. Dalleo and Machado Sáez, *The Latino/a Canon*, 139.
86. Ben Jacques, "Julia Alvarez: Real Flights of Imagination." *Americas* 53, no. 1 (January–February 2001): 27. Moreover, Luis points out that "in order to undergo a search for her origins," Alvarez—who, unlike Yolanda, was born in New York—also "had to change her place of birth, from the United States to the Dominican Republic; therefore, she trades places with her sister and assumes the identity of the third child, who was born on the island." Luis, *Dance*, 272.
87. "NEA Literature Fellowships: 40 Years of Supporting American Writers," National Endowment for the Arts, 2006, 12, https://www.arts.gov/about/publications/nea-literature-fellowships-40-years-supporting-american-writers.
88. Mark Bauerlein and Ellen Grantham, eds., *National Endowment for the Arts: A History, 1965–2008* (Washington, DC: National Endowment for the Arts, 2009), 186.
89. For more on the nomination process and the changes made to it in the 1970s and 1980s, see Bauerlein and Grantham, *National Endowment*, 186–87. For another study of the National Endowment for the Arts in this period, see Margaret Doherty, "State-Funded Fiction: Minimalism, National Memory, and the Return to Realism in the Post-Postmodern Age," *American Literary History* 27, no. 1 (2014): 79–101.
90. Quoted in Edward Arian, *The Unfulfilled Promise: Public Subsidy of the Arts in America* (Philadelphia: Temple University Press, 1989), 52.
91. Bauerlein and Grantham, *National Endowment*, 190.
92. "NEA Literature Fellowships," 3.
93. "NEA Literature Fellowships," 33, 19.
94. Machado Sáez, "Generation MFA," 370.

1. CONTEMPORARY FICTION IN REVERSE

95. Machado Sáez, *Market Aesthetics*, 33.
96. Jonathan Bing, "Julie [sic] Alvarez: Books That Cross Borders," *Publishers Weekly* 243, no. 51 (1996): 38.
97. Sirias, *Julia Alvarez*, 17.
98. Tom Vitale, "Julia Alvarez Reads from *How the García Girls Lost Their Accents*, and Talks About the Dominican-American Immigrant Experience," *Moveable Feast*, 1992.
99. McGrath, "Literary Agency," 357.
100. McGrath, "Literary Agency," 359.
101. Sirias, *Julia Alvarez*, 5.
102. Donna Rifkind, "Speaking American," review of *How the García Girls Lost Their Accents*, by Julia Alvarez, *New York Times*, October 6, 1991.
103. Machado Sáez, *Market Aesthetics*, 33–34.
104. Machado Sáez argues that the many student-teacher relationships depicted in Caribbean diasporic historical fiction function as "models for the reader-text relationship": "Framing the historical fiction as a lesson plan," she claims, "speaks to the mainstream market's demands for the genre and the ethical imperatives of Caribbean diasporic writers." Machado Sáez, *Market Aesthetics*, 34.
105. Focusing on Alvarez's bicultural protagonists in particular, McCracken has argued that these narrator figures are positioned as proxies for the author's white readers, using "ethnographic passages" to explain "cultural practices for the benefit of various groups of 'outsiders' " (5). Indeed, in the "postscript" to *In the Time of the Butterflies*, Alvarez goes so far as to explain that her goal was, first and foremost, "to immerse my readers in an epoch in the life of the Dominican Republic" and "deepen North Americans' understanding of the nightmare" that is recent Dominican history. Crucially, Alvarez's postscript then turns to a second audience, addressing "Dominicans separated by language from the world I have created" (324). "It is telling," Steve Criniti argues, that "even in her address directly to Dominican readers in the Postscript, Alvarez continues to keep English speaking North Americans as the primary focus of her purpose. In short, she is telling Dominican readers outright, not in so many words, 'this book is not for you.' " Steve Criniti, "Collecting Butterflies: Julia Alvarez's Revision of North American Collective Memory," *Modern Language Studies* 36, no. 2 (2007): 45. Describing an interview with Alvarez, Sirias explains that the author "visibly recoils when ... people attempt to relegate her to the margins of American literature: 'I am a Latina who writes, but not one who writes only for Latinos' " (6).
106. See, for example, Barbara Mujica, "On Politics and Literature," *Americas* 47, no. 2 (March–April 1995): 60.

1. CONTEMPORARY FICTION IN REVERSE

107. Michael Shnayerson, "The Four Amigas: Latina Literature's New Doyennes," *Vanity Fair*, September 1994, 128.
108. Jacques, "Julia Alvarez," 28.
109. *Homecoming: New and Collected Poems* (New York: Plume, 1996), 72.
110. One example of this discourse of interchangeability arrives in the opening pages of *The García Girls*, which include *Entertainment Weekly*'s description of the novel as "The Hispanic Joy Luck Club."
111. *Homecoming* (New York: Grove Press, 1984), 85–86.

2. THE MAKING OF THE GREATEST GENERATION

1. In that same period, the National Book Critics Circle, an American organization that nonetheless honors works of fiction from other countries and in other languages, shortlisted or selected World War II novels by Laurent Binet, Andrea Levy, Ian McEwan, and W. G. Sebald, among others.
2. Jenny Shank, "Dallas-Bound Luis Alberto Urrea Says 'House of Broken Angels' Is Like a Mexican Take on 'The Godfather,'" *Dallas Morning News*, March 6, 2018.
3. U.S. Congress, House, *Uniting and Strengthening America by Providing Appropriate Tools Required to Intercept and Obstruct Terrorism (USA PATRIOT ACT) Act of 2001*, HR 3162, 107th Cong., 1st sess., introduced in House October 23, 2001.
4. Shank, "Dallas-Bound." Urrea ultimately returned to the novel, published as *Good Night, Irene* in 2023.
5. Of the 107 works of historical fiction to win one of these three prizes from 1950 to 2019, more than a third take place, to some extent, in the 1940s.
6. Alexander Manshel, Laura B. McGrath, and J. D. Porter, "Who Cares About Literary Prizes?" *Public Books*, September 3, 2019, https://www.publicbooks.org/who-cares-about-literary-prizes/. For a comprehensive history and detailed analysis of literary awards, see James F. English, *The Economy of Prestige: Prizes, Awards, and the Circulation of Cultural Value* (Cambridge, MA: Harvard University Press, 2005).
7. This helps in part to explain why "post-45" has been such a prominent and *institutionalized* literary-critical term. Perhaps this period marker has less to do with changes in literary history during the mid–twentieth century than with the historical fiction of that period at century's end.
8. Toni Morrison, *Song of Solomon* (New York: Vintage International, 2004), 60.
9. Alice Walker, *The Color Purple* (New York: Washington Square Press, 1983), 231.

2. THE MAKING OF THE GREATEST GENERATION

10. "Minority Groups in World War II," U.S. Army Center of Military History, October 3, 2003, https://history.army.mil/documents/WWII/minst.html.
11. Walker, *The Color Purple*, 245.
12. Leslie Marmon Silko, *Ceremony* (New York: Penguin, 2006), 33; hereafter cited parenthetically.
13. Fiction of the 1940s—including novels about the war's multiple fronts and home fronts, the Holocaust, and Japanese American incarceration—is simply too vast to cover adequately in a single scholarly monograph, let alone a single chapter of one. For a broader history of World War II fiction, including more on early prizewinning novels by James Jones, Herman Wouk, and John Hersey, as well as war fiction by Norman Mailer, Chester Himes, and Ann Petry, see Elizabeth D. Samet, *Looking for the Good War: American Amnesia and the Violent Pursuit of Happiness* (New York: Farrar, Straus and Giroux, 2021); Roy Scranton, *Total Mobilization: World War II and American Literature* (Chicago: University of Chicago Press, 2019); Vaughn Rasberry, *Race and the Totalitarian Century: Geopolitics in the Black Literary Imagination* (Cambridge, MA: Harvard University Press, 2017); Joseph Darda, "Universality at War: Race, Nation, and Communism in Chester Himes's 'If He Hollers Let Him Go,'" *African American Review* 48, nos. 1–2 (Spring–Summer 2015): 157–73; Marina Mackay, "Introduction," in *The Cambridge Companion to the Literature of World War II*, ed. Marina Mackay (New York: Cambridge University Press, 2009), 1–10; James Dawes, "The American War Novel," in Mackay, *The Cambridge Companion to the Literature of World War II*, 56–66; John Limon, *Writing After War: American War Fiction from Realism to Postmodernism* (Oxford: Oxford University Press, 1994).
14. Joseph Heller, *Catch-22* (New York: Simon & Schuster, 2004), 387; hereafter cited parenthetically.
15. Orville Prescott, "Books of the Times," *New York Times*, October 23, 1961.
16. "Bureaucracy and War," panel at Florida State University, March 21, 1997, C-SPAN, c-span.org/video/?79870-1/bureaucracy-war#.
17. Kurt Vonnegut, *Slaughterhouse-Five* (New York: Vintage, 2000), 80–81; hereafter cited parenthetically.
18. Thomas Pynchon, *Gravity's Rainbow* (New York: Penguin, 2006); hereafter cited parenthetically.
19. The Pulitzer's three-member fiction jury—Benjamin DeMott, Elizabeth Hardwick, and Alfred Kazin—unanimously recommended Pynchon's novel for the prize, but the organization's board ultimately rejected their recommendation, calling the book "unreadable," "turgid," "overwritten," and "obscene." Peter Kihss, "Pulitzer Jurors Dismayed on Pynchon," *New York Times*, May 8, 1974.

2. THE MAKING OF THE GREATEST GENERATION

20. During World War II, Indigenous American communities had the "highest rate of voluntary enlistment in the military," with "70 percent of men" enlisting in some tribes. "1941–45: American Indian War Effort in World War II Is Remarkable," Native Voices, https://www.nlm.nih.gov/nativevoices/timeline/461.html.
21. George Lipsitz, *Time Passages: Collective Memory and American Popular Culture* (Minneapolis: University of Minnesota Press, 1990), 231.
22. Vonnegut, *Slaughterhouse-Five*, 17.
23. Joseph Frank, "Spatial Form in Modern Literature: An Essay in Two Parts," *Sewanee Review* 53, no. 2 (Spring 1945): 221–40.
24. Three years after the publication of *Ceremony*, the novel was awarded the Before Columbus Foundation's American Book Award, a nonhierarchical literary prize meant to honor the "multicultural, multiethnic, and multiracial diversity" of American letters. Quoted in Robert A. Lee, "Afro-America, The Before Columbus Foundation and The Literary Multiculturalization of America," *Journal of American Studies* 28, no. 3 (1994): 446.
25. Kenneth M. Roemer, "Silko's Arroyos as Mainstream: Processes and Implications of Canonical Identity," in *Leslie Marmon Silko's Ceremony: A Casebook*, ed. Allan Chavkin (Oxford: Oxford University Press, 2002), 223.
26. "Open Syllabus Explorer," Open Syllabus Project.
27. Roemer, "Silko's Arroyos," 227–229.
28. Twenty-eight of the thirty World War II novels shortlisted for the NBA, NBCC, and Pulitzer Prize between 1960 and 1979 were by white authors.
29. For a survey of criticism on the novel, see Chavkin, *Leslie Marmon Silko's Ceremony*. On the depictions of war and its aftermath in Silko's novel, see John Getz, "Healing the Soldier in White: *Ceremony* as War Novel," *WLA: War, Literature and the Arts* 9, no. 1 (1997): 123–40; Carrie Johnston, "Postwar Reentry Narratives in Leslie Marmon Silko's *Ceremony* and Ben Fountain's *Billy Lynn's Long Halftime Walk*," *Studies in the Novel* 49, no. 3 (Fall 2017): 400–418; Ben Railton, *History and Hope in American Literature: Models of Critical Patriotism* (New York: Rowman & Littlefield, 2017), ch. 2; and Alyssa A. Hunziker, "At the Intersections of Empire: *Ceremony*, Transnationalism, and American Indian–Filipino Exchange," *Studies in American Indian Literatures* 31, no. 3 (Fall 2019): 116–34.
30. Roemer, "Silko's Arroyos," 226.
31. Michael Rothberg, *Multidirectional Memory: Remembering the Holocaust in the Age of Decolonization* (Stanford, CA: Stanford University Press, 2009), 3, 5.
32. Stanley Crouch, "Literary Conjure Woman," *New Republic*, October 19, 1987. Both Morrison's epigraph and the figure it cites have been the source of much controversy and debate. On this, see Naomi Mandel, *Against the Unspeakable: Complicity, the Holocaust, and Slavery in America* (Charlottesville: University of Virginia Press, 2006), ch. 5.

2. THE MAKING OF THE GREATEST GENERATION

33. For a deft analysis of Ambrose's and Brokaw's contributions to the mythologizing of World War II, see Samet, *Looking for the Good War*, ch. 1. See also Scranton, who claims that *Saving Private Ryan* "betrays not so much a dedication to the past as an attempt to dominate it—an attempt by a baby boomer director to take ownership of his father's war" *Total Mobilization*, (236).
34. Samet, *Looking for the Good War*, 25–26.
35. Tom Brokaw, *The Greatest Generation* (New York: Random House, 1998), 183.
36. Walter Benn Michaels, *The Shape of the Signifier: 1967 to the End of History* (Princeton, NJ: Princeton University Press, 2004), 79.
37. Mackay, "Introduction," 6. That said, even for the generation of writers who experienced the period, the growing historical distance from the war and changing cultural perception of it may have gradually softened their cutting perspective. Take, for example, the 1997 panel on "Bureaucracy and War" described earlier. Asked about his thoughts on "the concept of a just war," Vonnegut answered: "I think we fought in a just war," adding, with Heller chuckling softly by his side, "I wouldn't have missed World War II for anything. It was a great adventure" ("Bureaucracy and War").
38. Amy Hungerford, *The Holocaust of Texts: Genocide, Literature, and Personification* (Chicago: University of Chicago Press, 2003), 96.
39. Thomas Keneally, *Schindler's List* (New York: Touchstone, 1993), 10.
40. Keneally, *Schindler's List*, 14.
41. English, *The Economy of Prestige*, 60.
42. Like her character Faye, Kim was born in the mid-1920s in Los Angeles, her father died when she was very young, and she was raised by a single mother who was a political organizer for multiple Korean and Korean American causes.
43. Ronyoung Kim, *Clay Walls* (New York: The Permanent Press, 1987), 50; hereafter cited parenthetically.
44. Samet, *Looking for the Good War*, 36.
45. Rasberry, *Race and the Totalitarian Century*, 10.
46. In a particularly moving passage at the end of the novel, Kim writes: "In my lifetime I have heard promises of trust from China and Japan while they helped themselves to our land. Germans and Frenchmen were on our soil digging out our gold. Americans looked the other way when we asked for recognition, and Russia considered us her legitimate spoil of war.... All we wanted from them was to be left alone" (115).
47. Box 1, Ronyoung Kim and Richard Hahn Papers, Collection no. 3010, Korean Heritage Library, USC Libraries, University of Southern California.
48. Box 1, Folder 51, Letter from Gloria Hahn [Ronyoung Kim] to Toni Morrison, May 7, 1982, Ronyoung Kim and Richard Hahn Papers.

2. THE MAKING OF THE GREATEST GENERATION

49. Box 11, Letter from Martin Shepard to Marilyn Hahn, August 7, 1987, Ronyoung Kim and Richard Hahn Papers; Box 1, Folder 17, "Assorted Personal Correspondence, 1965–1988," Letter from Melanie S. Hahn to Arthur Dong, Lorraine Dong, and Rebecca Soladay, April 15, 1988, Ronyoung Kim and Richard Hahn Papers.
50. Box 1, Folder 51, Letter from Gloria Hahn [Ronyoung Kim] to Toni Morrison. May 7, 1982, Ronyoung Kim and Richard Hahn Papers.
51. Scranton, *Total Mobilization*, 9.
52. Box 1, Folder 23, Letter from Gloria Hahn [Ronyoung Kim] to Leon Surmelian, April 7, 1977, Ronyoung Kim and Richard Hahn Papers.
53. Box 1, Folder 31, Letter from Gloria Hahn [Ronyoung Kim] to Susan Stamberg, April 11, 1983, Ronyoung Kim and Richard Hahn Papers.
54. Colson Whitehead, *The Nickel Boys* (New York: Doubleday, 2019), 71.
55. Colson Whitehead, *Harlem Shuffle* (New York: Penguin Random House, 2021), 73–75.
56. Rasberry, *Race and the Totalitarian Century*, 29.
57. Amy Hungerford, *Making Literature Now* (Stanford, CA: Stanford University Press, 2016), 125.
58. Heller, *Catch-22*, 110.
59. Anthony Doerr, *All the Light We Cannot See* (New York: Scribner, 2014), 13, 30; hereafter cited parenthetically.
60. Michael Chabon, *The Amazing Adventures of Kavalier & Clay* (New York: Random House, 2012); hereafter cited parenthetically.
61. Jonathan Safran Foer, *Everything Is Illuminated* (New York: Harper Perennial, 2003), 151; hereafter cited parenthetically.
62. Jennifer Egan, *Manhattan Beach* (New York: Scribner, 2018), 144; hereafter cited parenthetically.
63. This also explains the novels' insistence on the trope of simultaneity. Whether it is the image, from which Foer draws his title, of astronauts watching people all over the world make love at once (95), or Chabon and Doerr's shared fascination with radio transmissions, or the latter's present-tense narration of his twin protagonists, producing a near constant sense of *meanwhile*, both the plot and form of these novels betray a desire to feel contemporaneous with the war.
64. Sarah Lea, "Joseph Cornell: Wanderlust," in *Joseph Cornell: Wanderlust* (London: Royal Academy of Arts, 2015), 35.
65. Sarah Wasserman, *The Death of Things: Ephemera and the American Novel* (Minneapolis: University of Minnesota Press, 2020), 4.
66. Jeremy Rosen, *Minor Characters Have Their Day: Genre and the Contemporary Literary Marketplace* (New York: Columbia University Press, 2016), 184.
67. "2015 Pulitzer Prizes," The Pulitzer Prizes; "Judges Citation: *All the Light We Cannot See*," National Book Foundation.

2. THE MAKING OF THE GREATEST GENERATION

68. Deborah Treisman, "The Searcher," interview with Jonathan Safran Foer, *New Yorker*, June 10, 2001, https://www.newyorker.com/magazine/2001/06/18/the-searcher.
69. Jonathan Safran Foer, ed., *A Convergence of Birds: Original Fiction and Poetry Inspired by Joseph Cornell* (New York: Penguin, 2007). Foer's second novel, *Extremely Loud and Incredibly Close* (New York: Penguin, 2005), takes these aesthetics still further, incorporating photographs, business cards, annotated letters, and a flipbook of images, among other typographical ornaments.
70. Petra Rau, "The War in Contemporary Fiction," in Mackay, *The Cambridge Companion to the Literature of World War II*, 217.
71. For an example of how archival research has become part of the contemporary novelist's craft, "See Clayton Childress, *Under the Cover: The Creation, Production, and Reception of a Novel* (Princeton, NJ: Princeton University Press, 2017), 26–29.
72. Keneally, *Schindler's List*, 290; Doerr, *All the Light*, 135.
73. Philip Roth, *The Plot Against America* (New York: Vintage International, 2005). See Wasserman, *The Death of Things*, for deft readings of how ephemera functions in both Chabon and Roth.
74. Toni Morrison, *Playing in the Dark: Whiteness and the Literary Imagination* (New York: Vintage, 1993), 33, 59.
75. Morrison, *Playing in the Dark*, 17.
76. This is also reflected in the trope of disappearance that runs throughout these novels of the war. For a deft reading of vanishing in *Manhattan Beach*, see Allan Hepburn, "Vanishing Worlds: Epic Disappearance in *Manhattan Beach*," *PMLA* 134, no. 2 (March 2019): 384–90. On the trope of adolescence in World War II novels of the 1960s and 1970s, see Limon, *Writing After War*, 139–40.
77. On disability in Egan's *Manhattan Beach*, see Rachel Adams, "Siblings, Disability, Genre in Jennifer Egan's *Manhattan Beach*," *PMLA* 134, no. 2 (March 2019): 366–71; and Janet Lyon, "The Wheelchair: A Three-Part Drama," *PMLA* 134, no. 2 (March 2019): 405–11. See also Michael Chabon's follow-up to *Kavalier & Clay*, *The Final Solution: A Story of Detection* (New York: Harper Perennial, 2004), which is set in 1944 England and narrates an elderly Sherlock Holmes working to solve the mystery of a nine-year-old Jewish refugee who has lost the ability to speak.
78. Hungerford argues that Foer's chief "aesthetic innovation" in the novel "is not to be found in the book's typographical pyrotechnics and self-conscious structure" but rather "in its plot," which racks focus "from the victim's side of the Holocaust to the perpetrator's side" (*Making Literature Now*, 127).
79. Julie Otsuka, *When the Emperor Was Divine* (New York: Anchor Books, 2003); hereafter cited parenthetically.

2. THE MAKING OF THE GREATEST GENERATION

80. Julie Otsuka, "An Interview with Julie Otsuka," *BookBrowse*, January 6, 2010, https://www.bookbrowse.com/author_interviews/full/index.cfm/author_number/807/julie-otsuka.
81. Otsuka, "An Interview with Julie Otsuka."
82. Otsuka, "An Interview with Julie Otsuka."
83. Tim O'Brien, *The Things They Carried* (New York: Broadway Books, 1990), 68–69.
84. Josephine Park, "Alien Enemies in Julie Otsuka's *When the Emperor Was Divine*," *Modern Fiction Studies* 59, no. 1 (Spring 2013): 149, 151.
85. Tina Chen, "Towards an Ethics of Knowledge," *MELUS* 30, no. 2 (Summer 2005): 168.
86. "Phoenix Award," Children's Literature Association, https://chla.memberclicks.net/phoenix-award.

3. COLSON WHITEHEAD'S HISTORY OF THE UNITED STATES

1. Colson Whitehead, "What to Write Next," *New York Times Book Review*, November 1, 2009.
2. Andrew Hoberek, "Living with PASD," *Contemporary Literature* 53, no. 2 (2012): 406–13; Andrew Hoberek, "Cormac McCarthy and the Aesthetics of Exhaustion," *American Literary History* 23, no. 3 (2011): 483–99; Theodore Martin, *Contemporary Drift: Genre, Historicism, and the Problem of the Present* (New York: Columbia University Press, 2017); Jeremy Rosen, "Literary Fiction and the Genres of Genre Fiction," *Post45*, August 7, 2018, http://post45.research.yale.edu/2018/08/literary-fiction-and-the-genres-of-genre-fiction/.
3. Perry Anderson, "From Progress to Catastrophe," *London Review of Books* 33, no. 15 (2011): 27.
4. For an analysis of Whitehead's play with genre, see Stephanie Li, "Genre Trouble and History's Miseries in Colson Whitehead's *The Underground Railroad*," *MELUS* 44, no. 2 (2019): 1–23.
5. Colson Whitehead, *The Intuitionist* (New York: Anchor Books, 1999), 62, 58; hereafter cited parenthetically.
6. In order of quotations: Michael Bérubé, "Race and Modernity in Colson Whitehead's *The Intuitionist*," in *The Holodeck in the Garden: Science and Technology in Contemporary American Fiction*, ed. Peter Freese and Charles B. Harris (Normal, IL: Dalkey Archive Press, 2004), 163; Saundra Liggins, "The Urban Gothic Vision of Colson Whitehead's 'The Intuitionist' (1999)," *African American Review* 40, no. 2 (2006): 360; Ramón Saldívar, "The Second Elevation of the Novel: Race, Form, and the Postrace Aesthetic in Contemporary Narrative," *Narrative* 21, no. 1 (2013): 7.

3. COLSON WHITEHEAD'S HISTORY OF THE UNITED STATES

7. Walter Kirn, "The Promise of Verticality," review of *The Intuitionist*, by Colson Whitehead, *Time*, January 25, 1999.
8. Lauren Berlant, *Cruel Optimism* (Durham, NC: Duke University Press, 2011): 71.
9. Laura Miller, "Colson Whitehead's Alternate New York," review of *The Intuitionist*, by Colson Whitehead, *Salon*, January 12, 1999.
10. Liggins, "Urban Gothic," 361.
11. In order of quotations: Alison Russell, "Recalibrating the Past: Colson Whitehead's *The Intuitionist*," *Critique* 49, no. 1 (2007): 48; Saldívar, "Second Elevation," 9; Brian Norman, *Neo-Segregation Narratives: Jim Crow in Post–Civil Rights American Literature* (Athens: University of Georgia Press, 2010), 156.
12. In order of quotations: Julian Lucas, "New Black Worlds to Know," review of *The Underground Railroad*, by Colson Whitehead, *New York Review of Books*, September 29, 2016; Michele Elam, *The Souls of Mixed Folk: Race, Politics, and Aesthetics in the New Millennium* (Stanford, CA: Stanford University Press, 2011), 118; Jeffrey Allen Tucker, "'Verticality Is Such a Risky Enterprise': The Literary and Paraliterary Antecedents of Colson Whitehead's *The Intuitionist*," *Novel: A Forum on Fiction* 43, no. 1 (2010): 151.
13. Adam Kelly, "Freedom to Struggle: The Ironies of Colson Whitehead," *Open Library of Humanities* 4, no. 2 (2018): 3.
14. Fredric Jameson, *Postmodernism, or, The Cultural Logic of Late Capitalism* (Durham, NC: Duke University Press, 1991), 19–20.
15. Colson Whitehead, "The Year of Living Postracially," *New York Times*, November 3, 2009, http://www.nytimes.com/2009/11/04/opinion/04whitehead.html.
16. John Guillory has described this displacement as a kind of "imaginary politics" (i.e., "a politics of the *image*"), and, more recently, as "a form of surrogate politics." *Cultural Capital: The Problem of Literary Canon Formation* (Chicago: University of Chicago Press, 1993), 7; *Professing Criticism: Essays on the Organization of Literary Study* (Chicago: University of Chicago Press, 2022), 76.
17. William J. Bennett, *To Reclaim a Legacy: A Report on the Humanities in Higher Education* (Washington, DC: National Endowment for the Humanities, 1984), 29–30.
18. Allan Bloom, *The Closing of the American Mind: How Higher Education Has Failed Democracy and Impoverished the Souls of Today's Students* (New York: Simon & Schuster, 1987), 36.
19. Carol Iannone, "Literature by Quota," *Commentary* 51, no. 3 (March 1991): 50–53. That same year, the editors of the *New Criterion* described Charles Johnson's National Book Award for *Middle Passage* (1990)—only the second win for a Black author since Ellison's *Invisible Man* four decades earlier—as an example of how

3. COLSON WHITEHEAD'S HISTORY OF THE UNITED STATES

"the politics of affirmative action has finally destroyed the integrity" of the award: "Now [that] our major literary prizes have succumbed to the same political pressures ... ideology has supplanted literary excellence as the basis for these prizes." "Affirmative-action Book Prizes: On the Political Agenda of Certain National Book Award Jurors," *New Criterion*, January 1991, 1–2.

20. H. Aram Veeser, "Introduction," in *The New Historicism*, ed. H. Aram (New York: Routledge, 1989), xi.
21. Joseph North, *Literary Criticism: A Concise Political History* (Cambridge, MA: Harvard University Press, 2017), 8.
22. Bennett, *Legacy*, 30.
23. Henry Louis Gates, Jr., *Loose Canons: Notes on the Culture Wars* (New York: Oxford University Press, 1992), 35.
24. Guillory, *Cultural Capital*, 51, 32 (emphasis added).
25. David A. Plotz, "'Politically Correct' Thought Control," *Harvard Crimson*, February 5, 1990; Constance Chen, "Two Views on PC Ideology," *Harvard Crimson*, February 24, 1990; Paul Leonard, "The Flag Is Harassment," *Harvard Crimson*, February 20, 1990; Maggie S. Tucker, "Affirmative Action Debated: IOP Forums Sparks Lively Exchange of Opinions," *Harvard Crimson*, March 9, 1990; Gayle Beth Fenster, "Educators Urge Women, Minority Role Models," *Harvard Crimson*, February 24, 1990; Philip M. Rubin, "Obama Named New Law Review President: Student Becomes First Black Chief of the Publication," *Harvard Crimson*, February 6, 1990.
26. See Kelly A. E. Mason, "Stop Teaching English Lit," *Harvard Crimson*, December 13, 1990; Melanie R. Williams, "It's Not Just Ethnic Studies," *Harvard Crimson*, December 13, 1990.
27. Sharan Strange, "Dark Room Collective: Essay," *Mosaic* 16, Fall 2006, republished online May 12, 2013, https://mosaicmagazine.org/dark-room-collective-essay/. Strange explains, "We had named it 'The Dark Room ...' because it was housed in a former photographic darkroom on the third floor of the old Victorian house we shared with four other artists/students in Central Square.... Only afterwards did we realize the affinity with the Dark Tower—named after Countee Cullen's poem—the gathering of Harlem Renaissance artists in A'lelia [*sic*] Walker's salon." See also Brian Reed, "The Dark Room Collective and Post-Soul Poetics," *African American Review* 41, no. 4 (2007): 727–47; Sophia Nguyen, "Elbow Room: How the Dark Room Collective made space for a generation of African-American writers," *Harvard Magazine*, March–April 2016.
28. Strange, "Dark Room Collective."
29. Sophia Nguyen, "Elbow Room." See also Jenn Shapland, "Interview with Colson Whitehead," *Southwest Contemporary*, May 1, 2018, https://southwestcontemporary.com/interview-with-colson-whitehead/.

3. COLSON WHITEHEAD'S HISTORY OF THE UNITED STATES

30. Colson Whitehead, "Sylvia's Crime," *Diaspora: The Journal of Black Thought & Culture* (Fall–Winter 1989–1990): 5–9.
31. Kevin Young, "Editor's Note," *Diaspora: The Journal of Black Thought & Culture* (Fall–Winter 1989–1990).
32. Suzan Sherman, "Colson Whitehead," *BOMB*, no. 76 (2001): 78. See also Linda Selzer, "New Eclecticism: An Interview with Colson Whitehead," *Callaloo* 31, no. 2 (2008): 395–97.
33. Laura Miller, "Going Up," interview with Colson Whitehead, *Salon*, January 13, 1999. Reed served as a visiting professor in Harvard's Afro-American Studies Department in spring 1987, likely one semester before Whitehead matriculated.
34. Julian Lucas, "I Ain't Been Mean Enough: The Literary Provocations of Ishmael Reed," *New Yorker*, July 26, 2021, 44–53.
35. For Whitehead's reflections on this and other courses in Harvard's Department of African American Studies, see Liz Mineo, "An Imaginative Leap Into Real-life Horror," interview with Colson Whitehead, *Harvard Gazette*, September 20, 2016; Sabrina Li, "Colson Whitehead '91: Harvard Arts Medal Recipient," Office for the Arts at Harvard, April 21, 2018.
36. Toni Morrison, *Playing in the Dark: Whiteness and the Literary Imagination* (New York: Vintage, 1993), 5.
37. Morrison, *Playing in the Dark*, 53.
38. Joseph R. Palmore, "Afro-Am: Going Nowhere Fast," *Harvard Crimson*, February 2, 1990.
39. Steve Brown, "Why I Left the Afro-Am Dept.," *Harvard Crimson*, May 2, 1990; Roger G. Kuo, "The Troubled History of Afro-Am," *Harvard Crimson*, February 4, 1991.
40. Rebecca L. Walkowitz, "Afro-Am Activists Challenge Rosovsky," *Harvard Crimson*, November 17 1990; Walkowitz, "Afro-Am Beginning to Narrow Searches," *Harvard Crimson*, December 6 1990.
41. Julian E. Barnes, "Can He Save Afro-Am?," *Harvard Crimson*, January 31, 1991.
42. Gates, *Loose Canons*, 8.
43. Gates, *Loose Canons*, 10–11.
44. Gates, *Loose Canons*, 14.
45. Toni Morrison, "The Site of Memory," in *Inventing the Truth: The Art and Craft of Memoir*, ed. William Zinsser, 2nd ed. (New York: Houghton Mifflin, 1995), 85–102.
46. Lila Mae's method is not unlike Saidiya Hartman's practice of "critical fabulation." Saidiya Hartman, "Venus in Two Acts," *Small Axe* 12, no. 2 (2008): 11.
47. Georg Lukács, *The Historical Novel*, trans. Hannah Mitchell and Stanley Mitchell (Lincoln: University of Nebraska Press, 1983), 33.
48. Jameson, *Postmodernism*, 18–19.

49. Jameson, *Postmodernism*, 22.
50. Linda Hutcheon, "Historiographic Metafiction Parody and the Intertextuality of History," in *Intertextuality and Contemporary American Fiction*, ed. Patrick O'Donnell and Robert Davis (Baltimore: Johns Hopkins University Press, 1989), 3–32; Amy Elias, *Sublime Desire: History and Post-1960s Fiction* (Baltimore: Johns Hopkins University Press, 2001). For a reading of Whitehead's novels under the rubric of historiographic metafiction, see Derek C. Maus, *Understanding Colson Whitehead*, rev. ed. (Columbia: University of South Carolina Press, 2021).
51. Elias, *Sublime Desire*, xvii.
52. Guillory, *Cultural Capital*, 45.
53. My gratitude to Andrew Ward.
54. Madhu Dubey, "Museumizing Slavery: Living History in Colson Whitehead's *The Underground Railroad*," *American Literary History* 32, no. 1 (Spring 2020): 111.
55. See, e.g., William Ramsey, "An End of Southern History: The Down-Home Quests of Toni Morrison and Colson Whitehead," *African American Review* 41, no. 4 (2007): 769–85; Éva Tettenborn, "'A Mountain Full of Ghosts': Mourning African American Masculinities in Colson Whitehead's *John Henry Days*," *African American Review* 46, no. 2 (Summer–Fall 2013): 271–84; Peter Collins, "The Ghosts of Economics Past: *John Henry Days* and the Production of History," *African American Review* 46, no. 2 (Summer–Fall 2013): 285–300; Maus, *Understanding Colson Whitehead*. As if to emphasize the connection to his previous novel, at one point in *John Henry Days*, several characters debate a soon-to-be-published book "about two warring groups of chiropodists." "One group does it the natural way," a character explains, "looking for fungus and corns, and the other—" Here he is interrupted by another character. "The chiropodists are just the prologue," we are told. "The rest of the book is a social history, according to the *New Yorker*." Colson Whitehead, *John Henry Days* (New York: Anchor Books, 2001), 326; hereafter cited parenthetically.
56. "The Minds of Black Folk," *Vibe*, September 1997, 170–71.
57. Colson Whitehead, *Apex Hides the Hurt* (New York: Anchor Books, 2006), 22; hereafter cited parenthetically.
58. Stephanie Li connects Whitehead's satire in *Apex* to Obama-era calls for a new "postracial" United States, drawing out the similarities between the protagonist and the president himself. "As a black man in white-dominated institutions," Li argues, "the protagonist has learned to present a self that others want and expect of him and to hide the rest. . . . Much like Obama, the protagonist seems to ensure the promise of a color-blind meritocracy, a world in which racial difference does not matter." Although Whitehead skewers this dubious logic in *Apex Hides the Hurt*, the description of "a black [protagonist] in white-dominated

3. COLSON WHITEHEAD'S HISTORY OF THE UNITED STATES

institutions" is also an apt summary for many of Whitehead's novels. Stephanie Li, *Signifying Without Specifying: Racial Discourse in the Age of Obama* (New Brunswick, NJ: Rutgers University Press, 2011), 79.
59. My thanks to the anonymous peer reviewer who pointed this out.
60. Colson Whitehead, *Sag Harbor* (New York: Anchor Books, 2009), 212.
61. On this institutional position, see Mark McGurl, *The Program Era: Postwar Fiction and the Rise of Creative Writing* (Cambridge, MA: Harvard University Press, 2009), 335–38.
62. Laura Miller, "Colson Whitehead Is Still Just Doing His Weird Thing," *Slate*, September 12, 2021.
63. As Whitehead puts it, "A Negro in the world of academia must be twice the scholar, and twice the tactician, of his white colleagues" (157). On this aspect of the novel, see Collins, "Ghost of Economics Past," 287–88; Maus, *Understanding Colson Whitehead*, 49.
64. Cameron Leader-Picone, "Post-Black Stories: Colson Whitehead's *Sag Harbor* and Racial Individualism," *Contemporary Literature* 56, no. 3 (Fall 2015): 429.
65. "Oprah Reveals New Book Club Selection," *CBS This Morning*, August 2, 2016, www.youtube.com/watch?v=okcBr2h5zLc.
66. See, e.g., Li, "Genre Trouble."
67. Though many critics have asserted that *The Underground Railroad* is "as different as can be" from *Zone One*, others point up how Whitehead's zombie novel not only reanimates several of the central themes discussed earlier but also seems to be chewing on ideas explored in the author's meta–slave narrative (Juan Gabriel Vásquez, "In Colson Whitehead's Latest, the Underground Railroad Is More Than a Metaphor," review of *The Underground Railroad* by Colson Whitehead, *New York Times*, August 5, 2016). On the connections between these seemingly divergent novels and the zombie figure's "root[s] in the horrors of slavery," see Grace Heneks, "The American Subplot: Colson Whitehead's Post-Racial Allegory in *Zone One*," *The Comparatist* 42 (2018): 65–66. On history and historiography in *Zone One*, see Hoberek, "Living with PASD," 411–12; and Leif Sorensen, "Against the Post-Apocalyptic: Narrative Closure in Colson Whitehead's *Zone One*," *Contemporary Literature* 55 no. 3 (2014): 565–66.
68. Stephen Best, *None Like Us: Blackness, Belonging, Aesthetic Life* (Durham, NC: Duke University Press, 2018), 63.
69. Aida Levy-Hussen, *How to Read African American Literature: Post–Civil Rights Fiction and the Task of Interpretation* (New York: New York University Press, 2016), 6.
70. Stephanie Li argues that the novel is "mired in the demands of the literary marketplace," which celebrates Black artists "for bringing familiar stories of black

suffering to mainstream audiences" and rewards them "for fulfilling ... racialized literary expectations." "Great black writers write great books about slavery," Li concludes, "be they slave narratives, contemporary narratives of slavery, or the peculiar concoction that is *The Underground Railroad*" ("Genre Trouble," 4, 19–20).

71. Mineo, "An Imaginative Leap."
72. Colson Whitehead, *The Underground Railroad* (New York: Doubleday, 2016), 145; hereafter cited parenthetically.
73. Jennifer Schuessler, "Colson Whitehead on Slavery, Success and Writing the Novel That Really Scared Him," *New York Times*, August 2, 2016.
74. Jesse McCarthy, "A Literary Chameleon," *Harvard Magazine*, September–October 2016.
75. Schuessler, "Colson Whitehead."
76. Levy-Hussen, *How to Read*, 53.
77. Morrison, "The Site of Memory," 90–91.
78. Saidiya V. Hartman, *Scenes of Subjection: Terror, Slavery, and Self-Making in Nineteenth-Century America* (New York: Oxford University Press, 1997), 3.
79. Zora Neale Hurston, "What White Publishers Won't Print," in *Folklore, Memoirs, and Other Writings*, ed. Cheryl A. Wall (New York: Library of America, 1995), 879–81.
80. Dubey, "Museumizing Slavery," 112–14.
81. Michelle Singletary and Spencer S. Hsu, "Disney Says VA Park Will Be Serious Fun," *Washington Post*, November 12, 1993. Adding irony to both insult and injury, the theme park, which was ultimately abandoned, was set to be built on dubiously acquired land: for more than two years, "undercover Disney representatives secretly bought or obtained options on land in Prince William County," using "false names" to keep "Disney's interest in the area secret to prevent land prices from soaring."
82. Lee Konstantinou, "Critique Has Its Uses," *American Book Review* 38, no. 5 (2017): 18.
83. Levy-Hussen, *How to Read*, 6, 53.
84. Levy-Hussen, *How to Read*, 6.
85. "Responding to new conditions of public visibility rather than absence," Dubey argues, "the novel casts into bold relief the framing devices and mediating narratives used to contain the history of slavery even as it is opened up for affective, interactive consumption." Dubey, "Museumizing Slavery," 113.
86. Aida Levy-Hussen, "Boredom in Contemporary African American Literature," *Post45*, April 28, 2019, http://post45.research.yale.edu/2019/04/boredom-in-contemporary-african-american-literature/.
87. Elias, *Sublime Desire*, 113–14.

4. READING THE FAMILY TREE

88. "The Nickel Boys by Colson Whitehead," Penguin Random House, 2019, http://www.penguinrandomhouse.com/books/223161/the-nickel-boys-by-colson-whitehead/9780385537070.
89. Mitchell S. Jackson, "'I Carry It Within Me': Novelist Colson Whitehead Reminds Us How America's Racist History Lives On," *Time*, June 27, 2019.
90. For a fascinating study of the fugitive slave advertisement as a literary and historical genre, which draws on the same UNC archive, see Hannah Walser, "Under Description: The Fugitive Slave Advertisement as Genre," *American Literature* 92, no. 1 (2020): 61–89.
91. Colson Whitehead, *The Nickel Boys* (New York: Doubleday, 2019), 211; hereafter cited parenthetically.
92. The novel seems ready-made for the secondary school classroom: of all of Whitehead's novels, *Nickel* is the shortest, the most linear in its structure, the most accessible in its prose, and the least ironic in its tone.
93. Alexandra Alter, "Colson Whitehead's Next Novel Tackles Life Under Jim Crow," *New York Times*, October 10, 2018.
94. Maus, *Understanding Colson Whitehead*, 141.
95. Jennifer Wilson, "What Is Crime in a Country Built on It?" review of *Harlem Shuffle* by Colson Whitehead, *The Atlantic*, September 10, 2021.
96. Miller, "Colson Whitehead Is Still Just Doing His Weird Thing."
97. Miller, "Colson Whitehead Is Still Just Doing His Weird Thing."
98. Colson Whitehead, "Shaft vs. Action Jackson," *Diaspora: The Journal of Black Thought & Culture* (Fall–Winter 1989–1990): 30–31.
99. Ron Stodghill, "Why Colson Whitehead Keeps Bending the Rules of Fiction," *Wall Street Journal Magazine*, October 30, 2021, https://www.wsj.com/articles/colson-whitehead-harlem-interview-11635596651.

4. READING THE FAMILY TREE

1. Gyasi's seven-figure advance is said to have resulted from a ten-bidder auction in advance of the London Book Fair. As Laura Miller puts it, "that makes 'Homegoing' what publishers call a 'big book,' the object of promotion and marketing campaigns designed to present it as the glorious flowering of a precocious talent." Laura Miller, "Descendants," *New Yorker*, May 23, 2016, www.newyorker.com/magazine/2016/05/30/yaa-gyasis-homegoing.
2. As such, the genre both embodies and narrativizes what Lee Edelman has called "reproductive futurism." Lee Edelman, *No Future* (Durham, NC: Duke University Press, 2004).

4. READING THE FAMILY TREE

3. Julia Creet, *The Genealogical Sublime* (Amherst: University of Massachusetts Press, 2020), 4. Though the generational scope of the family saga genre varies from book to book, three or four generations—just long enough to imagine one's grandparents as children—is the most common.
4. Jill Owens, "Powell's Interview: Yaa Gyasi of *Homegoing*," Powell's Book Blog, May 23, 2016.
5. Ron Charles, "'Homegoing,' by Yaa Gyasi: A Bold Tale of Slavery for a New 'Roots' Generation," *Washington Post*, June 13, 2016.
6. Kimberly N. Parker, "*Homegoing* Teacher's Guide," Penguin Random House, 2018, www.penguinrandomhouse.com/books/533857/homegoing-by-yaa-gyasi/9781101971062/teachers-guide/.
7. Stanley E. Fish, "Interpreting the 'Variorum,'" *Critical Inquiry* 2, no. 3 (1976): 465–85. As Jeremy Rosen argues, literary genres "don't get 'seized on' . . . by accident, magic, or the extraordinary ken of great authors. A succession of interested agents—writers, editors, reviewers, scholars—actively search for and promote forms that will serve their interests and resonate with readers." Jeremy Rosen, *Minor Characters Have Their Day: Genre and the Contemporary Literary Marketplace* (New York: Columbia University Press, 2016), 30.
8. Yaa Gyasi, *Homegoing*, 2016 (New York: Vintage, 2017), 295; hereafter cited parenthetically.
9. Namwali Serpell and Maria Tumarkin, "Unethical Reading and the Limits of Empathy," *Yale Review*, Winter 2020, yalereview.yale.edu/unethical-reading-and-limits-empathy.
10. A. E. Zucker, "The Genealogical Novel, a New Genre," *PMLA: Publications of the Modern Language Association of America* 43, no. 2 (June 1928): 551.
11. Chronicle novel: q.v. in *The Oxford Dictionary of Literary Terms*, 4th ed., ed. Chris Baldick (Oxford: Oxford University Press, 2015); see also "Saga." Narrative of community: Sandra A. Zagarell, "Narrative of Community: The Identification of a Genre," *Signs* 13, no. 3 (1988): 498–527. See also Roxanne Harde, ed., *Narratives of Community: Women's Short Story Sequences* (Newcastle, UK: Cambridge Scholars Publishing, 2007), 3. Family novel: Anna A. Berman, "The Family Novel (and Its Curious Disappearance)," *Comparative Literature* 72, no. 1 (March 2020): 1–18; Yi-Ling Ru, "The Family Novel: Toward a Generic Definition," *Comparative Literature: East & West* 3, no. 1 (2001): 99–133. See also Lisa Saariluoma, "Virginia Woolf's *The Years*: Identity and Time in an Anti-Family Novel," *Orbis Litterarum: International Review of Literary Studies* 54, no. 4 (1999): 276–300.
12. Thomas Mann, *Buddenbrooks: The Decline of a Family*, trans. John E. Woods (New York: Vintage, 1993), 99. See Lothar Hönnighausen, "Thomas Mann's *Buddenbrooks* and William Faulkner's *Sartoris* as Family Novels," *Faulkner Journal* 6, no. 1 (1990): 33–45.

4. READING THE FAMILY TREE

13. Mann, *Buddenbrooks*: Napoleon and the July Monarchy, 23–25; Orsini and his bomb plot, 349–50; the 1842 Great Fire of Hamburg, 94; the 1848 Revolution, 176–90; the Austro-Prussian War, 427. Hereafter cited parenthetically.
14. Creet, *The Genealogical Sublime*, 16.
15. Throughout the novel Haley's characters directly address capital-H historical events, such as the British monarchy's role in the thirteen American colonies (227–28), the Revolutionary War (230–34), the Haitian Rebellion (295–96), the War of 1812 (379), Nat Turner's rebellion (438), Frederick Douglass's and Sojourner Truth's activism (468), Harriet Tubman and the "Unnergroun' Railroad" (469), the American Civil War (534), and the Emancipation Proclamation (547). Haley's discussion of these events often comes at the starts of chapters, setting in motion events in the lives of individual characters.
16. These include Louise Erdrich's *Love Medicine* (1984), Cristina García's *Dreaming in Cuban* (1992), Michael Cunningham's *Flesh and Blood* (1995), Rosario Ferré's *The House on the Lagoon* (1995), and Jeffrey Eugenides's *Middlesex* (2002), to name just a few.
17. Ru, "The Family Novel," 128.
18. Zucker, "The Genealogical Novel," 551. On the cultural impact of developments in genetic science, see Alondra Nelson, *The Social Life of DNA: Race, Reparations, and Reconciliation After the Genome* (Boston: Beacon Press, 2016). For a "postgenomic" reading of the multigenerational historical novel, see Patricia E. Chu, "D(NA) Coding the Ethnic: Jeffrey Eugenides's *Middlesex*," *Novel: A Forum on Fiction* 42, no. 2 (2009): 278–83. On *Finding Your Roots* and others like it, see Matthew Elliott, "The Inconvenient Ancestor: Slavery and Selective Remembrance on Genealogy Television," *Studies in Popular Culture* 39, no. 2 (2017): 73–90.
19. On this boom and its "genealogical imagination," see Jerome de Groot, "International Federation for Public History Plenary Address: On Genealogy," *The Public Historian* 37, no. 3 (2015): 106–7.
20. de Groot, "On Genealogy," 116.
21. Elena Machado Sáez, *Market Aesthetics: The Purchase of the Past in Caribbean Diasporic Fiction* (Charlottesville: University of Virginia Press, 2015), 26. See also Parker, "*Homegoing* Teacher's Guide."
22. Timothy Aubry, *Guilty Aesthetic Pleasures* (Cambridge, MA: Harvard University Press, 2018), 137.
23. Victoria Mills, "Fiction, Empathy and Teaching History," *Teaching History* 81 (October 1995): 7; Kevin Vanzant, "Problems with Narrative in the US Survey and How Fiction can Help," *The History Teacher* 52, no. 4 (2019): 687.
24. Dorothy J. Hale, *The Novel and the New Ethics* (Stanford, CA: Stanford University Press, 2020), 13. On the "empathy defense" of literature's value, see also Michael Fischer, "Literature and Empathy." *Philosophy and Literature* 41, no. 2

4. READING THE FAMILY TREE

(October 2017): 431–64. For a telling example of how the family saga genre relates to this defense, see Jeremy Knoll, "How 'Homegoing' Has Changed My Teaching," Learning for Justice, February 13, 2017, www.learningforjustice.org/magazine/how-homegoing-has-changed-my-teaching. On midcentury reading practices and "reading with feeling" in literary institutions, see Merve Emre, *Paraliterary: The Making of Bad Readers in Postwar America* (Chicago: University of Chicago Press, 2017), especially ch. 2.

25. Machado Sáez, *Market Aesthetics*, 21. Though Machado Sáez focuses particularly on fiction of the Caribbean diaspora, her theorization of what she calls "market aesthetics" is invaluable for understanding how racial and ethnic difference is commodified (by publishers and scholars alike) in the contemporary literary field.
26. "Open Syllabus Explorer," Open Syllabus; Campus Reads Penguin Random House, "Homegoing," Common Reads, www.commonreads.com/book/?isbn =9781101971062.
27. Machado Sáez, *Market Aesthetics*, 4.
28. Beth Driscoll, *The New Literary Middlebrow: Tastemakers and Reading in the Twenty-First Century* (Camden, NJ: Palgrave, 2014), 55.
29. Driscoll, *The New Literary Middlebrow*, 26, 32–33.
30. Timothy Aubry, *Reading as Therapy: What Contemporary Fiction Does for Middle-Class Americans* (Iowa City: University of Iowa Press, 2011), 14.
31. "Discussion Questions for 'Pachinko,'" *New York Times*, July 3, 2018.
32. Driscoll, *The New Literary Middlebrow*, 56.
33. Min Jin Lee, *Pachinko* (New York: Grand Central Publishing, 2017), 503–4.
34. Yaa Gyasi, "The Rumpus Interview with Yaa Gyasi," interview by Abigail Bereola, *The Rumpus*, July 29, 2016. See also Michiko Kakutani, "Review: In 'Homegoing,' What Slavery Costs One Family," review of *Homegoing* by Yaa Gyasi, *New York Times*, June 13, 2016.
35. Georg Lukács, *The Historical Novel*, trans. Hannah and Stanley Mitchell (Lincoln: University of Nebraska, 1983), 127–128.
36. Aubry, *Guilty*, 117.
37. Owens, "Powell's Interview" (emphasis added). See also Gyasi, "Rumpus Interview." This opposition between historicity and characterization is echoed in reviews of the novel. In the *New York Times*, for example, Michiko Kakutani explicitly contrasts the passages of the novel in which "we feel we are ... getting a history lesson" and those where readers are "hearing the stories of individual men and women we have come to know and understand." Kakutani, "Review."
38. Imani Roach, "Yaa Gyasi: Taking a Long View," *Guernica*, September 16, 2016, www.guernicamag.com/taking-a-long-view/.

4. READING THE FAMILY TREE

39. Leah Mirakhor, "More at Stake Here Than Beauty: An Interview with Yaa Gyasi," *Los Angeles Review of Books*, June 9, 2016, www.lareviewofbooks.org/article/stake-beauty-interview-yaa-gyasi/ (emphasis added).
40. When one interviewer described Ness's horrific scars as a kind of "callback," Gyasi broke in, finishing his sentence: "to the choke cherry tree [*sic*]." Ismail Muhammad, "'If You're Going to Tell the Story of Slavery, I'm Going to Listen All Day': Q&A with 'Homegoing' Author Yaa Gyasi," *ZYZZYVA*, June 21, 2016, www.zyzzyva.org/2016/07/21/if-youre-going-qa-with-yaa-gyasi/.
41. Gyasi cites Baldwin as "the gold standard for writing that is both beautiful and rigorous," adding that she "first encountered his work in college when a teacher assigned 'Sonny's Blues,'" a story that, she says, "I reread once a year." Mirakhor, "More at Stake."
42. Haley, *Roots*, 571–73. Lee, too, has been described as "a prodigious, inveterate researcher, who takes a journalistic approach to writing her novels," filling "more than ten Bankers Boxes with interview notes and other background material." Michael Luo, "What Min Jin Lee Wants Us to See," *New Yorker*, February 17, 2022, www.newyorker.com/culture/the-new-yorker-interview/what-min-jin-lee-wants-us-to-see.
43. Lisa Ze Winters, "Fiction and Slavery's Archive: Memory, Agency, and Finding Home," *Reviews in American History* 46, no. 2 (2018): 340.
44. Miller, "Descendants."
45. Walton Muyumba, "Yaa Gyasi's Transatlantic Epic," *New Republic*, July 5, 2016, www.newrepublic.com/article/134834/yaa-gyasis-transatlantic-epic.
46. Alex Woloch, *The One vs. the Many: Minor Characters and the Space of the Protagonist in the Novel* (Princeton, NJ: Princeton University Press, 2009), 13.
47. Lee, *Pachinko*, 9.
48. Woloch, *The One vs. the Many*, 19.
49. Owens, "Powell's Interview." On "the representation of a character's interiority . . . as a technology for enacting a kind of redistributive justice," see Rosen, *Minor Characters*, 27.
50. Charles, "'Homegoing,' by Yaa Gyasi."
51. "Reading Group Guide | *Pachinko* by Min Jin Lee," Grand Central Publishing, www.grandcentralpublishing.com/uncategorized/pachinko-reading-group-guide/. As with Gyasi, Lee's public comments reveal a tension in her thinking about characters as fictional people and as useful devices in a larger structure. On one hand, Lee stresses that "My characters are very real to me . . . and to be clear, dear reader, [writing] each death broke me." On the other, she explains, "It is possible that characters need to die for the author to make her moral point. . . . Certain characters die in *Pachinko*, and to me, their deaths were both natural to the plot and necessary symbolically. To me, the deaths were painfully inevitable."

52. Owens, "Powell's Interview." Initially, Gyasi planned for the book to "skip all of the in-between parts." During her time at the Iowa Writers' Workshop, however, she "realized that what [she] really wanted to do with this novel was to look at how something moves really subtly over a long period of time." Roach, "Yaa Gyasi: Taking a Long View."
53. Corina Selejan, "Fragmentation(s) and Realism(s): Has the Fragment Gone Mainstream?" *Anglica Wratislaviensia* 57 (2019): 107.
54. Woloch argues that "*every* minor character...by strict definition... disappear[s]," and it is this disappearance that most provokes the reader's "interest and outrage, painful concern or amused consent": "not simply their fate within the story (whether they marry or die, make their fortune or lose it, find a home or become exiled) but also in the narrative discourse itself (how they are finally overshadowed or absorbed into someone else's story, swallowed within or expelled from another person's plot)." Woloch, *The One vs. the Many*, 38.
55. Muhammad, "If You're Going to Tell the Story of Slavery."
56. Zucker, "The Genealogical Novel," 556.
57. Woloch, *The One vs. the Many*, 29.
58. Brian Yothers, "Contemporary African Immigration and the Legacy of Slavery in Yaa Gyasi's *Homegoing*," *The Immigrant Experience*, ed. Maryse Jayasuriya (Amenia, NY: Salem Press/Grey House Publishing, 2018), 209. See also Stephanie Li, *Pan–African American Literature: Signifyin(g) Immigrants in the Twenty-First Century* (New Brunswick, NJ: Rutgers University Press, 2018).
59. Mychal Denzel Smith, "The Truth About 'The Arc of the Moral Universe,'" *Huffington Post*, January 18, 2018, www.huffpost.com/entry/opinion-smith-obama-king_n_5a5903e0e4b04f3c55a252a4.
60. Muhammad, "If You're Going to Tell the Story of Slavery." Patricia Tobin, writing on García Márquez's *One Hundred Years of Solitude*, has described this way of thinking as a "genealogical imperative," a narrative structure that stresses "causality," and within which "seemingly random events and gratuitous details are brought into alignment at its conclusion, when all possibility has been converted into necessity in a kinship line of events." "Thus," Tobin concludes, "in both life and literature, a line has become legitimized—whether the family line, the timeline, or the story line—because our causal understanding" works ultimately to equate "descent and destiny." Patricia Tobin, "Response, 1: García Márquez and the Genealogical Imperative," *Diacritics: A Review of Contemporary Criticism* 4, no. 2 (1974): 53.
61. William Shakespeare, *Henry VI, Part Two*, ed. Barbara A. Mowat and Paul Werstine (New York: Simon & Schuster, 2008), 5.2.28.
62. Peter Brooks, *Reading for the Plot* (Cambridge, MA: Harvard University Press, 1984), 22.

4. READING THE FAMILY TREE

63. Wright problematizes this desire, adding: "Yet to what degree is our desire for knowing a desire for power and control, an urge to be at the top of the hierarchy?" Michelle Wright, "Diaspora and Entanglement," *Qui Parle* 28, no. 2 (2019): 233.
64. Lee, *Pachinko*, 263, 225.
65. Lee, *Pachinko*, 276; hereafter cited parenthetically.
66. Gyasi's father is a professor of francophone African literature. Kate Kellaway, "Yaa Gyasi: 'Slavery Is on People's Minds. It Affects Us Still,'" *The Guardian*, January 8, 2017. Owens, "Powell's Interview." Though Gyasi began the novel at Stanford, the University of Iowa, where Gyasi studied at the prestigious Iowa Writers' Workshop, was where it "really started to take shape." Wayne Catan, "Interview with Yaa Gyasi, 2017 PEN/Hemingway Award Winner," THR Blog, The Hemingway Foundation and Society, May 31, 2017, www.hemingway society.org/interview-yaa-gyasi-2017-penhemingway-award-winner. See also Mirakhor, "More at Stake"; Sam Scott, "The Story Behind 'Homegoing,'" *Stanford Magazine*, July–August 2017, stanfordmag.org/contents/the-story-behind-homegoing.
67. "Reading Group Guide | *Pachinko* by Min Jin Lee." See also Li, *Pachinko*, 481.
68. Claire Grossman, Stephanie Young, and Juliana Spahr, "Who Gets to Be a Writer," *Public Books*, April 1, 2021, www.publicbooks.org/who-gets-to-be-a-writer/. See also Claire Grossman, Juliana Spahr, and Stephanie Young, "Literature's Vexed Democratization," *American Literary History* 33, no. 2 (2021): 298–319.
69. Anton Dechand, "ILB interview: Yaa Gyasi," *EXBERLINER*, September 5, 2018, www.exberliner.com/whats-on/international-literature-festival-blog-yaa-gyasi-interview/.
70. Haley, *Roots*, 577–80 (original emphasis).
71. Muhammad, "If You're Going to Tell the Story of Slavery."
72. Barack Obama, "Remarks by the President at Cape Coast Castle," White House Archives, July 11, 2009, obamawhitehouse.archives.gov/the-press-office/remarks-president-cape-coast-castle.
73. Saidiya Hartman, *Lose Your Mother: A Journey Along the Atlantic Slave Route* (New York: Farrar, Straus and Giroux, 2007), 100.
74. Hartman, *Lose Your Mother*, 133.
75. Machado Sáez, *Market Aesthetics*, 30.
76. Mirakhor, "More at Stake."
77. Yaa Gyasi, "I'm Ghanaian-American. Am I Black?" *New York Times*, June 18, 2016.
78. Hanna Powers, "A Conversation with Author Margaret Wilkerson Sexton," *Sarasota*, July 25, 2019, www.sarasotamagazine.com/arts-and-entertainment/2019/07/margaret-wilkerson-sexton.

79. On the promotion of Sexton's novel, see the online publisher catalog platform Edelweiss+, www.edelweiss.plus/#dashboard. On "comps" and the politics of race, see Laura B. McGrath, "Comping White," *Los Angeles Review of Books*, January 21, 2019, www.lareviewofbooks.org/article/comping-white/.
80. Margaret Wilkerson Sexton, *A Kind of Freedom* (Berkeley: Counterpoint Press, 2017), 14, 107; hereafter cited parenthetically. Sexton writes that Evelyn's grandfather was the first Black doctor in the state of Louisiana and that her father's work delivering babies is an "awesome wonder" and a source of "pride."
81. On the Double V campaign, see Vaughn Rasberry, *Race and the Totalitarian Century: Geopolitics in the Black Literary Imagination* (Cambridge, MA: Harvard University Press, 2016): 29–30. See also Patrick S. Washburn, "The *Pittsburgh Courier*'s Double V Campaign in 1942," *American Journalism* 3, no. 2 (1986): 73–86.
82. See Lauren Berlant, *Cruel Optimism* (Durham, NC: Duke University Press, 2011).
83. Jesse McCarthy, "'A Kind of Freedom' Follows Three Generations of a Black Family in New Orleans," *New York Times*, September 5, 2017.
84. For Colored Girls Book Club, "For Colored Girls Book Club + Margaret Wilkerson Sexton," www.forcoloredgirlsbookclub.com/interviews/interview-with-margaret-wilkerson-sexton.
85. Richard Wright, *Native Son* (New York: Harper Perennial, 2005), 13.
86. Marian Kaufman, "Interview with Margaret Wilkerson Sexton," *Bayou Magazine*, January 2018, bayoumagazine.org/interview-with-margaret-wilkerson-sexton/.
87. Jesse McCarthy, "On Afropessimism," *Los Angeles Review of Books*, July 20, 2020, www.lareviewofbooks.org/article/on-afropessimism/.
88. As of February 2023, *Homegoing* had been rated nearly 292,000 times and reviewed more than 31,000 times; *A Kind of Freedom* had been rated 5,200 times and reviewed only 700 times. Though Gyasi's novel was published thirteen months before Sexton's, this is unlikely to account for the disparity. "Homegoing," Goodreads; "A Kind of Freedom," Goodreads.
89. "Open Syllabus Explorer," Open Syllabus.
90. Ann Mayhew, "The Canon: Books to Read in September," *The Riveter*, September 7, 2017.
91. Driscoll, *The New Literary Middlebrow*, 66.
92. Namwali Serpell, "The Banality of Empathy," *New York Review of Books*, March 2, 2019, www.nybooks.com/daily/2019/03/02/the-banality-of-empathy/. Gyasi, too, has lamented that the work of so many minoritized writers is treated "as though it were a kind of medicine," prescribed after "the murders of black people [for] the subsequent 'listening and learning' of white people." Yaa Gyasi, "White

5. THE RISE OF THE RECENT HISTORICAL NOVEL

People, Black Authors Are Not Your Medicine," *The Guardian*, March 20, 2021, www.theguardian.com/books/2021/mar/20/white-people-black-authors-are-not-your-medicine.

5. THE RISE OF THE RECENT HISTORICAL NOVEL

1. Hannah Seidlitz (@HannahSeidlitz), "what I'm really most afraid of that's incubating in my neighbors' homes is the next character-driven, pulitzer shoo-in pandemic novel," Twitter post, March 13, 2020, 10:37 a.m., https://twitter.com/HannahSeidlitz/status/1238519540838993920?s=20&t=uf4iLSkjJNx2XsMd1aSgEA.
2. Sloane Crosley, "Someday, We'll Look Back on All of This and Write a Novel," *New York Times*, March 17, 2020, https://www.nytimes.com/2020/03/17/books/review/sloane-crosley-pandemic-novel-coronavirus.html.
3. Alexandra Alter, "The Problem with the Pandemic Plot," *New York Times*, February 20, 2022, https://www.nytimes.com/2022/02/20/books/pandemic-fiction.html.
4. Fredric Jameson, *The Antinomies of Realism* (London: Verso, 2013), 263, 259.
5. This trend also includes popular thrillers such as David Videcette's *The Theseus Paradox* (2015), young adult literature such as Jewell Parker Rhodes's *Ninth Ward* (2010), and short fiction: Hassan Blasim's *The Corpse Exhibition* (2014), Deborah Eisenberg's *Twilight of the Superheroes* (2006), Jhumpa Lahiri's "Going Ashore" (in *Unaccustomed Earth*, 2008), Laila Laliami's "Echo" (2011), Patrick McGrath's *Ghost Town* (2005), David Foster Wallace's "The Suffering Channel" (*Oblivion*, 2004), et al.
6. Walter Scott, *Waverley or 'Tis Sixty Years Since* (New York: Penguin, 1985), 33–36. In his dazzling introduction, Scott defines the novel as "neither a romance of chivalry, nor a tale of modern manners," since those two genres, "to be interesting, must either refer to antiquity so great as to have become venerable, or . . . must bear a vivid reflection of those scenes which are passing daily before our eyes, and are interesting from their novelty." By contrast, Scott explains, "My hero will neither have iron on his shoulders, as of yore, nor on the heels of his boots, as is the present fashion of Bond Street."
7. "About the Prize," Walter Scott Prize for Historical Fiction.
8. James F. English, "Now, Not Now: Counting Time in Contemporary Fiction Studies," *Modern Language Quarterly* 77, no. 3 (2016): 395–418.
9. English, "Now, Not Now," 406.
10. On the decade novel as a genre in contemporary fiction, see Theodore Martin, *Contemporary Drift: Genre, Historicism, and the Problem of the Present* (New York: Columbia University Press, 2017), ch. 1.

5. THE RISE OF THE RECENT HISTORICAL NOVEL

11. Nicholas Dames, "'The People v. O.J. Simpson' as Historical Fiction," Public Books, April 1, 2016, http://www.publicbooks.org/the-people-v-o-j-simpson-as-historical-fiction/. Dames draws connections between nineteenth-century novels and contemporary television, both of which bear out "the idea that realism's gaze was sharpest when focused on the recent past, neither beyond living memory nor quite like the contemporary world."
12. Ben Lerner, *The Topeka School* (New York: Farrar, Straus and Giroux, 2019); Lerner, *Leaving the Atocha Station* (Minneapolis: Coffee House Press, 2011); Lerner, *10:04* (New York: Picador, 2014); all hereafter cited parenthetically.
13. Dames, "'The People v. O.J. Simpson' as Historical Fiction." Under this rubric, Pynchon's *Bleeding Edge* represents a kind of limit case. Despite the many connections between the novel and the conventions discussed here, the work—set during the first dot-com bubble in the spring and fall of 2001—also works hard to conjure and define a "period style" for the early 2000s. In this way, the evolution of the so-called 9/11 novel over the last two decades represents a study in how the conventions described in this chapter give way over time to those of historical fiction as it is traditionally understood.
14. In a 1984 letter from Alice Bradley Sheldon (better known by her pseudonym, James Tiptree, Jr.) to Isaac and Shauna Asimov, Sheldon writes: "if a book is finished in 1983, as of right-up-to-the-minute 1983-ness[,] but not published [until] 1985, it's already a historical novel of a sort. Short of sending something out page-by-page hot from the typer, I see no way of publishing a book in the present." As I argue here, however, part of how authors set their novels "in the present," is by removing certain details that denote their "right-up-to-the-minute"-ness. On the topic of how writers deploy and/or omit contemporary technologies in their fiction as a means of achieving either timeliness or timelessness, see Alexander Manshel, "The Lag: Technology and Fiction in the Twentieth Century," *PMLA* 135, no. 1 (January 2020): 40–58. James Tiptree, Jr., letter to Isaac and Shauna Asimov, February 28, 1984, University of Oregon Special Collections, Coll 455, Box 62, Folder 8. My gratitude to Arthur Wang for this treasure from the archives.
15. Scott, *Waverley*, 34 (emphasis added).
16. Scott, *Waverley*, 36.
17. Gérard Genette, *Narrative Discourse Revisited*, trans. Jane E. Lewin (Ithaca, NY: Cornell University Press, 1988), 80.
18. Ruth Ozeki, *A Tale for the Time Being* (New York: Penguin, 2013); hereafter cited parenthetically. In sketching out "the rough contours of this genre," I take my cues from Rick Altman's "semantic/syntactic approach." For Altman, any literary genre can be divided into its "*semantic* elements," or "building blocks," such as

5. THE RISE OF THE RECENT HISTORICAL NOVEL

"common traits," "key scenes, character types," settings or formal techniques—and its *syntactic* aspects": the "meaning-bearing structures" that organize those building blocks, such as plot structure, character arc, and theme. A Hollywood western, for example, can be characterized by the presence of horses, sheriffs, saloon gunfights, and the use of fast tracking shots; but it is also defined thematically, as a narrative of negotiating "the border between two lands," "two eras," or "two value systems." Rick Altman, *Film/Genre* (London: BFI Publishing, 1999), 89; Altman, "A Semantic/Syntactic Approach to Film Genre," *Cinema Journal* 23, no. 3 (1984): 10–11.

19. Linda Hutcheon, *A Poetics of Postmodernism: History, Theory, Fiction* (New York: Routledge, 1988); Fredric Jameson, *Postmodernism, Or, The Cultural Logic of Late Capitalism* (Durham, NC: Duke University Press, 1991), 18–20; Amy Elias, *Sublime Desire: History and Post-1960s Fiction* (Baltimore: Johns Hopkins University Press, 2001).
20. Jameson, *Postmodernism*, 19–20.
21. Kevin Caners, "Ben Lerner on *10:04*, The Politics of Imagination, and the Craft of Writing," audio blog post, The Public, March 16, 2015, https://thepublicradio.org/tag/ben-lerner/. In the same interview, Lerner comments that part of his project in *10:04* was to "explore the seam between reality and fiction": to make "[a] kind of flickering edge" between the two genres "explicitly part of the work." See also David Shields, *Reality Hunger: A Manifesto* (New York: Vintage, 2011), 3–5.
22. Felicia R. Lee, "What the Tide Brought In," review of *A Tale for the Time Being*, by Ruth Ozeki, *New York Times*, March 12, 2013. Likewise, Alter mentions that the novelist Weike Wang "had just finished a draft of her new novel, 'Joan Is Okay,' which centers on an Asian American emergency room doctor in New York, when Covid erupted. She decided to revise the story to reflect how the virus overwhelmed hospitals." Alter, "The Problem with the Pandemic Plot."
23. Perry Anderson, "From Progress to Catastrophe," *London Review of Books* 33, no. 15 (2011): 27.
24. Lerner has asserted that "a fundamental human anxiety about what counts as authentic experience [is] really fundamental to the novel as a form." Caners, "Ben Lerner."
25. Perry Anderson makes a similar point in "From Progress to Catastrophe," although his focus is on the historical fiction of what he calls the genre's "postmodern revival": "Military tyranny; race murder; omnipresent surveillance; technological war; and programmed genocide. The persistent backdrops to the historical fiction of the postmodern period are at the antipodes of its classical forms. Not the emergence of the nation, but the ravages of empire; not progress as emancipation, but impending or consummated catastrophe" (28).

5. THE RISE OF THE RECENT HISTORICAL NOVEL

26. Jean-Luc Nancy, *After Fukushima: The Equivalence of Catastrophes*, trans. Charlotte Mandell (New York: Fordham University Press, 2014), 3–4, 29–30. Nancy claims that as a result of the interconnection and interdependence of technologies, economies, and communities, "every kind of disaster hereafter will bear the mark of that paradigm represented by nuclear risk" (3–4). As such, the Fukushima disaster is "a powerfully exemplary event" (29–30).
27. Georg Lukács, *The Historical Novel*, trans. Hannah and Stanley Mitchell (Lincoln: University of Nebraska Press, 1983), 41–42, 127–28. As Lukács puts it, "Certain crises in the personal destinies" of the central characters must "coincide and interweave [with] the determining context of an historical crisis" (41).
28. Lukács, *The Historical Novel*, 128.
29. Lukács, *The Historical Novel*, 128.
30. All of the novels discussed in this chapter feature writers as their central characters, emphasizing the overlap between recent historical fiction and the increasingly popular genre of autofiction. One way of accounting for this is to read the genre's novelist-as-protagonist as a contemporary manifestation of Lukács's "middle-of-the-road hero," "always . . . more or less mediocre, average" (*The Historical Novel*, 33–38). In the context of contemporary social media, the author figure has become an emblem of the widespread compulsion to publicly narrate the events of daily life and curate reactions to global crises. Lukács claims that "Scott's greatness lies in his capacity to give living human embodiment to historical-social types. The typically human terms in which great historical trends become tangible" (35). Perhaps the same is true for these author-narrators and the historical trend of ubiquitous self-narration. *Writers, they're just like us.*
31. Lukács, *The Historical Novel*, 42.
32. Lauren Berlant argues that the concepts of "crisis ordinariness" and "slow death" are more helpful than the rhetoric of catastrophe, as it "belies the constitutive point that slow death . . . is neither a state of exception nor the opposite, mere banality, but a domain where an upsetting scene of living is revealed to be interwoven with ordinary life." *Cruel Optimism* (Durham, NC: Duke University Press, 2011), 102.
33. Wallace Stevens, *The Collected Poems of Wallace Stevens* (New York: Vintage, 2015), 136.
34. The use of news media in historical fiction is at least as old as John Dos Passos's *U.S.A.* trilogy and his iconic "newsreel" sequences. That said, the recent historical novel's use of news mediation does not merely evoke a historical background— what Lukács would call "the historical *milieu*"—but is instead tied inextricably to these novels' narration of historical events.
35. Echoes of DeLillo's influence on Lerner are apparent throughout *10:04*. Like DeLillo, Lerner ventriloquizes and personifies the various "voices" of the

5. THE RISE OF THE RECENT HISTORICAL NOVEL

modern mediascape, rendering them as dialogue alongside and between the voices of his characters: "'Get tested for HIV today,' said the poster on the D" (31). Moreover, Lerner also employs the characteristically DeLillovian trinity (e.g. "Visa, Mastercard, American Express") as a kind of punctuating flourish: "I frankly admired how she appeared capable of taking or leaving me, of taking and leaving me simultaneously, found it exciting, inspiring even, as if the energy we had generated were now free to circulate more generally, charging everything a little—bodies, streetlights, mixed media" (29). Don DeLillo, *White Noise* (New York: Penguin, 1986).

36. Kelly describes New Sincerity as a kind of "post-postmodern embrace of 'single-entendre' principles" that nonetheless "must be informed by a study of postmodernist fiction." Adam Kelly, "The New Sincerity," in *Postmodern/Postwar—and After: Rethinking American Literature*, ed. Jason Gladstone, Andrew Hoberek, and Daniel Worden (Iowa City: University of Iowa, 2016), 197–208. Lee Konstantinou outlines a similar jettisoning of postmodern irony, if not postmodern form, claiming that contemporary "postironists" draw on "techniques associated with postmodern metafiction" in order to "help readers cultivate belief." *Cool Characters: Irony and American Fiction* (Cambridge, MA: Harvard University Press, 2016), 168, 174.

37. For an earlier account of this phenomenon specific to television news, see Mary Ann Doane, "Information, Crisis, Catastrophe," in *Logics of Television: Essays in Cultural Criticism* (Bloomington: Indiana University Press, 1990), 222–39. Doane argues that there is "a certain slippage between the notion that television covers important events in order to validate itself as a medium and the idea that because an event is covered by television—because it is, in effect deemed televisual—it is important. This is the significance of the media event, where the referent becomes indissociable from the medium" (222).

38. At one point in *Leaving the Atocha Station*, Lerner's narrator cannot discern the exact temporality—or ontology—of the events he is seeing on screen. Lerner emphasizes this confusion with a convenient pun, made possible by the narrator's mediocre Spanish: "I passed a bar that had a TV on and I could see images of a swarming crowd. . . . At first I thought it was footage from earlier in the day, but then I noticed it was dark. Is this living, I asked the bartender, pointing to the screen. He blinked at me. Is this live, I corrected myself. He nodded. I drank and watched and eventually went home and fell asleep" (137). Compare this, for example, to Niklas Luhmann's claim in the opening of *The Reality of the Mass Media*: "Whatever we know about our society, or indeed about the world in which we live, we know through the mass media." Luhmann, *The Reality of the Mass Media* (Cambridge: Polity Press, 2000), 1.

5. THE RISE OF THE RECENT HISTORICAL NOVEL

39. Alan Barth, "Synthetic Misanthrope," review of *The Autobiography of a Curmudgeon*, by Harold L. Ickes, *New Republic* May 17, 1943; Ezra Pound, *ABC of Reading* (New York: Faber and Faber, 1934), 29.
40. For a brief discussion of the New Journalism in the context of historical realism, as well as a reading of Joan Didion's *The Last Thing He Wanted* (1996), a recent historical novel that engages this same triangulation of journalism, fiction, and recent history, see Samuel Cohen, *After the End of History: American Fiction in the 1990s* (Iowa City: University of Iowa Press, 2009), 17–8, 138–53. On the "Instant Book" in midcentury publishing, see Kenneth C. Davis, *Two-Bit Culture: The Paperbacking of America* (Boston: Houghton Mifflin, 1984).
41. Davis, *Two-Bit Culture*, 345–47, 81–82.
42. Davis, *Two-Bit Culture*, 347.
43. Benedict Anderson, *Imagined Communities: Reflections on the Origin and Spread of Nationalism* (London: Verso, 2006), 34–35.
44. According to Luhmann, the logic or "reality" of mass media dictates that news outlets must convey "the impression that something [has] already happened, *but only just* . . . that what has just gone into the past is still present, is still interesting and informative." He continues, "Events have to be dramatized *as events*" given that their observation "now occurs almost as the same time as the events themselves." This explains both "live" coverage of the "aftermath" of an event, as well as the production of that event's own signature title sequence and theme music, packaging that works to brand events as multiday stories rather than mere one-offs. That said, like the news narratives that structure them, novels of recent history appear far more interested in the event itself than its aftermath, the sudden catastrophe rather than the slow process of rebuilding in its wake. Luhmann, *The Reality of the Mass Media*, 25–26, (emphasis added).
45. Alter, "The Problem with the Pandemic Plot."
46. Elias, *Sublime Desire*, 22–23 (original emphasis).
47. This line is drawn from Feuchtwanger's remarks at the Paris Congress for the Defense of Culture in 1935 and quoted in Lukács's *The Historical Novel*, 235–36. Feuchtwanger's solution to this problem—especially in "a very hectic age" which "very rapidly turns all that is present into history"—is, quite unlike Lerner and Ozeki, to turn to the distant past. "If to-day's *milieu* will in any case be historical in five years' time, then why should I not just as well choose a *milieu* which lies as far back as I please, if I want to express a theme which I hope will still be alive in five years' time?"
48. Maurice Halbwachs, *The Collective Memory* (New York: Harper & Row, 1980), 82.
49. Rebecca Makkai, *The Great Believers* (New York: Penguin, 2018), 246.

5. THE RISE OF THE RECENT HISTORICAL NOVEL

50. Makkai, *The Great Believers*, 316–17.
51. Lukács, *The Historical Novel*, 31.
52. Anderson, *Imagined Communities*, 24–25 (original emphasis).
53. Jameson, *Antinomies*, 266, 260.
54. Anderson, *Imagined Communities*, 25.
55. Anderson, *Imagined Communities*, 32–33, 63.
56. Rebecca L. Walkowitz, *Born Translated: The Contemporary Novel in an Age of World Literature* (New York: Columbia University Press, 2015).
57. Hartmut Rosa, "Social Acceleration: Ethical and Political Consequences of a Desynchronized High-Speed Society," *Constellations* 10, no. 1 (2003): 22; Harry Harootunian, "Remembering the Historical Present," *Critical Inquiry* 33, no. 3 (2007): 471–94. According to Harootunian, "wherever both capital and science succeeded in implanting their exemplars" there arose a totalizing notion of contemporaneity that "displaced and diminished awareness of . . . coexisting temporalities . . . exporting the image of dissonant rhythms to the periphery, where it became a sign of a rift between modernity and nonmodernity" (479).
58. Consider, for example, twenty-first-century British works of recent historical fiction, such as Ian McEwan's *Saturday* (2005), Kamila Shamsie's *Burnt Shadows* (2009), Ali Smith's *Seasonal Quartet* (2016–2020), Olivia Laing's *Crudo* (2018), Roddy Doyle's *Life Without Children* (2021), Hermione Hoby's *Virtue* (2021), Sarah Moss's *The Fell* (2021), and McEwan's *Lessons* (2022).
59. Rosa, "Social Acceleration," 20.
60. Rosa, "Social Acceleration," 20.
61. Rosa, "Social Acceleration," 19 (original emphasis). In the years since Rosa's essay was published, the language of contingency with regard to political affiliation ("*voting Republican* rather than *being a Republican*") has waned considerably.
62. Lukács, *The Historical Novel*, 53.
63. Lukács, *The Historical Novel*, 235.
64. Makkai, *The Great Believers*, 331.
65. Rosa points out that "despite widespread acceleration and flexibilization which create the appearance of total contingency, hyper-optionality, and unlimited openness, 'real' change is in fact no longer possible: the system of modern society is closing in and history is coming to an end in a 'hyper-accelerated standstill' or 'polar inertia'" (16–17).
66. See Benjamin Kunkel, who cites Lerner's *10:04* as "the exception proving the rule that the contemporary experience of climate change has so far eluded the grasp of literature." Though Kunkel reads the novel as "set in the present," Lerner's fictionalization of the recent past only further strengthens Kunkel's central point. The novel's pastness suggests not only that the catastrophic effects

5. THE RISE OF THE RECENT HISTORICAL NOVEL

of man-made climate change have already arrived, but also that the present period is of historical importance. Kunkel, "Inventing Climate-Change Literature," *New Yorker*, October 24, 2014.

67. Altman, *Film/Genre*, 156.
68. Mark Currie, "The Novel and the Moving Now," *Novel: A Forum on Fiction* 42, no. 2 (2009): 322.
69. Theodore Martin, "The Currency of the Contemporary," in Gladstone, Hoberek, and Worden, *Postmodern/Postwar—and After: Rethinking American Literature*, 231. See also Martin, *Contemporary Drift*.
70. Martin, "The Currency of the Contemporary," 231.
71. Zadie Smith, "Two Paths for the Novel," *New York Review of Books*, November 20, 2008.
72. Jay N. Shelat, "Pattern Recognition: The Enduring Whiteness of 9/11 Literary Studies," *Post45*, September 11, 2021, https://post45.org/2021/09/pattern-recognition-the-enduring-whiteness-of-9-11-literary-studies/.
73. My thanks to Tabitha Sparks for first pointing me in this direction.
74. Merve Emre, "Jonathan Franzen Thinks People Can Change," *Vulture*, September 30, 2021, https://www.vulture.com/article/interview-jonathan-franzen-crossroads.html.
75. Jess Row, *White Flights: Race, Fiction, and the American Imagination* (Minneapolis: Graywolf Press, 2019), 144, 117. Row asks of Franzen's 2001 novel *The Corrections*, "How do you create a wide-ranging novel, set primarily in cities on the East Coast in the 1990s, and create the illusion of a panorama that doesn't include people of color?" (143). In *The Topeka School*, Lerner works to address the implicit whiteness of his earlier novels head on. In this way, the novel resembles a Lukácsian historical novel better than Lerner's previous two novels in how it turns to the 1990s as "the clearest manifestation of a crisis in white masculinity" that has reverberated powerfully in the late 2010s and since. Lerner, *The Topeka School*, 127.
76. Makkai, *The Great Believers*, 316–17.
77. DeLillo, *White Noise*, 114.
78. Jesmyn Ward, *Salvage the Bones* (New York: Bloomsbury, 2012), 255.
79. Shelat, "Pattern Recognition."
80. Jameson, *Postmodernism*, 22.
81. Elias, *Sublime Desire*, 46.

CODA

1. Hayden White, *Metahistory: The Historical Imagination in Nineteenth-Century Europe* (Baltimore: Johns Hopkins University Press, 1973), 6.

2. John Guillory, *Cultural Capital: The Problem of Literary Canon Formation* (Chicago: University of Chicago Press, 1993), x.
3. Toni Morrison, *Playing in the Dark: Whiteness and the Literary Imagination* (New York: Vintage, 1993), 53.
4. Viet Thanh Nguyen, *The Sympathizer* (New York: Grove Press, 2015), 1.
5. Jesmyn Ward, *Sing, Unburied, Sing* (New York: Scribner, 2017); Valeria Luiselli, *Lost Children Archive* (New York: Vintage, 2019); Tommy Orange, *There There* (New York: Knopf, 2018); all cited parenthetically hereafter.
6. Louis Elliott, "Ghosts of History: An Interview with Jesmyn Ward by Louis Elliott," *BOMB*, November 10, 2017. The likeness between the characters of Richie and Beloved is so uncanny, it almost seems as if the former is the child the latter might have given birth to at the end of Morrison's novel. In several passages, the two are almost indistinguishable, such as when Richie narrates his own spectral rebirth: "I woke in a stand of young pine trees on a cloudy, half-lit day. I could not remember how I came to be crouching in the pine needles.... I watched the tops of the trees toss, and I tried to remember how I got there. Who I was before this place, before this quiet haunt" (134). Richie's description of his childhood home also calls to mind *Beloved*'s iconic "rememory" passage: "Home ain't always about a place. The house I grew up in is gone. Ain't nothing but a field and some woods, but even if the house was still there, it ain't about that" (182).
7. Elliott, "Ghosts of History."
8. For a reading of *Lost Children Archive* as an "archive novel," see Patricia Stuelke, "Writing Refugee Crisis in the Age of Amazon: *Lost Children Archive*'s Reenactment Play," *Genre* 54, no. 1 (April 2021): 43–66.
9. As Matt Cohen argues, "History qua history ... is palpably held off" in the novel: the massacre at Sand Creek is "vividly described ... but brought up only once," and the book's brief sequence set during the Indian occupation of Alcatraz in 1969 is decidedly "sidelined." Matt Cohen, "Hacking Colonialism," *PMLA* 135, no. 2 (May 2020): 561.
10. Chris Kopacz, "Tommy Orange Hints About Upcoming Sequel to 'There There,'" *Indian Country Today*, July 6, 2021.
11. "Let Us Descend | Book by Jesmyn Ward | Official Publisher Page | Simon & Schuster," Simon & Schuster, https://www.simonandschuster.com/books/Let-Us-Descend/Jesmyn-Ward/9781982104498.

WORKS CITED

"1941–45: American Indian War Effort in World War II Is Remarkable." Native Voices. https://www.nlm.nih.gov/nativevoices/timeline/461.html.
"2015 Pulitzer Prizes." Pulitzer Prizes. https://www.pulitzer.org/prize-winners-by-year/2015.
"About the Prize." Walter Scott Prize for Historical Fiction. http://www.walterscottprize.co.uk/about-the-prize/.
Acocella, Joan. "Martin Amis's 'Experience.'" *New Yorker*, June 19, 2000.
Adams, Rachel. "Siblings, Disability, Genre in Jennifer Egan's *Manhattan Beach*." *PMLA* 134, no. 2 (March 2019): 366–71.
"Affirmative-Action Book Prizes: On the Political Agenda of Certain National Book Award Jurors." *New Criterion*, January 1991.
Allen, Bruce. "Well-Made Novel Sifts Black History." Review of *The Chaneysville Incident*, by David Bradley. *Christian Science Monitor*, May 20, 1981.
Als, Hilton. "Toni Morrison and the Ghosts in the House." *New Yorker*, October 27, 2003. www.newyorker.com/magazine/2003/10/27/ghosts-in-the-house.
Alter, Alexandra. "Colson Whitehead's Next Novel Tackles Life Under Jim Crow." *New York Times*, October 10, 2018.
———. "The Problem with the Pandemic Plot." *New York Times*, February 20, 2022. https://www.nytimes.com/2022/02/20/books/pandemic-fiction.html.
Altman, Rick. *Film/Genre*. London: BFI Publishing, 1999.

———. "A Semantic/Syntactic Approach to Film Genre." *Cinema Journal* 23, no. 3 (1984): 6–18.
Alvarez, Julia. *Homecoming*. New York: Grove Press, 1984.
———. *Homecoming: New and Collected Poems*. New York: Plume, 1996.
———. *How the García Girls Lost Their Accents*. 1991. Chapel Hill, NC: Algonquin Books, 2010.
———. *In the Time of the Butterflies*. 1994. New York: Plume, 1995.
———. *The Other Side / El Otro Lado*. New York: Dutton, 1995.
Amis, Martin. "Career Move." *New Yorker*, June 29, 1992.
———. *Einstein's Monsters*. New York: Harmony, 1987.
———. *The Information*. New York: Vintage, 1995.
———. *The Moronic Inferno, and Other Visits to America*. London: Jonathan Cape, 1986.
———. *Time's Arrow: Or the Nature of the Offence*. New York: Vintage, 1991.
———. *Visiting Mrs. Nabokov, and Other Excursions*. London: Jonathan Cape, 1993.
———. "When Amis Met Updike." *The Guardian*, January 31, 2009.
Anderson, Benedict. *Imagined Communities: Reflections on the Origin and Spread of Nationalism*. London: Verso, 2006.
Anderson, Perry. "From Progress to Catastrophe." *London Review of Books* 33, no. 15 (2011): 27.
Arian, Edward. *The Unfulfilled Promise: Public Subsidy of the Arts in America*. Philadelphia: Temple University Press, 1989.
Aubry, Timothy. *Guilty Aesthetic Pleasures*. Cambridge, MA: Harvard University Press, 2018.
———. *Reading as Therapy: What Contemporary Fiction Does for Middle-Class Americans*. Iowa City: University of Iowa Press, 2011.
August, Timothy K. "Spies Like Us: A Professor Undercover in the Literary Marketplace." *Lit: Literature Interpretation Theory* 29, no. 1 (2018): 60–79.
Baldick, Chris, ed. *The Oxford Dictionary of Literary Terms*, 4th ed. Oxford: Oxford University Press, 2015.
Barak, Julie. "'Turning and Turning in the Widening Gyre': A Second Coming into Language in Julia Alvarez's *How the Garcia Girls Lost Their Accents*." *MELUS* 23, no. 1 (March 1998): 159–76.
Barnes, Julian E. "Can He Save Afro-Am?" *Harvard Crimson*, January 31, 1991. https://www.thecrimson.com/article/1991/1/31/can-he-save-afro-am-pharvard-at/.
Barth, Alan. "Synthetic Misanthrope." Review of *The Autobiography of a Curmudgeon*, by Harold L. Ickes. *New Republic*, May 17, 1943.
Bauerlein, Mark, and Ellen Grantham, eds. *National Endowment for the Arts: A History, 1965–2008*. Washington, DC: National Endowment for the Arts, 2009.

WORKS CITED

Bellante, Carl, and John Bellante. "Unlike Father, Like Son. An Interview with Martin Amis." *Bloomsbury Review* 12, no. 2 (1992): 4–5, 16.
Bennett, William J. *To Reclaim a Legacy: A Report on the Humanities in Higher Education*. Washington, DC: National Endowment for the Humanities, 1984.
Bereola, Abigail. "The Rumpus Interview with Yaa Gyasi." *The Rumpus*, July 29, 2016.
Berlant, Lauren. *Cruel Optimism*. Durham, NC: Duke University Press, 2011.
Berman, Anna A. "The Family Novel (and Its Curious Disappearance)." *Comparative Literature* 72, no. 1 (March 2020): 1–18.
Bérubé, Michael. "Race and Modernity in Colson Whitehead's *The Intuitionist*." In *The Holodeck in the Garden: Science and Technology in Contemporary American Fiction*, ed. Peter Freese and Charles B. Harris, 163–78. Normal, IL: Dalkey Archive Press, 2004.
Best, Stephen. *None Like Us: Blackness, Belonging, Aesthetic Life*. Durham, NC: Duke University Press, 2018.
Bigsby, Christopher. *Writers in Conversation: Volume One*. Norwich, UK: Pen & Ink Press, School of English and American Studies, University of East Anglia, 2000.
Bing, Jonathan. "Julie [sic] Alvarez: Books That Cross Borders." *Publishers Weekly* 243, no. 51 (1996): 38–39.
Bishop, Ferman. "Henry James Criticizes *The Tory Lover*." *American Literature* (1955): 262–64.
Bloom, Allan. *The Closing of the American Mind*. New York: Simon & Schuster, 1987.
Bonetti, Kay. "David Bradley Interview with Kay Bonetti." American Audio Prose Library, February 1992. https://searchworks.stanford.edu/view/2403852.
Bourdieu, Pierre. *The Rules of Art: Genesis and Structure of the Literary Field*. Trans. Susan Emanuel. Stanford, CA: Stanford University Press, 1996.
Bourjaily, Vance. "Thirteen Runaway Slaves and David Bradley." Review of *The Chaneysville Incident*, by David Bradley. *New York Times*, April 19, 1981.
Bradley, David. *The Chaneysville Incident*. New York: Harper & Row, 1981.
——. "Novelist Alice Walker Telling the Black Woman's Story." *New York Times*, January 8, 1984.
Brier, Evan. "Unliterary History: Toni Morrison, *The Black Book*, and 'Real Black Publishing.'" *American Literature* 94, no. 4 (2022): 651–76.
Brigham, Cathy. "Identity, Masculinity, and Desire in David Bradley's Fiction." *Contemporary Literature* 36, no. 2 (1995): 289–316.
Brokaw, Tom. *The Greatest Generation*. New York: Random House, 1998.
Brooks, Peter. *Reading for the Plot*. Cambridge, MA: Harvard University Press, 1984.
Brown, Steve. "Why I Left the Afro-Am Dept." *Harvard Crimson*, May 2, 1990.

WORKS CITED

"Bureaucracy and War." Panel at Florida State University. March 21, 1997. C-SPAN. www.c-span.org/video/?79870-1/bureaucracy-war.

Campus Reads Penguin Random House. "Homegoing." www.commonreads.com/book/?isbn=9781101971062.

Caners, Kevin. "Ben Lerner on *10:04*, The Politics of Imagination, and the Craft of Writing." Audio blog post, The Public. March 16, 2015. https://thepublicradio.org/tag/ben-lerner/.

Catan, Wayne. "Interview with Yaa Gyasi, 2017 PEN/Hemingway Award Winner." THR Blog, The Hemingway Foundation and Society, May 31, 2017. www.hemingwaysociety.org/interview-yaa-gyasi-2017-penhemingway-award-winner.

Chabon, Michael. *The Amazing Adventures of Kavalier & Clay*. New York: Random House, 2012.

———. *The Final Solution: A Story of Detection*. New York: Harper Perennial, 2004.

Chandra, Sarika. "Re-Producing a Nationalist Literature in the Age of Globalization: Reading (Im)migration in Julia Alvarez's *How the García Girls Lost Their Accents*." *American Quarterly* 60, no. 3 (September 2008): 829–50.

Charles, Ann. "'Chaneysville Incident': Gripping, Provocative Story." Review of *The Chaneysville Incident*, by David Bradley. *New York Amsterdam News*, January 24, 1981.

Charles, Ron. "'Homegoing,' by Yaa Gyasi: A Bold Tale of Slavery for a New 'Roots' Generation." *Washington Post*, June 13, 2016. www.washingtonpost.com/entertainment/books/homegoing-by-yaa-gyasi-a-bold-tale-of-slavery-for-a-new-roots-generation/2016/06/13/f5802cee-2e85-11e6-9de3-6e6e7a14000c_story.html.

Chatman, Seymour. "Backwards." *Narrative* 17, no. 1 (January 2009): 31–55.

Chavkin, Allan, ed. *Leslie Marmon Silko's Ceremony: A Casebook*. Oxford: Oxford University Press, 2002.

Chen, Constance. "Two Views on PC Ideology." *Harvard Crimson*, February 24, 1990.

Chen, Tina. *Double Agency: Acts of Impersonation in Asian American Literature and Culture*. Stanford, CA: Stanford University Press, 2005.

———. "Towards an Ethics of Knowledge." *MELUS* 30, no. 2 (Summer 2005): 157–73.

Chiang, Mark. *The Cultural Capital of Asian American Studies: Autonomy and Representation in the University*. New York: New York University Press, 2018.

Chihaya, Sarah. "Slips and Slides." *PMLA* 133, no. 2 (2018): 364–70.

Childress, Clayton. *Under the Cover: The Creation, Production, and Reception of a Novel*. Princeton, NJ: Princeton University Press, 2017.

Chin, Frank, et al., eds. *Aiiieeeee! An Anthology of Asian American Writers*. Washington, DC: Howard University Press, 1974.

WORKS CITED

Chong, Phillipa K. *Inside the Critics' Circle: Book Reviewing in Uncertain Times.* Princeton, NJ: Princeton University Press, 2020.

Chu, Patricia E. "D(NA) Coding the Ethnic: Jeffrey Eugenides's *Middlesex.*" *Novel: A Forum on Fiction* 42, no. 2 (2009): 278–83.

Cohen, Matt. "Hacking Colonialism." *PMLA* 135, no. 2 (May 2020): 559–71.

Cohen, Samuel. *After the End of History: American Fiction in the 1990s.* Iowa City: University of Iowa Press, 2009.

Collins, Peter. "The Ghosts of Economics Past: *John Henry Days* and the Production of History." *African American Review* 46, no. 2 (Summer/Fall 2013): 285–300.

Cornell, Joseph. *Untitled (To Marguerite Blachas).* Madrid, Museo Nacional Centro de Arte Reina.

Criniti, Steve. "Collecting Butterflies: Julia Alvarez's Revision of North American Collective Memory." *Modern Language Studies* 36, no. 2 (2007): 42–63.

Crosley, Sloane. "Someday, We'll Look Back on All of This and Write a Novel." *New York Times*, March 17, 2020. https://www.nytimes.com/2020/03/17/books/review/sloane-crosley-pandemic-novel-coronavirus.html.

Crouch, Stanley. "Literary Conjure Woman." *New Republic*, October 19, 1987.

Currie, Mark. *About Time: Narrative, Fiction and the Philosophy of Time.* Edinburgh: Edinburgh University Press, 2007.

———. "The Novel and the Moving Now." *Novel: A Forum on Fiction* 42, no. 2 (2009): 318–25.

Dalleo, Raphael, and Elena Machado Sáez. *The Latino/a Canon and the Emergence of Post-Sixties Literature.* New York: Palgrave Macmillan, 2007.

Dames, Nicholas. "'The People v. O.J. Simpson' as Historical Fiction." *Public Books*, April 1, 2016. http://www.publicbooks.org/the-people-v-o-j-simpson-as-historical-fiction/.

Darda, Joseph. "Universality at War: Race, Nation, and Communism in Chester Himes's 'If He Hollers Let Him Go.'" *African American Review* 48, nos. 1–2 (Spring–Summer 2015): 157–73.

Davis, Kenneth C. *Two-Bit Culture: The Paperbacking of America.* Boston: Houghton Mifflin, 1984.

Dawes, James. "The American War Novel." In *The Cambridge Companion to the Literature of World War II*, ed. Marina Mackay, 56–66. Cambridge: Cambridge University Press, 2009.

Dechand, Anton. "ILB Interview: Yaa Gyasi." *EXBERLINER*, September 5, 2018. www.exberliner.com/whats-on/international-literature-festival-blog-yaa-gyasi-interview/.

DeCurtis, Anthony. "Britain's Mavericks." *Harper's Bazaar*, November 1991.

de Groot, Jerome. "International Federation for Public History Plenary Address: On Genealogy." *Public Historian* 37, no. 3 (2015): 102–27.
DeLillo, Don. *White Noise*. New York: Penguin, 1986.
Dern, John A. *Martians, Monsters and Madonna: Fiction and Form in the World of Martin Amis*. New York: Peter Lang, 2000.
"Discussion Questions for 'Pachinko.'" *New York Times*, July 3, 2018. www.nytimes.com/2018/07/03/books/discussion-questions-for-pachinko.html.
Doane, Mary Ann. "Information, Crisis, Catastrophe." In *Logics of Television: Essays in Cultural Criticism*, 222–39. Bloomington: Indiana University Press, 1990.
Doerr, Anthony. *All the Light We Cannot See*. New York: Scribner, 2014.
Doherty, Margaret. "State-Funded Fiction: Minimalism, National Memory, and the Return to Realism in the Post-Postmodern Age." *American Literary History* 27, no. 1 (2014): 79–101.
Driscoll, Beth. *The New Literary Middlebrow: Tastemakers and Reading in the Twenty-First Century*. London: Palgrave Macmillan, 2014.
Dubey, Madhu. "Museumizing Slavery: Living History in Colson Whitehead's *The Underground Railroad*." *American Literary History* 32, no. 1 (Spring 2020): 111–39.
Edelman, Lee. *No Future*. Durham, NC: Duke University Press, 2004.
Egan, Jennifer. *Manhattan Beach*. 2017. New York: Scribner, 2018.
Elam, Michele. *The Souls of Mixed Folk : Race, Politics, and Aesthetics in the New Millennium*. Stanford, CA: Stanford University Press, 2011.
Elias, Amy. *Sublime Desire: History and Post-1960s Fiction*. Baltimore: Johns Hopkins University Press, 2001.
Elliott, Louis. "Ghosts of History: An Interview with Jesmyn Ward by Louis Elliott." *BOMB*, November 10, 2017. https://bombmagazine.org/articles/ghosts-of-history-an-interview-with-jesmyn-ward/.
Elliott, Matthew. "The Inconvenient Ancestor: Slavery and Selective Remembrance on Genealogy Television." *Studies in Popular Culture* 39, no. 2 (2017): 73–90.
Ellison, Ralph. *Invisible Man*. New York: Vintage International, 1995.
Emre, Merve. "Jonathan Franzen Thinks People Can Change." Interview with Jonathan Franzen. *Vulture*, September 30, 2021. https://www.vulture.com/article/interview-jonathan-franzen-crossroads.html.
——. *Paraliterary: The Making of Bad Readers in Postwar America*. Chicago: University of Chicago Press, 2018.
English, James F. *The Economy of Prestige: Prizes, Awards, and the Circulation of Cultural Value*. Cambridge, MA: Harvard University Press, 2008.
——. "Now, Not Now: Counting Time in Contemporary Fiction Studies." *Modern Language Quarterly* 77, no. 3 (2016): 395–418.

WORKS CITED

Ensslen, Klaus. "Fictionalizing History: David Bradley's *The Chaneysville Incident*." *Callaloo* 35 (1988): 280–96.
Fenster, Gayle Beth. "Educators Urge Women, Minority Role Models." *Harvard Crimson*, February 24, 1990.
Ferguson, Roderick A. *The Reorder of Things: The University and Its Pedagogies of Minority Difference*. Minneapolis: University of Minnesota Press, 2012.
Finney, Brian. *Martin Amis*. New York: Routledge, 2008.
Fischer, Michael. "Literature and Empathy." *Philosophy and Literature* 41, no. 2 (October 2017): 431–64.
Fish, Stanley E. "Interpreting the 'Variorum.'" *Critical Inquiry* 2, no. 3 (1976): 465–85.
Fitzpatrick, Kathleen. *The Anxiety of Obsolescence: The American Novel in the Age of Television*. Nashville, TN: Vanderbilt University Press, 2006.
Foer, Jonathan Safran. *A Convergence of Birds: Original Fiction and Poetry Inspired by Joseph Cornell*. New York: Penguin, 2007.
———. *Everything Is Illuminated*. New York: Harper Perennial, 2003.
———. *Extremely Loud and Incredibly Close*. New York: Penguin, 2005.
For Colored Girls Book Club. "For Colored Girls Book Club + Margaret Wilkerson Sexton." www.forcoloredgirlsbookclub.com/interviews/interview-with-margaret-wilkerson-sexton.
Frank, Joseph. "Spatial Form in Modern Literature: An Essay in Two Parts." *Sewanee Review* 53, no. 2 (Spring 1945): 221–40.
Fregoso, Rosa-Linda. "Julia Alvarez, *In the Time of the Butterflies*." In *Reading U.S. Latina Writers: Remapping American Literature*, ed. Alvina E. Quintana. 7–14. New York: Palgrave Macmillan, 2003.
Gannon, Thomas. "The Chaneysville Incident." Review of *The Chaneysville Incident* by David Bradley. *America* 144, no. 21 (May 30, 1981): 449.
Gates, Henry Louis, Jr. *Loose Canons: Notes on the Culture Wars*. New York: Oxford University Press, 1992.
Genette, Gérard. *Narrative Discourse Revisited*. Trans. Jane E. Lewin. Ithaca, NY: Cornell University Press, 1988.
Getz, John. "Healing the Soldier in White: *Ceremony* as War Novel." *WLA: War, Literature and the Arts* 9, no. 1 (1997): 123–40.
Gilbert, Sandra M., and Susan Gubar. *The Madwoman in the Attic: The Woman Writer and the Nineteenth-Century Literary Imagination*. 1979. New Haven, CT: Yale University Press, 2020.
Gladstone, Jason, Andrew Hoberek, and Daniel Worden, eds. *Postmodern/Postwar and After: Rethinking American Literature*. Iowa City: University of Iowa Press, 2016.

Glaser, Jennifer. *Borrowed Voices: Writing and Racial Ventriloquism in the Jewish American Imagination*. New Brunswick, NJ: Rutgers University Press, 2016.
Glass, Loren, ed. *After the Program Era: The Past, Present, and Future of Creative Writing in the University*. Iowa City: University of Iowa Press, 2017.
Goodreads.com. "Homegoing." www.goodreads.com/book/show/27071490-home going.
———. "A Kind of Freedom." www.goodreads.com/book/show/33946142-a-kind-of -freedom.
Goyal, Yogita. "Un-American: Refugees and the Vietnam War." *PMLA* 133, no. 2 (2018): 378–83.
Greenblatt, Stephen. *The Power of Forms in the English Renaissance*. Ann Arbor: University of Michigan Press, 1982.
———. *Shakespearean Negotiations: The Circulation of Social Energy in Renaissance England*. Berkeley: University of California Press, 1988.
Grossman, Claire, Juliana Spahr, and Stephanie Young. "Literature's Vexed Democratization." *American Literary History* 33, no. 2 (Summer 2021): 298–319.
———. "Who Gets to Be a Writer." *Public Books*, April 15, 2021. www.publicbooks.org/who-gets-to-be-a-writer/.
Guillory, John. *Cultural Capital: The Problem of Literary Canon Formation*. Chicago: University of Chicago Press, 1993.
———. *Professing Criticism: Essays on the Organization of Literary Study*. Chicago: University of Chicago Press, 2022.
Gyasi, Yaa. *Homegoing*. New York: Vintage, 2017.
———. "I'm Ghanaian-American. Am I Black?" *New York Times*, June 18, 2016. www.nytimes.com/2016/06/19/opinion/sunday/im-ghanaian-american-am-i -black.html.
———. "White People, Black Authors Are Not Your Medicine." *Guardian*, March 20, 2021. www.theguardian.com/books/2021/mar/20/white-people-black-authors-are -not-your-medicine.
Halbwachs, Maurice. *The Collective Memory*. New York: Harper & Row, 1980.
Hale, Dorothy J. *The Novel and the New Ethics*. Stanford, CA: Stanford University Press, 2020.
Haley, Alex. *Roots: The Saga of an American Family*. New York: Doubleday, 1976.
Harde, Roxanne, ed. *Narratives of Community: Women's Short Story Sequences*. Newcastle, UK: Cambridge Scholars Publishing, 2007.
Harootunian, Harry. "Remembering the Historical Present." *Critical Inquiry* 33, no. 3 (2007): 471–94.
Harrison, M. John. "Speeding from Cradle to Grave." *Times Literary Supplement*, September 20, 1991.

Hart, Matthew. *Extraterritorial: A Political Geography of Contemporary Fiction*. New York: Columbia University Press, 2020.
Hartman, Saidiya. *Lose Your Mother: A Journey Along the Atlantic Slave Route*. New York: Farrar, Straus and Giroux, 2007.
———. *Scenes of Subjection: Terror, Slavery, and Self-Making in Nineteenth-Century America*. New York: Oxford University Press, 1997.
———. "Venus in Two Acts." *Small Axe* 12, no. 2 (2008): 1–14.
Heller, Joseph. *Catch-22*. 1961. New York: Simon & Schuster, 2004.
Heneks, Grace. "The American Subplot: Colson Whitehead's Post-Racial Allegory in *Zone One*." *The Comparatist* 42 (2018): 60–79.
Hepburn, Allan. "Vanishing Worlds: Epic Disappearance in *Manhattan Beach*." *PMLA* 134, no. 2 (March 2019): 384–90.
Hill, Michael DeRell. *The Ethics of Swagger: Prizewinning African American Novels, 1977–1993*. Columbus: Ohio State University Press, 2013.
Hoberek, Andrew. "Cormac McCarthy and the Aesthetics of Exhaustion." *American Literary History* 23, no. 3 (2011): 483–99.
———. "Living with PASD." *Contemporary Literature* 53, no. 2 (2012): 406–13.
Hönnighausen, Lothar. "Thomas Mann's *Buddenbrooks* and William Faulkner's *Sartoris* as Family Novels." *Faulkner Journal* 6, no. 1 (1990): 33–45.
Houston, Shannon M. "*Homegoing*: An Interview with Yaa Gyasi, Author of the Most Powerful Debut Novel of 2016." *Paste Magazine*, June 9, 2016. www.pastemagazine.com/books/yaa-gyasi-homegoing/.
Hungerford, Amy. *The Holocaust of Texts: Genocide, Literature, and Personification*. Chicago: University of Chicago Press, 2003.
———. *Making Literature Now*. Stanford, CA: Stanford University Press, 2016.
———. "On the Period Formerly Known as Contemporary." *American Literary History* 20, no. 1 (2008): 410–19.
Hunziker, Alyssa A. "At the Intersections of Empire: *Ceremony*, Transnationalism, and American Indian–Filipino Exchange." *Studies in American Indian Literatures* 31, no. 3 (Fall 2019): 116–34.
Hurston, Zora Neale. "What White Publishers Won't Print." In *Folklore, Memoirs, and Other Writings*, ed. Cheryl A. Wall, 878–83. New York: Library of America, 1995.
Hutcheon, Linda. "Historiographic Metafiction Parody and the Intertextuality of History." In *Intertextuality and Contemporary American Fiction*, ed. Patrick O'Donnell and Robert Davis, 3–32. Baltimore: Johns Hopkins University Press, 1989.
———. *A Poetics of Postmodernism: History, Theory, Fiction*. New York: Routledge, 1988.

WORKS CITED

Hyde, Emily, and Sarah Wasserman. "The Contemporary." *Literature Compass* 14, no. 9 (2017).
Iannone, Carol. "Literature by Quota." *Commentary* 51, no. 3 (March 1991): 50–53.
Ireland, Ken. "Peeling the Onion: Outcomes to Origins in Retrograde Narrative." *Journal of Literary Semantics* 39, no. 1 (2010): 29–41.
Jablow, Martha. "Novelist Has All the Moves." *Philadelphia Daily News*, September 12, 1983.
Jackson, Mitchell S. "'I Carry It Within Me': Novelist Colson Whitehead Reminds Us How America's Racist History Lives On." *Time*, June 27, 2019.
Jacques, Ben. "Julia Alvarez: Real Flights of Imagination." *Americas* 53, no. 1 (January–February 2001): 22–29.
Jameson, Fredric. *The Antinomies of Realism*. London: Verso, 2013.
———. *Postmodernism, Or, The Cultural Logic of Late Capitalism*. Durham, NC: Duke University Press, 1991.
Johnson, Kelli Lyon. *Julia Alvarez: Writing a New Place on the Map*. Albuquerque: University of New Mexico Press, 2005.
Johnston, Carrie. "Postwar Reentry Narratives in Leslie Marmon Silko's *Ceremony* and Ben Fountain's *Billy Lynn's Long Halftime Walk*." *Studies in the Novel* 49, no. 3 (Fall 2017): 400–418.
"Judges Citation: *All the Light We Cannot See*." National Book Foundation. https://www.nationalbook.org/books/all-the-light-we-cannot-see/.
Kakutani, Michiko. "Review: In 'Homegoing,' What Slavery Costs One Family." *New York Times*, June 13, 2016. www.nytimes.com/2016/06/14/books/review-homegoing-by-yaa-gyasi.html.
Karem, Jeff. *The Romance of Authenticity: The Cultural Politics of Regional and Ethnic Literatures*. Charlottesville: University of Virginia Press, 2004.
Kaufman, Marian. "Interview with Margaret Wilkerson Sexton." *Bayou Magazine*, January 2018. bayoumagazine.org/interview-with-margaret-wilkerson-sexton/.
Kellaway, Kate. "Yaa Gyasi: 'Slavery Is on People's Minds. It Affects Us Still.'" *The Guardian*, January 8, 2017. www.theguardian.com/books/2017/jan/08/yaa-gyasi-slavery-is-on-peoples-minds-it-affects-us-still-interview-homegoing-observer-new-review.
Kelly, Adam. "David Foster Wallace and the New Sincerity in American Fiction." In *Consider David Foster Wallace: Critical Essays*, ed. David Hering, 131–46. Los Angeles: Sideshow Media Group Press, 2010.
———. "Freedom to Struggle: The Ironies of Colson Whitehead." *Open Library of Humanities* 4, no. 2 (2018): 1–35.

———. "The New Sincerity." In *Postmodern/Postwar—and After: Rethinking American Literature*, ed. Jason Gladstone, Andrew Hoberek, and Daniel Worden, 197–208. Iowa City: University of Iowa Press, 2016.

Keneally, Thomas. *Schindler's List*. New York: Touchstone, 1993.

Kermode, Frank. "In Reverse." Review of *Time's Arrow*, by Martin Amis. *London Review of Books*, September 12, 1991.

Kihss, Peter. "Pulitzer Jurors Dismayed on Pynchon." *New York Times*, May 8, 1974.

Kim, Ronyoung. *Clay Walls*. New York: Permanent Press, 1987.

Kim, Ronyoung, and Richard Hahn Papers. Collection no. 3010, Korean Heritage Library, USC Libraries, University of Southern California.

Kirn, Walter. "The Promise of Verticality." *Time*, January 25, 1999.

Kissel, Howard. "David Bradley: Writing Beyond the Rage." *Women's Wear Daily*, April 7, 1981.

Knoll, Jeremy. "How 'Homegoing' Has Changed My Teaching." Learning for Justice, February 13, 2017. www.learningforjustice.org/magazine/how-homegoing-has-changed-my-teaching.

Konstantinou, Lee. *Cool Characters: Irony and American Fiction*. Cambridge, MA: Harvard University Press, 2016.

———. "Critique Has Its Uses." *American Book Review* 38, no. 5 (2017): 15–18.

Kopacz, Chris. "Tommy Orange Hints About Upcoming Sequel to 'There There.'" *Indian Country Today*, July 6, 2021. https://indiancountrytoday.com/news/tommy-orange-hints-about-upcoming-sequel-to-there-there.

Kubitschek, Missy Dehn. "'So You Want a History, Do You?': Epistemologies and 'The Chaneysville Incident.'" *Mississippi Quarterly* 49, no. 4 (1996): 755–74.

Kunkel, Benjamin. "Inventing Climate-Change Literature." *New Yorker*, October 24, 2014. http://www.newyorker.com/culture/cultural-comment/problem-climate-change-novel.

Kuo, Roger G. "The Troubled History of Afro-Am." *Harvard Crimson*, February 4, 1991.

Lam, Andrew. "Viet Thanh Nguyen in Conversation with Andrew Lam." *Asian American Literature: Discourses & Pedagogies* 9 (2018): 8–19.

Lambert, Josh. *The Literary Mafia: Jews, Publishing, and Postwar American Literature*. New Haven, CT: Yale University Press, 2022.

Lea, Sarah. "Joseph Cornell: Wanderlust." In *Joseph Cornell: Wanderlust*, 19–39. London: Royal Academy of Arts, 2015.

Leader-Picone, Cameron. "Post-Black Stories: Colson Whitehead's *Sag Harbor* and Racial Individualism." *Contemporary Literature* 56, no. 3 (Fall 2015): 421–49.

WORKS CITED

Lee, A. Robert. "Afro-America, The Before Columbus Foundation and The Literary Multiculturalization of America." *Journal of American Studies* 28, no. 3 (1994): 433–50.

Lee, Felicia R. "What the Tide Brought In." Review of *A Tale for the Time Being*, by Ruth Ozeki. *New York Times*, March 12, 2013.

Lee, Min Jin. *Pachinko*. New York: Grand Central Publishing, 2017.

Le-Khac, Long. *Giving Form to an Asian and Latinx America*. Stanford, CA: Stanford University Press, 2020.

Lehman, David. "From Death to Birth." Review of *Time's Arrow*, by Martin Amis. *New York Times Book Review*, November 17, 1991.

Lehmann-Haupt, Christopher. "Books of the Times." Review of *The Chaneysville Incident*, by David Bradley. *New York Times*, May 12, 1981.

LeMahieu, Michael, Angela Naimou, and Viet Thanh Nguyen. "An Interview with Viet Thanh Nguyen." *Contemporary Literature* 58, no. 4 (2017): 438–61.

Leonard, Paul. "The Flag Is Harassment." *Harvard Crimson*, February 20, 1990.

Lerner, Ben. *10:04*. New York: Picador, 2014.

———. *Leaving the Atocha Station*. Minneapolis: Coffee House Press, 2011.

———. *The Topeka School*. New York: Farrar, Straus and Giroux, 2019.

"Let Us Descend | Book by Jesmyn Ward | Official Publisher Page | Simon & Schuster." Simon & Schuster. https://www.simonandschuster.com/books/Let-Us-Descend/Jesmyn-Ward/9781982104498.

Levy-Hussen, Aida. "Boredom in Contemporary African American Literature." *Post45*, April 28, 2019. http://post45.research.yale.edu/2019/04/boredom-in-contemporary-african-american-literature/.

———. *How to Read African American Literature: Post–Civil Rights Fiction and the Task of Interpretation*. New York: New York University Press, 2016.

Li, Sabrina. "Colson Whitehead '91: Harvard Arts Medal Recipient." Office of the Arts at Harvard Blog, April 21, 2018.

Li, Stephanie. "Genre Trouble and History's Miseries in Colson Whitehead's *The Underground Railroad*." *MELUS* 44, no. 2 (2019): 1–23.

———. *Pan–African American Literature: Signifyin(g) Immigrants in the Twenty-First Century*. New Brunswick, NJ: Rutgers University Press, 2018.

———. *Signifying Without Specifying: Racial Discourse in the Age of Obama*. New Brunswick, NJ: Rutgers University Press, 2011.

Liggins, Saundra. "The Urban Gothic Vision of Colson Whitehead's 'The Intuitionist' (1999)." *African American Review* 40, no. 2 (2006): 359–69.

Lim, Jeehyun. *Bilingual Brokers: Race, Literature, and Language as Human Capital*. New York: Fordham University Press, 2017.

Limon, John. *Writing After War: American War Fiction from Realism to Postmodernism.* Oxford: Oxford University Press, 1994.

Lipsitz, George. *Time Passages: Collective Memory and American Popular Culture.* Minneapolis: University of Minnesota, 1990.

Lowe, Lisa. "Canon, Institutionalization, Identity: Contradictions for Asian American Studies." In *The Ethnic Canon: Histories, Institutions, and Interventions*, ed. David Palumbo-Liu, 48–68. Minneapolis: University of Minnesota Press, 1995.

Lucas, Julian. "I Ain't Been Mean Enough: The Literary Provocations of Ishmael Reed." *New Yorker*, July 26, 2021.

———. "New Black Worlds to Know." Review of *The Underground Railroad*, by Colson Whitehead. *New York Review of Books*, September 29, 2016.

Luhmann, Niklas. *The Reality of the Mass Media.* Cambridge: Polity Press, 2000.

Luis, William. *Dance Between Two Cultures: Latino Caribbean Literature Written in the United States.* Nashville, TN: Vanderbilt University Press, 1997.

Luiselli, Valeria. *Lost Children Archive.* New York: Vintage, 2019.

Lukács, Georg. *The Historical Novel.* Trans. Hannah and Stanley Mitchell. Lincoln: University of Nebraska Press, 1983.

Luo, Michael. "What Min Jin Lee Wants Us to See." *New Yorker*, February 17, 2022. www.newyorker.com/culture/the-new-yorker-interview/what-min-jin-lee-wants-us-to-see.

Lyon, Janet. "The Wheelchair: A Three-Part Drama." *PMLA* 134, no. 2 (March 2019): 405–11.

Machado Sáez, Elena. "Generation MFA: Neoliberalism and the Shifting Cultural Capital of US Latinx Writers." *Latino Studies* 16, no. 3 (2018): 361–83.

———. *Market Aesthetics: The Purchase of the Past in Caribbean Diasporic Fiction.* Charlottesville: University of Virginia Press, 2015.

Mackay, Marina. "Introduction." In *The Cambridge Companion to the Literature of World War II*, ed. Marina Mackay, 1–10. New York: Cambridge University Press, 2009.

Makkai, Rebecca. *The Great Believers.* New York: Penguin, 2018.

Mandel, Naomi. *Against the Unspeakable: Complicity, the Holocaust, and Slavery in America.* Charlottesville: University of Virginia Press, 2006.

Mann, Thomas. *Buddenbrooks: The Decline of a Family.* Trans. John E. Woods. New York: Vintage, 1993.

Manshel, Alexander. "The Lag: Technology and Fiction in the Twentieth Century." *PMLA* 135, no. 1 (2020): 40–58.

Manshel, Alexander, Laura B. McGrath, and J. D. Porter. "Who Cares About Literary Prizes?" *Public Books*, September 3, 2019. https://www.publicbooks.org/who-cares-about-literary-prizes/.
Martin, Theodore. *Contemporary Drift: Genre, Historicism, and the Problem of the Present*. New York: Columbia University Press, 2017.
———. "Contemporary, Inc." *Representations* 142, no. 1 (Spring 2018): 124–44.
———. "The Currency of the Contemporary." In *Postmodern/Postwar—and After: Rethinking American Literature*, ed. Jason Gladstone, Andrew Hoberek, and Daniel Worden, 227–39. Iowa City: University of Iowa Press, 2016.
Martínez, Elizabeth Coonrod. "Julia Alvarez: Progenitor of a Movement." *Americas* 59, no. 2 (March–April 2007): 6–13.
Mason, Kelly A. E. "A Poet Who Is Wary of the 'Burden of Representation.'" *Harvard Crimson*, June 4, 1992.
———. "Stop Teaching English Lit." *Harvard Crimson*, December 13, 1990.
Maus, Derek C. *Understanding Colson Whitehead*. Rev. ed. Columbia: University of South Carolina Press, 2021.
Mayhew, Ann. "The Canon: Books to Read in September." *The Riveter*, September 7, 2017. www.therivetermagazine.com/the-canon-books-to-read-in-september/.
McCarthy, Dermot. "The Limits of Irony: The Chronillogical World of Martin Amis' *Time's Arrow*." *War, Literature, and the Arts: An International Journal of the Humanities* 11, no. 1 (1999): 294–320.
McCarthy, Jesse. "'A Kind of Freedom' Follows Three Generations of a Black Family in New Orleans." *New York Times*, September 5, 2017. www.nytimes.com/2017/09/05/books/review/a-kind-of-freedom-margaret-wilkerson-sexton.html.
———. "A Literary Chameleon." *Harvard Magazine*, September–October 2016.
———. "On Afropessimism." *Los Angeles Review of Books*, July 20, 2020. www.lareviewofbooks.org/article/on-afropessimism/.
McCracken, Ellen. *New Latina Narrative: The Feminine Space of Postmodern Ethnicity*. Tucson: University of Arizona Press, 1999.
McDowell, Edwin. "'Chaneysville Incident' Wins Faulkner Award." *New York Times*, April 11, 1982.
McGrath, Laura B. "Comping White." *Los Angeles Review of Books*, January 21, 2019. www.lareviewofbooks.org/article/comping-white/.
———. "Literary Agency." *American Literary History* 33, no. 2 (Summer 2021): 350–70.
McGurl, Mark. *The Program Era: Postwar Fiction and the Rise of Creative Writing*. Cambridge, MA: Harvard University Press, 2009.

WORKS CITED

Melamed, Jodi. *Represent and Destroy: Rationalizing Violence in the New Racial Capitalism*. Minneapolis: University of Minnesota Press, 2011.
Menke, Richard. "Narrative Reversals and the Thermodynamics of History in Martin Amis's *Time's Arrow*." *MFS: Modern Fiction Studies* 44, no. 4 (1998): 959–80.
Michaels, Walter Benn. *The Shape of the Signifier: 1967 to the End of History*. Princeton, NJ: Princeton University Press, 2004.
Miller, Laura. "Colson Whitehead's Alternate New York." *Salon*, January 12, 1999.
———. "Colson Whitehead Is Still Just Doing His Weird Thing." *Slate*, September 12, 2021.
———. "Descendants." *New Yorker*, May 23, 2016. www.newyorker.com/magazine/2016/05/30/yaa-gyasis-homegoing.
———. "Going Up." *Salon*, January 13, 1999. www.salon.com/1999/01/12/cov_si_12int/.
Miller, Laura J. *Reluctant Capitalists: Bookselling and the Culture of Consumption*. Chicago: University of Chicago Press, 2008.
Mills, Victoria. "Fiction, Empathy and Teaching History." *Teaching History* 81 (October 1995): 7–9.
"The Minds of Black Folk." *Vibe*, September 1997.
Mineo, Liz. "An Imaginative Leap into Real-Life Horror." Interview with Colson Whitehead. *Harvard Gazette*, March 7, 2003.
"Minority Groups in World War II." U.S. Army Center of Military History, October 3, 2003. https://history.army.mil/documents/WWII/minst.html.
Mirakhor, Leah. "More at Stake Here Than Beauty: An Interview with Yaa Gyasi." *Los Angeles Review of Books*, June 9, 2016. www.lareviewofbooks.org/article/stake-beauty-interview-yaa-gyasi/.
"MLA International Bibliography." Modern Language Association. www.mla.org/Publications/MLA-International-Bibliography.
"Monitor Manuscripts: 'The Chaneysville Incident.'" Review of *The Chaneysville Incident*, by David Bradley. *New York Amsterdam News*, August 28, 1982.
Morrison, Toni. *Beloved*. New York: Vintage, 1987.
———. *Playing in the Dark: Whiteness and the Literary Imagination*. New York: Vintage, 1993.
———. "The Site of Memory." In *Inventing the Truth: The Art and Craft of Memoir*, ed. William Zinsser, 2nd ed., 85–102. Boston: Houghton Mifflin, 1995.
———. *Song of Solomon*. 1977. New York: Vintage International, 2004.
Muhammad, Ismail. "'If You're Going to Tell the Story of Slavery, I'm Going to Listen All Day': Q&A with 'Homegoing' Author Yaa Gyasi." *ZYZZYVA*, June 21, 2016. www.zyzzyva.org/2016/07/21/if-youre-going-qa-with-yaa-gyasi/.

WORKS CITED

Mujica, Barbara. "On Politics and Literature." *Americas* 47, no. 2 (March/April 1995): 60.

Murray, Simone. *The Adaptation Industry: The Cultural Economy of Contemporary Literary Adaptation*. New York: Routledge, 2011.

Muyumba, Walton. "Yaa Gyasi's Transatlantic Epic." *New Republic*, July 5, 2016. www.newrepublic.com/article/134834/yaa-gyasis-transatlantic-epic.

Nadiminti, Kalyan. "The Global Program Era: Contemporary International Fiction in the American Creative Economy." *Novel: A Forum on Fiction* 51, no. 3 (2018): 375–98.

Nancy, Jean-Luc. *After Fukushima: The Equivalence of Catastrophes*. Trans. Charlotte Mandell. New York: Fordham University Press, 2014.

"NEA Literature Fellowships: 40 Years of Supporting American Writers." National Endowment for the Arts, 2006. https://www.arts.gov/about/publications/nea-literature-fellowships-40-years-supporting-american-writers.

Nelson, Alondra. *The Social Life of DNA: Race, Reparations, and Reconciliation after the Genome*. Boston: Beacon Press, 2016.

Nguyen, Sophia. "Elbow Room: How the Dark Room Collective Made Space for a Generation of African-American Writers." *Harvard Magazine*, March–April 2016. https://www.harvardmagazine.com/2016/03/elbow-room.

Nguyen, Viet Thanh. "Canon Fodder." *Washington Post*, May 3, 2018. www.washingtonpost.com/news/posteverything/wp/2018/05/03/feature/books-by-immigrants-foreigners-and-minorities-dont-diminish-the-classic-curriculum/.

——. *Nothing Ever Dies: Vietnam and the Memory of War*. Cambridge, MA: Harvard University Press, 2016.

——. *Race and Resistance: Literature and Politics in Asian America*. New York: Oxford University Press, 2002.

——. *The Sympathizer*. New York: Grove Press, 2015.

"The Nickel Boys by Colson Whitehead." Penguin Random House, 2019. http://www.penguinrandomhouse.com/books/223161/the-nickel-boys-by-colson-whitehead/9780385537070.

Nishikawa, Kinohi. *Street Players: Black Pulp Fiction and the Making of a Literary Underground*. Chicago: University of Chicago Press, 2018.

Norman, Brian. *Neo-Segregation Narratives*. Athens: University of Georgia Press, 2010.

North, Joseph. *Literary Criticism: A Concise Political History*. Cambridge, MA: Harvard University Press, 2017.

"Notes & Comments." Editorial. *New Criterion*, January 1991.

Obama, Barack. "Remarks by the President at Cape Coast Castle." White House Archives, July 11, 2009. obamawhitehouse.archives.gov/the-press-office/remarks-president-cape-coast-castle.

WORKS CITED

O'Brien, Tim. *The Things They Carried*. New York: Broadway Books, 1990.
"On Viet Thanh Nguyen's *The Sympathizer*, *The Refugees*, and *Nothing Ever Dies*." *PMLA* 133, no. 2 (March 2018): 364–436.
"Open Syllabus Explorer." Open Syllabus Project, https://explorer.opensyllabus.org/.
"Oprah Reveals New Book Club Selection." *CBS This Morning*, August 2, 2016. www.youtube.com/watch?v=okcBr2h5zLc.
Orange, Tommy. *There There*. New York: Knopf, 2018.
Ortiz-Vilarelle, Julia. "Julia Alvarez and the Autobiographical *Antojo*." In *Inhabiting La Patria: Identity, Agency, and Antojo in the Work of Julia Alvarez*, ed. Rebecca L. Harrison and Emily Hipchen, 21–42. Albany: State University of New York Press, 2013.
Otsuka, Julie. "An Interview with Julie Otsuka." *BookBrowse*. January 6, 2010. https://www.bookbrowse.com/author_interviews/full/index.cfm/author_number/807/julie-otsuka.
———. *When the Emperor Was Divine*. New York: Anchor Books, 2003.
Owens, Jill. "Powell's Interview: Yaa Gyasi of *Homegoing*." Powell's Book Blog, May 23, 2016. www.powells.com/post/interviews/powells-interview-yaa-gyasi-of-homegoing-.
Ozeki, Ruth. *A Tale for the Time Being*. New York: Penguin, 2013.
Palmore, Joseph R. "Afro-Am: Going Nowhere Fast." *Harvard Crimson*, February 2, 1990.
Palumbo-Liu, David. "Introduction." In *The Ethnic Canon: Histories, Institutions, and Interventions*, ed. David Palumbo-Liu, 1–27. Minneapolis: University of Minnesota Press, 1995.
Park, Josephine. "Alien Enemies in Julie Otsuka's *When the Emperor Was Divine*." *Modern Fiction Studies* 59, no. 1 (Spring 2013): 135–55.
Parker, Kimberly N. "*Homegoing* Teacher's Guide." Penguin Random House, 2018. www.penguinrandomhouse.com/books/533857/homegoing-by-yaa-gyasi/9781101971062/teachers-guide/.
Perlmutter, Ruby. "Interview with Viet Thanh Nguyen." *Lit: Literature Interpretation Theory* 29, no. 1 (2018): 80–89.
Phelan, James. *Somebody Telling Somebody Else: A Rhetorical Poetics of Narrative*. Columbus: Ohio State University Press, 2017.
"Phoenix Award." Children's Literature Association. https://chla.memberclicks.net/phoenix-award.
Piercy, Marge. "A Historian Obsessed by Ghosts of Past." Review of *The Chaneysville Incident*, by David Bradley. *Chicago Tribune*, April 26, 1981.
Plotz, David A. "'Politically Correct' Thought Control." *Harvard Crimson*, February 5, 1990.

WORKS CITED

Porter, J. D. "Popularity/Prestige." *Literary Lab*, Pamphlet 17, 2018. https://litlab.stanford.edu/assets/pdf/LiteraryLabPamphlet17.pdf.

Pound, Ezra. *ABC of Reading*. New York: Faber and Faber, 1934.

Powers, Hanna. "A Conversation with Author Margaret Wilkerson Sexton." *Sarasota*, July 25, 2019. www.sarasotamagazine.com/arts-and-entertainment/2019/07/margaret-wilkerson-sexton.

Prescott, Orville. "Books of the Times." *New York Times*, October 23, 1961.

Pruett, Jordan. "Managed Abundance: A Quantitative History of American Fiction, 1931–2009." PhD dissertation, University of Chicago, 2022.

Pynchon, Thomas. *Gravity's Rainbow*. New York: Penguin, 1973.

Railton, Ben. *History and Hope in American Literature: Models of Critical Patriotism*. New York: Rowman & Littlefield, 2017.

Ramsey, William. "An End of Southern History: The Down-Home Quests of Toni Morrison and Colson Whitehead." *African American Review* 41, no. 4 (2007): 769–85.

Rasberry, Vaughn. *Race and the Totalitarian Century: Geopolitics in the Black Literary Imagination*. Cambridge, MA: Harvard University Press, 2016.

Rau, Petra. "The War in Contemporary Fiction." In *The Cambridge Companion to the Literature of World War II*, ed. Marina Mackay, 207–19. Cambridge: Cambridge University Press, 2009.

"Reading Group Guide | *Pachinko* by Min Jin Lee." Grand Central Publishing. www.grandcentralpublishing.com/uncategorized/pachinko-reading-group-guide/.

Reed, Brian. "The Dark Room Collective and Post-Soul Poetics." *African American Review* 41, no. 4 (2007): 727–47.

Rifkind, Donna. "Speaking American." Review of *How the García Girls Lost Their Accents*, by Julia Alvarez. *New York Times*, October 6, 1991. https://www.nytimes.com/1991/10/06/books/speaking-american.html.

Roach, Imani. "Yaa Gyasi: Taking a Long View." *Guernica*, September 16, 2016. www.guernicamag.com/taking-a-long-view/.

Rody, Caroline. "Between 'I' and 'We': Viet Thanh Nguyen's Interethnic Multitudes." *PMLA* 133, no. 2 (2018): 396–405.

———. *The Interethnic Imagination: Roots and Passages in Contemporary Asian American Fiction*. Oxford: Oxford University Press, 2009.

Roemer, Kenneth M. "Silko's Arroyos as Mainstream: Processes and Implications of Canonical Identity." In *Leslie Marmon Silko's Ceremony: A Casebook*, ed. Allan Chavkin, 223–39. Oxford: Oxford University Press, 2002.

Romagnolo, Catherine. *Opening Acts: Narrative Beginnings in Twentieth-Century Feminist Fiction*. Lincoln: University of Nebraska Press, 2015.

WORKS CITED

Rosa, Hartmut. "Social Acceleration: Ethical and Political Consequences of a Desynchronized High-Speed Society." *Constellations* 10, no. 1 (2003): 3–33.
Rosen, Jeremy. "Literary Fiction and the Genres of Genre Fiction." *Post45*, August 7, 2018. http://post45.research.yale.edu/2018/08/literary-fiction-and-the-genres-of-genre-fiction/.
———. *Minor Characters Have Their Day: Genre and the Contemporary Literary Marketplace.* New York: Columbia University Press, 2016.
Roth, Philip. *The Human Stain.* New York: Vintage International, 2001.
———. *The Plot Against America.* New York: Vintage International, 2005.
Rothberg, Michael. *Multidirectional Memory: Remembering the Holocaust in the Age of Decolonization.* Stanford, CA: Stanford University Press, 2009.
Row, Jess. *White Flights: Race, Fiction, and the American Imagination.* Minneapolis: Graywolf Press, 2019.
Ru, Yi-Ling. "The Family Novel: Toward a Generic Definition." *Comparative Literature: East & West* 3, no. 1 (2001): 99–133.
Rubin, Philip M. "Obama Named New Law Review President." *Harvard Crimson*, February 6, 1990.
Rushdy, Ashraf H. A. *Remembering Generations: Race and Family in Contemporary African American Fiction.* Chapel Hill: University of North Carolina Press, 2001.
Russell, Alison. "Recalibrating the Past: Colson Whitehead's *The Intuitionist*." *Critique* 49, no. 1 (2007): 46–60, 112.
Saariluoma, Liisa. "Virginia Woolf's *The Years*: Identity and Time in an Anti-Family Novel." *Orbis Litterarum: International Review of Literary Studies* 54, no. 4 (1999): 276–300.
Saldívar, Ramón. "The Second Elevation of the Novel: Race, Form, and the Post-race Aesthetic in Contemporary Narrative." *Narrative* 21, no. 1 (2013): 1–18.
Samet, Elizabeth D. *Looking for the Good War: American Amnesia and the Violent Pursuit of Happiness.* New York: Farrar, Straus and Giroux, 2021.
Santin, Bryan M. *Postwar American Fiction and the Rise of Modern Conservatism: A Literary History, 1945–2008.* Cambridge: Cambridge University Press, 2021.
Schuessler, Jennifer. "Colson Whitehead on Slavery, Success and Writing the Novel That Really Scared Him." *New York Times*, August 2, 2016.
Scott, Sam. "The Story Behind 'Homegoing.'" *Stanford Magazine*, July–August 2017. stanfordmag.org/contents/the-story-behind-homegoing.
Scott, Walter. *Waverley or 'Tis Sixty Years Since.* New York: Penguin, 1985.
Scranton, Roy. *Total Mobilization: World War II and American Literature.* Chicago: University of Chicago Press, 2019.

WORKS CITED

Seidenbaum, Art. "Superior Saga Tracks Heritage from Slave Times." Review of *The Chaneysville Incident*, by David Bradley. *Los Angeles Times*, April 8, 1981.

Seidlitz, Hannah (@HannahSeidlitz). "what I'm really most afraid of that's incubating in my neighbors' homes is the next character-driven, pulitzer shoo-in pandemic novel." Twitter post, March 13, 2020, 10:37 a.m. https://twitter.com/HannahSeidlitz/status/1238519540838993920?s=20&t=uf4iLSkjJNx2XsMd1aSgEA.

Selejan, Corina. "Fragmentation(s) and Realism(s): Has the Fragment Gone Mainstream?" *Anglica Wratislaviensia* 57 (2019): 103–12.

Selzer, Linda. "New Eclecticism: An Interview with Colson Whitehead." *Callaloo* 31, no. 2 (2008): 393–401.

Serpell, Namwali. "The Banality of Empathy." *New York Review of Books*, March 2, 2019. www.nybooks.com/daily/2019/03/02/the-banality-of-empathy/.

———. *The Old Drift*. New York: Hogarth Books, 2019.

Serpell, Namwali, and Maria Tumarkin. "Unethical Reading and the Limits of Empathy." *Yale Review*, Winter 2020. yalereview.yale.edu/unethical-reading-and-limits-empathy.

Sexton, Margaret Wilkerson. *A Kind of Freedom*. Berkeley: Counterpoint Press, 2017.

Shakespeare, William. *Hamlet*. Ed. Barbara A. Mowat and Paul Werstine. New York: Simon & Schuster, 1992.

———. *Henry VI, Part Two*. Ed. Barbara A. Mowat and Paul Werstine. New York: Simon & Schuster, 2008.

Shank, Jenny. "Dallas-Bound Luis Alberto Urrea says 'House of Broken Angels' Is Like a Mexican Take on 'The Godfather.'" *Dallas Morning News*, March 6, 2018. https://www.dallasnews.com/arts-entertainment/books/2018/03/06/dallas-bound-luis-alberto-urrea-says-house-of-broken-angels-is-like-a-mexican-take-on-the-godfather/.

Shapland, Jenn. "Interview with Colson Whitehead." *Southwest Contemporary*, May 1, 2018. https://southwestcontemporary.com/interview-with-colson-whitehead/.

Shelat, Jay N. "Pattern Recognition: The Enduring Whiteness of 9/11 Literary Studies." *Post45*, September 11, 2021. https://post45.org/2021/09/pattern-recognition-the-enduring-whiteness-of-9-11-literary-studies/.

Shemak, April. *Asylum Speakers: Caribbean Refugees and Testimonial Discourse*. Philadelphia: Temple University Press, 2010.

Sherman, Suzan. "Colson Whitehead." *BOMB* 76 (2001): 74–80.

Shields, David. *Reality Hunger: A Manifesto*. New York: Vintage, 2011.

Shnayerson, Michael. "The Four Amigas: Latina Literature's New Doyennes." *Vanity Fair*, September 1994.

Silko, Leslie Marmon. *Ceremony*. New York: Penguin, 2006.

WORKS CITED

Singletary, Michelle, and Spencer S. Hsu. "Disney Says VA Park Will Be Serious Fun." *Washington Post*, November 12, 1993.

Sinykin, Dan N. "The Conglomerate Era: Publishing, Authorship, and Literary Form, 1965–2007." *Contemporary Literature* 58, no. 4 (2017): 462–91.

Sirias, Silvio. *Julia Alvarez: A Critical Companion*. Westport, CT: Greenwood, 2001.

Slater, Maya. "Problems When Time Moves Backwards: Martin Amis's *Time's Arrow*." *English: The Journal of the English Association* 42, no. 173 (1993):141–52.

Smith, Mychal Denzel. "The Truth About 'The Arc of the Moral Universe.'" *Huffington Post*, January 18, 2018. www.huffpost.com/entry/opinion-smith-obama-king_n_5a5903e0e4b04f3c55a252a4.

Smith, Zadie. "Two Paths for the Novel." *New York Review of Books*, November 20, 2008.

So, Richard Jean. *Redlining Culture: A Data History of Racial Inequality and Postwar Fiction*. New York: Columbia University Press, 2020.

Song, Min Hyoung. *The Children of 1965: On Writing, and Not Writing, as an Asian American*. Durham, NC: Duke University Press, 2013.

——. "Viet Thanh Nguyen and the Scholar–Public Intellectual." *PMLA* 133, no. 2 (2018): 406–12.

Sorensen, Leif. "Against the Post-Apocalyptic: Narrative Closure in Colson Whitehead's *Zone One*." *Contemporary Literature* 55, no. 3 (2014): 559–92.

Squires, Claire. *Marketing Literature: The Making of Contemporary Writing in Britain*. London: Palgrave, 2007.

Stanton, Ali. "David Bradley's New Book Tells of 13 Slave Martyrs." *New York Amsterdam News*, April 18, 1981.

Stefanko, Jacqueline. "New Ways of Telling: Latinas' Narratives of Exile and Return." *Frontiers: A Journal of Women Studies* 17, no. 2 (1996): 50–69.

Steier, Rod. "Trying for Another 'Roots' Saga." Review of *The Chaneysville Incident*, by David Bradley. *Hartford Courant*, April 9, 1981.

Stevens, Wallace. *The Collected Poems of Wallace Stevens*. New York: Vintage, 2015.

Stodghill, Ron. "Why Colson Whitehead Keeps Bending the Rules of Fiction." *Wall Street Journal Magazine*, October 31, 2021. https://www.wsj.com/articles/colson-whitehead-harlem-interview-11635596651.

Strange, Sharan. "Dark Room Collective: Essay." *Mosaic* 16 (Fall 2006). Republished online May 12, 2013. https://mosaicmagazine.org/dark-room-collective-essay/.

Stuelke, Patricia. "Writing Refugee Crisis in the Age of Amazon: *Lost Children Archive*'s Reenactment Play." *Genre* 54, no. 1 (April 2021): 43–66.

WORKS CITED

Tettenborn, Éva. "'A Mountain Full of Ghosts': Mourning African American Masculinities in Colson Whitehead's *John Henry Days*." *African American Review* 46, no. 2 (Summer–Fall 2013): 271–84.

Thompson, John B. *Book Wars: The Digital Revolution in Publishing*. London: Polity Press, 2021.

———. *Merchants of Culture: The Publishing Business in the Twenty-First Century*. London: Polity Press, 2013.

Thurman, Deborah. "Professions of Craft: Program Era Pedagogy in Julia Alvarez's ¡Yo!." *Arizona Quarterly: A Journal of American Literature, Culture, and Theory* 77, no. 4 (2021): 61–86.

Tiptree, James Jr. Letter to Isaac and Shauna Asimov, February 28, 1984. University of Oregon Special Collections, Coll. 455, Box 62, Folder 8.

Tobin, Patricia. "Response, 1: García Márquez and the Genealogical Imperative." *Diacritics: A Review of Contemporary Criticism* 4, no. 2 (1974): 52–55.

Tran, Ben. "The Literary Dubbing of Confession." *PMLA* 133, no. 2 (2018): 413–19.

Tran, Paul. "Viet Thanh Nguyen: Anger in the Asian American Novel." Asian American Writers Workshop, June 29, 2015. aaww.org/viet-thanh-nguyen-anger-asian-american-novel/.

Tredell, Nicolas. *The Fiction of Martin Amis*. London: Icon Books, 2000.

Treisman, Deborah. "The Searcher." Interview with Jonathan Safran Foer. *New Yorker*, June 10, 2001. https://www.newyorker.com/magazine/2001/06/18/the-searcher.

Trueheart, Charles. "Through a Mirror, Darkly." Review of *Time's Arrow*, by Martin Amis. *Washington Post*, November 26, 1991.

Tucker, Jeffrey Allen. "'Verticality Is Such a Risky Enterprise': The Literary and Paraliterary Antecedents of Colson Whitehead's *The Intuitionist*." *Novel: A Forum on Fiction* 43, no. 1 (2010): 148–56.

Tucker, Maggie S. "Affirmative Action Debated." *Harvard Crimson*, March 9, 1990.

Updike, John. "Nobody Gets Away with Everything." *New Yorker*, May 25, 1992.

U.S. Congress. Uniting and Strengthening America by Providing Appropriate Tools Required to Intercept and Obstruct Terrorism (USA PATRIOT ACT) Act of 2001. HR 3162, 107th Cong., 1st sess., introduced in House October 23, 2001. https://www.gpo.gov/fdsys/pkg/BILLS107hr3162ih/pdf/BILLS-107hr3162ih.pdf.

Vanzant, Kevin. "Problems with Narrative in the US Survey and How Fiction Can Help." *The History Teacher* 52, no. 4 (2019): 677–96.

Vazquez, David J. *Triangulations: Narrative Strategies for Navigating Latino Identity*. Minneapolis: University of Minnesota Press, 2011.

WORKS CITED

Vásquez, Juan Gabriel. "In Colson Whitehead's Latest, the Underground Railroad Is More Than a Metaphor." Review of *The Underground Railroad* by Colson Whitehead. *New York Times*, August 5, 2016.

Veeser, H. Aram. "Introduction." In *The New Historicism*, ed. H. Aram Veeser, ix–xvi. New York: Routledge, 1989.

Vice, Susan. *Holocaust Fiction*. New York: Routledge, 2000.

Vitale, Tom. "Julia Alvarez Reads from *How the García Girls Lost Their Accents*, and Talks About the Dominican-American Immigrant Experience." Moveable Feast, 1992. Sound recording. https://searchworks.stanford.edu/view/2857576.

Vonnegut, Kurt. *Slaughterhouse-Five, or The Children's Crusade*. New York: Vintage, 2000.

Wagers, Kelley. "Seeing 'from the Far Side of the Hill': Narrative, History, and Understanding in *Kindred* and *The Chaneysville Incident*." *MELUS* 34, no. 1 (2009): 23–45.

Walker, Alice. "The Black Woman's Story." *New York Times*, February 12, 1984.

——. *The Color Purple*. 1982. New York: Washington Square Press, 1983.

Walkowitz, Rebecca L. "Afro-Am Activists Challenge Rosovsky." *Harvard Crimson*, November 17, 1990.

——. "Afro-Am Beginning to Narrow Searches." *Harvard Crimson*, December 6, 1990.

——. *Born Translated: The Contemporary Novel in an Age of World Literature*. New York: Columbia University Press, 2015.

Walser, Hannah. "Under Description: The Fugitive Slave Advertisement as Genre." *American Literature* 92, no. 1 (2020): 61–89.

Ward, Jesmyn. *Men We Reaped: A Memoir*. New York: Bloomsbury, 2013.

——. *Salvage the Bones*. New York: Bloomsbury, 2012.

——. *Sing, Unburied, Sing*. New York: Scribner, 2017.

Warga, Wayne. "An English Professor's Historical Tale." *Los Angeles Times*, April 24, 1981.

Warren, Kenneth W. *What Was African American Literature?* Cambridge, MA: Harvard University Press, 2011.

Washburn, Patrick S. "The *Pittsburgh Courier*'s Double V Campaign in 1942." *American Journalism* 3, no. 2 (1986): 73–86.

Washington, Mary Helen. "Black History: His Story or Hers?" Review of *The Chaneysville Incident*, by David Bradley. *Washington Post*, April 12, 1981.

Wasserman, Sarah. *The Death of Things: Ephemera and the American Novel*. Minneapolis: University of Minnesota Press, 2020.

White, Hayden. *Metahistory: The Historical Imagination in Nineteenth-Century Europe*. Baltimore: Johns Hopkins University Press, 1973.

WORKS CITED

Whitehead, Colson. *Apex Hides the Hurt*. New York: Anchor Books, 2006.
———. *Harlem Shuffle*. New York: Penguin Random House, 2021.
———. *The Intuitionist*. New York: Anchor Books, 2000.
———. *John Henry Days*. New York: Anchor Books, 2001.
———. *The Nickel Boys*. New York: Doubleday, 2019.
———. "Picking a Genre." *New York Times Book Review*, November 1, 2009.
———. *Sag Harbor*. New York: Anchor Books, 2009.
———. "Shaft vs. Action Jackson." *Diaspora: The Journal of Black Thought & Culture* (Fall–Winter 1989–1990): 29–34.
———. "Sylvia's Crime." *Diaspora: The Journal of Black Thought & Culture* (Fall–Winter 1989–1990): 5–9.
———. *The Underground Railroad*. Doubleday, 2016.
———. "The Year of Living Postracially." *New York Times*, November 3, 2009.
———. *Zone One*. New York: Anchor Books, 2011.
Wiley, Catherine. "Memory Is Already the Story You Made Up About the Past: An Interview with Julia Alvarez." *Bloomsbury Review* 12, no. 2 (1992): 9–10.
Wilkens, Matthew. "Contemporary Fiction by the Numbers." *Post45*, March 11, 2011. https://post45.research.yale.edu/2011/03/contemporary-fiction-by-the-numbers/.
Williams, Melanie R. "It's Not Just Ethnic Studies." *Harvard Crimson*, December 13, 1990.
Wilson, Jennifer. "What Is Crime in a Country Built on It?" Review of *Harlem Shuffle* by Colson Whitehead. *The Atlantic*, September 10, 2021. https://www.theatlantic.com/magazine/archive/2021/10/colson-whitehead-harlem-shuffle/619821/.
Wilson, Judith. "Books." *Essence* 12, no. 4 (August 1981): 22.
Winters, Lisa Ze. "Fiction and Slavery's Archive: Memory, Agency, and Finding Home." *Reviews in American History* 46, no. 2 (2018): 338–44.
Woloch, Alex. *The One vs. the Many: Minor Characters and the Space of the Protagonist in the Novel*. Princeton, NJ: Princeton University Press, 2009.
Wright, Michelle M. "Diaspora and Entanglement." *Qui Parle* 28, no. 2 (2019): 219–40.
Wright, Richard. *Native Son*. New York: Harper Perennial, 2005.
Xiang, Sunny. "The Ethnic Author Represents the Body Count." *PMLA* 133, no. 2 (2018): 420–27.
Yothers, Brian. "Contemporary African Immigration and the Legacy of Slavery in Yaa Gyasi's *Homegoing*." In *The Immigrant Experience*, ed. Maryse Jayasuriya, 209–25. Amenia, NY: Salem Press/Grey House Publishing, 2018.

WORKS CITED

Young, Kevin. "Editor's Note." *Diaspora: The Journal of Black Thought & Culture* (Fall–Winter 1989–1990).

Zagarell, Sandra A. "Narrative of Community: The Identification of a Genre." *Signs* 13, no. 3 (1988): 498–527.

Zucker, A. E. "The Genealogical Novel, a New Genre." *PMLA* 43, no. 2 (June 1928): 551–60.

INDEX

10:04 (Lerner), 14, 30, 38, 210, 211, 213–16, 222, 223, 224, 227–228, 230, 234, 237, 238, 291n21, 292n35, 295n66; catastrophe in, 213–15, 223, 228, 234; microhistory in, 30; multiple temporalities in, 227–28, 238, as novel of recent history, 211, 213, 222, 230; sincerity in, 222

11-M Bombings, 223, 230

2008 financial crisis, 9; fiction of, 208

9/11 novel, 235–36, 290n13. *See also* September 11 attacks

Achebe, Chinua, 254n34

adaptation, 62–63, 96, 147, 172

Adichie, Chimamanda Ngozi: *Americanah*, 208

advances, 44, 59, 63, 165, 213, 281n1

aesthetic value, 3, 4, 10, 14, 18, 32, 34, 35, 45, 58, 74, 75, 85, 119, 243, 263n57

African American literature, 3, 5, 6, 27, 29, 47, 51, 52, 95, 105, 133–35, 140, 148, 153–54, 180, 190, 192, 244, 250n6, 251n11, 257n61, 275n19, 279n70. *See also* Dark Room Collective

African American studies. *See* Black studies

Ahmed, Nawaaz: *Radiant Fugitives*, 208

Alderman, Naomi: *The Power*, 254n36

Alexander, Elizabeth, 133

allegory, 34, 35, 37, 43, 89, 123, 125, 146; in *The Intuitionist*, 37, 123, 125, 146

Allende, Isabel: *Violeta*, 205

Alter, Alexandra, 206, 221, 291n22

Alvarez, Julia, 30, 35, 43–45, 64–79, 265n80, 266n83, 266n86, 267n105; *Before We Were Free*, 77; *Homecoming*, 77–79; *How the García Girls Lost Their Accents*, 30, 35, 43–45, 64–72, 74–77, 79; *In the Name of Salomé*, 77; *In the Time of the Butterflies*, 76, 79, 267n105; *Saving the World*, 77; *¡Yo!*, 77, 265n80. See also *How the García Girls Lost Their Accents* (Alvarez)

INDEX

Altman, Rick, 232, 290n18
Ambrose, Stephen: *Band of Brothers*, 96, 97; *D–Day: June 6, 1944*, 96
Amis, Martin, 30, 35, 43–46, 54–64, 65, 66, 75, 78, 129, 262n40, 263n51, 263n57, 266n84; "Career Move," 59–60, 62; early career of, 44, 58; *House of Meetings*, 60; *The Information*, 59; *The Pregnant Widow*, 60; *Saturn 3*, 63; *Time's Arrow*, 30, 35, 43–45, 54–64, 71, 263n51, 263n57, 266n84; *The Zone of Interest*, 60. See also *Time's Arrow* (Amis)
anachronism, 11, 17, 19, 89, 148, 155, 159; and *Flight to Canada*, 155; and *The Intuitionist*, 148; and *The Underground Railroad*, 148, 155
Anderson, Benedict, 220, 225, 226, 227
Anderson, Perry, 16, 255n40, 291n25
Antoon, Sinan: *The Corpse Washer*, 207
Apex Hides the Hurt (Whitehead), 121, 143–44, 146, 278n58; university in, 143–44, 146
Apocalypse Now (Coppola), 31
Appiah, Kwame Anthony, 143
Asian American literature, 5, 21, 27, 29, 99, 104, 244, 256n56, 257n61, 258n81
Asian American studies, 24
assemblage, 106, 108, 110–11, 227
Atwood, Margaret, 122, 254n34, 254n36; *The Handmaid's Tale*, 254n36
Aubry, Timothy, 174, 175, 178
autobiographical novel, 43, 99, 145, 195
autofiction, 65, 232, 292n30

Back to the Future (Zemeckis), 238
Baldwin, James, 47, 52, 132, 133, 160, 180, 246, 250n6, 285n41; *Giovanni's Room*, 250n6; *Notes of a Native Son*, 160
Bambara, Toni Cade, 8, 133
Banks, Russell: *Cloudsplitter*, 95
Baptist, Edward, 149
Barker, Pat, 254n34
Barth, Alan, 219
Barzun, Jacques, 136
Begley, Louis: *Wartime Lies*, 95
Behn, Aphra, 21, 149; *Oroonoko*, 149
Beloved (Morrison), 1–4, 6–7, 14, 20, 22, 35, 39, 42, 46–47, 50, 51, 95, 103, 131, 149–50, 156, 157, 180, 245, 249n2, 259n83, 262n33, 297n6; canonicity of, 1, 6, 47; ghosts in, 245; history in, 1–3, 46, 131, 157, 259n83; and Nguyen, Viet Thanh, 22; "rememory" in, 3, 50; and prizes, 1, 103, 251n16; trauma in, 3, 42, 51; and Whitehead, Colson, 149–50, 156. See also rememory
Benjamin, Walter: "Theses on the Philosophy of History," 214
Bennett, William, 128, 129, 130, 132
Bergholz, Susan, 74, 75
Berlant, Lauren, 125, 292n32
Best, Stephen, 148, 156
bestsellers, 17–18, 79, 83, 96–97, 157, 220, 255n40, 257n67
bildungsroman, 65, 71, 121, 122, 123, 185, 188, 217; ethnic, 122, 123. See also *un-bildungsroman*
Black studies, 7, 24, 30, 131, 133, 135, 142–43, 148, 153, 251n20, 258n79, 277n35
Bloom, Allan, 128, 129
Bloom, Harold, 136
book clubs, 7, 37, 47, 121, 147, 168, 175–76, 191, 202, 203, 206, 241;

INDEX

Oprah Winfrey's book club, 7, 121, 147
Bourdieu, Pierre, 9, 257n67
Bradley, David, 6, 7, 35, 43, 45–53, 250n6, 260n9, 260n16, 261n31; career of, 46; *The Chaneysville Incident*, 35, 43, 45–53, 250n60, 262n33. See also *Chaneysville Incident, The* (Bradley)
Brokaw, Tom: *The Greatest Generation*, 96, 97
Brooks, Peter, 187
Brown v. Board of Education, 9
Brown, Michael, 159, 160
Bulosan, Carlos, 21
Butler, Octavia: *Kindred*, 254n36

campus novel, the, 28, 65, 127, 158. See also satire: academic
canon wars, 7, 22, 25, 37, 123, 127, 130, 136, 138, 141, 148, 188, 242, 257n62. See also literary canon
catastrophe, 32, 211, 212–16, 220–21, 227, 228–29, 231–32, 234, 236, 237, 246, 291n25, 292n32, 294n44. See also 11-M Bombings; *Challenger* disaster; Hurricane Irene; Hurricane Katrina; Hurricane Sandy; September 11 attacks; Tōhoku earthquake (2011); trauma
Cather, Willa, 16
Ceremony (Silko), 36, 74, 84, 87–94, 99, 117, 270n24; canonization of, 93–94; regional specificity of, 84, 88, 92; tone of, 88–89; and war fiction, 36, 84, 87–88, 91–92
Chabon, Michael, 30, 36, 81, 85, 106, 107, 108, 109, 110, 111, 112, 113, 114, 115, 122, 208, 236, 272n63, 273n77; *The Amazing Adventures of Kavalier &*

Clay, 107, 111, 112, 113, 118; *Telegraph Avenue*, 208
Challenger disaster, 215, 216, 223, 224
Chandler, Raymond, 21
Chaneysville Incident, The (Bradley), 35, 43, 45–53, 250n60, 262n33; anger and, 45, 52–53; criticism of, 50–51; grief in, 45; underrecognition of, 47–48, 51–53
Chang, Jade: *The Wangs vs. the World*, 208
Charles, Ron, 167
Chatman, Seymour, 55, 57, 61
Cheever, John, 104
Chen, Tina, 118
Chiang, Mark, 30
Chihaya, Sarah, 256n49
Chin, Frank, 21
Chu, Seo-Young, 253n26
Clay Walls (Kim), 36, 84, 99–105, 117, 118, 271n46; publication of, 99, 103; racialized contradictions in, 100, 102; wartime discrimination in, 36, 99–100, 102, 104
Cohen, Matt, 297n9
Cohen, Samuel, 43, 259n4
comedy, 17, 54, 56, 57, 60, 62, 71, 81. See also satire
Common Reads programs, 33, 174, 191
contemporary narratives of slavery, 13, 34, 37, 122, 123, 147–50, 154, 155, 242, 279n67, 280n70; limits of, 123
contemporary, the: periodizing problems of, 234
Corin, Lucy: *Swank Hotel*, 208
Cornell, Joseph, 108–10
Covid-19 pandemic, 9, 206, 216, 221, 235. See also pandemic novel
Coward, Noël, 21

INDEX

creative writing programs, 9, 10, 35, 43, 46, 51, 66–69, 72, 241, 265n80, 265n82, 266n83. *See also* Iowa Writers' Workshop
Creet, Julia, 166
crime fiction, 162
Criniti, Steve, 267n105
Crosley, Sloane, 205
Currie, Mark, 233

Dalleo, Raphael, 72
Dames, Nicholas, 209, 290n11
Dark Room Collective, 132–33
Davis, Angela, 8
de Groot, Jerome, 173
Delany, Samuel, 133
DeLillo, Don, 43, 207, 217, 218, 237, 292n35; *Falling Man*, 207; *Underworld*, 43; *White Noise*, 217, 237, 292n35
Desai, Kiran, 254n34
Dickens, Charles, 21, 188, 258n74
Didion, Joan, 21
Doane, Mary Ann, 293n37
Doctorow, E. L.: *Ragtime*, 17
Doerr, Anthony, 30, 36, 85, 106–109, 110, 111, 113, 114, 118, 272n63; *All the Light We Cannot See*, 107, 109–13, 114,
Dos Passos, John: *U.S.A.* trilogy, 292n34
Douglass, Frederick, 156, 178, 180, 283n15
Driscoll, Beth, 175–76, 203
Dubey, Madhu, 142, 152, 280n85
Du Bois, W. E. B., 23

Edelman, Lee, 281n2
Egan, Jennifer, 36, 85, 106, 107, 108, 110, 111, 112, 113, 122; *Manhattan Beach*, 107, 112

Eggers, Dave: *What Is the What*, 208
Elias, Amy, 17, 19, 140, 155, 211, 221, 238
Eliot, George, 191
Eliot, T. S., 21, 136
Ellis, Thomas Sayers, 132
Ellis, Trey, 133
Ellison, Ralph: *Invisible Man*, 3, 4, 15, 20–21, 23, 39, 47, 125, 160, 180, 256n50, 275n19
Emerson, Ralph Waldo, 21
Emre, Merve, 236
English departments. *See* university English departments
English, James F., 9, 98, 209, 253n32, 263n57, 268n6
English Patient, The (Minghella), 96
Erdrich, Louise, 7, 21, 74, 165, 246; *Love Medicine*, 74, 165, 174
ethnic studies, 7, 24, 29, 30, 128, 257n61
Eugenides, Jeffrey: *Middlesex*, 71, 174, 284n16

family tree novel. *See* multigenerational family saga
Faulkner, William, 16, 21, 121, 166, 170, 172, 246
Ferguson, Roderick, 24, 258n83
Fitzpatrick, Kathleen, 62
Foer, Jonathan Safran: *Everything is Illuminated*, 30, 36, 85, 106, 110, 113, 114–15, 118, 272n63, 273n78; *Extremely Loud and Incredibly Close*, 273n69
Foner, Eric, 149
Fountain, Ben: *Billy Lynn's Long Halftime Walk*, 207
Franzen, Jonathan, 236–37; *The Corrections*, 296n75
Frazier, Charles: *Cold Mountain*, 95

· 328 ·

INDEX

Gallagher, Catherine, 178
Gallagher, Matt: *Youngblood*, 207
Galsworthy, John: *The Forsyte Saga*, 170, 171
García, Cristina: *Dreaming in Cuban*, 165, 174; *Monkey Hunting*, 74
García Márquez, Gabriel, 166, 172, 286n60
Garner, Eric, 159–60
Garner, Margaret, 157
Gates, Jr., Henry Louis, 130, 135–36, 139, 143, 148, 173; "Canon Confidential," 136; *Finding Your Roots*, 173; *Loose Canons*, 136
genealogical novel, 170, 172
Genette, Gérard, 211
genre, 12–13, 14, 57, 71, 75, 105, 130, 139, 141, 147, 149, 150, 156, 175, 194, 203, 211, 213, 232, 290n18; experimentation, 69; fiction, 123; and genealogy, 165–73; mass-market, 17, 122, 147; and mode, 12–13; and pastiche, 19; play, 122–23; turn, 122. *See also* autofiction; campus novel; historical fiction; meta–slave narrative; multigenerational family saga; satire: academic; and whiteness, 112; World War II novel
Ghosh, Amitav, 254n34
ghosts: in *Beloved*, 2, 7, 180, 186, 245; in Greenblatt, Stephen, 7
Glaser, Jennifer, 28
Greenblatt, Stephen, 7, 48, 178
Greene, Graham, 21
Grossman, Claire, 190, 255n44
Guillory, John: *Cultural Capital*, 25–26, 32–34, 130, 141, 243, 275n16

Gyasi, Yaa, 14, 22, 27, 32, 37, 38, 155, 165–70, 176–95, 197–200, 202, 285n40, 285n41, 285n51, 286n52, 287n66, 288n92; *Homegoing*, 14, 22, 32, 37, 38, 155, 165–70, 176–95, 197–200, 202–203, 281n1, 288n88. *See also Homegoing* (Gyasi)

Halaby, Laila: *Once in a Promised Land*, 207
Halbwachs, Maurice, 222
Haley, Alex: *Roots*, 47, 50, 52, 165, 172, 180, 184, 192–93, 283n15
Hamid, Mohsin: *The Reluctant Fundamentalist*, 207
Harlem Renaissance, 38, 125, 126, 178, 189, 276n27
Harlem Shuffle (Whitehead), 37, 105, 122, 123–24, 134, 145–46, 157, 159, 162–63; and canonization, 123–24, 157; historical setting in, 162; work in, 145–46
Harootunian, Harry, 227, 295n57
Hartman, Saidiya, 49, 151, 193–94, 277n46
Heinemann, Larry: *Paco's Story*, 95
heist thriller, 162
Heller, Joseph, 17, 36, 84, 86, 87, 106, 254n32, 271n37; *Catch-22*, 86, 87, 254n32
Hemingway, Ernest, 134, 246
Higginbotham, Evelyn Brooks, 143
Hijuelos, Oscar: *The Mambo Kings Play Songs of Love*, 74
historical analogy, 37, 124, 157, 160–62, 195, 244, 260n83
historical distance, 12–13, 14–15, 16, 38, 53, 107–108, 113, 209, 220, 222, 234, 271n37

· 329 ·

INDEX

historical fiction, 4–7, 10–19, 26–31, 33–39, 43–45, 48–50, 53–60, 108, 122–23, 130, 221, 231, 233, 241–45, 248, 250n4, 253n32, 255n40; and the American Civil War, 84, 94, 95, 96; contemporary narratives of slavery, 13, 34, 37, 123, 147–48, 149, 154, 155, 242, 279n67, 280n70; critique of, 125, 139, 212; and film, 63; geographical scale of, 15; Holocaust fiction, 13, 29, 34, 46, 73, 85, 106, 111, 114, 269n13, 273n78; immigration narratives, 13–14, 34, 46, 64–65, 71, 172, 236, 242; limits of, 156, 161, 169, 212, 244; logics of, 254n36; minoritized writers of, 4–5, 7, 10, 18, 22, 26, 29–31, 39, 43, 65, 72–75, 82, 97–98, 102, 106, 113, 120, 131, 148, 172–74, 191, 203, 212, 236, 244, 247, 255n44; multigenerational, 13–14, 34, 37–38, 165–71, 173, 175–77, 183, 185, 187, 191, 194, 202, 204, 206, 242; novels of recent history, 205–48, 294n44; policing of, 242; postmodern, 17–19, 49, 61, 88, 98, 140, 211, 217–18, 222, 238, 291n25; prestige of, 206–207, 209, 212, 241, 247, 250n9, 250n10, 257n71, 260n17; recent historical novel, 15, 38–39, 205–48, 258n74, 292n30, 292n34; twenty-first-century, 12, 22, 39, 105, 106, 119, 123, 168, 186; and the university, 7, 33, 47, 93, 130, 174, 202, 234, 249n2, 250n8, 254n34, 267n104; and the Vietnam War, 94, 95; whiteness of, 85, 94–105, 111–15, 236, 238; and World War II, 13–14, 29, 30, 34, 84, 85, 87–88, 94, 97, 106, 108, 113, 119–20, 233, 268n5. *See also* contemporary narratives of slavery; historical novel, the; Holocaust fiction; multigenerational family saga; World War II fiction

historical novel, the, 11–12, 13, 15, 17, 21, 32, 34–35, 38, 63, 139, 160, 204, 206, 208, 210, 225, 229, 254n33; recent, 15, 38–39, 207, 209–20, 221, 222, 224, 226–39, 242, 246, 258n74, 292n30, 292n34

historical self-consciousness, 85, 206

historical setting, 3, 5, 13, 34, 35, 38, 74, 78, 82, 84–85, 88, 104, 119, 123, 125–26, 139, 155, 158, 162, 166, 196–200, 208–209, 241, 247, 253n29, 253n32

historiography, 5, 12, 15, 17, 19, 30, 38, 49, 50, 88, 99, 126, 140, 142, 146, 209, 211, 233

Hoberek, Andrew, 122

Holocaust fiction, 13, 29, 34, 46, 73, 85, 106, 111, 114, 269n13, 273n78; and *All the Light We Cannot See*, 112, 114; and *Beloved*, 95; and *Time's Arrow*, 55–56, 263n57

Homegoing (Gyasi), 14, 22, 32, 37, 38, 155, 165–70, 176–95, 197–200, 202–203, 281n1, 288n88; and book clubs, 175–76, 202; and empathy, 183–84, 203; family tree in, 166–67, 179; historical scope of, 168–69, 180, 189, 192, 199; limits of, 176, 178, 181, 183–84; and personalized history, 168; scenes of instruction in, 174, 180, 189–90; and the university, 174–75, 190–91, 202

How the García Girls Lost Their Accents (Alvarez), 30, 35, 43–45, 64–72, 74–77, 79; and metafiction, 69; as un-Künstlerroman, 66, 71

• 330 •

INDEX

Hughes, Langston, 180, 189
Hungerford, Amy, 26, 98, 106, 273n78
Hurricane Irene, 213, 214, 217, 223
Hurricane Katrina, 14, 195, 200, 216, 237–38
Hurricane Sandy, 213, 227, 228, 231, 237, 238
Hurston, Zora Neale, 152, 180: "What White Publishers Won't Print," 152
Hutcheon, Linda, 17, 61, 140, 211

Iannone, Carol, 128
immigration narratives, 13–14, 34, 46, 64–65, 71, 172, 236, 242
internet, 9, 219, 264n71
Intuitionist, The (Whitehead), 36–37, 121, 123–29, 131–34, 136–47, 149, 151, 155, 156, 158, 180, 188; as academic satire, 123, 127–28, 131–32, 141, 142, 188; temporal indeterminacy of, 124–26, 155
Iowa Writers' Workshop, 9, 286n52, 287n66
Indigenous American literature, 5, 27, 29, 84, 88, 93–94, 244, 246–47
irony, 17, 36, 86, 87, 98, 119, 183, 187, 198, 200, 222, 280n81; dramatic, 161, 201, 220, 221, 231; historical, 54, 161, 187, 197, 231; post- 19; postmodern, 19, 106, 293n36. *See also* new historical sincerity; postmodernism
Ishiguro, Kazuo, 122, 254n34

Jacobs, Harriet, 149, 156
James, Henry, 16, 134
Jameson, Fredric, 13, 48, 125, 129, 139, 211–12, 225, 229, 238; *The Antinomies of Realism*, 206, 254n33; on contemporary historical fiction 125, 139, 212, 225; on postmodernism, 211, 238
Jenkins, Barry, 147
Jewish American fiction, 28–29, 30, 85, 111: de-ethnicizing of, 29, 111
John Henry Days (Whitehead); 121, 123, 142–43; institutional memory in, 142–43
Johnson, Charles: *Middle Passage*, 95; *Oxherding Tale*, 74
Jones, Edward P.: *The Known World*, 155
Jones, Gayl, 8
Jones, James: *The Thin Red Line*, 96
journalism, 34, 39, 46, 135, 206, 211, 217–21, 224, 225–27, 229, 232, 237, 238, 241, 246, 292n34, 294n44

Kakutani, Michiko, 284n37
Kelly, Adam, 19, 217, 293n36
Kenan, Randall, 133
Keneally, Thomas: *Schindler's Ark* (*Schindler's List*), 48, 95, 98, 110
Khakpour, Porochista: *The Last Illusion*, 207
Kim, Ronyoung, 36, 78, 84–85, 99–105, 117–18, 271n42, 271n46; *Clay Walls*, 36, 84, 99–105, 117, 118, 271n46. See also *Clay Walls* (Kim)
Kind of Freedom, A (Sexton), 14, 27, 37–38, 156, 168–69, 186, 195–204; cyclical structure of, 196–200
King, Jr., Martin Luther, 125, 158, 186
Kingsolver, Barbara: *Unsheltered*, 208
Kingston, Maxine Hong, 21, 104
Klay, Phil: *Redeployment*, 208
Kobek, Jarett: *Atta*, 207
Komunyakaa, Yusef, 133
Konstantinou, Lee, 19, 152, 293n36

INDEX

Kubitschek, Missy Dehn, 48, 260n16
Kunkel, Benjamin, 295n66
Künstlerroman, 44, 66, 71

Lamb, Wally: *The Hour I First Believed*, 208
Lambert, Josh, 28, 257n73
Lanchester, John: *Capital*, 208
Larsen, Nella, 22, 180
Latinx literature, 5, 27, 29, 65, 74, 82, 97, 244, 265n82, 266n83
Leader-Picone, Cameron, 146
Leaving the Atocha Station (Lerner), 30, 38, 210, 211, 212, 215, 222, 226, 230, 234, 293n38; catastrophe in, 215, 230; history in, 222–23, 293n38; microhistory in, 30
Lee, Min Jin, 26, 37, 183–84, 174–76, 188, 190–92, 285n42, 285n51; *Pachinko*, 14, 37, 168, 174–76, 183–84, 188, 190, 191, 192, 285n51. See also *Pachinko* (Lee)
Legér, Dimitry Elias: *God Loves Haiti*, 208
Lerner, Ben: *10:04*, 14, 30, 38, 210, 211, 213–15, 222, 223, 224, 227–228, 230, 234, 237, 238, 291n21, 292n35, 295n66; *Leaving the Atocha Station*, 30, 38, 210, 211, 212, 215, 222, 226, 230, 234, 293n38; *The Topeka School*, 210, 296n75
Lethem, Jonathan: *The Feral Detective*, 208
Levy-Hussen, Aida, 148, 150, 153, 154, 262n33
Li, Stephanie, 278n58, 279n70
Life is Beautiful (Benigni), 96
Lipsitz, George, 88
litany, 78, 106, 110, 111

literary agents, 9, 10, 35, 44, 59, 74, 75, 103, 120, 222, 241, 259n5, 282n7
literary canon, 1, 5–10, 14, 16, 18, 22, 24–30, 32–34, 37, 39–40, 47, 50, 51, 58, 69, 78, 83–84, 86, 94, 106, 121, 123, 127–28, 129–30, 133–34, 136, 138, 141, 148, 166, 173, 185, 188–89, 236, 241–42, 243, 244, 248, 257n67, 259n83; and Black history, 134; and canon wars, 7, 22, 25, 37, 123, 127, 130, 136, 138, 141, 148, 188, 242, 257n62; contemporary, 1, 4, 18, 29, 32, 34, 39, 166, 185, 259n83; critique of, 24; and culture wars, 6, 25, 28, 127, 128, 131; deformation of, 130; formation of, 6, 10, 34, 37, 123, 166, 242; meta, 21–22, 24, 134, 188, 246, 247; and multiculturalists, 7, 10, 20, 26, 29, 128, 129, 130, 144, 189; and traditionalists, 7, 25, 121, 129
literary editors, 28, 46, 74, 103, 259n5, 282n7
literary institutions. *See* book clubs; Common Reads programs; creative writing programs; editors; literary prizes; publishers; secondary schools; university English departments
literary labor, 8
literary prizes: Arthur C. Clarke Award, 165; Booker Prize, 59, 63, 95, 96, 254n34, 263n57; F. Scott Fitzgerald Award for Outstanding Achievement in American Literature, 77; Hispanic Heritage Award in Literature, 77; Library of Congress Lifetime Achievement Award, 121; MacArthur Grant, 121; National Book Award, 1, 3, 6, 17, 33, 81, 82, 83, 86, 87, 93, 95, 96, 109,

118, 119, 121, 147, 157, 165, 195, 209, 250n6, 250n9, 255n43, 260n17, 275n19; National Book Critics Circle Award, 1, 6, 7, 76, 81, 82, 118, 209, 250n9, 255n43, 260n17; National Medal of Arts, 77; Nobel Prize, 8; PEN/Faulkner Award, 47; PEN Oakland/Josephine Miles Award, 75; Pulitzer Prize, 1, 6, 8, 33, 81, 82, 83, 87, 93, 94, 103, 104, 109, 118, 121, 147, 157, 209, 250n9, 255n26, 270n28,
literary value. *See* aesthetic value
Lowe, Janice, 133
Lowe, Lisa, 29
Luhmann, Niklas, 293n38, 294n44
Luis, William, 266n86
Luiselli, Valeria, 22, 27, 39, 244–246, 247, 248; *Lost Children Archive*, 22, 244–46
Lukács, Georg: *The Historical Novel*, 139, 178, 211, 215, 225, 250n4, 292n27, 292n30, 292n34

Machado Sáez, Elena, 71, 74, 75, 174, 175, 194, 267n104, 284n25
Mackay, Marina, 97
Mahajan, Karan: *The Association of Small Bombs*, 208
Makkai, Rebecca: *The Great Believers*, 208, 224–25, 231, 236, 237
Mann, Thomas, 166; *Buddenbrooks: The Decline of a Family*, 170–72, 185–86, 188, 203–204
Mantel, Hilary, 254n34
Martin, Theodore, 122, 234, 249n3
Mbue, Imbolo: *Behold the Dreamers*, 208
McCarthy, Cormac, 122, 174
McCarthy, Jesse, 197, 202

McCracken, Ellen, 267n105
McEwan, Ian, 206, 254n34, 268n1, 295n58; *Lessons*, 206
McGrath, Laura B., 44, 75, 259n5
McGurl, Mark, 10, 258n76, 265n82
McInerney, Jay: *The Good Life*, 207, 236
memory: collective, 36, 88, 92, 94–96, 222, 232, 242; counter-, 88, 92; cultural, 40, 84, 238; historical, 22, 25, 95, 104, 142, 147, 207, 218, 220–21; news, 220; public, 83, 94, 96, 114, 117, 159; racial politics of, 147; "site of," 137, 150; traumatic, 262n33; war, 99, 106, 117. *See also* rememory
Menke, Richard, 61
Messud, Claire: *The Emperor's Children*, 207, 236
metacanonical, the, 21–22, 24, 134, 188, 246, 247
metafiction, 17, 19, 21, 49, 66, 69, 140, 156, 211, 293n36
meta–slave narratives, 37, 122, 123, 147–50, 154, 155, 242, 279n67; limits of, 149. *See also* contemporary narratives of slavery
Michaels, Walter Benn, 97
microhistory, 20, 30
middlebrow, the, 37, 168, 206, 241
Miller, Laura, 145, 181, 281n1
miniaturization, 105–14, 189
Mitchell, David: *Cloud Atlas*, 254n36
Momaday, N. Scott: *House Made of Dawn*, 94
Morrison, Toni, 1–4, 6–9, 14, 20, 21, 22, 35, 39, 42, 46, 47, 50, 51, 73, 95, 103–104, 111, 112, 131, 134–36, 137, 149–50, 156, 157, 180, 244, 245, 249n2, 250n6, 251n20, 259n83, 262n33, 297n6; *Beloved*, 1–4, 6–7, 14, 20, 22,

Morrison, Toni (*continued*)
35, 39, 42, 46, 47, 50, 51, 95, 103, 131, 149–50, 156, 157, 180, 245, 249n2, 259n83, 262n33, 297n6; career of, 7–8, 22; *Playing in the Dark*, 8–9, 111, 134, 137, 139; "The Site of Memory," 137, 150; *Song of Solomon*, 82; *Sula*, 250n6. See also *Beloved* (Morrison)
Moshfegh, Ottessa: *My Year of Rest and Relaxation*, 254n32
multiculturalism, 7, 10, 20, 25–26, 29, 128–30, 139, 144, 189
multigenerational family saga, 13, 14, 34, 37, 38, 165–71, 173, 175–77, 183, 185, 187, 191, 194, 202, 204, 206, 242; limits of, 203.
Muyumba, Walton, 181

Nancy, Jean-Luc, 214, 292n26
Naqvi, H. M.: *Home Boy*, 207
National Endowment for the Arts (NEA), 5–6, 17, 35, 72–74, 75
nationalism, 22, 86, 90, 91, 96, 225, 254n33
neo–slave narratives, 155. *See also* contemporary narratives of slavery
new historical sincerity, 10–19, 106, 217
New Historicism, 7, 10, 19, 26, 48, 129, 139, 173–74, 178
New Journalism, 219
Nguyen, Viet Thanh, 19–25, 30–31, 32, 41–43, 81, 122, 186, 244, 256n49, 259n83; "Canon Fodder," 25; *Nothing Ever Dies*, 22, 81; *The Sympathizer*, 19–25, 30–31, 32, 41–43, 244, 256n49, 259n83. See also *Sympathizer, The* (Nguyen)
Nickel Boys, The (Whitehead), 37, 105, 122, 123, 156–61; and canonization, 124, 156–57; politics of, 160

Noonan, Peggy, 216
North, Joseph, 26, 129

Obama, Barack, 77, 131, 169, 186, 193, 200, 202, 208, 229, 278n58
O'Brien, Tim: *The Things They Carried*, 97, 115
O'Connor, Flannery, 134
Occupy Wall Street, 230
O'Hehir, Diana: *I Wish This War Were Over*, 95
Ondaatje, Michael: *The English Patient*, 96
O'Neill, Joseph: *Netherland*, 235
Orange, Tommy, 6, 21, 27, 39; *There There*, 244, 246–48
Otsuka, Julie, 6, 36, 85, 114–19; *When the Emperor Was Divine*, 36, 85, 114–19
Oyler, Lauren: *Fake Accounts*, 208, 236
Ozeki, Ruth: *A Tale for the Time Being*, 14, 15, 19, 32, 38, 211, 213–14, 217–19, 222–23, 226–32, 236, 238, 294n47. *See also* *Tale for the Time Being, A* (Ozeki)

Pachinko (Lee), 14, 37, 168, 174–76, 183–84, 188, 190, 191, 192, 285n51; and empathy, 184; history in, 191; and the metacanonical, 188
pandemic novel, 205–206. *See also* Covid-19 pandemic
Parker, Kimberly N., 167
Phillips, Carl, 133
Picoult, Jodi: *Wish You Were Here*, 205
Poe, Edgar Allan, 21, 134
postapocalyptic fiction, 121, 122
postmodernism, 5, 17–19, 35, 44, 48, 49, 60, 61, 63, 85, 88–89, 98, 106, 122, 124, 140, 152, 211, 217–18, 222, 238, 291n25, 293n36

INDEX

Pound, Ezra, 219
Powers, J. F.: *Wheat That Springeth Green*, 95
Powers, Kevin: *The Yellow Birds*, 208
presentism, 57
prestige: of contemporaneity, 58, 63; cultural, 17, 63; of historical fiction, 6, 33, 60, 94, 206, 212, 214; of historicity, 58, 63, 211, 241; literary, 14, 17, 33, 35–36, 78, 82, 85, 95, 98, 119, 235, 236; and World War II, 36, 82, 85. *See also* literary prizes
prolepsis, 159, 220; in *Leaving the Atocha Station*, 220
Pruett, Jordan, 255n40
publishers, 9, 10, 44, 51, 74, 103, 120, 152, 175–76, 203, 219, 281n1, 284n25; Bantam, 219, 220; the Big Five, 9, 203; Counterpoint Press, 203; Holloway House, 9; McSweeney's, 9; Penguin, 79;
Penguin Random House, 167, 176, 203; Pocket Books, 219; Random House, 7, 8, 18, 46, 103;
Pynchon, Thomas, 17, 20, 84, 86, 87, 88, 106, 134, 180, 207, 218, 236, 269n19, 290n13; *Bleeding Edge*, 207, 290n13; *The Crying of Lot 49*, 134; *Gravity's Rainbow*, 86, 87, 88, 134

Rasberry, Vaughn, 102, 105
Rau, Petra, 110
Ravenel, Shannon, 74–75
Reagan, Ronald, 9, 54, 197, 200, 216, 223, 224
Reed, Ishmael, 17, 74, 134, 149, 155, 156, 180, 250n6; *Flight to Canada*, 74, 149, 155; *Mumbo Jumbo*, 250n6

rememory, 3, 50, 154, 297n6. *See also Beloved* (Morrison)
Robinson, Marilynne: *Housekeeping*, 47, 174
Roemer, Kenneth M., 93
Rosa, Hartmut, 227, 295n61, 295n65
Rosen, Jeremy, 108, 122, 282n7
Roth, Philip, 21, 28–29, 81, 95, 111, 258n74, 258n76; *American Pastoral*, 95; *The Human Stain*, 28, 258n74; *The Plot Against America*, 111
Rothberg, Michael, 95–96
Row, Jess, 237
Roy, Arundhati, 254n34
Rushdie, Salman, 254n34; *The Golden House*, 208
Rushdy, Ashraf, 49, 261n21

Saving Private Ryan (Spielberg), 96, 271n33
Samet, Elizabeth, 96–97
satire, 36, 59, 86, 87, 98, 121, 122, 123, 127, 136, 144, 158, 278n58; academic, 36, 123, 127, 136, 158
Saunders, George: "Love Letter," 254n36
Schindler's List (Spielberg), 96
science fiction, 13, 59, 63, 253n26
Scott, Walter, 14, 38, 170, 208, 210, 219, 253n31, 289n6; *Waverley*, 170, 208, 210, 253n31, 289n6
Sebald, W. G., *Austerlitz*, 118
secondary school, 159, 173, 188–89, 281n92
Seidlitz, Hannah, 205
September 11 attacks; 9, 11, 207, 223, 234–36, 238, 254n32, 290n13. *See also* 9/11 novel
Serpell, Namwali, 165, 169, 203; "The Banality of Empathy," 203; *The Old Drift*, 165

· 335 ·

Sexton, Margaret Wilkinson: *A Kind of Freedom* 14, 27, 37–38, 156, 168–69, 186, 195–204. See also *Kind of Freedom, A* (Sexton)
Shaft (Parks), 162–63
Shakespeare, William, 21, 187
Shange, Ntozake, 133
Shelat, Jay N., 236, 238
Shteyngart, Gary, 205, 206, 236; *Lake Success*, 208; *Our Country Friends*, 205
Silko, Leslie Marmon: *Ceremony*, 36, 74, 84, 87–94, 99, 117, 270n24. See also *Ceremony* (Silko)
sincerity, 10, 19, 98, 106, 119, 217–18, 222, 233, 235, 293n36. *See also* new historical sincerity
Smith, Tracy K., 133
Smith, Zadie, 235
So, Richard Jean, 5, 18
Spahr, Juliana, 190, 255n44
Spiegelman, Art: *Maus*, 95, 98
Stevens, Wallace: "The Idea of Order at Key West," 216
Stowe, Harriet Beecher, 21
Strange, Sharan, 132, 133, 276n27
syllabi, 18, 25, 31, 33, 34, 47, 78, 93, 128, 130, 134, 174, 202, 234, 248, 249n2, 250n8, 257n70
Sympathizer, The (Nguyen), 19–25, 30–31, 32, 41–43, 244, 256n49, 259n83; reverse history in, 41–42
Styron, William: *Sophie's Choice*, 95

Tale for the Time Being, A (Ozeki), 14, 15, 19, 32, 38, 211, 213–14, 217–19, 222–23, 226–32, 236, 238; and catastrophe, 213; extranational logic of, 226–27; history in, 222–23, 238

technology, 63, 108, 113, 125, 212, 213, 229, 233, 242, 247, 264n71
Thurman, Deborah, 265n80, 266n83
Thin Red Line, The (Malick), 96
Time's Arrow (Amis), 30, 35, 43–46, 54–64, 71, 263n51, 263n57, 266n84; generic drift in, 57–58; historical logic of, 43, 54–55; historical trauma in, 44–45; media in, 62–63
Tiptree, Jr., James, 290n14
Tōhoku earthquake (2011), 14, 213, 227
trauma, 2, 3, 20, 35, 45, 78, 85, 89, 104, 114, 146, 153, 172, 194, 198, 215, 231; historical, 35, 78, 194; intergenerational, 45, 114; and memory, 262n33
Trueheart, Charles, 58
Trump, Donald, 159, 208, 210, 229, 236
Twain, Mark, 211
Tyler, Anne: *French Braid*, 206

un-bildungsroman, 35, 64
Underground Railroad, The (Whitehead), 14, 21, 32, 37, 122, 123, 147–56, 157, 160, 161, 244, 279n67; and *Beloved*, 150; as meta–slave narrative, 150, 154; reenactment in, 151–53, 160; violence in, 151
university English departments, 6, 9, 10, 25, 37, 128, 131, 147, 168, 174, 175, 176, 191, 241, 243, 251n20, 259n83
Updike, John, 54, 56–57, 121, 263n51
Urrea, Luis Alberto: *The House of Broken Angels*, 81–82

Vendler, Helen, 136
Vidal, Gore: *Burr*, 17
Vietnam War fiction, 22, 31, 84, 94–97, 253n29

INDEX

Vonnegut, Kurt, 17, 36, 62, 84, 86–87, 88, 106, 271n37; *Slaughterhouse Five*, 62, 86–87, 88

Walcott, Derek, 133
Waldman, Amy: *The Submission*, 207
Walker, Alice, 6, 74, 133, 134, 250n6, 261n31; *The Color Purple*, 74, 134, 250n6, 261n31
Walkowitz, Rebecca L., 135, 226
War on Drugs, 192, 195
War in Iraq, 207–208, 216, 226
War on Terror, 223, 234
Ward, Andrew, 278n53
Ward, Jesmyn, 6, 26, 39, 237–38, 244, 245, 246, 247, 248, 297n6; *Let Us Descend*, 248; *Salvage the Bones*, 208, 237–38; *Sing, Unburied, Sing*, 244, 245
Warren, Kenneth, 27, 260n9
Wasserman, Sarah, 108
West, Cornel, 143
Wharton, William: *Birdy*, 95
When the Emperor Was Divine (Otsuka), 36, 85, 114–19; sparseness of, 115–16, 118; and World War II fiction, 117
White, Hayden, 17
Whitehead, Colson, 6, 14, 19, 21, 26, 32, 36–37, 105, 121–63; *Apex Hides the Hurt*, 121, 143–44, 146, 278n58; *Crook Manifesto*, 163; *Harlem Shuffle*, 37, 105, 122, 123–24, 134, 145–46, 157, 159, 162–63; *John Henry Days*, 121, 123, 142–43; *The Intuitionist*, 36–37, 121, 123–29, 131–34, 136–47, 149, 151, 155, 156, 158, 180, 188; *The Nickel Boys*, 37, 105, 122, 123, 156–61; "Picking a Genre," 122; *Sag Harbor*, 121, 123, 145; *The Underground Railroad*, 14, 21, 32, 37, 122, 123, 147–56, 157, 160, 161, 244,

279n67; *Zone One*, 122, 147, 279n67. See also *Apex Hides the Hurt* (Whitehead); *Harlem Shuffle* (Whitehead); *Intuitionist, The* (Whitehead); *John Henry Days* (Whitehead)
whiteness, 29–30, 46, 92, 111–14, 135, 153, 210; and 9/11 fiction, 236, 238; and war memory, 83–85, 97, 99, 111–12, 117
white writers, 18, 29–30, 35–36, 39, 72, 82, 84, 85, 94, 97, 99, 106, 107, 111–12, 172, 188–89, 212, 236–238, 244, 255n44, 288n79
Whitman, Walt, 21, 70, 222
Wideman, John Edgar, 133
Winters, Lisa Ze, 181
Woloch, Alex, 181, 183, 286n54
Woolf, Virginia, 166, 171
World War II fiction, 13–14, 29, 30, 34, 84, 85, 87–88, 94, 97, 106, 108, 113, 119–20, 233, 268n5; adolescence of, 119; aesthetics of, 36; and the "Double V" campaign, 196; whiteness of, 94–105, 106, 111–14, 120; and writers of color, 106
Wouk, Herman: *War and Remembrance*, 95
Wright, Michelle, 187, 287n63
Wright, Richard: *Native Son*, 52, 200
Wylie, Andrew, 59

Yapa, Sunil: *Your Heart is a Muscle the Size of a Fist*, 208
Yothers, Brian, 186
Young, Kevin, 133, 149
Young, Stephanie, 190, 255n44

zombie novel, 121, 122, 279n67
Zucker, A. E., 170, 172

LITERATURE NOW

Literature Now offers a distinct vision of late-twentieth- and
early-twenty-first-century literary culture. Addressing contemporary literature
and the ways we understand its meaning, the series includes books that are
comparative and transnational in scope as well as those that focus
on national and regional literary cultures.

Matthew Hart, David James, and Rebecca L. Walkowitz, Series Editors

Glenda Carpio, *Migrant Aesthetics: Contemporary Fiction, Global Migration, and the Limits of Empathy*
John Brooks, *The Racial Unfamiliar: Illegibility in Black Literature and Culture*
Vidyan Ravinthiran, *Worlds Woven Together: Essays on Poetry and Poetics*
Ellen Jones, *Literature in Motion: Translating Multilingualism Across the Americas*
Thomas Heise, *The Gentrification Plot: New York and the Postindustrial Crime Novel*
Sunny Xiang, *Tonal Intelligence: The Aesthetics of Asian Inscrutability During the Long Cold War*
Jessica Pressman, *Bookishness: Loving Books in a Digital Age*
Heather Houser, *Infowhelm: Environmental Art and Literature in an Age of Data*
Christy Wampole, *Degenerative Realism: Novel and Nation in Twenty-First-Century France*
Sarah Chihaya, Merve Emre, Katherine Hill, and Jill Richards, *The Ferrante Letters: An Experiment in Collective Criticism*
Peter Morey, *Islamophobia and the Novel*
Gloria Fisk, *Orhan Pamuk and the Good of World Literature*
Zara Dinnen, *The Digital Banal: New Media and American Literature and Culture*
Theodore Martin, *Contemporary Drift: Genre, Historicism, and the Problem of the Present*
Ashley T. Shelden, *Unmaking Love: The Contemporary Novel and the Impossibility of Union*
Jesse Matz, *Lasting Impressions: The Legacies of Impressionism in Contemporary Culture*
Jeremy Rosen, *Minor Characters Have Their Day: Genre and the Contemporary Literary Marketplace*
Sarah Phillips Casteel, *Calypso Jews: Jewishness in the Caribbean Literary Imagination*
Carol Jacobs, *Sebald's Vision*
For a complete list of books in the series, please see the Columbia University Press website.

GPSR Authorized Representative: Easy Access System Europe, Mustamäe tee
50, 10621 Tallinn, Estonia, gpsr.requests@easproject.com

www.ingramcontent.com/pod-product-compliance
Lightning Source LLC
Chambersburg PA
CBHW031231290426
44109CB00012B/252